THE
Knapps
LIVED HERE

BY *Ken Spooner*

E&M

ELM & MᶜKINLEY BOOKS

The information provided in this book is based on sources that the author believes to be reliable. All such information regarding individuals, products, and companies is current as of July 2010.

ELM & McKINLEY BOOKS
P. O. Box 2752
New York, New York 10116

Visit E&M online at **ELMANDMCKINLEY.COM**

First Edition September 2010

ISBN No.: 978-0-578-06236-5

Book design by Erik Spooner | erikspooner.com

This book is typeset using a combination of the
Eldorado family for display, by The Font Bureau, Boston, MA,
and Sentinel by Hoefler & Freer-Jones, New York, NY.
Flourishes and ornaments are all from the Woodcuts series
by Adobe Systems, San Jose, CA.

Contents

FOR DONALD DENNING

1945-2008

A Summer Friend for All Seasons

Moving To "The Country"

On Saturday November 18th, 1950 the Walter C. Joseph family, all five of them, picked up and moved from the city to the country. Walter Charles age 38, his wife Amelia just 31, and their three children Geraldine Marjorie aka "Gerry"10, Walter John aka "Butchie" 6.5 and "Kenny"aka Kenneth Charles (when he was in trouble) age 3.5 exactly! Now I'm fairly sure the three children had no say in this big move to the country or would of protested if they did. Speaking for the youngest of them, I can say that I can't recall if I even knew the name of the place we were moving to. To me it was just "the country", but it seemed to hold a lot more promise for the wide eyed adventures that would hallmark my childhood, than the immediate neighborhood around our house at 131, 134th Street, South Ozone Park, Queens ever did. Not to say I wouldn't of had an adventurous childhood — it just would of been one very different.

When I was old enough to understand such things, I would learn that it was the "going downhill" of South Ozone Park that prompted our parents to look elsewhere for a better life for all of us. They would say the straw that broke the camels back was when our house was burglarized, an event I was too young to recall because I was still in my mothers womb. That's probably the only reason I don't recall it, because without meaning to be a braggart, I was truly blessed with an amazing memory that has always astonished my family and friends for over 60 years. In fact it was my vivid memory that started this entire saga, when in 2000, I decided it would be fun to write a series of short stories about growing up in "the country".

We discovered our new house that summer while out in "the country" visiting with Grandpa and Grandma Joseph, who had lived there since 1940. It wasn't but a stones throw from their three room bungalow that always smelled of kerosene from the brown box metal heater planted in their main room. "The country" was a fairly primitive place (electricity only having arrived there 18 years before) and most of the homes there were never designed for the all year round living we would be doing. Thankfully our house didn't hold that smell or construction. It was built with blown in rock wool insulation, diagonal sheathing, a real oil burner that provided steam heat to radiators, and indoor plumbing, which believe it or not was an option with many of the homes around us! Besides the surrounding houses, which to me were strangely empty, there was a whole lot of woods with trees that were much bigger than anything I ever saw in a city park. On our property alone, which was a 100 x 100 foot corner lot, there were three large pines, an oak, two maples. two peach, a pear and an apple tree. Not to mention a two story house that sported a knotty pine living room with exposed beams, cathedral ceiling, stone fireplace, stained glass windows, two loft bedrooms, a master bedroom with two doors, an enclosed porch, kitchen, with separate pantry and one tiny bathroom with just a shower that our mother despised. That closet sized bathroom almost put the kibosh deal. Mom would suffer with it for nine years before we enlarged the place and she got her new bathroom with green fixtures that included a tub. If Mom had to get by with a cramped bath, Pop had to deal with a half basement, that only Butchie and me could stand upright in. He built a workbench in it, but never spent much time down there. The unique feature was a sump pump that would shoot a geyser of ever seeping water out into our backyard several times a day.

"The Country's" official name was Mastic Beach and I have to say its developers aptly named it back in 1926. It was about 60 miles east of New York City on Long Island's south shore. There was water everywhere both near and sometimes under our house. Across Elm Road, deep in the woods, was the rusted remains of a metal canoe they said was rowed straight down Elm Rd. during a hurricane. Less than a half mile east, south, and west was a lagoon, a bay and a creek. Put a shovel in the ground in our yard and you would hit water less than two feet down. Grandpa's house, which wasn't 300 feet from ours, was on a road that had the unofficial name of "swamp road" because that's where it led to. Right into acres of cattails, marshes, and drainage ditches, eventually it dead ended at "Beach Ten". As for actual beaches, there were only four of them in the immediate area, One, Ten, Four and Five. The numbers referred to the ten sections that made up the town. Beach Ten was the closest to our house at the foot of Jefferson Drive. Most of the roads around us seemed to be named for either historical figures or botanicals. Our house was on the corner of McKinley and Elm. Jefferson Drive, was a hundred feet west of our property, followed by Lafayette, Polk, and Monroe. Cedar, Dogwood, Locust, Magnolia, Cypress and Dahlia, chris crossed grid like throughout the beach. Of course most of this info was not realized by a 3 and half year old, that couldn't read yet, but I did listen closely, even back then and most of the details I just relayed to you, were well entrenched in my little expanding skull before I was five.

I MENTIONED THAT THERE WERE SEVERAL HOUSES AROUND OURS BUT no one living in them when we moved there. They would remain that way, many with their windows shuttered, until the summer when the whole place changed overnight. Initially playmates were not missed by me because I didn't really have any of my own in the city either. Butch and Gerry were my first playmates and the friends they made in South Ozone Park were mine too. Butch and Gerry were in first and sixth grades then, so they got their kid fix in the little school they went to in Moriches, a hamlet about four miles away. My mother said she was amazed at how I seemed to entertain myself all day long while they were in school. Thing is there was plenty for me to do and see right in our yard. I do recall going into the woods alone once to get a closer look at that canoe I had only seen silhouetted from the safety of our yard. When I got up close to it, I got scared, as I only equated canoes with Indians and I thought there might be some lurking in the woods. I beat a hasty retreat back across Elm and into our yard before Mom even missed me. There were several other things of interest in our immediate neighborhood that I didn't know at the time of discovery, but would find out much later, were directly connected to the Knapps, the main subjects of this book. Just around the corner from us on Jefferson Drive were two towers in the woods. One had a wooden water tank on it and the other had something I never saw before. Butch said it was a windmill and one day we decided to take a closer look.

The Small, Small World
of Butchie & Me

I'm a little fuzzy on the time or events that prompted Butchie and me to go take a closer look at the windmill and water tower. They were just beyond the border of our allowed play area, which at first was basically our property. I'm sure it was Butch's idea and just as sure that we had to have seen them several times before we decided to mount an expedition to get a closer look. The grid like, named "Roads" in Mastic Beach ran east-west, and the "Drives," north-south. We had a semi-circular driveway on the McKinley Drive side of our house and by living on a corner, Mom or Pop could head off in all four directions on their way to town and beyond. Often on return trips from places like Fisher's market, we would head south off of Neighborhood Road (the main drag) onto Jefferson Drive, and I would always notice these two barns as we neared our house and the towers sticking above the trees. Those towers always fascinated me especially the windmill.

But if there was one main event that inspired us to visit the towers, it was probably the day our sister took us for a little walk to see something special she discovered with the other kids at her school. We had lived in Mastic Beach just about a year, as it was the fall of 1951. Ever the explorer, Gerry was allowed a lot more liberty than her kid brothers were. I recall it was a Sunday afternoon and our grandmother, Anna Spooner was visiting with us from Ja-

maica, Queens. It was always a treat to drive on a Friday night, to the little victorian Mastic Station to meet Grandma at the train. When the big GM diesel
approached, Butchie and me always got a thrill as the ground shook and the
station master handed the engineer a note on a long stick. Grandma always
had a "little something" for us that she bought at the 5 & 10 cent store, in her
green quilted shopping bag. A bag of marbles, a bottle of bubbles, a Tootsie-
Toy car or truck; always one for each of us.

Mom and Pop were somewhere that Sunday and Grandma was in charge.
Gerry, who was very persuasive, when she wanted to do something, convinced
Grandma to go for a "little" walk with her, to see this fantastic big house in the
woods that she had discovered. She had already been to it probably more than
once. Grandma asked how far it was and Gerry said, "Oh it's not far at all it's
right by Dick's." Dick's was a little grocery, variety, soda fountain and bus stop
over in section one, about a mile away. So off we went; Gerry, Grandma, Butchie
and me, to see this "mansion in the woods with lots of barns around it." We headed east on Elm Road, then turned north on Whittier Drive at the lagoon. By the
time we reached Dick's, both Grandma and I were getting tired legs. Gerry and
Butch were walking much faster and always had to stop to wait up for us. After
we walked a few blocks past Dick's, Grandma was starting to have some real
worry in her voice. "Gerry, how much further is it?" "Just a little ways Gram."
We started heading north again down this road in the woods and soon the pave-
ment turned to sand. Finally we came to a grassy path with tire tracks worn in
it., just wide enough for one car to travel on. Gerry said, "This is it, here's the
driveway." The trees that lined it were huge and there was a chain across it. The
driveway went on as far as you could see and several of the trees had signs on
them that said POSTED. This seemed to cause great concern for Grandma but
Gerry said it was OK, as she knew the owner. "Who is the owner?" Grandma asked.
"William Floyd, but he's been dead a long time. His relatives own it now and they
only use it once in a while". The word dead must have hit home with Butch, because
he now stuck much closer to us as we walked along this very shady path that seemed
to go on forever and get darker as the woods grew even thicker. We came to a fork in
the path and took the left one. I don't think anybody questioned Gerry any further
on how she knew the owner. The fact was, she didn't know anyone. She just knew
what she learned from her school friends who showed her the place.

WILLIAM FLOYD WAS INDEED DEAD A LONG TIME. He was entitled to
be; signing the Declaration of Independence when he was 42, Floyd
lived to the ripe old age of 87, breathing his last in 1821. In a year or two we
would start going to a brand new school they were building, named for him.
Of course none of this impressed me then, but as we finally reached a clearing,
the sight of all those ancient barns did. Gerry said one of them was built over
a pit of quicksand (to scare Butch). Most of them had no doors and Butch
stayed far back from their shadowy entrances. And there, in the field next to
one of the barns, was a windmill and water tower just like the ones around
the corner from our house. We approached the main house from the rear and

never did get to see the front. It was a two story white rambling place, that looked very old. It did have that certain intrinsic spookiness to it that any kid would equate with an old house. There seemed to be no one around, and Gerry said even if there was, we were not allowed inside anyway. So there was nothing to do but turn around and head for home.

On the return trip my legs gave out completely. Butchie and Gerry took turns carrying me. Grandma had to stop several times to rest and when we finally got home our folks were back. They actually had gone driving around to look for us as Mom was worried about our whereabouts. Gerry got yelled at for stressing out Grandma and was told to never go there again. She probably didn't, instead trading out her prohibition for exploring the Dana estate, which was further north in Mastic and far spookier. It would certainly not be the last time though that Butchie and me would wander in and get chased out of the Floyd estate.

It could well be that because there were barns near the windmill and a water tower on Jefferson, that Butch may have figured there would be a big house or mansion around here too. As for me, I was always up for anything my big brother wanted to do. It was a winter afternoon and we were playing in our backyard by the pine tree tire swing when Butch said "You wanna go look at the water tower and windmill?" We took the shortcut through the Jordans' (our next door summer neighbors) backyard. In the years that followed, we actually wore a path through the Jordans' yard, not because of the towers, but because of whom we would meet there for the first time that day. The towers were probably only 20 feet or so off the road. We both stood in the middle of Jefferson, looking up at them for some time before Butch said "follow me" and into the stickers, poison ivy and brush we went. When we got to the towers, we saw two wells. One round and one square. The round one was made of bricks and pretty well filled up with junk. The square one was partially covered with old wide boards, but you could see water in it. We were only there a minute or so when we heard someone coming our way through the woods. It was a little kid, about my age, and a brown dog. His name was Larry and his dog was Skippy. He lived on the other side of the woods and said the towers and wells that we were looking at were Mr. Clark's. "Who is Mr. Clark"? Butch asked. "He's our neighbor who lives in a barn in my backyard," Larry replied, as he pointed to the barn roof just behind him. When we followed Larry into his yard, we got our first close up look at Mr. Clark's barn. It had house windows in it and a small doghouse dormer in the roof. I'm not sure if we saw Mr. Clark that day, but when we finally did, he kind of scared me. He just walked around on his property, never really acknowledging us kids. There was a small shed attached to the rear of his barn that he seemed to always be going in and out of. Thinking back, he looked like the character who was cast in Christine, the Stephen King movie. In his felt hat and farmer's denim overalls, Mr. Clark indeed looked like the old man who sold Christine, his dead brother's car. We got to be fast friends with Larry that day and it grew stronger in the growing weeks. I really liked having someone my own age to play with when Butch went to school, but it all came to a screeching halt in about a month. Larry's Dad took a job in Maryland and the Schulz family moved away. I never thought I'd see him again. Sometimes I would walk by his empty house on Tennis Place, kind of hoping he'd be there. After a year or so the house remained empty and I gave up. Then one day the tower and the wind mill just disappeared. The tiny world of Butchie and me was changing and it seemed Larry wasn't coming back into it. It wasn't the first time I was wrong about events connected to this story, but I was only 4 and this story continues on and off for another 55 + years.

A Tale of Two Barns, Two Cousins, Two Towns & One Mansion

Of the two barns I mentioned that were near our house, I haven't said much about the second one. Reasons being, first, that it was a little further over our ever-expanding play area boundary, though not out of sight. The second and bigger reason: it was much more foreboding looking than Mr. Clark's Barn, even with him walking like a sentry around his grounds. It was abandoned and sat on the overgrown vine weeded corner of Jefferson Drive and Dogwood Road, shaded by trees. You could see in the partially open barn doors as we rode past it in the car, but it did not look very inviting; it looked spooky and really torn up. Adding to that spookiness was a small charcoal black, weathered outbuilding, which sat near it, with a white skull and crossbones and the words KEEP OUT painted on the door. *Keep out?!* More like creep out! The site of both of them were enough to make any kid keep their distance. The second barn was much larger than Mr. Clark's and it was twice as forboding looking. On the center of its roof, it had a long cupola that would become a BB gun pillbox for some of the older kids. Ruffians that went up there to rain their Daisies down on us smaller kids, probably had a lot to do with tearing up the interior. And if that wasn't enough to convince you to give it a wide berth, then how about *bats!* Yes, bats up in the hayloft and cupola that would come out at dusk in the summer time. Once, one got into Gerry's bedroom and she chased it out with a broom. All I knew about bats then was that they could get tangled in your hair and if they bit you, then you had to get a bunch of rabies shots, which hurt a whole lot. This was probably five years or so before any of us kids would see Dracula on the Saturday night horror movies they showed on WOR-TV and learn the true danger of bats. It would be several years too, before I learned that the barn was known as Schulte's Barn, or dared step foot in it. But a half-century after I did, it would provide the first dots to the rest of the Knapp story.

O F THE THREE OF US JOSEPH KIDS, I guess I had the easiest time adjusting to our new town. In recent conversations with my sister, she has confessed that her first years in Mastic Beach were not easy for her. I found that to be surprising because she seemed to have the most friends and was always involved with lots of activities. One of the earliest was the Girl Scouts. I can recall a photo of her uniform, next to the flagpole on our front lawn while the 48 stars of Old Glory fluttered in the summer breeze. As for Butchie's memories, I sadly can't really say what they are, other than my interpretations of them based on my recall, the closeness of our relationship back then and the adventures we shared, especially the first decade we lived there. I say that not because he has passed on, but rather has estranged himself from both Gerry and I with no explanation for over twenty years. It was in fact my desire to preserve those memories that first led me to write a series of short stories titled *Buzz and Pee Wee, Butchie & Me*, that in turn led me to write this book.

Buzz and Pee Wee were two brothers I'd meet years later, who actually had a similar childhood to mine, but they grew up in South Carolina. They could have just as easily been known as Donald and Patty, and for the purposes of this book they are. Butchie and me first met Donald and Patty in the summer of 1951. And we didn't have to go traipsing into the poison ivy and woods risking our necks by some dangerous wells to do so. Do I hear some resentment towards Larry Schulz for leaving town? No, to find Donald and Patty we didn't have to look all the way south of the Mason-Dixon line either, we just had to look 80 feet north of our driveway and there they were, on the other side of McKinley Drive playing with their cars and trucks in the white sand that bordered the road. Well before you could say Jack Robinson, we were standing over them and asking if we could play too. In no time flat, Donald was running in his house to get some more toys to share. That was the beginning of an annual summer friendship that endured until we moved away in 1964.

Donald and Patty (who seemed as close as any brothers could be) were actually first cousins Donald and Donald Denning. Their grandmother gave one of them the nickname Patty so they would know who she was speaking to. Patty also went by Donny, which I believe he preferred, just as my brother always wanted to be called Walt instead of Butch. It seemed no one ever paid either of them any heed. Their grandmother, Nora Denning, whose bungalow it was, took care of them through the summers while their parents worked in Brooklyn. On most weekends, the Dennings, all 13 of them, would convene at the bungalow. How they managed to fit in there I'll never know. I do know that by 1953 they added on to the place and included an indoor bathroom, having had put up with an outhouse since the place was built in 1938.

Their grandmother was probably the first person I ever heard any history of Mastic Beach or the word Knapp from. I noticed Donald and Patty always referred to the shopping areas as old town and new town or sometimes big town and small town. Big town was really not very big, which made small town a real misnomer. You could call it tiny town. But the fact is it was the first town, started in the first section of Mastic Beach to be developed. It had two general stores that sold gasoline, later on in the '30s and '40s it had three stores, but then one turned into a bar. And talk about optimism, in 1927 it had a 15 room hotel. By 1930 Paul Schulte, the proprietor of the hotel, saw more opportunity to the west side of the rapidly expanding summer development, and built a store at the 5 corners that would be the anchor for New Town. Unbeknownst to me and many others except the folks that were there in the '20s and '30s, was that both towns were separated by a 200 acre private estate in the middle of it all. And once upon a time in the middle of those two hundred acres sat the very elegant residence of one Joseph F. Knapp. I also had no idea at that time that our house and those of all our neighbors were sitting on what once was Mr. Knapp's property.

If the Denning Irish clan helped swell the Mastic Beach population in the summers, they were nothing compared to our next door neighbors the Yodices who lived just over the fence in our backyard. The Anthony Yodice family were Italian and could number up to 50 or more on holiday weekends. Their half acre property extended from McKinley to Jefferson and in addition to an average size home, they had a guest house and a garage with upstairs living quarters to accommodate all the relatives. At one point, Mr. Yodice, to the dismay of all on the block, cleared four lots of woods (80' x 100'), opposite his front door just to park the cars. He put a small cement slab on the field and briefly had one of the first above-ground swimming pools in Mastic Beach. I remember he tried to fill it with a garden hose, but gave up after a day or so and called the Fire Department to finish the job. Mr. Yodice, who was a dock boss in Brooklyn, had a huge voice that could be heard for blocks. I think the two times I heard it at maximum DB, were when Butchie and Denning cousin Georgie Lang (later known as "Spike") were playing with matches and set a little fire under his big black '51 Cadillac Fleetwood. The other time Mr. Yodice could be heard for miles, was when his daughter Sally Ann poked a hole in the swimming pool sidewall and flooded the field.

Of the actual immediate Yodice family, there were probably only 7 or 8 members, with three of them, Sally Ann, Mary Ann and Anthony being kids of our of age. They would become a big part of the nucleus of our summer friends. Along with the Dennings and Butchie and me, we all shared a bunch of great kid adventures, all through the '50s, including exploring the two barns and eventually the Knapp mansion.

As I mentioned, one of Gerry's first social activities was with the Girl Scouts that she joined in the spring of '51. That was how I first heard about the mansion in our midst, but didn't know yet how close that was. This mansion was used as a community center then, and I knew she usually walked to it, but I had no idea how close to our house it was, because with Gerry, a little walk could be a hike. After her first meeting there, she talked more about the mansion than what she did at the scout meeting. She said it had a huge ballroom with big fireplace, a knight's armor and great circular stairway. All of this really caught my attention.

It seems that St. Jude's, the local catholic church, had bought this place a few months before we moved to Mastic Beach. They planned to turn it into a school, but for now were using it as a parish house and a community center. Of course all these details were not of any interest to me. I just wanted to look around inside and was wondering when I would get a chance to. One day when Gerry was at a meeting, Mom told me to get in the car with her as she needed something from the store. I can't recall why Butch wasn't with us, but the next thing I know we were heading down that old coal covered road that passed between Mr. Clark's Barn and that skull & crossbones shack. It was then I saw it for the first time, looming up over the tree tops. *Holy Cow!* I couldn't believe the size of it, nor that I never noticed it before, as Jefferson Drive wasn't even 500 feet away. Probably because I was always looking up at the towers. It was big, and white, with blue shutters on lots of windows and it had several chimneys. We passed the front of it and I noticed terraced balconies on each side, then Mom turned the corner headed north a short distance, then veered to the right and pulled into the grounds, stopping the car in the back yard driveway. What she did next might be one of the main reasons I would get deeply involved half a century later in the years of research it took to do this book. She told me to wait in the car... *ohhhh, nooo...*DRAT! Crestfallen, I watched her walk inside. Being that it was summer, it was getting real hot in the car, so I got out and sat on the running board. There was an old man mowing the grass with a big farm style mower and I noticed a long very old looking garage with a window on the side. I wandered over there to take a look and saw a large car in it. I think it was a Packard, but I'm not sure. Whatever it was, it probably belonged to Father Skelly, who I would later learn was the main driving force for the church's buying the mansion. He certainly wound up with a fine place to live for awhile. The man mowing the grass kept a close eye on me, and he was most likely Willie Schluder, the custodian at the fire department, who I also would find out in later years was connected with the estate. Willie was the last caretaker for the Knapps. Mom and Gerry finally came out and off we went. That was probably my only chance to ever see the inside of it the way it was. Soon, Gerry traded in her Girl Scout uniform for one from the Mastic Beach Fire Department Band. Not long after that, Father Skelly moved out. It would be at least three or more years before I finally got to go inside the mansion, and by then it was "remodeled" dramatically.

CHAPTER
3

The Seven Year Itch:

1952-1959

If MY FIRST TWO YEARS IN MASTIC BEACH WOULD START THE GROUND breaking for this saga, it was the events of the following seven odd years, that held the entire foundation of the Knapp story, I would start to pursue fifty years later. Of course I didn't know that then. I probably only heard their name twice over the course of those seven years and like many other Mastic Beach folks, probably never gave a thought to how Knapp Road, got it's name. But then again I was just 5 years old in May of '52 and would only be 12 in October of 1959, which is where this part of Knapp Road ends. In looking back, recalling the kid things that happened to me, my sister, brother and our friends, I have been able to use them time and time again to help understand most of the stories that were yet to unfold in my lap. At times when I thought, well that's it, I've learned all I could ever hope to about the Knapps, something else from those seven years would connect another set of dots and my batteries would get recharged. It's my hope that what you will learn in this chapter, will also return again to your mind as you read beyond it, thereby making your discoveries of who the Knapps were, as close as I can to my own experience. They would turn out to be a very interesting family, and some of them lived in my little town.

By 1952 the big town west of our house on Neighborhood Rd. and 5 corners of Mastic Beach had merchants and stores that pretty much carried or catered to every essential need anyone could want. There were three grocery stores, Fisher's, Harer's, and Stop & Shop, Smith's fish market, two hardware stores, Izzy's and Watrous', and three gas stations, Pat & Mike's Texaco, at one end, Triangle Shell, at the other and a Gulf station between them. There was also Mae Bowery's Gift Shop, Lagumis Liquors, Joe Orlando's Barber shop, Sunflower Coffee Shop, Anchor Inn and Red Barn Restaurant, Schulte's Tavern, Beachcomber Tavern, Shannon Bar, Neighborhood Pizzeria, Fannie's Bowling Alley, a shoemaker or two, Allan and Marty' s pharmacy, and several delis, like Ben and Anita Siriani's. There were many seasonal places too, open from Memorial through Labor Day, Kate's produce stand, Kozy Korner ice cream parlor and Mrs. Distel's frozen custard stand (later known as Ann Harrington's). By 1952 Mastic Beach was well established with a Fire Department, Post Office, four houses of worship ; Episcopal, Lutheran, Catholic, and Hebrew and even it's own hospital, located in Richard Floyd's "Pattersquash," a circa 1700's mansion that was one of the original huge colonial estates the entire area was carved from. And speaking of estates, Mastic Beach had at least four or five real estate offices, most of them owned by former salesmen from the Home Guardian Company, who started Mastic Beach on the east side of the Knapp estate in 1926 with the 315 acre Revolutinary war General Woodhull's estate. From 1952 through 1959, many other small business opened up; Bohouris Lumber, Walt's Miniature Golf, Bell's 5 & 10 cent store, Jean's Soda Fountain,a real teen age hangout, along with more delis, gas stations, barber shops, and pizza places, including De Carlo's Polly-0 deli that sold pizza dough, pans, and cheeses, and last, but not least in my book, Jo-Don's Hobby Shop which was my second home in 1959.

For the total shopping experience though there was only one place to go and that was go west young shopper, to Patchogue. Just seven miles away, almost a small city, it had been around since the 1800s. It had several department stores like Sears, Swezey's and the Bee Hive, an F. W. Woolworth, W. T. Grant and S.S. Kressge 5 & 10 cent stores, John's Bargain Store, two music stores, which two pet shops, several opticians, auto supply stores, supermarkets like A&P, Bohack, Grand Union and Safeway, The Rialto, Granada and Patchogue theatres, all kinds of clothing and shoe jewelry, sporting goods stores, auto dealerships for every US make of car, banks, multiple restaurants including Chinese and Kosher, utility companies like PELCO and the NY Telephone Company, where my father spent his entire adult working life. Clearly, for shopping and really "taking care of business," Patchogue was it. But if Patchogue was too much town for you, then you could always go about five miles east of Mastic Beach to the very provincial town of Center Moriches (formerly Centre Moriches), which was about half the size of Patchogue.

Some of my earliest memories of our shopping trips to Patchogue were of visiting with my grandfather, who worked at Justus Roe Co. manufacturing steel tape measures. Grandpa Joseph was a semi-retired machinist who spent his last working years there. Though he still drove until the day he died in 1957, he would mainly commute with Pop in our 1934 Buick Coupe. We must've had enough different length 25′, 50′, 100′ and 200′ brown leather covered tape measures in our cellar, to measure the distance from our house to the 5 corners, about a mile away.

I REMEMBER HEARING A COMMOTION, late one winter evening in our living room. Butch and I slept in the loft overhead and it woke us up. We peered over the balcony wall and saw our parents and my sister downstairs. My sister was crying and holding her little brown dog Cocoa by the fireplace, which was the only illumination in the room. That afternoon while out playing with her in the yard, Cocoa had run off and still wasn't home by our bedtime. She came home around midnight and apparently had been poisoned. By morning our father had already buried Cocoa in the backyard before he went to work.

My mother was in tears all morning and she kept Gerry and Butch home from school. At 4 years old the full concept of death wasn't in my little brain yet, but I felt the sadness all around me and I knew Cocoa wasn't coming back. By noon my mother and Gerry had not stopped crying and Mom told all three of us to get in our Hudson and off we drove to Patchogue. It was not a shopping trip, just a one stop mission to the pet shop on South Ocean Avenue. There we all picked out a little jet black puppy with four white feet. He was a mix of Labrador retriever and Boxer and cost seven dollars. We named him Boots. That evening my father also brought home a puppy that he got from one of his co-workers. That pup was cute too, but we were already attached strongly to Boots and Pop gave back the unnamed pup the next day.

The third early shopping trip I recall was most likely multi-purpose, but the main thing we went to Patchogue for was to get my sister's 12th birthday present. Her birthday is August 3rd and just a few weeks before, they had opened the doors to the latest big deal to hit Mastic Beach: a roller skating rink. Actually it was much more than a roller rink, it was the newly built St. Jude's Auditorium and Youth Center. Our Dad, who worked part time weekends with radio and TV repairman Paul Fueling, had helped Paul install the sound system in the place. Roller skating was an immediate hit with kids and adults from as far away as Center Moriches. Gerry was quickly becoming a roller derby queen in her sparkling white Chicago brand roller skates complete with blue metal carrying case. Little did I know then, that this beautiful new building with the blue tinted windows, was built in the "wrong place" and where it did wind up played an early role in my Knapp Mansion mystery. That discovery too would take another 50 years to find out.

1952 also saw the opening of the brand new William Floyd School located in the new town of Shirley. Originally named Mastic Acres in 1946, the town was surprisingly re-named by it's living developer Walter T. Shirley by establishing a Post Office there. Shirley, NY sat on the western border of Mastic Beach. Parts of it were still called Mastic Beach by the press all through the '50s much to the frustration of Walter T. Ever the promoter, he even tried to get the phone exchange named for himself, as well as the school building he donated the land for. At an early planning session for the school when

William Floyd's name emerged as the front runner, Shirley, turned to one of his aides and said something like, "Who the hell is this guy Floyd? I never heard of him." William Floyd, you may recall, was the dead guy we met in chapter two on that long walk to his estate. His claim to fame again was that he signed the Declaration of Independence. One might say that Will's roots in the community ran slightly deeper than Walter's, who only started rapidly buying up bargain property there after WWII. William Floyd was initially designed to be an elementary school, but in four years grew into a high school too. I started in Kindergarten, the day the building opened there in September of '52, then transferred into the little annex in Moriches for grades one through three. I skipped the fourth grade and returned to the newly finished wing of the Floyd school in 1956, finishing up in 1964.

Two months after I started kindergarten, a gentleman of 60 years age would pass away from heart failure, some 25 miles away to the east, in the town of Hampton Bays,. Although his obituary was in the New York Daily News, Mirror. Tribune, and Times, I doubt that anyone in Mastic Beach with the possible exception of Willie and Honey Schluder knew about it. I know I certainly didn't and even if I did know, the name Joseph Fairchild Knapp would mean nothing to this 5 $\frac{1}{2}$ year old.

IT WAS MOST LIKELY IN '52, PERHAPS EVEN EARLIER, that our dad joined the Mastic Beach Volunteer Fire Department, Mom signed onto their Ladies Auxiliary and Gerry joined the marching band. Their doing so, would provide adventurous encounters, that years later would also help me connect a bunch of dots in the big picture of what went on in our little town years before we ever moved there. One was meeting Willie Schluder, the Fire Department custodian and his wife. While the department held their testy with lots of shouting, lively but boring for us, committee meetings upstairs, my brother and I would get to play downstairs on the fire trucks. Willie stayed down there too, and kind of kept an eye on us. One time he let us set off the 6 PM whistle, something he did daily at noon and six. First he would call the telephone operator and ask for the time, then he would throw the switch, and YOWSA! the whole town knew what time it was. Although the siren was on the roof, inside the garage it was deafening. Honey Schluder was in the Ladies Auxiliary with our Mom. I recall Mom mentioning that Honey and Willie were the caretakers for "the people" that owned "the mansion", just about every time we drove past their little cottage on Neighborhood Road and Monroe Drive. Their cottage, which also was the mansions gatehouse dates back to the 19th century. It has caught fire at least twice, most recently in 2004, but has always survived. I recently learned there is a tunnel that connected it to the mansion a quarter mile away.

In 1953, I entered the first grade and was split up from my brother who remained in the new school in Shirley. This caused a bit of anxiety as I always felt better in new situations with my big brother nearby. My classroom was in a Quonset hut attached to the Moriches school now known as the annex. I can still see the portrait of George Washington, up on the wall behind my desk, looking down on us. Our teacher, Mrs. Whitman was telling us about the "father of our coun-try" on the first day of school. when the kid who sat along side of me and looked familiar, told me his birthday was on the same day as Washington's It was then I realized he was the same kid I had met under the twin towers three years ago.. Larry Schulz was back!

I couldn't wait to get home and tell Butch. We wasted no time after school, going over to Larry's to play. Skippy was still with him and now he had a kid brother Dennis, that although was still pretty much a toddler, really added to the fun. Mr. Clark was still around too, just to keep me a bit wary, yet fascinated by his barn home and his actions. It turns out he was the culprit who took the towers down to sell their iron for scrap, much to the disapproval of Larry's Mom and Dad, who seemed to have questions about whose property the towers actually stood on. But these were matters for adults to deal with. As kids we were taught to respect private property, but pretty much played our games of hide and seek, cowboys and indians, all through our neighborhood and in most everyone's yard save for Mr. Dorer's and Mr. Scimeca's, who were two very grumpy old men. Later on, followed by the erections of TV antennas on our roofs, our games changed to almost daily re enactments of episodes of Flash Gordon, Rin Tin Tin and Davy Crockett. With most of the homes still empty in the fall, winter and spring, we had acres of property to play on, open fields for baseball and lots of woods with some amazing trees.

The trees we climbed were very old and very tall. We had two "Fire Island" trees, one just across McKinley Drive from our house and one on Phyllis Drive just about 200 feet from Larry's yard. "Fire Island" trees were the ones tall enough that you could see all way down to bay and across it to Fire Island, a good half mile or more. When the Atlantic was pounding. you could even see the spray behind the dunes. If either of our parents, who also became friends through the years, ever knew we were up in trees that high, that early in our lives, we proba-bly would been grounded to our respective yards until we graduated high school. Thinking back, I believe my first big climb was in the tree across from our house and that would have had to been with our summer kid gang of the Dennings and Yodices, who just by living in the city, always seemed to be much further ad-vanced in daring do than their country bumpkin sidekicks. I can still see myself standing in our front yard looking up at Donald Denning in the crows nest of the big pine in the woods across the street. He was soon joined by his cousin Patty, who emerged from the camouflage of the huge branches and enticed the rest of us to come on up and take a look. It was probably several days before I found enough nerve to go all the way up to the top. I know I made several attempts, only to get about halfway there and then return to the safety of the soft pine needle covered earth with nothing to show for it but pine sap all over my hands.

The Fire Island tree by Larry's was a very different pine from the one by our house. It was much closer to the kind you see being putting up at Rockefeller Center during Christmas. It also was in an arrangement of trees. that I realize now, was landscaped rather than natural. I remember the first time I went up it, climbing in a circular fashion to utilize all the thickest branches. I was about three quarters of the way to the top and above the treetops of most of the sur-rounding trees. Looking northward I found myself staring at something I had sort of forgotten about. There not two hundred yards from my eye level were the third story windows and the gable of the mansion looking back at me. I continued to ascend and when I got to the top, found the view of Fire Island in this tree was different. Either the tree was taller than the one by my house or the dunes were lower, cause you could actually see the Atlantic Ocean and if you turned around you could look down on the terraces and rooftop of the mansion.

Another tree of great interest was the one in Mr. Clark's front yard. It was an oak and it was massive in thickness. What was really interesting was that it had a hole in the center of the main trunk that was caused by the lopping of it back in the early 1700's. Lopping trees was a way the farmers had of partially cutting them, so they would grow sideways, thereby making natural fences to contain their livestock. This tree had seen it's way to grow back together and create a tunnel in the middle of its main trunk. The branch that was lopped and pointed in the direction of Mr. Clarks barn was also huge and us "four musketeers" would spend lots of time sitting on it. Sometimes we would pretend it was an elephant we were riding, ala Rama Of The Jungle. Of course this was after Mr. Clark had left the scene. He had taken ill about 1953 and his son took him to a nursing home. His barn, which was built about 1850 would remain empty for many years. Also on Mr. Clark's property was a large cement lined "swimming pool sized" livestock watering hole that had a ramp on one side and probably three foot walls on the others. There was also a cement lined trough that supplied it, that led off to the south and to the water tower. We used the pool which was filled with pine needles mainly as a fort like the Alamo. It was directly across the road from where the bad guys were holed up in the skull and crossbones shack.

For Larry and me the bad guys then were mainly Joey Castellano, Eugene Tyres and Adolph Almasy. They weren't really bad guys, just strangers because although they lived in the neighborhood, they went to St. John's School where I'm sure the strict discipline enforced on them by the nuns resulted in their overly aggressive behavior towards us. They were like Skut Farkas and Grover Dill, those two rapscallions in Jean Shepherd's stories about Ralphy, Flick and company. If you have ever watched film The Christmas Story with it's famous line "You'll Shoot Your Eye Out, Kid", then you know exactly what I mean. I think the first time Larry and I encountered them it was just Joey and Eugene and they were hiding inside the skull and cross bones shack. As we walked into the field, Joey who was definitely the gang leader, came out of the shack war whooping. He was wearing a feathered headband and had a tomahawk in his hand. I don't know if Joey's tomahawk was real or just a rubber souvenir from the Pow Wows they used to hold on the Poosepatuck Indian Reservation in Mastic. We didn't hang around to find out. Larry and I took off like scared rabbits. The other encounter I recall over there was when we thought it was safe to explore the shack. Joey, Eugene and Adolph were up in the cupola of Schulte's barn shooting their Daisy BB guns at us. Adolph who became a friend and band mate of mine in high school, swears his was only a smoke rifle. It did not matter, as three rifle barrels pointed down at us were three too many for the two of us and we really only had smoke rifles. BB's were zinging all around us.

Once again we fled. For some reason Butch was never around when Larry and I got attacked by Joey and his "gang". I never knew then what that shack was built for, but now have a pretty good idea. We spent days of our childhood playing among the ruins of the Knapp estate. Skippy, who was part chow, gave birth to a litter of puppies in that shack. I'm pretty sure with what I now know is that shack was part of Claire Knapp's, Clairedale show dog kennels and Clairedale specialized in chows. During one of the Easter vacations from school in the '50s, I heard fire engines coming our way, saw the smoke from our backyard and ran over to Jefferson Drive just as the fire trucks pulled up to where the shack was. People were already gathered there. When I got closer, the flames were leaping through the roof and the fire had skipped across the road to Mr. Clark's property. Firemen were using Indian Canteens and brooms to put out grass fires all over the area. I can't say I missed the shack.

I'M NOT SURE WHAT YEAR IT WAS, BUT I KNOW IT WAS A RAINY DAY, in the early 1950s. I was probably seven or eight. Butchie, me, Larry and Dennis were together at the Schulz house playing with clay or something in his kitchen. Mrs. Schulz was on the phone. She was telling someone to get over to the mansion as soon as possible and get what they wanted before it was all gone. Larry filled in the blanks for me. It seems that St. Jude's had given up on plans of making a school out of the place and left it wide open for folks to just help themselves to all sorts of things. Whether or not this was official church policy or just someone who took it upon themselves to justify the community looting, is still unresolved to this day. For the record, the Schulzs were active members of St. Andrew's church, just across the street from St. Jude's. The Scimecas, their neighbors, across the street from the Schulz house, were very active members of St. Jude's and Mrs. Schulz would often go to card parties, held in the mansion ballroom with Rose Scimeca. But to get back to the phone conversation, I was straining to concentrate on, Larry said he was in the mansion with his parents a few nights before and had seen lots of neat things, like a treasure chest, and a roulette wheel, English darts and all kinds of swords and guns. He said people were just helping themselves to it all, even antique furniture. I mentioned the free stuff several times to Mom when we got home, but she seemed to have no interest at all in it. Again I just wanted to be able to go inside the mansion once, to see what it was that caused everyone's jaw to drop open when they went in there.

IN THE GOOD OLD SUMMERTIME; for some reason, come summer, Larry and Dennis and Butchie and me would always go our separate ways. Perhaps we just wanted some variety in who we spent our time with. I know we could not desert our summer friends as they were the only friends we had our first two years in Mastic Beach. I for one always felt kind of bad that Larry didn't seem to want to play with our summer friends, but then again I didn't care too much for his summer friends either. Especially the Whitten brothers, who lived down the end of his road. I played baseball with them a few times. They had an empty field at the back of their house that backed up to that "coal covered road" and it was directly in front of the mansion's front side. I can still recall standing in the outfield and looking up at the asymmetrical tower side of the mansion and wondering what that place was like inside. The third story windows and the tower gable always held some intrigue for me. But I would not dare go inside the place, even though I knew by then it was empty. That would be just too scary for a 7 year old. On the western border of the Whitten property, there was a small patch of woods and in it was another cement lined trough that was completely dry. I never thought much about it then, but now realize it was also part of some landscaping. In fact most of acres of land in front of the mansion's south face had an entire different look to it than the rest of our neighborhood. Back then I didn't know why.

IT WAS PROBABLY OUR THIRD SUMMER IN MASTIC BEACH, when we really started to spread our wings a bit beyond our respective yards. As I said. the city kids who we palled around with always seemed more advanced. Most of them save for Patty Denning, and Mary Ann Yodice, were a year or two older than me. Sally Ann Yodice was the oldest, even older than Butch by a few months. Back then it seemed even days counted. I know some years later, the first time our Mom allowed us to go the beach alone without her, it was only because Sally Ann was with us and had taken lifeguard training.

It was Anthony Yodice who suggested we go explore Schulte's Barn. I think he was already in it once or twice with his older relatives. So off we all went, Sally Ann, Mary Ann, Anthony, Donald, Patty, Butchie and me. Marching north on McKinley Drive, past the Nelsons and the Dorers, all the way up to Dogwood Rd. where we turned left by the Gailbraith's tar paper covered house. Then it was one very short block over to Jefferson. There it stood looking back at us in the shade of it's trees and overgrown grass, daring us to enter. By now I think the doors were either wide open or had fallen off. There was safety in numbers however as Anthony and Butch led the way. Walking inside of it was no big deal and there really wasn't much of anything to see, just a big empty barn, that is until we went up the stairs. In single file we hugged the wall. There was no railing and I think a few of us, might of crawled up the stairs. As soon as we got into the loft though, all fears were forgotten, save for keeping a look out for bats that supposedly slept in the daytime. The loft held all kinds of airplane parts, now scattered all over the place. It could of been a plane factory once. There were dashboards with gauges and those half circle airplane steering wheels, and more. Most of the stuff was all smashed up, but to us it was great. Then there was what seemed like endless heaps of wire that looked like an explosion in a Ronzoni spaghetti factory. In the middle of the loft there were some large metal cabinets filled with radio equipment with plates on them that said property of US Navy with dates going back to 1917. It didn't take us long to go home and get some wagons to haul the best of the loot back to our yard. There we set it up and played " Idelwild Airport" (known today as Kennedy) with it. When our Dad got home, he asked us where in the world did we find this stuff? At first he seemed interested in it, especially the radio equipment as he was a radio operator in WWII, but by the weekend he carted off our aviation treasures to the town dump.

I'LL NEVER FORGET NEW YEARS DAY 1955, EITHER. I was in the second grade and we were enjoying the end of our Christmas vacation. Mr. Clark's barn had been empty for some time and was getting nearly as torn up as Schulte's Barn. But because it was literally in the Schulz's backyard, Larry's parents kept a fairly close eye on it and would often chase kids out of it. I'm sure they didn't want it torched as the shack had been. For some reason though, they seemed to tolerate letting us play in it, even though it was not a very safe environment. Several windows had been broken out by kids and to add to that, Mr. Clark kept a cache of medicine and chemical bottles in the shed on the back. Many of them had found their way into the main room and kids obviously were throwing them around, resulting in a whole lot of broken glass on the wood floor. At the rear of the barn, where Mr. Clark had a makeshift kitchen, there was a stairway to the loft. It was not in good shape either and like Schulte's barn, it had no railing. Up in the hayloft itself, that always smelled very musty, the loft doors were wide open with a cement apron directly below them that led to the main barn doors. In short, the place would not pass muster with any playground inspector. That Christmas, Santa had brought me a double 6 gun cap shooter holster set. New Years day was clear and crisp and the four of us were playing Wyatt Earp or something like it. Butchie and Dennis were the bad guys and Larry and me were the marshals who were gonna bring them in dead or alive. It started out like a game of hide and seek, they took off while Larry and I counted to a hundred. We checked several places before we thought they might be holed up in the Clark barn.

Larry and I cautiously approached the barn doors, each one of us taking a side and opening them very slowly using them for cover. Peering around the edge, the room looked empty, so we slowly walked in with our guns drawn. We were about midway in the room when Dennis started making shooting noises *bang bang!* They were up in the loft and we were had. Larry yelled, *AMBUSH! Hit the dirt!* I dove to the floor and when I came back up, felt a sharp pain in my ankle. Long story short, I spent the afternoon at Doctor Remy's in Center Moriches getting glass taken out and stitches put in. I still have the scar and the memory.

I've mentioned a few times the "coal covered road" that ran east and west between Jefferson and Monroe Drives and passed in front of Mr. Clark's Barn on the east end and the mansion on the west. Looking now at my 1938 file map of Section 10, that road was 840 feet long and at one time in the early '50s, I think it had a name other than Ramshorn Rd. the one it has had since the late '50s. Only one other person I have talked with, seems to recall too that Ramshorn once had a different name. It's a small detail, but at least it tells me I'm not imagining things. I can still see the vertical 4x4 signpost that might of said Lawrence Rd. on it and just disappeared one day, like the twin towers did.

What I want to talk about here though is a second "coal covered road" located about a ½ mile south on Jefferson Dr. that led to the water. This one never had a signpost, but on the map it has a name, a very appropriate one, Dock Road. It forked off to the right of Jefferson just where Jefferson makes a straight beeline for Beach Ten. Dock Road, which today is completely hidden,was surrounded then on both sides by catails but when you got to the water there was much more than just a dock, It was a man made small lagoon about 60 long x 40 feet wide, fully bulkheaded and opened into a wider natural cove that in turn opened out to the bay with a very small island at its mouth. Pattersquash Island was directly out across the bay from it. My first time going down Dock Road, I was with Butch, Pop and grandpa Joseph. Grandpa kept his rowboat in that cove for a short time. His boat always looked lonely there all by itself and I wondered why no else kept their boats there, because the bulkhead part was really first class. (as if a 5 year old future commercial fisherman would know a first class bulkhead when he saw one) Gramp's rowboat leaked bad and he hauled it home one day where it sat in his yard till he passed away. My grandmother always said she was going to put a flower bed in it, as many other homes around the Beach had done, but I don't recall that ever happening. I think my Uncle Les may of hauled the boat off to his house in Center Moriches. Uncle Les, the youngest of the three sons always seemed to be getting his hands on Grandpa Joseph's stuff and fixing it up and selling it. When Grandpa died, in November of '57, I was a ten year old certified car nut with big plans to build a stock car and race it on Riverhead Raceway someday. I really wanted to inherit Grandpa's '47 Ford coupe and asked my Dad if I could have it. I never got a chance as Uncle Les towed it home and had sold it before Grandpa's headstone was in place. However, when I finally got my chance to race in 1965, guess what I drove: A 1947 Ford Coupe, that was built in East Moriches. I always liked to think it may of well of been Grandpa's own car, that I went bouncing off the walls and swapping paint with at Riverhead Raceway that summer. But getting back to the sea.

Larry's Dad, who was a carpenter, built a very massive and sturdy rowboat. He kept it at that "old lagoon" on Dock Rd. as it was sometimes called. He used a 3-horsepower Evinrude on it, that was so underpowered you could row faster, but gradually he upped the horsepower over the years to where the boat could stay ahead of the tide. Besides Larry's, the only other boat I recall ever seeing tied up there for a season or two was Pete Scimeca's runabout. Pete kept his boat in the main bulkhead area and it too looked very lonely, sitting in this big bulkhead most everyone thought was meant to be Mastic Beach Lagoon number two. It wasn't, but it would be 50 years before I'd find out the rest of the story and see what once was moored there or realize how the two coal covered roads were connected.

Another connection it would take years to make, was our discovery of the secret pond or what it's original purpose was. This would be another summer gang discovery that was enjoyed for years by all the kids in the neighborhood year round. The pond was fed from a stream that branched off from the Dock Road lagoon. But that is not how we found it.

I can't recall exactly when it was when we first discovered the secret pond, but I'm pretty sure it was in the summer of '56. That was a real big discovery year for Butchie and me and our summer pals from the city. By the mid '50s, we were old enough to be allowed to venture a little further from our cluster of houses and yards and bold enough to take chances. We hiked and biked all over back then, going up to big town by ourselves, to the town dump to scavenge buggy wheels for making soap box cars, over to Beach One and Ten for swimming, and of course the pilgrimage to the mother of all explorations, finally gathering the nerve to enter the abandoned and "haunted" Knapp Mansion.

We really weren't following Henry Thoreau's lead when we discovered the secret pond, actually we were drawn there by a large piece of industrial sculpture. A '40's Chrysler Imperial Taxi Cab. Some part time summer resident had permanently parked it on the side yard of his bungalow on Lafayette Drive. I never saw it move, much less pick up a fare in the 14 years, I lived in Mastic Beach. How many kids can ya get in one of these babies? Well let's see; there was Sally Ann, Mary Ann and Anthony Yodice, Donald and Patty Denning, their cousin Georgie Lang, Butchie and Me. That would be 8 of us and there was room for more. I'm driving, SHOTGUN! I called it—no I did— hey quit shoving—Hey, check out these jump seats back here.

Well with 8 kids piled into an old musty mohair cab in the summer time, you can bet they were not going to stay in there very long. We bailed out pretty quick and for some reason crossed the road and walked along the cattails that bordered the property of another closed up summer bungalow. A lot of folks only came out on weekends or for a week or two in the summer. Just in the back of this cottage, there was a path going off into the woods and so we followed it. A few yards into the woods, you had to bend down to get through an arch of trees.

I don't think any of us were prepared for what we saw, about 50 feet further into what felt like enchanted woods. There was big pond with an island in the middle of it! We walked around most of its eastern bank, just amazed at our discovery. For a week or two the 'secret pond', so named because somehow we thought we were the only ones who must know about it, was one of our main play destinations. Before long we were talking about building a raft to sail out to the island. The first raft never got built, mainly because we all got tired of trying to cut up some green locust tree logs with dull rusty saws. Several years later, some other kids left a small raft in there. It was made from some old wood flooring and when you stood on it, it sank. Exploring the island someday would always stick in my mind.

One family custom I used to look forward to at the end of each school year was the promotion gift. I think it was year I got promoted from 3rd grade into 5th, that I got an Ideal Toy Co, wind up speedboat. As soon as I got home I wasted no time in getting over to the pond.

I tied some string to the transom cleat, wound it up and watched her go... sort of. Though it resembled the great Chris Craft, Dodge and Gar Wood classic mahogany speedboats, speed it did not have, it barely moved, giving one options for litigation over the false advertising on the box cover. But just as that dis-appointment was sinking in, true disaster struck. About 20 feet out the string came loose and I watched helplessly as my brand new boat headed for Gilligan's Island with no definitive way of returning from a "3 hour cruise". I already knew that you didn't want to try wading out in this pond, because of my past experiences with the shoddy raft. Two feet under the dark brown and green water lay a bottom of pure mud. So I was at the mercy of the breeze and that June day there wasn't any.

The engine soon unwound and my little craft stopped dead out there. It slowly drifted around for what seemed forever, before it started to drift back in my direction. Fueled with hope that I might get it back before I had to go home for supper, I climbed a tree and broke off a fairly long branch. It took a while, but I got my new boat back and kept it high and dry in my room after that. I wish I still had it though, as I saw one on eBay recently sell for $150.00. Quite an appreciation for some molded plastic and a spring motor that Mom spent $2.98 for at the 5 & 10 in town.

About 3 years passed before I would go boating in the pond again but this time it was for real. Butchie's friend Doug Percoco had got hold of a real kayak. It was made of green canvas stretched over a wood frame and looked just like the ones the Eskimos had. And what better time for me to try it out than in Eskimo weather, the dead of winter.

It was either in December of 1958 or January of '59. I know that for sure because of who was with me the last time I took it out. I had been out in it a few times solo after school and always got back ok, even though it did leak some. The canvas was fairly old and dried out. My last trip may of occurred during Christmas recess or a school snow day in January. I had told Guido Michelini, a classmate about it. We were in 7th grade together and just starting to hang around a bit with each other. Guido's Mom, worked with mine at Howard Johnson's. Guido came over one very snowy day and we lit out for the pond. He seemed to doubt that the kayak could safely hold us both, but got in and we shoved off. We were just a little ways out from shore when Guido yelled "HEY! We're sinking" Sure enough a tree branch came through the bottom and we were taking on water like the Titanic. I bailed out taking about two or three giant leaps through the water. Each time feeling myself sink deep into the muck. I turned around on the bank and there was Guido standing up holding the paddle, as the little craft disappeared. He then slowly walked into shore getting thoroughly soaked. It was about a half mile back to my house and we arrived looking like two Eskimo Pies. My Mom called his and then she washed and dried his clothes. We spent the afternoon playing with my Marx Cape Canaveral play set and although we continued with four and a half more years of school, that was the last time Guido ever came over to my house.

GUIDO LIVED UP IN SECTION **4**, which was on the other side of Patterquash Creek and that was where the actual big town was located. There was another mansion located up there, too. This one was very old, dating back before the Revolutionary War, It was built by William Floyd's cousin Richard. Richard Floyd took the "wrong side" during the Revolutionary War and had to beat it to Nova Scotia when the war was over. His 3,500 acre estate was confiscated by the victors. During the entire Revolution, the British army occupied all of Long Island partly because General Woodhull, also of Mastic. who's estate was but a stones throw from his brother in law

William Floyd's, had gotten himself wounded and captured in the Battle of Long Island in August of 1776. He died a month later from his wounds. About ten years after the town of Mastic Beach was started, the few year round locals decided it would be a good idea to honor the General every Memorial Day with a parade that started in "new town" and proceeded east to the Woodhull graveyard over in Section One. There they gave the General a 21 gun salute. As a kid it was a big deal to rush in through the gates to try and get a souvenir cartridge. The big kids always seemed to get them. For me though just watching the parade was good enough.

For a kid who seemed to be interested with old houses and mansions, I never thought of Richard Floyd's place that way, probably because of how it looked when I first went inside of it, in November 1958. Had I been there say two years earlier when it was still wearing it's colonial exterior face, I know I would have thought differently. In 1946 a local physician, Doctor Calabro bought it and decided to make a hospital out of it. Fortunately I stayed hospital free through the '50's, save for my eye operation that was performed in Riverhead Hospital in 1955. By 1957, Bayview Hospital hit the national news because of it's most famous patient, Benny Hooper, a little boy who was trapped in a well for several days recooped there. By then it's exterior had been totally covered in brick and by 1959. It had a modern brick addition attached to it. However, when I did go inside of it with about three quarters of my entire school, who had got food poisoning from the Thanksgiving turkey lunch, I did notice it was a pretty old house. Fifty years later thanks to the Knapps, I would learn so much more about it's fascinating history and all the estates that once made up a place called Mastic.

Once again here I am going to turn to my web site and the original words that I wrote in 2000 about exploring the innards of our center piece, because at the time I wrote them, there was no thought of ever doing anything with it other than telling the story from a kids perspective, as close to the way it happened, not embellished by anything, I have learned since. At the risk of repeating a few facts you may already know, I think it's the best way to again let you experience it for the first time, just the way I did.

I seem to recall once hearing the mansion was built by the Knapps, who we thought we were relatives of the Floyds [they weren't] Actually the Floyds built several very large mansions in the Mastic area, but none just around the corner from our house. This one was three stories high and had a whole lot of fireplaces and chimneys. It sat on a couple of acres bordered by three roads and a grove of trees. It was white with Greek blue shutters on the windows and a reddish copper metal? roof. One day around 1954, the church people that lived there, just walked away from it. They never even locked the doors! Before long folks were hauling off carved furniture, statues, antiques, musical instruments and God knows what.

After a while "older kids" started hanging out in there and vandalizing the place. Before long it took on the look of a full fledged haunted house and all the kids I knew, gave it a wide berth. True we all would look at it on our bikes from a distance and fantasize about what it would be like to explore the innards, but no one dared go inside. Rumors even sprung up their was a dungeon in it.

By 1956 our "Summer Kids" gang had grown a bit. There was Spike a cousin of Donald and Patty who was now old enough to hang around with us and the Yodices. It was probably Anthony Yodice who first suggested to our bored little group that we go explore the mansion. At first a lot of us looked at each other to try and figure out what the other one was thinking. Somehow we must have felt safety in numbers because before long we were heading out for it with the eagerness of Miss Rosado's 5th graders on a field trip. However, you could feel the tension building as we approached the grounds.

For a while we just circled it, wondering who was going to go in first. There were doors on all sides with the main front doors on the south side. All of them were boarded up, but the porch windows were broken out and it was just a matter of stepping inside right off the huge stoop. I don't recall if we chose for who would go first, but I think it was Butch and Anthony who led the way. Then the rest of us. like Jefferson in a Charlie Chan movie said. " Wait For Me! " The porch was all windows and didn't seem too scary. It was a good room to get your feet wet at being in a place like one, that I'm sure none of us had ever been in before. The floor was covered with broken glass and debris. We huddled together and went into the hall way. Off to the right side was a spiral staircase, we decided to stay downstairs for now. To the left of the hall way was this huge dark room. It had to be at least 50' long and was all wood paneled. It must have been the great hall Gerry had told us about.

There were alcoves in it and small pedestals that probably housed the statues and the knights armour Gerry had spoke of. Several of us looked for a secret passage, that we thought must be in there somewhere. (there were several) At the far end were a set of French doors that led to the west entrance.

There may have been a table or desk left, but other than that it was very dark and empty. Wandering out a doorway we found several smaller rooms and a bathroom or two. Eventually we came upon the kitchen. It too was enormous and though it had windows to the east, seemed very gloomy. It had a dumbwaiter,the first one I ever saw outside of an Abbott & Costello or Charlie Chan movie. And several of us took turns riding in it, till the rope broke. The musty smell in the whole place was very distinctive and almost overbearing. There was an entire wall of refrigerator compartments, huge commercial stoves and a sink you could sail a boat in.

Going out the other kitchen doors took us back into another hall and we wound up at the stairway again. No one seemed too eager, so I became the show off and decided to climb it. We came to a landing with a sun room off of it and a terrace. Then up the second flight and we came to the master bedroom. It was over the great hall and had a terrace that you could have hosted a party for a 100 on. Up another flight and the rooms got smaller, probably servants quarters and lots of walk in closets. One had a ladder to the roof. The view from the roof was incredible. You could see the bay and Fire Island, which gave us a perspective of how high up we were. The roof was both flat in the center with pretty steeply pitched edges, but the terraces below us on both the west and east sides gave a false sense of security that if you slid off or fell you wouldn't go all the way down.

We must have spent at least an hour in it the first time and gathered on the front stoop to compare notes and take it all in before heading home. The only place we had not explored was the basement, as none of us were ready for that yet. We were also breathing a sigh of relief that the cops hadn't showed up to chase us out. We had heard that the Church had asked them to patrol it when it first started to get vandalized and they would haul you off to jail. Before we all left though, Anthony burst into the opening of *My Prayer* which was a new song by the Platters. I was amazed at how good he was. *"When the twilight is gone, and no songbirds are singing..."*

F OR MOST OF THAT SUMMER, the Knapp place occupied most of our attention. We devised this great escape plan to get away from the cops, in case they came for us. We actually had ropes tied to beams in upper rooms that we could go out the windows on all sides of it. While doing an escape rehearsal, Butchie cut his arm on a broken outside light fixture. He was bleeding pretty good but made a temporary bandage out of his undershirt. He ran home to get bandaged and soon rejoined us. I can't recall how he explained that to our Mom. The place had around 22 rooms, so there were some great places to hide. We played hide and go seek in it a whole lot. One time nobody could find Donald, some of us thought he might be in the cellar, but no one dared go look. I was in one of the first floor rooms that had a fireplace and I heard his voice. He was stuck in the chimney. Several of us ran up to the roof and sure enough, there he was laughing his head off a few feet down in it, but stuck none the less. We used one of the escape ropes to haul him out. We were lucky kids, but we were pushing our luck.

We made an unofficial ritual of all gathering on the front steps before we headed home ever since our first visit. It seems each time we went, we'd spend more time in there and push things a little further. After one long noisy afternoon, we were sitting on the stoop when we all froze. There were two of them and I can still see them coming at us from both sides. The boys in blue from the Brookhaven Town Police. One of them was Sgt. Burkhardt, who's teen age son Jackie, was one of the older kids who initially helped wreck the place when the church first left it. We all were pretty scared, but all that happened was a lecture from them and they made us promise to stay out of it for our own safety. I asked Sgt. Burkhardt, if the church really cared about what was happening to it, why didn't they take better care of boarding it up. He had no answer.

We had found out that the people who lived on the other side of the pine trees had called the cops. So we stayed away for a week, but one thing kept calling us. The fact that we never went down the cellar. Mary Ann Yodice repeatedly provoked us, saying we boys were too scared. What a troublemaker she was. So a plan was hatched, first we would split up and take different routes so the nosy neighbors wouldn't see a gang of kids heading for the joint. We brought along candles and flashlights. Donald and I led the way down the stairs. We went down them in twos and when we got to the bottom step, Donald blew out the candles. All the rest of them screamed and tore back up the steps. I had only got a glimpse of what was down there and really wasn't eager to go again. But after we all caught our breath, Mary Ann gave us her flashlight, took control of the candles, and we headed back down. You could hardly see anything, just the huge coal furnace. By the stairs was a door and it took a whole lot of nerve to open it. It was pitch black inside and its a good thing we shined the light on the floor first. There was none, it was a coal bin of undetermined depth. Then somebody said, "I see a rat." That did it: another mad scramble for stairway and that was the last visit any of us ever made to the cellar. We knew enough not to hang out on the stoop anymore, so when we all regrouped over at the Yodice house, everyone's imagination contributed to what they really saw down there. From chains on the walls to skeletons. Needless to say, no one wanted to return to verify or contest it.

For the first year or two it was a lot of fun and adventure over there. I remember smoking my first cigarette while sitting on the corner of the roof. It was a Newport and I got real dizzy and almost fell off. One day Butch said we could make a fortune selling the brass hardware in the ballroom. We visited the mansion with screwdrivers, hammers and chisels and stripped the ballroom of all its door handles and elaborate window mechanisms with these long half round brass rods. We had a wagon full of brass and hauled it back to our yard. Butch called a junky who said he'd be right over, while we salivated at the thought of blowing our new found riches at the Kozy Korner Ice Cream parlour and the Carnival behind Pat and Mike's gas station. But the junky must have got lost or distracted by a field of old Packards or LaSalles, because he never showed up.

We would go in the mansion in the winter time too, with a whole different group of kids, like the Schulz brothers and Doug Percoco. I remember an after school game of hide and go seek where I really fooled them all, pulled a Donald Denning and hid in the chimney. Trouble was they all gave up on me and went home. It gets dark early in the winter and when I no longer heard anyone's voice, I started to call out. Realizing I was alone and having to come down three flights of stairs in the dusk and getting the hell out of there was the scariest few moments I had ever experienced in my 10 years on earth. The last few steps I took through that big gloomy kitchen is forever encased in my fear locker.

There was this whole other group of "winter kids" in the neighborhood that we knew of, but didn't hang around with very much. You could say we were kind of leery of them. In high school Butchie would become friends with their unofficial leader Willy Conklin. It was around the fall of 1958 that Willy fell off the mansion roof and onto the porch roof below, breaking his leg in the process. The place was getting really torn up and just wasn't as much fun anymore. The summer kids would really notice the difference when they came out. The last summer we spent there, the entire stair railings had been ripped out, steps were missing and I don't think there was a single unbroken window. It was getting to be very dangerous.

I THINK THE SUMMER OF '58 WAS ALSO THE LAST SUMMER our original gang spent together. The Yodices were the ones who kind of went their own way. Sally Ann was first to stop hanging around with us, followed by Anthony who now had a a speed boat and started hanging out with older kids on the bay. Mary Ann who was my first girlfriend when we were around 5 stayed with us that summer. I think the last time we were together, it was up in the hayloft of Mr. Clark's barn.

It was the Dennings, their cousin Spike, Butchie and me and Mary Ann. Playing an early version of Truth or Dare. Well Mister Show off, perhaps to try and impress her, does a pre David Letterman stunt and pushes the lone piece of furniture, an old beat up dresser out the hayloft doors. It hit the cement apron and folded up like a cheap suitcase, but made a hell of a racket. We nearly all fell over each other scrambling down the hayloft stairs and as we ran out I saw Larry and his Mom coming out their back door to see what had happened. The Schulz family were now the owners of it, having purchased it at a back tax auction. I don't think I ever told Larry, who I am still in touch with, that it was me who did that, but I guess he knows now.

That fall Dave Schulz who was a fine carpenter and furniture maker, started to fix up Mr. Clark's barn. He originally purchased the place as a property buffer. Mastic Beach was rapidly expanding as an all year round community in the 50's and property was starting to get scarce. Sam Cole a local bulldozer operator had recently tore down Schulte's barn, though it would be at least 15 years before anyone built there. Mr. Schulz was originally was going to tear down, Clark's barn too, but when he saw how well it was constructed, decided to renovate it into a bonafide house. Larry, Dennis, Butchie and me had a big time watching him do that, not to mention getting in his way a lot. I can still hear him say *"Larry — DON'T mess with that!"* He put a center room staircase in it and divided the hayloft into two bedrooms. It was really neat and cozy. That same fall of 1958 my Mom started working as a nanny for a Floyd school teacher, who lived just down the road from the school. I was in 7th grade then and used to go there after school until Mrs. Nelson got home about, then ride home with Mom. The Nelsons lived in one of those Shirley Pre Fab homes that sprung up like weeds in the mid '50s. They were very affordable, modern looking and promoted to the hilt. We too bought property in Shirley in 1955 and almost had one put up. The main reason we never did though was Butchie and me said we didn't want to leave our friends both summer and winter. By 1958 our parents resold the uncleared lot and by summer of 1959 built an extension on the rear of our house instead.

Dorice Nelson was a striking looking woman. Very tall and slender with red hair and temper to match. At one time she had been a fashion model. I know for a fact she was many a young male Floyd students' fantasy and lots of my friends couldn't believe how lucky I was to get to go over to her house everyday after school. Thing is, we soon left after she got home, as Mom had to get dinner ready for us. That is unless Mrs. Nelson wanted to talk with my Mom. She was going through a messy divorce then and didn't want to stay in that house, even though it was only two blocks from her job. My Mom said she couldn't blame her because the house was drafty as hell and already falling apart after only two years, She also said I'm so glad we never bought one. I chimed in me too, for other reasons though, because good friends were always important to me. To make a short story longer, Mom suggested that Dorice look at the Schulz place that was soon going to be available and she did. It was very cheery looking with its canary yellow exterior, pastel colored bedrooms, bright kitchen, brand new bathroom. Mrs. Nelson moved in it around Christmas of 1958 with her three young children. Steven who was in kindergarten and the twins Lee and Mikey who were around three. For

Mom it was really convenient as now she could walk around the corner to work, also shuttle back and forth to get a jump start on making dinner for us. And for me, well, it might have kept me out of going to jail at the age of 11.

O N SUNDAY, FEBRUARY 15TH 1959, my dad took me to Commack about twenty some miles from Mastic Beach to see some Go Kart races. Go Karts were the rage in the late '50s and I really wanted one. Watching them race in a parking lot, just made me long more for them. But what I really wanted back then was Street Rod, like a '32 Ford and a jalopy stock car to race at Riverhead. I'd have to wait about six more years for both. I got home around 4 o'clock and was telling Butch and his friend Doug Percoco about the races and was all jacked up. Though I was excited, they were bored and I think it was Doug who said, "You want to go over to the mansion before it gets dark?"

We walked on over and when we turned off Jefferson Drive onto Ramshorn, I think we all saw it at once. As you know by now, the mansion was down the end of the road, but you could see the top half of it over the trees. I can still see the smoke pouring out of one the top windows. It was acting like a chimney sending puffs like smoke signals—*help, help!* As we turned around to run home and call the fire department, along came Charlie Ratigan in his forest green '58 Ford Brookhaven Town Police car (who said there's never a cop around when you need one?). Butch flagged him down and we yelled in unison *the mansion's on fire!* He called it in on the radio, then took off for it and with us running behind him.

As we were running, we heard the fire alarm blasting, the one Willie Schluder probably set off. I would give a jar of pennies and more for what his thoughts were that day. Of course we were there when the first fire truck arrived a few minutes later. A couple of fireman ran into it to see if there was anyone in there. I think one of them fell down the staircase winding up in Bayview hospital. Charlie went inside it too, then he came over to take our names. Soon the grounds were covered with fire trucks from Mastic Beach, Mastic and Brookhaven Fire Departments. I think I saw the whole Almasy family, who lived just across from the north side of it, gather to watch. I know Mr. Almasy for sure was there. Once upon a time he was a self appointed guardian for the place, when St. Judes first abandoned it. He tried hard to keep kids out of it, but got frustrated over the years. Word soon passed through the gathering spectators, that a decision had been made to let it burn. Back then I couldn't understand why they decided that, because with what little I knew about fire fighting from watching my Dad and company put out many a blaze in the early 50's, I knew they could have easily put this one out. I felt sick to my stomach and I had a lot of mixed emotions that afternoon. Most folks seemed to watch like it was a fireworks display and when the copper roof was fully engulfed it was extremely dramatic against the night sky. Others would tell me years later you could see it for miles around. Larry Schulz's dad even took home movies of it. When the roof collapsed, it was time to go home. The firemen stayed till 4 AM.

It's a good thing I went to the Go Kart races that day, because it became part of the alibi I had to use. Charlie Ratigan thought for sure we did it. Several neighbors spoke up for us though. None stronger however than Dorice Nelson who knew Charlie and told him he was pissing in the wind and he had the wrong kids. Everyone just assumed the arson was the work of kids. By Monday morning we were off his prime suspect list. For a long time there was lots of speculation about who did set it ablaze. Willy Conklin was a prime suspect as was any kid who was ever in it. Several years later another kid who was an Honor Boy Scout was fingered for it. Although he was a true firebug and was caught red handed about 1962 torching a house and admitted to having set numerous places on fire including the one that destroyed St. Andrew's church, he too wasn't the culprit. That discovery for me would also take 50 years to uncover.

The following day I returned to the property after school. Sam Cole was there with his dump truck. He was taking down the chimneys and told me to stand back. As each one toppled the ground shook. After he drove off it was starting to get dark. I took a quick look through the rubble and thought about all the great times I had playing in it. As I walked slowly home, I wondered again what it must have been like when — The Knapps Lived Here.

O NE NIGHT A WEEK MRS. NELSON TOOK A CLASS AT HOFSTRA UNIVERSITY, and Mom naturally babysat. I would often go over there with her as I liked being in Mr. Clark's barn. One evening a few weeks after the fire, the Schulz family came over with a movie projector. There was the Knapp mansion ablaze again, on a portable screen, in living color and total silence, save for the whir-ring of the projector.

Several times that spring, I returned to the huge pile of rubble and charred timbers and bricks that was probably ten feet high. I never thought to take home a souvenir though. Besides there was all those brass parts from the ballroom we were going to get rich on, still lying in the woodpile in our backyard. They are probably still under the dirt back there.

I think it was in the spring that Sam Cole returned with his bulldozer and plowed the mansion rubble under the earth. Bet there's still stuff under there too.

That summer of 1959, we had a lot of other things to occupy our attention. The biggest, was putting the addition on to our house. That took up most of August. That early autumn our grandparents the Spooners moved in with us. By fall the tall grass had erased any trace that a mansion was ever there. On October 25, 1959, some twenty five miles away to the east, again in Hampton Bays, Claire Antoinette Knapp, age 70 by just three short days, would pass away. That too would take me 42 years to find out.

CHAPTER

4

Back & Forth to the Future

The last five years that I lived in Mastic Beach, I don't think I went past the area of where the mansion once stood, more than a half dozen times. Probably thought of it even less. Mrs. Nelson moved out of Clark's Barn and upstate to Albany at the end of the 1960 school year. But before she did my Mom took a flying leap down the barn stairway and wound up in Bayview Hospital for a few days. My visits to her there did nothing to remind me of what Bayview Hospital once was, as she was in the new wing. Same thing a year or so later when trying to water ski on a 1941 Chevrolet car hood out of the cove at the end of Dock Road, behind Larry's grossly underpowered rowboat boat. That stunt resulted in my return to Bayview to have Dr. Calabro put some more stitches in my leg. (same side just higher up above the knee) and this time I got a Tetanus shot. Even in 1962, when I returned to the scene of the crime or ground zero if you will, carrying the battery from my Mom's '61 Falcon to start up an old '50 Plymouth, that Joey Castellano had stashed in the field where the mansion once stood. I was really whooping it up and don't think the mansion crossed my mind that day as I drove round and round, making a track through the tall, tall grass until the old motor in the Plymouth overheated. In retrospect the infield of my makeshift speedway was the actual footprint of the grand old house.

Probably the last time I was in the vicinity of the place was in April of '65 when

I returned to the Beach in my new 1933 Ford street rod with a full tilt exposed, chromed '54 Caddy engine. It was cut down, bright yellow with no fenders and could smoke the tires and turn heads wherever I went. The first day I had it, I went from Patchogue, where I would live for the next ten years to Mastic Beach to visit my old friends. One of them was Adolph, who you might recall was one of the "Bad Guys" in the very early '50s holed up in the cupola of Schulte's Barn with Joey, raining BB's and supposedly harmless smoke down upon Larry and me. Adolph, who still lived in his house, that was directly across Dogwood road where the backside of the mansion overlooked its squatters, suggested we drive over to show Peter and John. Peter and John were two members of the large Dermody family, who lived just around the corner in a very old home circa 1860, directly across from the mansions west face. Though I had walked past their house many times over the years, I never thought much about it until that day as I wheeled into their driveway. Even then I never connected it to what once stood across the road. Actually, there were two other houses all architecturally similar to the Dermody place, not more than a block and a half apart. Each was beautifully landscaped with tall pines, and unlike any others in Mastic Beach. Each one is connected with the Knapp estate. But my thoughts that day and theirs too were on hot rods, not house and garden tours. They all piled in and we went cruising around town, up to Skippy's Drive-In for burgers and thick shakes.

"Life is what happens to you while your making other plans"

—*Gamble Rogers*

THE LAST TEN YEARS THAT I LIVED ON LONG ISLAND, IN PATCHOGUE, Patchogue Shores, Bay Shore, Mastic and Easthampton, I can't say that old houses occupied much of my thoughts. Even when surrounded by 18th century ones in Easthampton or when I moved back to Mastic in 1973 and Susan and I purchased a new replica of a Colonial Salt Box home. Now, fast-forward to 1987. I'm a long way from Long Island, living on Florida's west coast. I had been there for nine years and suddenly its moving day again. I'm heading back north, this time to the hills of Nashville, Tennessee. With me is my wife Anne and 3 $\frac{1}{2}$ year old son Erik. It's Erik's first move and I'll be darned if he's not the same age as I was when I made my first move to the country in 1950.

After we settled in a bit, we started to explore Nashville on the weekends. One of the earliest places we visited was The Hermitage, the home of Andrew Jackson, seventh President of the United States. As we walked up the tree lined driveway to the front of the home, I was transported immediately just as fast as Marty McFly was, when he first drove Dr. Brown's DeLorean in the movie *Back To The Future*. I even went back to the same year that Marty did—1955! Yes, I was transported to the summer of '55 at the Shirley Drive In and approaching the Hermitage exactly from the same viewpoint the cameras of Walt Disney did, as Davy Crockett first paid a call on "Old Hickory"! I don't think I said too much about it to Anne that day, but it just was an overwhelming feeling of deja vu

*—Davy, Davy Crockett king of the wild frontier—*my hero and the hero of million more young boys. As we approached the balcony where Old Hickory stood telling Davy to come on in, I recalled the way Larry and I used to re-enact each weekly TV episode of "The Adventures Davy Crockett". Fess Parker was my idol back then and thinking back, Larry always identified with Buddy Ebsen. It was never even discussed between us as to who should play Davy and who should play his sidekick Georgie Russell. Larry carried his Daisy Smoke Rifle that spewed smoke when you poured household oil down its barrel the same way Buddy Ebsen did and I carried mine "Old Betsy" the same way Fess Parker did. Traipsing through the woods and fields around Mr. Clark's and Schulte's barns, fighting Creek Indians, bears, and bad guys, we had some of the best years of our lives. Going inside Jackson's main hall, did nothing to put the brakes on my back to the future journey. I knew the staircase from the movie, I knew the wallpaper. Disney had used this actual house for his film, which was nothing more than all the TV episodes joined together *but in living color—*and on a *big screen!*

I don't think I heard too much of what our costumed tour guide said, until we reached the second floor, but as we reached the first landing of the spiral staircase, I flashed for a minute what it felt like the first day I climbed the stairs in the Knapp mansion. After that, perhaps because I was thinking about my own youth, I focused on Erik's reaction to the whole deal. He was *fascinated,* and that's all he could talk about for days on end. That led us to take him to more and more old homes and plantations around Tennessee. He just lived and breathed it for years. He and I returned to the Hermitage several years later with his third grade class. This time I was a chaperone and keeping track of a bunch of wild 9 year olds, didn't leave the luxury of time traveling to my own childhood. What I did take notice of though, because it was so strong, was Erik's recollection of the place and he actually played tour guide to a group of four or five of his classmates, pointing out details of the place and the rooms that were absolutely uncanny. He seemed frustrated when they didn't pay close attention to all he was saying. For months after it he would speak of Jackson's family as if he was once part of it!

For several years at home, the main thing he played with was a whole lot of wood blocks and for about a year or so they occupied a permanent place in the living room of our apartment. He also said he wanted to be an architect when he grew up. An unlikely choice for a nine year old and Anne and I just looked at each other. Not long after I noticed his strong fascination with old houses, I began to tell him stories about my adventures in the mansion. He really wanted to see it and I told him I would try to find a picture of it for him. I did recall seeing a photo of it, in a newspaper story about the fire. The hometown paper had ceased publication by then, so my first effort was to call the Moriches Bay Historical Society. They had never even heard of anything called The Knapp Mansion, nor did they seem to have much info at all on the Mastic area other than the usual stuff about The Manor Of St. George and The William Floyd estate. My second choice was to call the people who last owned it, St. Jude's. A woman in the parish office took my number and said the Father would get back to me. He never did. I tried calling again but got the same results. My attempts to draw a picture of it were not very satisfying to me. I kept seeing the tower in the front, but could not seem to get it right on paper. I don't think Erik was as frustrated as I was.

IN THE SUMMER OF 1994, I VENTURED BACK TO LONG ISLAND to work on my first book, *Long Ride On A Short Track,* a doumented history of auto racing on Long Island. Erik came with me, it was our first long father and son trip alone. We were there for about ten days. Although the bulk of my time was spent interviewing former retired race drivers. that I first saw when I was Erik's age, and who inspired me to follow them out on the track in the summer 1965, I did manage to spend a day and a half showing him my hometown and all places he had only heard about in my stories. We had ourselves quite a time as we drove and parked and walked through the town itself with Erik holding a video camera and me being tour guide. He repeated almost everything I said as he pointed the camera at the places I was pointing at with dizzying cinematic results. But to me that video tape is priceless. The very first place he wanted to see was the mansion, fully knowing that it wasn't there. In showing him where the mansion once stood, I decided to take the route from my house to it. As we turned onto that "coal covered road" we of course paused in front of Mr. Clark's Barn. It was still yellow. The huge tree with the hole in it was still standing strong. I couldn't believe it. As we slowly drove at 5 mph down Ramshorn Rd., we came to the end of it, where the mansion once stood proudly. To my surprise there was a fairly large split level home there looking back at us. But it was not in the exact place where the mansion was. There were also two other houses on the west and north sides of the remaining 3 ½ acres the mansion once stood on. All were quite large and largest one was very contemporary, kind of like what you would see in the Hamptons, certainly out of place in Mastic Beach. The one thing that struck me though was that the footprint of where the Knapp Mansion once stood towering over the tree tops, remained unbuilt on and served as common back yard to all three "squatters". We drove off and I would think no more about it for another six years. Wanting to give Erik a real Mastic mansion fix, we tried to visit the Floyd Estate the last day we were there. It had been willed to the NATIONAL PARK SERVICE as a museum, but because of budget cutbacks, was closed that day. We did manage to get in a whirlwind tour of The Manor Of St. George, another colonial estate-turned-museum though and that seemed to satisfy him.

As we travel on, throughout this book, you will learn as I did, much more, about the roles these great estates played in Mastic, as my mission unfolds to try and find out just who were, the family you are about to meet. Another little side trip to Long Island in 2001, sent me on a journey down Knapp Road, that I would have never ever dreamed of taking.

I'm Forever Blowing Bubbles

Knapp Road is nothing like most roads in Mastic Beach. Most roads there run very grid like, laid out with definite east west and north south precision. Considering the crude equipment they used to build them with from 1926-1938 and the condition of some of the road builders (fetch the jug and bring it here) as they labored to plow through the scrub pine and oak, sometimes with horse drawn plows, it's amazing they turned out as straight as they did. Knapp Road however runs on an angle with twists and turns that have been there since the 19th century. Throughout this book it will become a metaphor for how I found out what Paul Harvey used to call "The Rest Of The Story"...

Happy New Year
When I was a full time songwriter, I always tried to write one song at the end of the year and one on the first day of the year. Seeing that it worked well for me there, I tried to apply the same work ethic to writing stories. Not that I could write a book in December and another in January, but because I had now determined to do a short story series and had written my first Buzz & Pee Wee, Butchie & Me adventure "You Better Watch Out" just before Christmas, I decided

to follow it up with another story of that ilk on New Years Eve. It was most likely New Years Eve morning of 2000 that I started to tap out with my right index finger what happened to Butchie & Me in "The Mansion" By late afternoon it was a done deal and uploaded to my Spoonytunes website. Again this time, but now within a year instead of fifty, I would find out one of the many odd coincidences associated with my timing and choices of what to do next.

I'm not sure if I even knew what genealogy was when I started, but I'd soon find out as I enlisted the wonderful world wide web, to help me in my search. I actually had little choice back then, as here I was in Nashville, a long way south of Mastic Beach. But then again I had no plans to pursue the history of Mastic Beach or the Knapp mansion for that matter. My curiosity to dig a little (actually very little) may of been initially spurred by a telephone conversation with Kenny Vitellaro. Kenny was a newly re acquainted, old high school friend and former band-mate too. Back on New Years Eve of 1963, we did a gig at the Mastic Beach Yacht Club together with Larry Schulz on guitar and Bobby Green on drums. It was an all Floyd High combo, although Kenny was a refugee from St. John's, only having entered Floyd in high school with Adolph, the other St. John's accordion player I worked with back then.

Kenny, who now is a contractor, takes care of several of the fine homes in the Hamptons. He has a strong interest in old houses and buildings in general too. He had read "The Mansion" online and asked me "When do you think it was built?" He had only seen it briefly up close once when he was at Adolph's house and Adolph was very reluctant to even enter it. He recalls it being really torn up inside, and said they did most of their exploring from the exterior, but may of been inside on the first floor briefly. Kenny was asking me all kinds of building details, like what was the roof like, the windows, gutters etc. He felt it wasn't as old as most folks thought and was probably built in the early 1900's. I told him that a newspaper, most likely the Moriches Tribune published a photo of it after the fire, that showed it as it once was. I can still see it standing, especially that tower part, tall and proud. At my request, he went to the Center Moriches library looking through the microfilm. He found the story but the only pictures in the paper were one of it ablaze, one of it the morning after, with three naked chimneys reaching skyward above the rubble through the morning mist and one of a fireman re-cooperating in the Bayview hospital. He told me the last time he saw the Knapp Mansion, it was from a great distance, when he was riding with his Dad down Mastic Road right where Knapp Road forks off it to the left. That is about a mile or so away from where the house itself was. What he saw was the entire sky lit up bright orange that Sunday evening in 1959. It may well of been our phone call that spurred on what happened next and nearly sent me a long way from Mastic Beach, all the way to Philadelphia, and far beyond to Wurtenberg, Germany!

Meet M. J. Knapp and Family
They say genealogy and the interest in it has taken giant steps with the invention of the internet. As one who has been online since 1994, I can certainly

agree with that, if only to know how fantastic the internet is as a means of find-ing folks and info about things that would probably never have seen the light of day without it. Communications and the reach of it, are only really coming into full appreciation in the last decade, as libraries and data bases start to publish digitally. There are also all sorts of people with all sorts of intentions both good and bad out in cyberspace. I know without it though, there would be no web site or book The Knapps Lived Here, at least not from me. But in the very infancy of my initial curiosity, the internet took me smack to a dead end on Knapp Road.

It was one of the many genealogy message boards or forums as they are also called, where I first ran into one Michael Joseph Knapp. He left word he was looking for info on the F. A. Knapp family of New York and Philadelphia and I responded to him that I was also looking for a Knapp family in New York who once owned a place on Long Island called the Knapp Mansion. About a day or so later I received a short reply. "HOW CAN I HELP YOU?" Mike Knapp. Several emails flew back and forth between us, then AOL Instant messages which eventually led to phone calls, followed by faxes.

His initial story was fascinating and just what it took to sort of make me drop everything else I was doing and concentrate on the Knapp story. Though I continued with more Buzz & Pee Wee stories, the more I learned about Mike Knapp's family, the more I wanted to do the research for a book on them. And why not, because here is what he told me.

H IS GRANDFATHER WHO HE SPENT A LOT OF TIME WITH in Fort Lauder-dale, Florida was the first one who told him about the mansion in New York and the lost fortune of their family. Mike didn't know the exact location in NY, but from what he described to me over the phone, it sounded like the place I knew. His grandfather Harry was born in Brooklyn in 1901 and as young boy Harry said the entire family would gather at this summer mansion around 1910 -1915 and the young cousins would play in the dumbwaiter and moon passerby's from the roof top dormers. Amusing story, but I was in doubt as to who could be possibly pass-ing by in Mastic in 1910. Estate workers, cows? There was no town, just private estates_ a minor detail. He said at the gatherings, the patriarch F. A. Knapp would often come from Philadelphia to the NY mansion and the kids would play practi-cal jokes on him and he would chase them down the staircases. The staircase too, that he described was that of what was in the Knapp Mansion as were the terraces and balconies. Again every mansion worth it's salt has them. But what he also said was, he could get his hands on the blue prints and architects drawings for it as they were in Ft. Lauderdale. I knew if I saw them then I could confirm it. For me that was his "snake in the bag"

His great grandfather, was a German immigrant named Frederick A. Knapp. He initially settled in Philadelphia and became a wealthy merchant with a large estate in Knob Hill. He made his money several ways. He had a distillery and retail liquor business with Julius Kessler, and he also had a company known as The Knapp Barrel Organ Works, that besides barrel organs,made the music machinery for carousels. This was during the era of the great carousels of companies like Loof and Dentzel that are now prized museum pieces. Barrel organs are what the organ grinders used crank on the street corners, while their trained monkeys did tricks and passed the hat.

F. A.'s sons became wood and stone carvers and moved to Brooklyn. And somewhere, someone, he didn't know who, got a hold of the family fortune and left the others in the cold. Many of Mike's family moved to Florida. His grandfather's theme song was "I'm Forever Blowing Bubbles" which if there ever was a better song to fit his sad story, it hasn't been written yet.

> *I'm Forever Blowing Bubbles*
> *Pretty bubbles in the air*
> *They fly so high, Nearly reach the sky*
> *Then like my dreams, they fade and die*
> *Fortune's always hiding*
> *I've looked everywhere*
> *I'm forever blowing bubbles*
> *Pretty bubbles in the air*

I can still recall hearing it in the last scene of an early James Cagney gangster flick, Public Enemy, made in 1931. I first saw it on TV in Mastic Beach around 1954. What follows is from the film's plot description:

The song, I'm Forever Blowing Bubbles, plays on the Victrola phonograph when a phone call to the Powers home reports that Tommy (Cagney) is coming home. His mother cheerfully goes upstairs and hums to herself as she prepares his room for his home-coming: "Oh, it's wonderful. I'll get his room ready. I knew my baby would come home."

In the rival gang's gruesome plan, Tommy's bullet-ridden, rope- and blanket-wrapped 'mummified' corpse/body is gift-delivered by a knock on the door. When brother Mike answers the front door, Tommy appears alive, bound from head to foot except for his exposed, bandaged and bloody face. It is the film's final memorable bone-chilling image - he tetter-totters on the doorstep, and then his mummy-body falls and crashes with a dull thud - face-first onto the floor. The needle on the revolving phonograph record becomes stuck, sounding like a heart-beat...

ON A LIGHTER NOTE, I found a barrel organ version of the song and sent it out to Mike. We were staying in touch daily. He asked me if I would be interested in doing family research for him, for which he said he could pay me because he could not afford to take off time from his car towing business in the city of Los Angeles. He wanted me to go to Brooklyn, Philly and possibly if things were working to our mutual satisfaction, he was willing to send me to Wurtenberg, Germany to do an in depth search of his family. He sounded serious! He also said if I could help him find one of the two very rare mechanical instruments his family built (the exact name of it escapes me) that we would all become very wealthy, as they reportedly were worth over $100,000. Seems odd but that didn't impress me, as much as finding out if they were indeed the Knapps that had the Mastic Beach mansion and if I could help solve the mystery of what happened to their family fortune.

Most of this happened within the months of January and February of 2001. With Erik's approaching trip to Brooklyn coming up in mid March, to look at Pratt Institute for college, I felt it would be quite easy to test the waters and look at some Brooklyn property address Mike gave me. One was on Bedford Ave. another on Monitor St. and another on one 5th or 3rd Avenue. To help me find my way around I called on old friend Doug Percoco, who knows Brooklyn better than any cab driver.

About the same time all this was going on, a person from my past re entered my life through the wonders of the internet. My ex wife Susan, who I had not heard from in well over 25 years or more, had a vivid dream about me. So she took it upon herself to look me up on the internet. Because of my music business success in Nashville, she had very little trouble finding me and proceeded to learn about a book I had written, about my life in music. I was prompted to write it because of two reasons. The death of a dear friend and co writer Walter (Pee Wee) Hyatt, in the Valu Jet disaster on my 49th birthday and the diagnosis from doctors a year or so earlier that I had a very serious disease. If that's not enough motivation for a writer to put down memoirs of a 40 year career in music, especially when they involve names like Bob Dylan, David Bowie, and Billy Joel, then they have no business thinking of themselves as a writer. Susan who played bass and sang in our band, shared a big part of it with me in the late '60s early '70s, was naturally curious what I might have written about her. Seeing that I treated her fairly in the book without any bitterness, she became a casual friend again. Something I always hoped would be possible before I auditioned for a harp seat. As we caught up with each others lives, I learned she was an investigator and CPA for a huge financial concern. When I told her about what was occupying my time these days, she said I would want to look in at the Register Of Deeds, as they would hold much of the info I was seeking as far as property owners. I had never heard of such a place or resource and she said when she went back to Long Island in the summer, she would be happy to do some initial searching for me, providing I could give her the names of who I was looking for. It was an offer I could not refuse because I had no clue on how to perform property searches. And she was right as rain, it opened up everything. The one person who wasn't happy with Sue's findings though was Michael Joseph Knapp.

Actually Mike Knapp and I were having some difficulty just before I left for NY and even more so when I returned in March with what Erik and I found. He kept promising to send me those blueprints and drawings, but it always seemed one thing or another why he didn't. Also he didn't seem too thrilled when I told him that I always heard as a kid, the mansion was given away to St. Jude's or that under their ownership they just abandoned it and let it fall into ruin. He spoke about taking legal action,which I thought was pretty premature at this stage. He seemed to enjoy seeing photos of the house of his grandfathers birth on Monitor Street. It was a mid 19th century row house and he didn't mind that the other address turned out to be an empty lot, and an abandoned building. But when Erik and I went to the library in Shirley, Erik found something that confused us all for a bit and eventually changed everything. There in a file cabinet in the local history room was a pamphlet with the title a brief history of Mastic Beach. It talked about the different sections and when they were developed and from whom the developer, Home Guardian Company, bought the land from. When it got to the last part of the town to be added in it said: *Maps IX and X former land owners were John Lawrence, Frank and Louise Lawrence and J. F. Knapp*. Well there was a Knapp alright but not F. A. Knapp. I asked Mike if he ever heard of J. F. Knapp? He didn't have an answer other than to say it must be a cousin or uncle. I thought could it be a J & A typo? While we were in Mastic Beach that day, we took photos of the houses that sat on the mansion grounds and the Dermody house across the street. We chatted briefly with its owner too who saw us standing in the middle of Locust Dr. aiming our camera at her house. Her name was Joan Larkin and she had owned it for over 10 years. She said it was built in the mid 1800's and when Mrs. Dermody sold it to her, she told her about a mansion that used to be just across the road and once upon a time that her house and the mansion as well as the two other real old homes just down the road were once all part of a large estate. Then we went down to the old dock and took pictures there too, because by now I felt there was a connection of the two coal covered roads. I even took a piece of the old bulkhead, which by now was detoriated badly, home with me. We also took pics of Mr. Clark's barn which was still yellow and of Willie Schluder's house.

Before I left for the trip, I had done a little more research on the St. Jude's connection. Adolph Almasy, whose parents were active church members at St. Jude's, told me he had attended a 50th anniversary celebration of the church recently, and on display there was a photo taken at a Rosary Society breakfast in the early '50s. No one else at the party knew where that photo was taken except Adolph. It was taken the Knapp mansion ballroom. Erik and I stopped in at the parish office and inquired about the photo, and we were told who owned the picture. The church secretary said she would inquire about getting me a copy. We never heard anything more. I told Adolph whose photo it was and he said "Oh Yes, Mrs. Fuzie, she was a good friend of my Mom's." I wrote to Mrs. Fuzie and her children, but never heard anything back. I also wrote to the Diocese in Rockville Center, LI, and they in turn referred me to their archives, located in Huntington. I called and tried to get an appointment with the Diocese archivist. We made contact, but I was told I could not just come there to browse through their files. Thing is, I didn't want to browse, I knew exactly what I was looking for and I was convinced they had to have it. Photos of the mansion they once owned. She took down my info and promised she would research it for me when she had time. I was a little disappointed, but all in all it was a trip that would lay out the future not only for me but for Erik, too. He enrolled at Pratt in August of 2002.

Alphabet Soup
Back home I now had a name to work with, J. F. Knapp. I googled it and came up with some guy who was in on the ground floor of Metropolitan Life Insurance

company. Mrs. Denning's words from 1956 came back to me. "The Knapps were millionaires from the city, that were in the insurance business" Her other words "Stay out of their mansion" once again fell on deaf ears. I wrote to Dan May, the archivist at Met Life and he was very helpful. He wound up sending me a lot of material, including a photo of one Joseph Fairchild Knapp, the second president of Metropolitan Life Insurance from 1872 -1891. I now thought I knew just who J. F. Knapp was and I sent copies of this stuff to Mike Knapp. "Oh yeah; He's related all right—he has that Knapp nose!" was the initial reaction from Mike. When he read that J. F. Knapp was indeed a millionaire, Mike was sure that this was where some of his family fortune went. He said some of it was grabbed by Knapp's partner in the booze biz, one Julius "Smooth As Silk" Kessler. I was not convinced of anything, in fact I was really beginning to think I may have two different families here, but still was not about to make any conclusions. Again I asked about the blueprints and architects drawings of the house. Mike put me on a three way conference call with an aunt or cousin in Virginia and I listened as they talked about their family members from Ft. Lauderdale; Elwin, Edwin, Arlette, Orville, Henry and more. When we hung up I was convinced I would have something on paper to look at soon, other than the faxes Mike had sent of 19th century city directories from Brooklyn and Philadelphia with F. A. Knapp & Sons and the Knapp Barrel Organ Works.

So I went well into the spring trying to piece together tidbits on the Knapps of Philadelphia and Brooklyn—which was where J. F. Knapp had lived. I also had another piece of the puzzle to look at. It seems that J. F. Knapp had a second major business concern, one he was involved with before the insurance business and that had nothing to do with merry-go-rounds, barrel organs or whiskey. It seems he was a lithographer. I also knew that he could not have given his mansion away to St. Jude's in 1950 for one simple reason: he was born in 1832, and his tenure as the president of Met Life ended in 1891, when he died. Could there be a son? There was, but his name was J. P. Knapp. Also a lithographer, J. P. Knapp was alive until January of 1951. The Knapp merry go round had just begun to spin a little faster.

I continued my research into carousel builders and even bought several books on it. The wood carving part was quite an art. It was a pleasant part of the research and even led me to reacquaint myself with an 8th grade teacher history teacher I had, who turned up on the internet. His name was Gerry Holzman and after his retirement, he had become a full time wood carver. Gerry was involved with the creation of the Empire State Carousel, that was at that time housed in another mansion in Islip, Long Island known as Brookwood Hall. Brookwood Hall was built by NY millionaire H. K. Knapp! Mr. Holzman had studied wood carving for years, especially as it applied to carousel making, and he turned me on to all sorts of material on the great carvers of both Coney Island and Philadelphia, the two main places that all the great merry go rounds were built. He did not know of the name Knapp associated with carousels though. But Mike Knapp insisted there was much more for me to find in the Knapp world of merry go rounds. He was right about that, at least about the name Knapp. There was much, much more to discover and the ride was far from over.

WITH THE KNAPP NAMES, ESPECIALLY THEIR INITIALS, FLYING ALL over the Spooner house that spring, Anne and Erik got me a gag birthday gift of a dry erase board with a bunch of color dry erase markers. Gag or not it came in handy, as I tried to post a crude genealogical chart of who was who in the Knapp line as I knew it then. It looked like one in a Kojak's squad room. When I would talk about the Knapps using their initials, they both would roll their eyes. Thing is, I was just as confused as they were. About that same time I got an envelope from Jean Wassong, the archivest of the Diocese. Along with a letter saying she had found several items pertaining to their ownership of the mansion, was a photo copy of the silver anniversary program St. Jude's held in the 1970s. Right smack in the middle of a page was a small 2 x 3 inch photo of "The Mansion" which is what they called it, too. It stopped me in my tracks. So much came rushing back and of course I said to myself if they have this, then they must have more! Jean mentioned in her letter there was more "material" but she had to get permission from the Bishop in Rockville Center, before she could send it to me. A month or so later another letter came. She said the Bishops lawyers said this was all they could let me see. A memo from the 1980s about them deciding to dispose of the property and that was partly redacted. DAMN!—what the heck do they have to hide?— was my first thought.

Word got around town in Mastic Beach and the internet that I was pursuing this Knapp story from all angles in earnest. And info began to trickle in, some seemed totally innocuous and some of it was a major eye opener at the time, only to be topped through the years. as more and more magically seemed to find its way to me. Rest assured, you will eventually learn what I have over the years, but it will have to be added in to this book where I think the most appropriate places in the overall story are. As the spring drew to a close and summer came around, I had already learned who really torched the mansion. It wasn't who most thought it was and was also met with "I DON'T BELIEVE IT" from some true believers. I also learned that the Knapp family, who once lived there had a wireless radio station, and a Navy seaplane base during WWI. They also had a private golf course and on top of that an enclosed helicopter would land there as early as 1933! The helicopter was described to me by Nassau County town historian, Jim York who's family spent summers on the western border of the Knapp estate since the late 1920s. His Mom was around 12 then. She used to climb this large observation tower with several sets of stairs as soon as they arrived out there. I checked into helicopters that were around in the thirties and there were'nt any. Actually Igor Sikorski, who is considered the father of the helicopter, was working on them in the thirties, but his were only one man. very crude affairs that looked like a lawn chair with a motor attached. Digging deeper I found that there were things called Auto-Gyros in the early thirties,but they too looked mighty crude, some were WWI era plane fuselages with these cumbersome huge blades attached on a mess of pipes that looked like the roll cages on a 1980s era sprint car. And they were all open cockpit affairs. I checked back with Jim, "Are you sure about the year and that it was enclosed?" I asked. He double checked with his Mom. who was now in her 80s and living in Florida. Yes it was 1933 or 34 and yes it was enclosed and three or four people would get out of it. It came down on Knapp's golf course, right behind his Mom's house.

She saw it land and take off several times. Jim sent me photos of his grandparents bungalow near the south end of Locust Dr, taken from up on the observation tower and one of the tower itself. That was good enough for me I thought and I dug a little deeper. Lo and behold there was a gyro copter like she described made during those years. But it wasn't made in the USA, it was made in France. It was enclosed and it looked like something right out of Buck Rogers or Flash Gordon, but with huge helicopter blades on top. Coupled with that was the info I already had from Metropolitan Life Insurance, that the J. F. Knapps had a strong French connection. In fact J. F. Knapp and his wife were coming back from France, aboard a ship when he died at sea in 1891. It also seems the family traveled often to France and other parts of Europe, all through the late 18 and early 1900s. So owning a helicopter made in France and flying it into Mastic Beach in 1933, wouldn't be much of a leap now, especially since I knew there had been flying going on at their estate since April of 1917. The other thing Jim told me was even more intriguing and started to connect a few memories with what we found in Schulte's barn in the early '50s. He said, "Did you know that Knapp was a rum runner?" No kidding, I said. "No kidding," said Jim. Hmmm, I thought. Now that's colorful. Colorful indeed, as unbeknownst to me at the time, within a few months it would make certain people see red.

In My Mind I'm Going To Carolina

Googling either J. F. Knapp or J. P. Knapp or all versions of their names back then yielded probably no more than a dozen entries in 2001, but it was enough to send me off in 4 directions North, South, East and West around the country and the globe, as I'd pick up a tid bit here and there. The two most recurring things I'd find were; Joseph Palmer Knapp and his association with the state of North Carolina and Mrs. Joseph F. Knapp (his mother), who much to my interest turned out to be a songwriter. I was really enjoying getting to know about these people. There was a first person account of how Joseph Palmer Knapp, a wealthy publisher and sportsman from New York almost single handedly supported the North Carolina school system in Currituck, during the great depression. Publisher? another avenue to explore. It seems that Phoebe Palmer. Knapp (nee Phoebe Worrall Palmer) was an "amateur" musician and wife of a Brooklyn millionaire, J. F. Knapp. She had written a melody that her dear friend Fanny Crosby, a poor blind woman supplied the lyrics for. The song "Blessed Assurance" is staple in just about every denomination of Christian church hymnals. It has been recorded literally, several hundred times. What impressed me even more as a professional songwriter however, was how beautiful her melody was. If Phoebe Palmer Knapp was an amateur, then Ken Spooner, a proud member of the ASCAP Number One Club was a hack!

It seems J. P. Knapp had his own 2,500 acre island in a place called Currituck, near the outer banks of North Carolina and Virginia border. Wow, this guy had some dough I thought. There were schools and bridges named for him and he was also credited with founding an organization called "Ducks Unlimited" Hmmm—Long Island was once a place of unlimited duck farms, and with that I soon discovered a large Long Island history website. LongIslandGenealogy.

com, run by Mac Titmus. a former classmate of mine, whose family ran the Swift Stream Duck Farm in Mastic. Though Mac had no info about the Knapps per se, what he did have was a connection to a family, that opened up almost everything for me. He had the Penneys and they would eventually lead me to a treasure trove of all things Knapp as it applied to Mastic Beach and beyond.

I started putting my still meager findings online under my Spoonytunes umbrella website, that encompassed my music stuff, my Buzz and Pee Wee Short Stories and my fledgling history of Mastic Beach and the Knapp family. Thanks to the internet and the search engines that crawl through websites, linking keywords together, a few folks from around the globe started to correspond for all sorts of reasons. I heard from people in Connecticut, North Carolina, Long Island and as far away as England! A few of them were interested in the genealogy of the Knapp family, some were interested in the history of Mastic Beach and were happy to finally see some positive things written about the place. The town started slipping into decline in the early '70s and has never fully recovered, though there are still ongoing efforts to restore the town. I for one hope they succeed, as it was a great place to grow up.

One of the early email pals was, Kay Ann Donaldson who now lives in Yaphank. She was born in Bayview hospital, grew up in Mastic Beach and was thrilled that someone was trying to write about the glory days of it. She knew I was mainly interested in the transformation period of the Mastics in general as they passed from private estates into towns and she sent along this tidbit about a gentleman named Merritt Cash Penney. He was born in 1854 and died in 1941. He was a "Man Of All Work", a Sunday School teacher at the Moriches Bible Church and the superintendent for the Dana Estate. The name Dana Estate sure caught my attention, as I remember it from my early childhood. It was a huge rambling Victorian mansion, located north of the Floyd estate up in Mastic near the Poosepatuck Indian Reservation. My sister Gerry visited it either with her school class or with the girl scouts and Mrs. Dana gave her a little wooden crib from this big doll house that was in the living room. I remember the crib being in my sisters room for years and just wish I knew what happened to it. Anyway just by the fact that he was connected to an estate, I certainly decided to look further into who Mr. Merritt Cash Penney was.

From England and a gentleman named Nigel Brassington, came this e mail. *I have been studying the Knapp family for years all the way back to the year 1200. I might have some things of interest for you and good luck on your research.* After a few emails and pleasantries were exchanged, I found myself in receipt of a copy of the *Last Will and Testament Of Joseph Palmer Knapp*! In it was mention of a daughter, Claire A. Dixon and a son Joseph F. Knapp. My goodness I thought, at this rate I probably will have this wrapped up by the time I get up to Long Island in August.

All the while communications were getting less frequent and more tense with Mike Knapp in California. When I asked again about the drawings, he said his Aunt had just mailed them and I would have them anyday. When they didn't arrive, that was changed to, she was just about to mail them but had a stroke and passed away. Something was feeling VERY strange and I felt I could certainly put my Passport back into mothballs. I wasn't wild about Wurtenberg anyway.

In July, I received an e mail from Susan, who was on Long Island visiting her sister. *Kenny: Yesterday on my way to Nancy's, I stopped in at the Suffolk County Register Of Deeds. I have been in many a registry before, but have never seen one so poorly organized or in such bad shape. It was a madhouse in there. I spent most of my time trying to figure out their system and hope to return later on in the week. I did find one lease from 1894 where a Joseph P. Knapp rented Carmen's River from the Tangier Smith family to go hunting on. Hopefully I will find more for you later on. Regards, Sue.*

I was more than hopeful she would, I knew my ex wife pretty well since she was in college. She's a very bright person, marrying me may of been the dumbest thing she ever did. A few days later came this second e mail.

Kenny, I still can't believe what a disaster this place is, but after awhile it almost became fun. dealing with their broken down copy machines that should of been in the dumpster 20 years ago. Not to mention it's an absolute madhouse in here with people pulling libres and indexes out all over and not putting them back. However that said, I think I found some of what you are looking for. It seems that in 1938 a Joseph F. Knapp of Isle Of Palms in Ft. Lauderdale, Fl, sold off large chunks of land in Mastic Beach sections nine and ten in installments to a company known as Home Guardian of New York. I made copies of some of the deeds for you and will send them along with directions on how to do the research here. It's not easy. but I'm sure you will be able to figure it out. Best of luck, Sue.

Well I still had no clue as to what she was referring to about Libres and Indexes, but I did know my sections and Section Ten was where my house was and the mansion was literally in my backyard. The fact that there was someone named Joseph F. Knapp alive and well in 1938, was icing on the cake and the fact that he lived in Ft. Lauderdale was of interest too, because although I was now thinking that Mike Knapp and his story was a dead end street for me, I knew he did grow up in Ft. Lauderdale. That told me I probably was not quite at the end of his Knapp Road yet either. Yes indeed, in July of 2001, I was in much better shape than James Cagney as Tom Powers was in 1931, when his brother Mike opened that door.

Fortune's always hiding
I've looked everywhere
I'm forever blowing bubbles
Pretty bubbles in the air

CHAPTER

6

Back To The Beach

I decided, well actually my budget did, that I would coordinate the research trip to Mastic Beach with the annual Riverhead, Islip, Freeport Speedway Reunion that had been running steady for the last few years, helped along by the arrival of my book Long Ride On A Short Track in 1998. Besides that, I always looked forward to it because I think I got more laps (albeit parade laps) in on Old Timers Day at the track, than I ever did when I actually tried to race there. Parade laps or not. I relived every heat race and the one feature I did qualify for in the summer of '65, while driving around the $^1/_4$ mile oval in Axel Anderson's '37 Plymouth Coupe, one of the same kind of cars I raced in and as a bonus Nippy Commandinger's '37 Chevy, 327 powered modified. This year it was going to be extra special, because a week before I left, Donald Denning called me and said he would try and get together with me this time out. He tentatively planned to meet me at the track reunion, but had my number where I was staying in case he could not. I had been trying to see him since 1994 when I first came back to start writing the Long Ride book. Ironically the very last time I saw Donald, was in August of 1965 ,when he watched me get T Boned in the drivers door at Riverhead in turn 4. That was my last night for ever driving a stock car in competition.

"You Gotta Have Friends"

Remember that song by Bette Midler? It was written by Buzzy Linhart, a folkie, I'd often see perform at the Cafe Au Go Go in Greenwich Village in the sixties. Buzzy opened shows for the Blues Project and their larger reincarnation, Blood Sweat & Tears. I want to say at the outset, that this trip and all those that followed would of never been possible without the help of old friends and band mates of mine from sixties, Kenny Vitellaro and Doug Percoco. Their offers of places to stay and placing transportation at my disposal is the only reason you are able to be reading this. Without it it, well it just would not of happened–period end of story. I landed at McArthur Airport in Islip on a Friday, August 24th just before the Sunday deal at Riverhead. Kenny met me at the plane and we were off to his house in Shirley, taking the scenic and long way home on Montauk Highway through Blue Point, Patchogue and then down South Country Road through East Patchogue, Bellport and Brookhaven, South Haven, approaching the town of Shirley the only way you could before the Sunrise Highway was extended out that far in 1960s. Having lived in the area for well over a quarter a century, and even though as much time had passed since I did, I could still write a book, just on the memories of traveling along those roads.

On Friday evening, I met with Larry Schulz and he took me over to see his Mom who I had not seen since about 1969. Before we got to Larry's house, he stopped to show me a place he had just bought as an investment. It wasn't my house, but it was as close as you could get. It was it's twin, on the corner of Monroe and Cedar that was built about the same time in 1939. Other than choosing Redwood for the living room, instead Knotty Pine, Brick instead of Stone for the fireplace and a full basement over our half , it was exactly like going inside my home again. Not only that, Larry had bought it off it's original owners who kept it totally original. It was near sunset, when Larry and I arrived and the electricity was off. I took a picture of the fireplace, that came out so dark it wasn't visible, but the light coming through the two identical stained glass windows, was all it took to send my memory drive into high gear every time look at it. At first I could not believe how small it felt inside. Even in the living room, with its high cathedral ceiling and balcony loft bedrooms. Going up in the loft where Butchie and me bunked for the first 8 years was amazing. As was looking down over the exposed beams into the living room, where we first saw a colorful cat named Elvis, shake the entire black and white world up on the Tommy Dorsey show in January of 1956. Our Mom couldn't believe what she was seeing that night and yelled for our Dad, "Wally! come here and look at this, your not going to believe this guy!" Butchie and me were still awake and as we peered over the balcony wall at our 17" Halicrafters console flickering in the corner of the living room, we became true believers. Then it was down the road a bit to Phyliss Dr. When we first got to the Schulz house, we walked around the property, looked at the remains of the wells in the woods, where we first had met 51 years earlier. We were in his backyard looking at "Mr. Clark's" Barn, when the soon to be 76 year old, Mrs. Estelle Parr Schulz appeared on her elevated back deck, looked down and said "MY GOD–IT'S WALLY!" When I took off my hat and bowed, she said,

"Kenny Joseph, your a spitting image your father, come on up here and let me get a good look at you." As I climbed the stairs She said, "It seems like only yesterday. I'd look out this door and see you and your brother playing with my Larry and Dennis." As much as an emotional meeting as it was for me, I know had to be for her too, as she had just lost her husband Dave to cancer a year ago. We had a nice reunion that night and set up a date for me to return in a few days for an official "for the book" interview and to look through her family photographs. Estelle has lived in Mastic since the 1920s, and her father's business activities played a part in my fledgling Knapp and what seemed to be developing too, Mastic area history story. Larry took me back to Kenny's and as we drove along Neighborhood Road, I was thinking who ever said you can't go home again, apparently hadn't asked me.

Kenny Vitellaro is a car collector and has a nice assortment of vintage cars and trucks, some Studebakers, a DeSoto, a Buick, Oldsmobile etc. On Saturday, he fired up his newest acquisition, a 1948 Hudson Commander and off we went. Our first stop being just around the block, at the Manor Of St. George, as that is where the whole "Grand Estate" or Manor thing started in Mastic in the 1600's. The manor is literally in his backyard and he never tires of talking about it or Miss Eugenie Smith (1866-1954), the last Tangier Smith to live and die there. Kenny recalls meeting her a time or two when he was a real youngster. From there we pressed on into Mastic Beach and made the rounds, the Riveria as the bayfront is known on both sides of Patterquash Creek, the area around the Knapp Mansion, that includes the Dermody. Wetzel and Muse 18th century houses, the Lagoon and more. All the while, I was snapping away with my camera like a Papparazzi. We stopped in the Woodhull graveyard in section one and I photographed all the headstones, as I knew there was some kind of connection between the Lawrences who are buried in there with how the Knapps wound up with the Lawrence estate. Just didn't know exactly what it was yet. I find headstones are like little genealogical charts. We also drove over the Smith Point Bridge to look at the ocean and cruised by the Island View Manor which I already had learned from Mrs. Schulz was once known as the Tolfree estate. There was so much to learn and I only ten days to do it in. Before the second day I thought I would have to be coming back, to put in more time at this.

SUNDAY I TOOK A LITTLE BREAK FROM IT ALL BY SPENDING THE DAY AT Riverhead Raceway. I got out there around 10 and was walking around talking and meeting with my newly adopted racing family, that had graced the pages of my book, when I saw a guy standing alone in the distance looking at me. I immediately knew it was Donald and he likewise, even though thirty six Augusts had come and gone since we last saw each other. Well suddenly my racing days in the summer of 1965 from that point went to the rear of the field, bowing to our personal reunion, that goes back to the summer of 1951. That was only bolstered further about an hour later when Doug Percoco showed up, Donald and I started to hang out with Doug back in 1958. Later that afternoon, we stopped in at a diner and Doug and I caught up with the life of Donald and we all shared our collective thoughts on the world in general today. Before we left we made an agreement to get together again, before I went back to Tennessee.

Monday morning I started research in earnest with a return visit to the Mastic Shirley Library. They had a large fairly large archive of 8 x 1 0 photos they had obtained from the Walter T. Shirley estate and others that they purchased from the Trypuc family. who ran the Center Moriches camera store. Phil Trypuc took many of the civic affairs photos and those of business establishments in the 1950s. It didn't take me long to strike a little gold (the gold standard for me is subject and period based) There in front of the new Shirley Post Office in 1952, were two Mastic Beach Fire Engines. No. the place was not on fire—Shirley had no Fire Department then, still doesn't today. It is protected jointly by Mastic, Mastic Beach and Brookhaven Departments with Brookhaven maintaining a sub station there since the mid '50s. Standing along side of and on the top of one of the fire engines. were a whole bunch of firemen in uniform, They had just returned from a parade in Coney Island of all places. On the rear of the truck, the last man standing was none other than my Father! Actually every photo in the binders was a trip down memory lane for me. A little further in, was the entire Mastic Beach Fire Dept. Marching Band, with my sister Gerry staring back at me from the dead center of the photo. Then I came upon a group of St. Jude's photos. Most had to do with erection of the roller rink-auditorium they put up along side of the church in 1952. But there were two photos in the group that gave me pause–real pause–and at first I could not figure out where they were taken. It showed a group of people standing in a large field. with a road and few bungalows in the background. There was a makeshift stage and a group of clergymen with hats you seldom see outside of the Vatican were standing on it. There was also a second shot of a man in a suit addressing the crowd. I recognized Fr. Skelly and though most of the crowd has it's back to the camera, I saw some familiar profiles. But it was what was off to the side of the crowd that rang the déjà vu bell with me. It was an old long building. Actually you could tell by the roof it had been added onto but both parts were old. I thought could this be taken at the rear of the mansion grounds and was that the garage I once wandered over to look in the window of, the day my Mom went into the ballroom to get my sister? The garage came down several years before the mansion burned down. It was probably demolished around the same time that Sam Cole took down Schulte's Barn circa 1957. I made digital copies of about 15 - 20 photos that day and was on my way to Center Moriches Library, when I decided to go back down to the Beach to the Knapp mansion site just to satisfy my curiosity. I turned off Neighborhood onto Monroe and then made the left onto Dogwood and Surprise! Surprise! — Holy Gomer Pyle, there they were. The three bungalows from the background of the photo. Two had been altered but the third one was still exactly the same. But what the heck was St. Jude's doing holding a ceremony in the back yard, when they had that huge 50 foot ballroom that could of easily held the crowd they had and half of St. Andrews congregation too? The answer would soon be revealed.

U P IN CENTER MORICHES, I PROBABLY SPENT TWO AND HALF DAYS IN the library looking at microfilm of The Moriches Tribune, a weekly paper from 1938-1950s. A good half day or more was wasted feuding with their worn out microfilm reader, that wouldn't stay in focus and obsolete printer that was even worse. The graphite copies it made, when it would make them at all, were barely readable even with a magnifying glass. Graphite heat copiers a new technology in the 1970s were about as obsolete in 2001 as the 1950 mimeograph machine was and they didn't even provide the nice fruity ink smell, we used to get back in elementary school. It's sad to know what could be a significant resource, was nearly unusable for lack of proper funding. Too add to my frustration, was that the microfilm company was very careless about focusing their cameras on far too many pages. I concentrated at first on the year 1938, because that is when one J. F. Knapp sold most of the estate to Home Guardian.

The first story that caught my eye happened in May, when Mastic Beach held it's first Memorial Day Parade. The marchers met at Paul Schulte's Tavern then proceeded easterly along Neighborhood Road, turning north on Locust Drive, then east again on Aspen (OK I'm with ya) then south on Alder. then east on Birch, where they proceeded to the grave-site? I knew all the roads except Birch. That was a new one on me. The story then gave the list of names and groups who were in attendance to honor General Woodhull, the first General killed in the American Revolution and they hoped it would become an annual event. Just below that story was a much shorter one, about something that was going on the same day just two blocks from the grave yard. It seems the police were called out to investigate somebody who was "stealing" lumber out of the General's mansion. When they arrived, the alleged thief showed them a bill of sale he had for the place. He told them he was taking the lumber out to the Hamptons for use in a home there. End of story? Of course not!

About week or two, into June, there was a mention of a meeting held at the Mastic Beach Property Owners Clubhouse re the recent acquisition of acreage from the J. F. Knapp estate. From it, new sections of Nine and Ten would be developed and new roads like McKinley. Jefferson, Hockey, Soccer, Tennis, Dock etc. would be cut into it. It said something to the effect that all the new road construction would be up to standard. Something that was apparently sorely lacking in earlier Sections 1-8. As I went through the years, I began to read more and more about the names of families I knew as a kid and the local doings of the town. At one point there were two correspondents sending in items about the goings on about town. There was nothing though, about the Knapps other than an occasional mention of the former Knapp estate.

When I hit the spring of 1950, I started to read stories about St. Jude's buying the Knapp Mansion and their plans for it. They wanted to use the ballroom as a community center for all kinds of civic and cultural affairs and then eventually build an even larger meeting hall. Then they planned to turn the mansion into a parochial school. They held an open house there in April of 1950, so folks could come in and see the place. There were no photos published of the open house story or of the summer school they ran at the mansion the first few months they owned it. Like any newspaper the use of photos and or illustrations is meant to draw the eye to the story, and in June of 1950, draw my eyes they did. There on top right of the page,was an architects drawing of the proposed St. Jude's Auditorium and Youth Center. I recognized it immediately as well as what else was looming over the back of it. The north face of the Knapp Mansion.

That issue also contained a photo, I had seen earlier that day of Father Skelly and two other clergy men with a shovel. So: St. Jude's was planning to build the auditorium, right in the back yard of the mansion. Now those two other photos of the crowd became perfectly clear. The full plan was once the auditorium was built, the mansion would be turned into a 4 room school house with the Nuns who would teach there, residing upstairs. They were hoping to open the school by September of 1951. Through the summer of 1950, the paper carried many stories about the fund raising going on to complete the project. They raised $58,000 of the $75,000 they needed to complete the auditorium in just 5 weeks. They also held several recitals, card parties, and dances in the ballroom the first summer they owned the place.

Sometime during that week I ventured back to Riverhead . This time it was to the county center to try my luck in the Register of Deeds. Not knowing what to expect. except that Sue told me it was real chaotic, I ventured inside with a notebook and her written instructions in hand and was immediately overwhelmed. First off, it was extremely busy, with people who obviously knew each other well, making small talk and opening and closing books and throwing them on top of two copy machines, that were beat to their socks, fast enough to make your head spin. I'd find that most of these folks were para legals, doing title searches for real estate transactions. I found someone to help me find Brookhaven Township and started to look in the indexes. After about a half hour I started to find a few things at least in the indexes. They were large, about 18″ x 24″ hand written Ledgers. The indexes held names of grantors and grantees of property, by year, last name then first name. The index would then refer you to the Libre Binders, that held the actual copies of the deeds themselves. I started to get the hang of it a little bit, then ventured into the numerical Libres. They were huge canvas covered binders that sat on roller shelves and I pulled my first document. It was a handwritten, with impeccable penmanship, lease between The Smith brothers and sisters William, Clarence, Martha and Eugenie and Joseph P. Knapp dated in the 1890's granting him gunning rights on Carmen's River for $50.00 per year. It was renewable from 1894-1899 and it was just like the one Sue had found for me a few months prior. With a little help from Ed, a retired lawyer, who was there at his realtor daughters behalf, I was soon pulling deeds almost like a veteran. Within an hour or so I had the deed of sale dated Oct 2, 1916 from a Frank M. and Louise C. M. Lawrence for 166 acres of property and all buildings to one Joseph F. Knapp. Eureka! I thought this is it. Soon after that I found another deed issued just two days later. This time Joseph F. Knapp (unmarried) of Moriches sold the same place to one Claire Antoinette Knapp (spinster) according to the deed. Soon I was pulling out deeds left and right with Knapp names on them. In June of 1917 ,Joseph P, Elizabeth, Claire and Joseph F. Knapp all signed a deed for a place in Greenlawn. Then in 1925, Claire A. Knapp sells the Mastic property back to

Joseph F. Knapp. Geez I thought these Knapps sure like to buy and sell property. Looking in the year 1938, I found a whole stack of deeds from Joseph F. Knapp to Home Guardian Co. On the second day there. I found the one for St. Jude's. It seems the Knapp mansion wasn't given to them by anyone, as the tale was told around Mastic Beach. Rather it was sold very reasonably. Ed the Lawyer showed me how to figure the sales price, based on the tax stamps on the deeds. On May 4. 1950 St. Jude's paid about $18, 000.00 to a George Sutter of Manhattan for the mansion and 3.5 acres of property around it. I found some real oldies too that pertained to the Knapp Mastic property, like an agreement between Charles Jefferey Smith and Henry Nichol over a boundary in 1862.

By the second day I had figured out how to trace the reference Libre numbers on the deeds, enabling me to skip looking through the indexes and soon found a deed from Home Guardian to George Sutter from January 8, 1941 which in turn led me to the sale of the home and the 12 acres immediately around it from one Joseph F. and Marion H. Knapp to Home Guardian company just 8 days earlier on December 31, 1940. Happy New Year. Things were starting to come into focus. I also asked Ed about the File Maps referenced in the deeds. He directed me to a room called micro - graphics and I walked out of the Register Of Deeds with large File Maps Titled Ninth & Tenth Map of MASTIC BEACH, Dated June 7, 1938 There upon them was my entire neighborhood, plus all the buildings and property a Mr. J. F. Knapp decided to hold onto in 1938, his mansion included YESSSSSS! INDEED! IT WAS A VERY GOOD DAY.

I spent some time in Patchogue Library one day, acting on the tip I got from Van Field. Their micro - film readers were in much better shape, and added to that was the fact they had computer scanner printers. As I didn't know the date of when it happened, it took me about an hour to find the account in April of 1917 of one James (sic) P. Knapp donating part of his estate in Mastic to the US Navy, for the creation of a wireless station and a seaplane base with three hangers. April of 1917 is when the US entered WWI. From that little news item I would learn a lot more through the years about the most obscure flying out-fit the US Navy ever had—Unit 3 , Aerial Coast Patrol Naval Reserve Squadron.

The week seemed to fly by and Saturday afternoon I spent with Mrs. Schulz on her deck, doing a lot of catching up, reminiscing and learning a ton of Mastic history. Her father William Parr, operated two automobile gas and repair stations in Mastic and Mastic Beach. from the early '20s until he passed away in the late 1940s. One of the services he offered, was house calls for all the private estate owners; the Danas, Floyds, Smiths, Tolfrees, Lawsons and the Knapps. Often Estelle and her sister would accompany him on these estate calls. She recalls in the 1930s meeting Eleanor Roosevelt at Moss Lots, the Dana mansion while her Dad worked on William S. Dana's two Rolls Royces. She then talked about the Tolfrees as having some large Rotweiler guard dogs as well as St. Bernards. Edward R. Tolfree was a show dog breeder and judge for the Westminster Kennel Club. She spoke of having milk and cookies in Miss Eugenie's kitchen at the Manor of St. George, while her Dad tinkered with The Smith's Stutz - Bearcat. When I asked her about the Knapps, she paused and said. "Well I don't know if I can tell you too much about the Knapps—I never saw them, just heard about them. You know that Willie Schluder was their caretaker right? Well my father used to take us swimming on the beach at the end of the Knapp Estate, you know the one that became Beach 10. He would always stop at Willie Schluder's house first and ask if it was ok. Willie said sure—he's not here, go right on through. You couldn't even cross town then on Neighborhood road—Knapp had it fenced off. Neighborhood dead ended at Locust Drive. You had to go up Locust and around the north side of his estate and then back down Alder on the east side. In Section One the road that is now Neighborhood was called Birch."

"I remember, sitting on Knapp's boat. while my father worked on the engine. He kept it at that dock down off the end of Jefferson Dr. where Dave kept our boat' 'How big was it?' I asked. "It was a regular cabin boat, I didn't pay that much attention to it." I asked if she was ever inside the mansion itself. "Not when Knapp had it, only after St. Jude's bought it. I would go to the card parties there, with Rose Scimeca. It was really something inside, absolutely fantastic. I recall one afternoon my father came home and announced with his chest out 'I've been invited to go out drinking with Doty Knapp! "Who was Doty Knapp?" I asked. "I don't know, I guess he was the Knapp that owned the estate, because my Dad couldn't stop talking about him: I'm going drinking with Doty Knapp!" I made a mental note of it.

We looked through her photos and besides the ones of Larry and Dennis as kids, there were several that really struck a chord with me. One was of their house under construction in the late '40s . Her husband Dave built it. Through the frame work, Mr. Clark's Barn was clearly visible. Estelle said, "That barn goes back to the mid 1800s, Denny Barnes figured out the construction date when he put a new roof on it for us. Knapp used it for a machine shop. Dave found some stuff about it in the loft and machine shop tools when we converted it into a house." You could also see the two towers off to the side in that photo. "When we came back from Maryland , I was so upset with old man Clark for taking down the windmill and watertower. They were beautiful. "Why did he do it?" I asked. "He sold the iron for scrap—probably to buy whiskey. I was really upset with him 'cause they were actually on our property. When we bought his place at auction, we had to research the deed and that's when we found out they were on our land not Clark's. Dave made our picnic table out of the wood from the water tank." "Anything else you remember about the Knapp estate?" I asked. "Not really, except he was very particular about his trees. You know he planted a lot of them as they are not like any other trees in this town. And he had a private golf course and tennis court. Home Guardian named the roads that ran across Knapp's property for all the sports they supposedly played there, once upon a time. Hockey, Soccer and LaCrosse. Our street was Tennis Place 'till Pete Scimeca got it changed to his daughters name. That too happened when we were away in Maryland. Not that I cared. Dave and I never got along with Pete and he couldn't stand any of you kids. YOU KIDS STAY OFF MY PROPERTY! I got along fine with Rose and their daughter Phyliss, but Pete was nothing but a grouch—Oh yes, between Clark's barn and Schulte's barn there used to be a house there. Knapp's secretary lived there in the 1930s. Knapp must of gave it or sold it to Paul Schulte, because Paul moved it behind his bar when Knapp sold out." "So I guess he gave Paul Schulte the barn on Dogwood too?" I asked. "He probably did, I remember when we first built the house, I asked Willie, if I could take some of the daffodils growing around the barn to plant in my yard. He said to ask Paul."

I mentioned that I heard that Knapp might of had some other dealings with Paul Schulte in regards to bootlegging. "I don't know about that, but Paul Schulte certainly was involved with bootlegging. There was a lot of bootleg liquor around here then and my father probably drank half of it. A lot of people just made it for their own use." I told her I had found a few stories about rum running around here in the micro film files. I also mentioned the story about them taking lumber out of the Woodhull mansion in 1938. "Now that was a perfect house, nothing wrong with it at all, other than being very old. It was boarded up for years, but one day Willie Schluder, just tore it down. 'So he was the one who took it down, the paper didn't name the person. I guess he was still working for Knapp then?' "Yes. it was Willie...*SCHLUUUDER*...is how he used to say it. He still worked for Knapp watching after the estate even after Knapp left town before WWII. During the war, Willie worked as a cook at Camp Upton. Willie and Honey used to say when Knapp sold out to Home Guardian, he gave them their house and property, which was the gate house to the whole estate. It caught on fire once and almost burned down. You know that the Dermody, Wetzel and Muse houses were all part of Knapps property too, don't you? They go way back to the 1800s." I brought up the the story about overhearing her talking on the phone to a girlfriend back in the early '50s regarding the fact that everyone was taking stuff from the Knapp mansion and asked her the same question I had asked many others who were old enough to remember back then. Why did St. Jude's just walk away from the place and let it go to ruin? She too had no answer. I left that afternoon with a handful of pics to copy and a headfull of memories and info to look into. She said she had a bunch more photos in another drawer but it was stuck shut and she was going to get Larry to open it for her. "Next time round," I said, knowing full well I'd be back.

Twenty Years Ago

Sunday and Monday were a wash for doing any library research and Kenny and I kinda goofed off riding bikes and stuff. We biked over to George Barnes' house in Section 5. George. was another classmate whose Dad a builder, went way back in the history of Mastic Beach. George was also interested in the history of Mastic Beach and he gave me some prints of photo postcard landmarks and a copy of the St. Andrew's Directory from 1942. It listed most everyone who lived there then, both all year round and summer. A great resource.

It was Monday, September 3rd, 2001 (Labor Day) that Donald Denning, Doug Percoco and myself got together for dinner in our old hometown. I was flying back to Nashville on Wednesday, winding up a very successful trip that I knew now, would not be my last for this story. We decided to go to Neighborhood Pizzeria. now known as Onofrio's, but is still in the same family, as when we were kids. We used to sit there many a winters night, without spending more than a dime for a cup of coffee. Though we would sometimes pool our resources and splurge on a large pie for a $1.25. Other than the moving of the entrance door and the removal of the booths, the place looks and feels the same. After dinner it was still early and we decided to walk through the town. It was while walking through it, that a whole lot of what happened to it, hit all of us. We couldn't believe how dead it was at 8 O'clock on Labor Day Weekend, compared to the way it was when we were kids, when cars and people lined both sides of the streets. There was nothing going on. Some guy was sitting in the doorway of a laundromat in what used to be Harers market, waiting for his clothes to dry. Schulte's was closed, Beachcomber was gone, O'Donnells was now called the Chas Mor Pub and just did not look too inviting. No Kozy Korner, No Harrington's Custard stand No Jean's, No nothing. But as we walked. a song of Wood Newton's, a friend and co writer of mine back in Nashville, came into my mind. You may know it, as Kenny Rogers had a big hit on it in the late 1980s.

TWENTY YEARS AGO
It's been a long time since I walked
Through this old town
But oh how the memories start to flow
And there's the old movie house
They finally closed it down
You could find me there every Friday night
Twenty years ago.

I worked the counter at the drugstore down the street
But nobody's left there I would know
On Saturday mornings that's where
All my friends would meet
You'd be surprised what a dime would buy
Twenty years ago.

All my memories from those days come gather round me
What I'd give if they could take me back in time
It almost seems like yesterday
Where do the good times go?
Life was so much easier twenty years ago.

IT WAS STILL WAY TOO EARLY TO CALL IT A NIGHT AND WE HEADED down to the lagoon, a place we all spent a whole lot of time at as kids and kept our boats there, when we were teens. We were standing by the launch ramp just across from the Yacht Club , when a voice came yelling— "I don't believe it! Doug Percoco, my old nemesis!" It was Larry Schulz and he was feeling no pain, as he was at least two and a half sheets to the wind. When he got closer, he was equally as amazed to see Donald Denning standing there. But he kept it up in a jovial sort of way about Doug being his old nemesis. This was as puzzling to me as it was to Doug. As I mentioned way back in the first chapters, Larry did not hang out with my summer friends and although Doug was a summer kid turned all year rounder, Mister Memory here could never recall any trouble between the two of them. I had many fist fights with Larry, most which I always won, until one day in the fall of 1959, he unleashed on me something fierce and gave me a heck of a bloody nose. We never fought from that day on. "Come on over to the club and let me buy you a drink, guys," Larry kept saying. None of us had to be asked twice, not for the alcohol, but for something to do. Donald and I both had cokes, Doug may of had a beer. I grabbed my loose leaf binder of stuff, I had been compiling on both the Knapps and Mastic Beach history that week to show Larry and whom-ever else may of been interested. On the cover, I had placed an enlargement of the Knapp Mansion photo the diocese had sent me. There weren't too many people sitting round the circular bar and it was the first time I had been inside the place since the New Years Eve in 1963 when Larry and I were part of the band. Larry introduced us all to the folks at the bar and said "Kenny here, is writing a history of Mastic Beach, he has a memory that you just won't believe." I soon found my-self playing a game of do you remember, with a guy sitting across from me.

Then across the room another guy walks in, sees us and says "I'll be dammed! it's Percoco," to which Doug replied. "Ray is that you?" It was Ray Farmer and they went to Mercy High in Riverhead together. After a bunch of how ya beens and you old coot you, Doug turns and says. "You remember Kenny Joseph don't you?" We shook hands and Ray looks at me like he might and says. "I remember a Walter Joseph." "He's my older brother," I said. Before I could say anything else, Ray saw my book laying on the bar top and says, "wow! I sure remember that place—The Mansion, where the hell did you get that picture? I haven't seen it since what—the sixties when it burned?" 'February 15, 1959 and neither has any-one else', came my wise guy reply. Doug interjected, "Kenny is working on a history of the place." Ray picked up the book and casually leaved through it, he was about halfway through when he said to me. "Do you remember, all the guns they had hidden behind the paintings in the ballroom?" WHOA! RAY HAD MY UNDIVIDED ATTENTION. 'No,' came my immediate answer, 'I was never in it until after it got wrecked. Tell me about them.' "Well there were wall safes behind these large paintings in that ballroom there and inside the safes were all kinds of antique firearms, dueling pistols, engraved shot guns and all sorts of weapons really fancy stuff." Before I could ask him another question, he turned back to Doug and they started reminiscing and then the guy next to me started playing do you remem-ber so and so again. Donald was kind of staring out the window and Larry was engaged talking with some of the locals. I really wanted to talk with Ray more about what he knew about the interior of the place, but never got a chance to that night. I made myself a mental note to talk with him again though. Doug, Donald and I all left around 11 and said we would have to get together again, before another thirty some years pass by. Donald followed my car and I drove down Elm to McKinley paused on the corner to look at my house in the dark, then did the same a few feet up McKinley in front of the Denning bungalow. When we hit Floyd Parkway, he honked as he turned north and I tuned south.

Tuesday was my last full day to do anything. I spent the morning back at the register of Deeds and grabbed up a few more. Then I drove down Route 24 to

Hampton Bays. My reason was simple. I had a short NY Times obituary that said Joseph F. Knapp of Ft. Lauderdale, who was associated with his father Joseph P. Knapp in the publishing business, died at his Hampton Bays home on October 23, 1952. It did not mention much else, like where he was buried. I thought I might try and see if there was any local coverage of it. When I got there, the place was undergoing renovations, but their card catalog told me they indeed had a weekly newspaper The Hampton Bays Chronicle. I asked at the reference desk and was told they did not have microfilm of it for that year, but instead the actual papers themselves. However because of the renovations, they were no longer stored on the premises. I thought well nice try. They then said if I wanted to wait a little bit, they would send someone to get the year I was interested in. Well sure I'll wait. After about twenty minutes, a gentleman handed me a hardbound and very dusty book of issues of the paper. Looking at the last issue for October, the front page had huge photos of Dwight D. Eisenhower and Richard M. Nixon on it. Obviously the paper, like much of Suffolk county was Republican because there was no mention of Adlia Stevenson at all, much less a photo of him. But there on the front page on the bottom of the fold was this headline:

JOSEPH FAIRCHILD

Joseph Fairchild Knapp retired New York printing executive, died at his summer home on Rampasture Road, Hampton Bays on Thursday October 23. His permanent residence was Isle of Palms in Florida.

Mr. Knapp was born February 3, 1892, the son of Joseph Palmer Knapp and Sylvia K. Knapp. For many years he served as chairman of the board of directors of the American Lithographic Company of New York which his father founded. He was a member of Howard Lodge No.35, F.A.M. of New York.

The body will be in repose at Leonard & Rogers Funeral Home in Riverhead until Sunday, when a funeral service will be held at St. Mary's Episcopal Church in Hampton Bays. Interment will be in the Southampton Cemetery.

Surviving Mr. Knapp are his wife. Mrs. Marion H. Knapp; a sister Mrs. Claire K. Dixon: and two nieces; Mrs Margaret P. Raynor of Hampton Bays and Mrs. Antoinette Willumsen of Southampton.

He's buried in Southampton! was my only thought as I laid the paper down on the copy machine. I got to get out there before they close the gates. It was around 3:30 and the drive to the cemetery seemed to take forever, even though it was probably not 20 minutes to the east. It was a large and a very old cemetery that's been there since the 1850s. I drove all over looking for the office, but could not find it. I finally found some caretakers mowing the grass, way in the back. I asked a guy on a ride on mower if he could tell me where the office was. He stood up on his machine, looked across to a white utility building way in the distance and said, "It's over there, but they are gone for the day." With nothing to lose, I said, "Would you by any chance know where a Joseph F. Knapp might be buried?—he died in '52." Rubbing his chin a bit he then asked me "Where is your car?" I pointed it out and he said. "Turn it around and follow me." And follow I did and he didn't stick to the roads. I found myself driving through the grass past headstones and monuments with all old Long Island names like Raynor, Penny, Osborne etc. After a few minutes, he paused his tractor in front of a group of hedges and pointed at them. "He's in there." I thanked him and tipped him (I don't know if you're supposed to or not but I did) There in a private plot were five small markers all the same and in the rear was a large monument that said KNAPP. Joseph F. Knapp Feb 3 1892-Oct 23 1952 was front and center IN LOVING MEMORY was inscribed across the top of his headstone. To the left of Joseph, was his sister Claire Knapp Dixon Oct 23 1889-Oct 25 1959. The second row had much newer but same size stones, Again with IN LOVING MEMORY on the top, Willis O. Penney Jan 11 1898-May 2 1972. Then one with flowers on it and a totally strange name to me, Robert B. Vojvoda Nov 18 1926-Sept 25 1999 and last but certainly not least, was one that said IN LOVING MEMORY Antoinette Vojvoda Oct 10, 1928-*blank!* Holy cow, there is a Knapp family member still alive! I drove back to Shirley thinking this could be the break I was hoping for. Even the historian at Met Life thought there were no living Knapp heirs. When I got back to Kenney's house, I looked in the phone book and there was one Vojvoda listed in Riverhead. I called the number and a very frail sounding woman answered. "Hello Mrs. Vojvoda , I'm a historian, visiting Long Island and ran across your last name as being possibly related to a family named Knapp. Would you know if you are?" There was a pause and she said, "I think I might be, but can't tell you much about that. If you call Mrs. George Penny in Southold, she can help you." I thanked her and looked up the name she gave me, but decided to wait until morning as it was the dinner hour.

September 5, 2001

I had a morning flight out of MacArthur and about nine am I dialed the number. A woman's voice answered and our conversation went something like this. Hello Mrs. Penny my name is Ken Spooner and for the last year or so I have been doing research on the history of some people you may be related to, named Knapp. I told her I visited the gravesite in Southampton and that's how I found out there were still living relatives. "Yes. my mother is Ann Vojvoda and, my grandmother was Claire Knapp." 'No Kidding!' I said—wow! I was not hiding any enthusiasm in my voice.

I then told her briefly about the Knapp mansion in my hometown of Mastic Beach and the stories I wrote about it. She didn't know about her grandmother ever living there, but when I mentioned Joseph F. Knapp she said "Oh, Uncle Doty" and I heard a smile in her voice—I said funny she mentioned the name Doty as I had just heard it for the first time a few days ago. but the person who told me did not know who Doty Knapp was, other than he was associated with the place. Then our conversation really started to flow. She told me about her great grandfather and playing at his desk in New York City as a child. Then she talked about his fish camp in upstate NY on the Beaverkill River and the fact that it's still there, run today as a fly fishing school by a woman named Joan Wulff. She talked quite a bit about her great grandfathers sporting activities of fly fishing and duck hunting. then told me about the Joe Knapp Club and the custom engraved shotguns with a oval medallion in the stock. I immediately flashed back to what Ray Farmer had said a few nights earlier. I asked her if she had any photos of her grandmother and uncle. She said she had one of her grandmother, on horseback taken in the early 1900s, and she would talk to her mother about it. She said to call her Sibby (short for Sylvia, her great grandmother's name) and she was quite enthused about my researching her family and said there were some real characters in it. She told me she tried to do something on the order of what I was doing, about ten years ago. but never got very far and commended me. I told her I had a little web site with what I had found so far and gave her the url address. She also said she would be talking to her mother, sister and aunt about me and took my number and address in Nashville. The conversation ended on a real high note. We said our goodbyes and I was left with a strong impression that it was the beginning of what I hoped to be the answer to all my questions as far as the Knapps were concerned.

I was jazzed all the way to the airport and it was an incredible day weather wise. crystal clear sky, We took off on time and in a few minutes the pilot came on the intercom to do his usual pilot talk, pointing out we were flying over NY City. It was an incredible view of the city and we were banked slightly, so you could really see everything. It was probably the first time, I ever saw the twin towers of the World Trade Center from the air.

CHAPTER
7

Back Home Again and
Happy Thanksgiving to You, Too!

It's always good to get home, and see Anne and Erik. This time was no exception. I was charged up with all the stuff I had found and could only imagine what I might find if I dug a little deeper. Of course the really big thing that had me excited was making contact with the Knapp family. I was not disappointed when I got home either, for there in my e mail was this note from Sibby:

Hello Ken:
It was great talking to you this morning on the phone. I have very much enjoyed all your information on the Knapps. I have to stop now and do some work. I did talk to my mother and sister this morning and told them about you. I am sure you will be hearing from them soon. The info that you have is very interesting especially about Mastic. It has been fun reading this information. THANK YOU!!!!

She then included her home address and said to please stay in touch. Wow! I thought all caps and four exclamation points on the last thank you. I felt like shouting too. YESSSSS!

A FEW DAYS LATER I WAS SETTLING IN, going through all the paper stuff I brought home (over 150 deeds alone) and scanning photos when I decided to give Marty Himes a call because I had left the Riverhead Raceway reunion early to spend time with Donald and Doug and wanted to get his take on the event. Marty is the chief spark-plug for it and supplies about 75% of the cars and nearly all the memorabilia they have on display. It was a Tuesday, a beautiful morning and clear as bell. When he answered I said. "Hey Marty, How did the rest of the reunion go?" I never got an answer. He said, "Is your TV on?" I said, "No, why?" He said, "It's the damndest thing—a plane has just flown into the World Trade Center, just like the one that went into the Empire State building. *(Marty has a piece of that plane, a B-25 that hit Empire State building in 1945, he is a collector of everything he can get his hands on)* It just happened and it's on all the stations." I turned on the TV and stayed on the line with him. No one knew anything yet and I saw the smoke coming out of the tower. They cut back to Matt and Katie and it was showing on a screen behind them, when what I saw next was as incredulous to my eyes as it had to be to anyone else that watched in real time. I yelled in the phone "MARTY! WHAT THE HELL WAS THAT?" I first thought what I saw was a replaying of the plane crashing along with the video of it burning. It took a second to realize that "JESUS CHRIST! IT'S TWO PLANES INTO TWO TOWERS—THAT'S NO FREAKING ACCIDENT." I'm not sure how much longer we talked, but the results of the raceway reunion never got discussed.

Well just like the rest of the world, it seems everything stopped in the Spooner world and totally in my Knapp world for several weeks. If David Letterman could take a week off from throwing watermelons and other items off the roof of the Ed Sullivan theatre, so could the kid who sent the old dresser flying out of the Knapp barn hayloft in 1958.

After three weeks I decided to give Sibby a follow up call. This time she was very reserved, but then again it seemed the whole world had changed forever. She gave me some more information about her great grandfather Joseph Palmer Knapp and his Joe Knapp Club, but seemed reluctant to say anything else. I asked if she had talked with her Mother about our first call and she said she had and that my project had been discussed with the family. There was a long uncomfortable pause and she said ," They don't object to you writing about the Knapps that are deceased, but no one living wants to be included in your history." I was taken back a bit and did not quite know what to say. But what I did say was, "I guess they are probably wondering what my reasons are for wanting to write about the Knapps?" This broke a little bit of the ice and she said, "Well yes, I guess we all are wondering about that." I told her truthfully I couldn't really pin point one specific reason, but my intentions were honorable and I would be happy to furnish them with references from people I interviewed and wrote about in my *Long Ride On A Short Track* book. I could sense a tone of frustration in her voice and that she just wanted to end the phone call. I followed it up with an email that provided three references. The real shocker was Sibby personally knew two of them and one of them for many years. A few more emails went back and forth along with one more phone call.

Before I had left for my trip in August, I had made several North Carolina contacts regarding the history of J. P. Knapp and his years in Currituck. It seems he was quite the philanthropist towards his adopted state, especially in the area of education. One fellow, Roy Sawyer sent me a photo of the Knapp home on Knott's Island. I told him I was hoping to write a book on the family based around the places they lived and wanted to visit Currituck. He said the government tore the home down years ago and it was now a wildlife refuge. He also cautioned me that folks at the Knapp Foundation could be "quite sensitive". He had some first hand knowledge of this, in regards to a grant they had made. He said "and of course you heard about the china incident right?" I said, "No... Knapp gave money to the Chinese?" "No not the country—the White House china—during the Reagan era." I told him I remembered something about that and recalled there was a lot of press on it at the time. He said, "When the hullabaloo in the media blew up about Nancy Reagan spending over $200,000 for new china, it was revealed that it was not taxpayer money, but rather a private gift given anonymously. When that did not stop the press from talking about it, someone from the Knapp Foundation came forward and revealed they were the donor." "Oh, that's interesting," I said and didn't think too much more about it at the time, but wondered a bit, what does supporting education have to do with a set of dishes? I researched the newspaper archives and saw the stories where Ann Vojvoda (Sibby's mom) explained her reason for the gift to the press. Now in light of this newly felt coolness I felt from Sibby and the fact that I now knew her mother was running the Knapp Foundation, I figured that it was probably this china incident that set them down the path of caution in dealing with anyone trying to write anything on the Knapps from that day on.

Since the the very first days that I learned that the Knapps were involved in lithography, I had started collecting actual lithos they had printed. They had to have printed a ton of stuff, for so much of it to survive. I had a really nice one called "Roses Rare" of a Victorian age lady and thought I would make a nice personal birthday card for Sibby's mom's approaching birthday in early October. I sent Sibby an e mail to tell her about it and asked for her Mom's address, but did not get a reply. So I sent off my custom card to the Knapp Foundation, which had a P. O. Box posted online. In all honesty I thought it could not hurt a relationship, that seemed to be concluding as quickly as it had started.

Speaking of conclusions by the time, I had returned from New York, I had determined that Mike Knapp in California was not a family member of this Knapp group and wanted to wrap up my dealings with him. I asked for a simple reimbursement just for my cost of materials I had laid out six months ago, about $50, I asked nothing for my time. My request was met with ultimate hostility from him and his wish that whatever disease I did have, would hurry up and take its course.

On a much more positive note, I was given the name of Merritt Cash Penney from Kay Donaldson, a website reader who was born and grew up in Mastic Beach. Because Merritt was the superintendent at the neighboring Dana estate, I decided to look a little further into who he was. The first light had came on re a deed I had, where J. F. Knapp's sister Claire, sells the Mastic estate back to J.F. in 1925. Her name is now Claire K. Penny. Now both Penney and Penny are large old Long Island family names that often get typo-ed , but I had a strong hunch there just might be a connection here between Claire K. Penny and Merritt C. Penney.

I found some information on Merritt online, along with his photo no less and those of some of his family on Long Island Genealogy.com . The site credited a Darby Penney with the photos and posted her email address. So I wrote to her asking about the Merritt. Darby turned out to be his great granddaughter, and was very helpful from the gitgo. She sent me on a path that went straight down the middle of Knapp Road and right inside the Knapp mansion when the Knapps lived there!

Merritt Cash Penney was born in Moriches in 1854. He was a man of all work including a fisherman and a member of the US Life Saving Service.(a progenitor of the US Coast Guard). They patrolled the ocean beaches, trying to save as many lives as they could from numerous shipwrecks that littered the coast. He had three sons, Clarence, Leonard. and Willis . His first two sons found employment with the private estate owners. Clarence, like his father was a man of all work as they were called then, listed his occupation in the 1910 census is that of a carpenter. Through the years he did all types of heavy construction work for the estate owners in Moriches and Mastic area including; building private islands in the bay for their hunting pursuits, road building, moving houses and barns, landscaping and constructing private golf courses. Leonard was a private chauffeur. Willis born in 1898, was the brother that no one seems to recall just what he did for a living in his younger days. Some say he may of been a chauffeur too. Whatever it was he did in 1920 is unknown. But he must of done something, as he was married by then. However for me those facts get far overshadowed in 1925 when he marries for a second time. And just who is the bride the second time around? Why none other than Claire Antoinette Knapp of Mastic that's who.

Now bear in mind most of the information you just read in the last paragraph and more came from just two e-mails from Darby Penney, who asked her Dad Arthur about the Knapps for me. Arthur was certainly in position to know too as he is the son of Clarence Penney and lived in the Moriches area from 1923-1940, when he became the first in his family to go off to college. In fact a year or so before I ever contacted Darby, she recorded an oral history of her family from her now late Dad, who was in his 80's at the time. In 2005 she provided me with the entire 3 hour recording. But from just what I learned from those emails in 2001, it was more than enough to fire me up and to want to pursue all knowledge of the Knapps regardless of what I might or might not ever learn from Sibby and her mother Antoinette.

Arthur had told her that his father had built the 9 hole golf course on the Knapp estate and that might of been how Willis met Claire. He said that both Claire's brother and her father strongly disapproved of her relationship with Willis and he had to hide in closets and climb out of upper story windows in the Mastic mansion whenever "Doad" as he called J.F. came home. Arthur also mentioned Frank and Louise M. Lawrence. Louise was a Mauran, a wealthy shipping family in Providence, RI . She was a friend of his grandparents Bart and Stella Ross of Moriches and used to board with the Ross' when Frank Lawrence (her cousin) courted her in the early 1900s. Arthur worked summers as a houseman for The Maurans when he was Brown University. and said Louise was less than thrilled about selling her Mastic estate to the Knapps and said "If we had known. what kind of people the Knapps were, we would of never sold them our estate". Darby asked her Dad to elaborate and he just said, I think the Knapps lived a little too fast for Louise.

He also spoke a little about Claire and Clairedale (her dog kennel) and of both her daughters who are a few years younger than he is. He said that Aunt Claire and her daughter Peggy are the only Mother and daughter to have ever both won Best In Show at Westminster. Darby added in that her mother is a dog fancier and she recalled going to Madison Square Garden as a kid, to see the show and meeting Peggy one time. And to think all this info came my way because a website reader gave me the name Merritt Cash Penney! To cap it off Arthur supplied both addresses of his cousins Peggy and Antoinette. I was darned if Peggy did not live but minutes away from my mother in law in Florida, which was where we were going for Thanksgiving! I took it upon myself to write her a letter, telling her I would be in Florida in a few days and hoping to have the pleasure of calling her, not knowing that I did not need to.

The day after Thanksgiving, the excitement was really building in me as I dialed the number, it was busy. A few minutes later success! — It was ringing and a woman answered. "Hello Mrs. Newcombe, this is Ken Spooner, did you receive my letter?" "YES I DID AND I DO NOT WISH TO TALK TO YOU ABOUT ANYTHING!" Startled I said, "Well I'm sorry to have bothered you, goodbye." As everyone else was out shopping, I had some solitude to think about what went so wrong, Roy's words came back: "Knapp heirs can be very sensitive." Mrs. Newcombe's words kept repeating themselves and it just didn't make sense.

When the shoppers returned, I told them what had happened and they too were startled and puzzled, but by now I was depressed. I went out and headed for the Clearwater Library. I returned with two digital copy printouts from the American Encyclopedia of Biography. One on Joseph Fairchild Knapp 1832-1891 and one of Joseph Palmer Knapp 1864-1951. Most of the info in the text I already knew, but both included fine portrait photos, that were of much higher quality than those I already had. It was a small consolation, but seemed only fair, as both father and son were the worlds leading printers of their day.

Letters—We Get Letters
We always take two days to drive back to Nashville from Florida and it gave me plenty of time to think about the next step. Drop the whole thing? Go back to my Butchie and Me stories? Incorporate what little I knew about the Knapps into a history of Mastic Beach?

The only thing I decided on, was to write a letter to Sibby and try to explain myself further and apologize for bothering them. I did that and also sent a copy of it to Peggy, only to have hers returned unopened. Sibby did not respond, but Ronald B. Lee (a kin of Robert E. perhaps?) of the law firm of Griswold & Lee, who represented her mother did.

Dear Mr. Spooner:

This firm represents the descendants of Joseph F. Knapp and Joseph P. Knapp. It has come to their attention that you have been compiling information about the Knapp family and publishing this information on the internet along with your own commentary on this information. This ongoing publication of information and contacts on the Internet is grossly inconsistent with your stated goal of compiling information about a property located in Mastic, NY and writing a book about this property.

Please understand that the family has long sought to maintain their privacy and does not seek any notoriety or publicity. Your publications on the internet go far afield of your stated preoccupation with the Mastic property. Further your unsolicited phone calls, cards, letters and e-mails directed to several family members have been unwelcome and caused distress. The family does not support your activities and wishes to be left undisturbed.

Please be advised that you are engaging in these activities without any authorization from current members of the family. The family requests you make no further effort to contact them as they have no desire for you to publish their family history. They request that you confine the statements made in your publications to actual facts substantiated by public record.

Any further efforts by you to contact family members will run afoul of the protections against invasion of privacy afforded to the family by state and federal laws. In particular I call your attention Section 4-21-701 of the Tennessee Code which affords members of the family the right to initiate a civil action against you for malicious harassment. This statute provides for recovery of both special and general damages including but not limited to damages for emotional distress, reasonable attorneys' fees and costs and punitive damages. Further any statements which you make which are injurious to the reputation of the family will be vigorously pursued under applicable defamation law.

The family respectfully asks you to honor their desire for privacy and respect these protections. Any further communications should be directed to this office. Thank you for your cooperation in these matters.

Sincerely yours,
Ronald B. Lee

Well there you go. At least now, I knew where I stood with them. However I was not convinced that Sibby truly felt that way. I knew I had to respond to the accusations their attorney was making. So I did, four full pages worth, explaining my side and future intentions. It was probably two more pages than needed, but Mr. Lee went silent. Through the years, I honored my commitment to not contact the heirs. However, it did not stop certain members of their family from contacting me, as some of them obviously, wanted to talk. In my letter to Mr. Lee I said. "The Knapps Lived Here", would certainly not be the first unauthorized biography ever written, but he could assure his clients, it would certainly be a respectful one.

CHAPTER
8

New York, New York

Ah, Christmas 2001 — a well needed break from the intensity of the past year. A time to spread joy and cheer and commune with family and friends. One of the most surprising Christmas gifts I would receive that year came from my son Erik. It was a large encyclopedic volume titled Long Island Country Houses 1860 - 1940, that according to it's editors was twenty years in the researching. It served as a sober reminder to what I had tried to do in the past year based on just one country house that of course was not in this excellent book or it seemed anywhere else in print. However there was another one that caught my eye. A place called Tenacre in Southampton, that was built in 1920's for publisher Joseph P. Knapp.

By the time New Years rolled around I sort of figured out what I was going to do. I called Kenny Vitellaro and Doug Percoco and asked them if they would mind my company for a week or two. My plan if you could call it that, was to do an extended study in both New York City and Long Island into just what might be available via public documents, and other sources on the original ground breaking Knapp Family of Joseph Fairchild and Phoebe, their children Antoinette & Joseph Palmer and his three wives, and two children Claire and Joseph F. with again the Mastic Beach Mansion sort of being the center of it all. I really felt there was a large diversified story here, probably most of it being about big J. F. as I called him and J. P. as they had certainly made their mark in history. Of course the one Knapp, who I still found most fascinating was Doty or Dodi or J. F. K. Jr. as I referred to him then. Probably because he seemed a stark contrast to his high achieving father and grandfather. But I really had no agenda, other than being slightly steamed that the Knapp heirs told me I couldn't write about anything other than the Mastic Beach mansion. I had faced challenges before; friends on Long Island in the 1970s telling me to give up commercial fishing, as I struggled through the first winter, by the summer I was taking my catch to market in the trunk of my vintage Bentley. In the '80s, it was friends in Florida, who cautioned that moving to Nashville to pursue songwriting was a real big gamble. I knew it was too; I had done the research. The odds of achieving success with writing a number one song was greater than being elected to US Senate! I'm not sure who came up with that statistic. Three years after I moved there, I had a number 1 song on the charts. So now I was going to focus on this group of very low profile Knapps, knowing that there was probably no one alive that could offer me anymore info than I already had. And the surviving heirs were not pleased at all with what I had already done, threatening legal action if I went any further. But hey, I already had invested a year of my time, so what's another few weeks?

I arrived in New York in mid January and spent the first few days at Doug's house in Elmont. I had set up appointments with the archive room of the Queensboro Library, Brooklyn Historical Society, NY Historical society and with Dan May, the archivist of Met Life. All proved to be extremely fruitful. The Long Island room of the Queensboro Library has a treasure trove of unique LI historical stuff that no one else seems to have. There I saw the huge Belcher & Hyde property atlases from the 19th and early 20th centuries, that showed Mastic as it was, when it was still entirely private estates. They also show the property owners and where the buildings were. It seems that a building in the location of the Knapp mansion, first appears on the Lawrence estate in 1906. So it looks like, although it was always known as the Knapp mansion, that the Lawrences built it or at least built something there. I also looked at the Long Island Press microfilm for coverage of the fire, as I knew one of the papers had carried a photo of the mansion intact during its glory days in the fire story. I struck out there, but then I was reading the Nassau edition of the paper and it could of appeared in just the Suffolk edition. I looked at Suffolk County phone books for the 1920s-50s and found The Knapp estate in Mastic Beach, listed in the late '30s and Joseph F. Knapp listed in the '40s and '50s in Hampton Bays as well as his sister Claire as Mrs. W. O. Penney in Stony Brook and Hampton Bays and also as Claire K. Dixon in the 1950s. The Queensboro library had quite a photo archive on computer too and I left with several rare photos of Bellport, Moriches and Mastic Beach including two of the colonial era Richard Floyd mansion, when Hollywood screenwriter John Howard Lawson owned it in the 1930s. This was the place, that was converted by Doctor Calabro into Bayview Hospital in the late 1940s.

The Brooklyn Historical Society, had some digital images of the original Joseph F. Knapp mansion in Williamsburg. Most were taken inside during the 1940s when it was a catering hall. They had just one very poor photo of the exterior, taken about 1910, which was about 15 years after the Knapps sold it. But I would find out that this was a very historic place, where the Knapps hosted several US

Presidents and other dignitaries in the latter 19th century. They also had several excellent photos of St. John's Methodist Church and Sunday School, which was just one block away. This church was strongly supported by the Knapps and J. F. was the president of the Sunday School which was huge. I visited these actual sites on Bedford Ave. in the Williamsburg section of Brooklyn, taking photos of the remaining buildings, from the era the Knapps lived there. Some were directly across the street at the corners of Bedford and Ross where a large Medical Office now sits on the property the original Knapp Mansion once stood.

The NY Historical Society, had photos of the original Metropolitan Life buildings, circa 1880s, a Memorial Day Parade from that same era, that passed the Knapp Mansion in Brooklyn and one of the entire staff of Major & Knapp Lithographers, circa 1879. There, about 20 some guys, most in suits are standing around a loading dock. In the center in vests, I believe, are none other than the owners Richard Major and Joseph F. Knapp. There is one young fellow, in the front row that could very well be, Joseph P. Knapp. He would be about 16 years old there. The society building is located on Central Park West. That afternoon I walked down west 72nd Street to the Hudson River and Riverside Drive and saw Number 322, which was the address of the Joseph Palmer Knapp family, lived in a 4 story brownstone in the 1890s. Some of those brownstones are still there.

New York Public Library had some city directories on microfilm that listed both Joseph Palmer Knapp and his son J.F. in the early 1900s-1930s. I also got to see copies of several different New York papers that ran obituaries on both. They also had microfilm of the Brooklyn Citizen newspaper which used subscription sales in the 1920s as the way to sell the new town of Mastic Beach. The display ads, some of them two full pages, provided some glimpses into my home town the way it was a quarter century before I moved there.

My visit to Metropolitan Life Insurance was a real eye opener. Dan May, the company archivist had been corresponding with me for some time. He was the one who first alerted me to the two Joseph F. Knapps. Big J. F., the grandfather and godfather of the company if you will and his namesake grandson that was born in February 1892, six months after the grandfather died. The grandson had nothing to do with the company, but his father Joseph Palmer certainly did. Even after he sold the family interest thereby allowing the company to mutualize in 1917, J. P. remained a director of the finance committee, thereby making critical decisions of where the company invested it's funds. Dan took me into the reconstructed 19th century boardroom. The sheer opulence was jaw dropping. On the hand-tooled leather covered walls, were huge oil portraits of all the Presidents of the company with Big J.F. hanging slightly above the others in the center of the room. I also got a personal tour of the company museum and left feeling I knew a little bit more about the president, who guided the company at the very shaky beginning (they nearly folded in the 1860s insuring soldiers in the Civil War) to one of the leading insurance companies in the world. I will have a lot more to say about the Knapps and this company in future chapters. It certainly could be summed up in their 1980s ad campaign, Get Met It Pays.

Probably the most profound experience I had on the New York leg of this trip however was my visit to Greenwood Cemetery. And even six years on, I don't think

I could convey that experience any better than I did when I wrote this and posted it on my website along with the photos I took that spring like January afternoon.

O VER THE 160 PLUS YEARS OF ITS EXISTENCE, the gates to Green Wood have probably been photographed more times than any cemetery in the world. Though many superb photos exist, this simple snapshot taken as I approached it on Thursday afternoon, January 17, 2002 is the one I chose, because for me it captures the mixed feelings I had that day. So near, yet so far— I had traveled a great distance to see the final resting places of the patriarch Knapp's, a family that never knew me nor I them, yet have been drawn to over the past year by forces I cannot readily explain. So I paused here for a minute, as if to give notice of my arrival and to receive some type of silent nod to enter.

The guard at the gate handed me a large map (it is 468 acres) and showed me where the office was. Pre-armed with both the section & burial plot numbers obtained from the Greenwood Internet site. I saw no need to stop at the office and set out on my way. According to the map, the Knapp's were way in the back of the place and I slowly snaked my way. through the maze of twisting roads, while taking in as much as I could all along the way. The place has been around since 1838 and was a leading tourist attraction by the 1850s according to what I had read about it. In the 1860s the New York Times wrote " It is the ambition of the New Yorker to live upon the 5th Avenue, to take his airings in Central Park and to sleep with his fathers at Greenwood. I do not know if that was Joseph F. Knapp's ambition, as his father is not buried there with him, his mother however- er is. With the exception of his little known, first born son Francis, who died as an infant, his other son Joseph Palmer, who would rise to even greater heights in the world than his father, lies elsewhere in North Carolina. But do not pity Mr. J. F. Knapp, as he has a good deal of company here , within his family circle.

The section I was looking for was not to difficult to find using the Green Wood Map. I parked and got out thinking I would not have any trouble. I knew there were at least a half dozen Knapp's buried here so I thought there would be a large marker easily spotted. Well after 40 minutes of combing the section, I realized I better drive back down to the main gate and office if I wanted to find the grave-site before dark.

On the drive back down I thought about how far the hearse had to travel from Williamsburg in 1891. Mentioning to the office clerk where the Knapp's lived, he estimated it would of taken the procession a half a day to arrive back then. After a few minutes of searching his records, he told me why I couldn't find it. The internet site listed the wrong section. He added by looking at his map,that he could tell by the size of the plot, I would not have any trouble seeing it. He gave me a print out of it and I could see it was indeed a very large circular plot.

W HEN I GOT BACK TO THE PROPER AREA THE CLERKS WORDS RANG very true. There they were, Joseph, Phoebe, Francis, Joseph's mother and daughter Antoinette, Edward his first born grandson, and more, all circled around a huge obelisk monument, that sat on pedestal with KNAPP chiseled boldly into the white marble. Out further on Long Island, discoveries too, were really started to pile up. One snowy day Kenny and I headed east and visited Tenacre, J. P. Knapp's 1920s home in Southampton (It was recently on the market for 12.5 million). We also visited the locations of Joseph F. Knapp's, three 1940s era home sites in Hampton Bays, including his last one on Smith creek and Hampton Harbor Road, that he died in. On the north shore of Hampton Bays (the Peconic Bay side) we drove through the area that was once known as "Clairedale" which was also the name of Claire Knapp's dog kennel. It became the estate of Mr. and Mrs. Willis O. Penney from 1933-1941 and after that, Mrs. Claire K. Dixon's estate until she passed on in 1959 and her daughters sold it. It is still a very wooded area and the ride on Clairedale Drive, was like going through a state park. Although I did not see the actual home she built there in 1933 this time out, I figured I was now in this Knapp story for the long haul and if it was meant to be, I would eventually find it and who knows what else.

CHAPTER
9

A Fairchild is Born in an
Unfair World

Poet Samuel F. Smith's "America", the tune most people know by its opening line "My Country Tis Of Thee" (and ironically sung to the British anthem "God Save The Queen") would first be sung in public in Boston, Massachusetts, for our nation's 56th birthday celebration in 1832. That Wednesday, July 4th, in our nation's capital, Congress was rushing renewal of the charter of The Second Bank of the United States. On that same day in New York City, the Fourth of July was hardly celebrated at all as a raging epidemic of cholera claimed hundreds of lives weekly. However, Sunday's child, the four-day-old Joseph Fairchild Knapp, second son of Antoinette and William Eben Knapp, was unaware of all these swirling events; he was simply trying very hard to survive, as the other denizens of New York were and would continue to for the months to come. Joseph F. was successful in ducking the fatal disease. Perhaps it was that early touch of grace, success, national events and song that would seem to stay with him for most of his extraordinary life.

But six days later on Tuesday, July 10th, President Andrew Jackson (who was running for reelection) killed the re-chartering of The Second Bank of the United States, a veto that marked one the major events of his presidency. On that same day, a major event would occur in Joseph Fairchild's 10-day-old life when his 25 year old father passed away, most likely from cholera. I say most likely, because the one obituary I have found on him, that appears in *The Working Man's Advocate* on July 14th, does not specify the exact cause of William E. Knapp's demise. It seems however it would either be cholera or grave misfortune. As the report does specify the causes and the ages of one hundred and ninety one persons, that died in NY City that week and among them William E. Knapp's name is surrounded with cholera victims.

That will not be the last reasonable assumption, I have to make on the history of this particular Knapp family. Some of the very reasons for that have already been established, in regard to the surviving Knapp heirs, who opposed from the outset, my writing a history of their family. I also have had to contend with the surviving public records or newspaper accounts of which some are very incomplete, some illegible, and some that seem to flat out contradict each other. It is only after many years of study that I venture reasonable guesses on the many blanks I would discover and the questions they raised within myself as I pondered them. I would also discover through confidential sources, that even if I did have the cooperation of the afore mentioned reluctant heirs, many of my questions, they could not answer either. I have discovered through nothing but innocent accident and my own detective work, that I now know some things that they don't. Not that it matters, for that discovery is really of no use in trying to achieve my desired intention, the whole Knapp story. Knowing and being comfortable that learning the whole Knapp story is an impossibility, let's move right along to my second reasonable assumption. The maiden name of Joseph Fairchild Knapp's mother Antoinette. It seems it was—drum roll please—**Fairchild**. Seems simple doesn't it? Downright logical too. However there is no definitive record that I have found, of what her maiden name was, even though her predecessors have theirs listed. So let me walk you through, how I arrived at this reasonable assumption (and I have learned not to make many with this family) and perhaps you will decide for yourself, if your unofficial Knapp historian, is a fairly reasonable person, possessing a logical deductive mind.

There has been a long published and sometimes revised Genealogy of the Knapp family in America, that goes back to the year 1606 when a Nicholas Knapp was said to have been born in Suffolk, England. It says Nicholas came to America with his wife Elinor about 1630. Others say Elinor did not exist. However Nicholas and seven more generations of Knapps did. But my Knapp story is really confined to the last three generations of this Knapp line. Joseph Fairchild Knapp 1832-1891, his son Joseph Palmer Knapp 1864-1951 and finally his son Joseph Fairchild Knapp 1892-1952, who never had any children, that I know of, but was the person who owned the Knapp mansion in my childhood backyard. My reaching back before the first Joseph Fairchild Knapp has been only to help shed some light on who the first J. F. Knapp, his son and namesake grandson was and of the genesis of their middle names, Fairchild and Palmer.

The very early census of the United States, from 1790 through early 1800s only lists the names of the heads of family. The rest of the members were enumerated as number of males under and over the age of 21 and the same for females. Also up until either the outlawing of, or the Civil war, are the number of slaves that belonged to each family. The Knapp family first settled in the Watertown, Mass. area and then it seems many of them migrated to Greenwhich, Connecticut around 1670. From there the first ones to show up in New York City area around 1820 are Eben 1746-1824 and Ruth 1773-1852 Knapp. the parents of three girls and four boys including William E. (Eben?) 1807-1832 and James Hobby Knapp 1824-1871. Ruth's maiden name was Hobby.

The census for 1790 shows a half dozen or more Hobby families enumerated near the Knapp families back in Greenwhich Ct. It also lists a large amount of Fairchilds (37) in Greenwhich, with several enumerated near the Knapps. William E. and Antoinette named their first son born in 1830 William Timothy Knapp and the name Timothy goes back to the first generation of Knapps born in America. The name Joseph also goes back to that generation. However there is no William until Eben & Ruth marry and no Fairchild until William E. Knapp marries one Antoinette. So does Antoinette Fairchild sound reasonable? Well it did to me, until I found one entry in the National Cyclopedia of Biography published about 1893. There in parenthesis, the name Chichester appears next to Antoinette. I have never seen it in any other biography or obituary on Joseph F. Knapp. I'm not saying it is wrong , but it certainly is not helpful in explaining where the name Fairchild came from. It certainly was not Joseph's complexion, which usually appeared in photos to be very dark, but in some portraits of him, like the one that dominates all others in the boardroom of the Metropolitan Life Insurance Co. appears to have been lightened to an exaggeration, by the artist.

I have not found too much written about Joseph Fairchild's early childhood other than he started public school in Williamsburg, Brooklyn, where the family had moved to and that his Mother then sent him to North Adams, Massachusetts to be further educated at a boarding school. There he stayed until he was around 15 years of age. An uncle is mentioned (not by name) several times in most of his bios, as the one who arranged for young Master Knapp's further education. Of the three possible uncles on Joseph's father's side, Sanford Reynolds Knapp, David A. Knapp my bet is on youngest one, James Hobby Knapp, who saw to it that Joseph would benefit from a very good education. One of young Knapp's tutors was the eminent educator of the day, Lyman Thompson who would later write of his pupil: "At first I was discouraged with Knapp–but in watching him closely, I discovered an inclination for mathematics so I began to develop that talent in him; it seemed to impose just enough concentration, strict system, and hard application to suit his bent; so I carried him from one arithmetic to another, through algebra upon algebra and finally into the classics, and stopped only when I could do no more. Now the way is paved, the track laid, and you may send any train you please over the road. Mark me, wherever Knapp goes, you may be sure he will be heard from."

And so young J. F. went back to Brooklyn and proved his tutor right and made his uncle and mother proud. As for Lyman Thompson, he used J. H. Knapp as a prominent endorser in advertisements for the Classical and Commercial Institute that Thompson would open in Port Chester, NY in the 1850's further adding credence to my reasonable assumption that James Hobby Knapp was indeed his nephew's "Dutch Uncle."

J. H. Knapp is listed as making a living as a teacher in the 1860 census and he is shown as living at Lyman Thompson' s residence in Rye, NY. There is a paper trail of news items that show J. H. Knapp would also stay involved with his promising nephew for most of his life. James H. Knapp Esq. had an office at 31 Pine St. in New York (a parallel block north of Wall Street) and was among other things, the executor of his widowed mother, Ruth Hobby Knapp's estate in the 1850s. He ran legal notices for those who might make claims against it for almost two years from her death in late September of 1852 at the age of 79 until February of 1854. This suggests to me, that there was some strong estate wealth there among the Knapps and contradicts the biographical info from several newspapers that makes claims of a poor beginning for young Joseph Fairchild, his brother William and his widowed mother. That is unless his mother was perhaps estranged or disinherited by her own mother.

In 1862 James Hobby Knapp still had an office on Pine St. NYC, but he was now an insurance agent for the territory of Chicago and the state of Illinois with the Security Life Insurance and Annuity Co. His 30 year old nephew was on the board of directors of that company. It has generally been said that Joseph F. Knapp got involved with the insurance business as a means of providing some sort of protection for his employes from the hazards of the printing business which like many occupations in the 19th century could often be fatal. However in "The Metropolitan Life," a very thoroughly researched text by Marquis James that was commissioned by the Metropolitan Life Insurance Company in 1946, the author states that Joseph Fairchild Knapp initially got into the insurance business as an investment and then began to be actively interested as a means of safeguarding his holdings. I believe there is much truth in both statements.

When J. F. became involved with The National Travelers Insurance Co (the original name of Met Life) in 1866 he gradually withdrew from Security Life and several other insurance companies he was invested and involved with. This decision at age 34 would be just one of the many that earned him the reputation among his friends and intimate peers as having an abundance of "innate sagacity" Within a decade after that decision Security Life Insurance and Annuity Co. was headline news, not unlike Enron would be centuries later and its chief officers were in prison.

Young Joseph's unbridled sense of patriotism and national pride may of also came from his Uncle James, who was a Major in The National Guard. In the latter part of the 19th century J. H, Knapp Esq. was the vice president in the Republican party for the state of NY. Other occupations he may of been involved with were those of superintendent of schools for Knox County and the city of Chicago, Ill. (as he was the insurance agent for that state) and possibly a banker in NY. Regardless of exactly whatever he was or was not, I think it is safe to assume that Uncle James Hobby Knapp, played a major role in the destiny that was to become the legacy of one Joseph Fairchild Knapp.

CHAPTER
10

Sarony, Major & Knapp, and Palmer

"New York is notoriously the largest and least loved of any of our great cities. Why should it be loved as a city? It is never the same city for a dozen years altogether. A man born forty years ago, finds nothing, absolutely nothing, of the New York he knew. If he chances to stumble upon a few old houses not yet leveled, he is fortunate. But the landmarks, the objects, which marked the city to him, as a city, are gone." — Harpers Bazaar 1856

$Just$ half of the dozen years that Harper's Bazaar claimed it would take to totally change the face of a loathed mid-19th century New York City had passed in the life of Joseph F. Knapp, since Assistant Marshall Richard Van Eyeck had taken that short ferry ride across the East River to the country in Kings County. There he knocked on broker Francis Dominick's door, in the Village of Williamsburg, on Sept 4th, 1850. Along with Mr. Dominick, he would find one Antoinette Knapp Dominick age 41 no occupation , William T. Knapp age 20, a seaman and Joseph F. Knapp age 18, a lithographer, living at that address. We know all this because of Mr. Van Eyecks beautiful penmanship, he so carefully applied to the Schedule 1, pre printed form of the sixth Federal Census of the United States. This was not the first, nor the last census, I would use to discover many facts of Knapp life over the course of seven some years. Like so many of my other discoveries, life had changed dramatically for Knapp over those early years and would continue to do so for his 41 more Septembers.

I would find no further mention of J.F.'s brother, William Timothy Knapp, other than his obituary in April of 1858. Like his father, William E., William T. had died well before he was 30. Joseph had returned from Massachusetts to Williamsburg about 1848 when he was 16. He soon found employment across the river as an apprentice for the lithography firm of Sarony & Major. He would live out his life on both sides of the east river working in what would become known as America's Greatest City and eventually residing in what was once called the finest home in the "Eastern District". For his entire life, Brooklyn was a separate city, from New York, with its own government. It was also the 4th largest city in America and one that Joseph was offered to head, on more than one occasion, but firmly declined. He had started as a vulnerable infant born less than 20 years before, in a very different city and in the path of a six week Cholera epidemic that most likely took his father along with more people than the World Trade Center attack. But during his fairly brief future life of about a half century, spent in the greater New York area, Joseph F. Knapp's family, fortunes, business decisions and landmarks he built on both sides of that river, would effect people world wide for many decades to come. One could argue it is still effecting them and yet very few know his name. Like her son, his mother Antoinette, continued to live in Williamsburg, ED., until she passed away on November 30, 1876 at the age of 66.

L ITHOGRAPHY WAS A PRINTING PROCESS THAT WAS INVENTED IN THE 1790s by German publisher, Alois Senefelder. In the mid 19th century when teenager Joseph F. first strapped on a leather apron, in the shop of Napolean Sarony and Henry B. Major. it was as different as it was in from Senefelder's day as to what it would be, when his son Joseph Palmer Knapp, would take over the firm that bore the family name 40 years later and was by then a multi million dollar enterprise. The major differences, would be its wide spread commercial use in creating prints and the advances in the use of color. It was still based on the same principles of creating an image from a drawing, made with grease crayons, pens and pencils off of a highly polished stone. Unlike engraving in intaglio or carving in relief, lithography images are transferred after a drawing is made on the flat surface and is washed with a solution of gum arabic and diluted nitric acid which fixes the greased image. Then it is washed in water and since water and grease repel each other, the ink sticks to the greasy image. When the paper is applied over it and sent through a press, a mirror image is reproduced. Early lithographs were monochromatic and if color was desired they were hand colored with paints. Hand tinted lithographs soon followed, in which two or three stones were used one for the image and the others for tints. These were followed by Chromo - Lithographs, that required at least three stones, each holding the image and a seperate color. This process was patented by Godefroy Engelmann, a French printer in 1837. Chromo Lithography is technically very complex, as it requires perfect registration and a highly sophisticated understanding of color.

The lithographer can be considered as much of an artist as the painter, engraver etc. That said, there has never been anything written about Joseph F. Knapp as an artist, other than his real artistry for business and later on when he was a very successful businessman his appreciation for art and his collecting of the same. The same cannot be said for Napoleon Sarony, who most likely leaned far to the artistic side and yet enjoyed both artistic and strong commercial acclaim in his later life, partly perhaps from the hiring or consenting of hiring with his partner of the young apprentice J. F. Knapp in 1848. The talents of the Majors both Henry who was an Engraver and his son Richard, who was just six years older than Joseph and would become Knapp's partner, most likely fell somewhere in the middle of Sarony and Knapp. During the 14 years that all were in business together, there is no doubt each one profited many times over from the association.

Napoleon Sarony was about ten years Knapp's senior and also was a child of a single parent. He lost his mother when he was around 10. In the 1830s he immigrated to NY city from Quebec, Canada, where his father was reportedly a lithographer. There he entered the lithographic trade in NY working for Henry Robinson and Nathaniel Currier of Currier & Ives. In the late 1840s he partnered with Currier & Ives, engraver Henry B. Major to form Sarony & Major. He also married Henry's sister Ellen. Both are enumerated as living with their family under Major's roof in Brooklyn in 1850. In most census forms that he appears in, Sarony lists his occupation as that of an "artist".

And that he certainly was, along with a promoter of that image. Standing just about 5 feet tall, sporting a goatee, Sarony was very animated and excitable when he spoke. He wore a fez along with other very picturesque attention getting attire, one would consider more of a costume than suitable for everyday wear. When Ellen died in 1858, Napoleon took the children and went to Europe for a few years. While there, he studied art in Berlin, Paris and London. While in England, a visit with his brother Oliver exposed him to the new possibilities of photography. Oliver was having tremendous financial success, not that Napoleon wasn't with the litho firm back in NY, that was running very smoothly and had provided him the luxury of the extended trip. He may of stayed in Europe for the entire duration of the Civil War, but he returned to NY afterwards to set up the first and most successful celebrity 19th century portrait studio in NY. City. There is a landmark US Supreme court case, involving copyrights of photos (Sarony Vs Burrow Giles Lithographic) that was settled in Sarony's favor in 1884. Napoleon re married the equally colorful and artistic Louise Thomas in NY. In the latter half of the 19th century, his portrait studios were the talk of the town and it is estimated he photographed over 30,000 world celebrities and over 200,000 people from the general public. In the late 1890s he liquidated most of his studio props, artwork and other items as it was said he was in deep financial difficulty. The interviews he gave the press, merely suggest he was tired of photography as an art form. After he died in November of 1896, the possession of half a million glass plate negatives were passed onto the trust of his son Otto. Otto soon sold the right to use the name Sarony and experienced a great deal of legal entanglements. He passed away in 1903. Although many original Sarony prints survive, the fate of Napoleon's glass plate negatives is unknown.

If Joseph Knapp learned anything artistic from Napoleon Sarony, it may of been the style in which he would sign his name, when he did it for posterity. He embellished it with the same wide flowing banner underneath that Sarony used. However when he signed office invoices or memos, it was quite ordinary and sometimes barely legible or perhaps just the mark of a very busy man.

After three years at Sarony & Major, Joseph F. Knapp was the foreman of the shop, Perhaps for financial reasons the company at times confusingly used the name Sarony & Co. during this era or it may of just been Napoleon Sarony's ego? From 1847 - 1860's they moved to several locations, all in what is considered today as the lower Manhattan, Wall Street area, but at the time was the center of the city. At one point in the 1850s, there was a Joseph Knapp lithographer listed on Ann St. in NYC which suggests perhaps Mr. Knapp struck out with his own company briefly. However by the time he was 21, Joseph was the general manager of Sarony & Major and year later by 1855, the name on the building at 449 Broadway was Sarony, Major & Knapp. It was also the year he became the life partner of 16 year old Phoebe Worrall Palmer.

PHOEBE BORN IN MARCH OF 1839, WAS THE 5TH CHILD OF DOCTOR. Walter Clarke Palmer, 1804-1883, a surgeon and his wife Phoebe Worrall Palmer 1807-1874. Three of the first four Palmer children all died in infancy, but probably none more horribly than their daughter Eliza. She was born in 1835 and died a few months later in 1836, when a nursery worker accidentally set fire to her crib netting while refilling an oil lamp. Their final child Walter Jr. would be born in 1842. Young Phoebe Palmer grew up in a methodist home, where her mother's fascination for theology and spiritual impressions deeply effected all aspects of family life. Order and comfort rather than self indulgence, were the cardinal rules. Bells would summon family, guests and servants to morning and evening prayers, meals began and ended with sung graces. In 1837, her mother claimed by faith, the experience of entire sanctification. Dr. Palmer soon followed suit at a camp meeting that summer. From that point on. the Palmers devoted their entire lives to evangelism and the promotion of the doctrine of Christian Holiness. Religious scholars call the work of Phoebe and 'The Beloved Physician" Walter C. Palmer, as some of the major cornerstones of the Holiness Methodist movement. They established missionaries and out reach programs in both the eastern United States and Canada. The 5 Points Mission, was the first inner city mission established in NYC by Phoebe Palmer in 1850. Five points, was the absolute worst part of NY City at that time and is the location at which the film "Gangs Of New York" takes place. In 1859, Dr. Palmer left his medical practice to devote his full time to the Palmer's ministry. It became a family business too, with the printing (by Major & Knapp) of periodicals like Guide To Holiness and song books, Walter Jr. became the publisher. Phoebe Worrall Palmer and her sister Sarah Lankford, established the Tuesday Meetings in NYC, that continued well past both of their deaths. Three years after Phoebe Palmers's death in 1874, from Brights disease, Dr. Walter C. Palmer married Sarah, his widowed sister in law. History professor Edith Blumhofer states in her book "Her Heart Can See, the life and hymns of Fanny J. Crosby " that Phoebe Palmer coveted her children's entire sanctification and perhaps marriage offered the best escape for young Phoebe. She had no quarrel with her mother's faith, but preferred activity and society to what some called her mothers "Spiritual Abstraction". Joseph F. was himself a devout Methodist, thanks to his mother Antoinette, but he also was engaged in a fast paced and glamorous high society world of both business and politics, that surely must of impressed a girl who just turned 16. On Thursday May 24, 1855 at the Allen Street ME Church, just around the corner from the Palmer's modest Rivington Street home, Phoebe Palmer became the bride of Joseph F. Knapp. The Reverend Bishop Matthew Simpson united the couple. Bishop Simpson was a lifelong friend of Abraham Lincoln (he delivered Lincoln's eulogy) and that gives credence to the reports that Lincoln might of been the first in a long line of US Presidents who would enjoy the hospitality of Mr. and Mrs. Joseph Fairchild Knapp of 84 Bedford Ave, Williamsburg, Brooklyn ED.

CHAPTER

11

The Knapps Lived Here
(On the Corner of Bedford & Ross)

Being a full partner in the firm of Sarony Major and Knapp, I can say Joseph and Phoebe probably could of set up their newly wed housekeeping right away in the large mansion at the corner of Bedford and Ross in Williamsburg. The fact is though, it may not of been built yet. I'm not sure of the construction date, but I saw a mid 1850's map once that showed the lots there as part of the Remsen farm property. An 1894 real estate sale report indicates "that the Knapps purchased the house for $35,000.00 years ago and invested an additional $100,000.00 into it" during the several decades they lived there." An 1857 city directory lists J. F. Knapp lithographer, residing at South 2nd Street in Williamsburg with offices both at Ann St, NYC (lower Manhattan) and Fulton St. Brooklyn. South 2nd Street was also the address of Mr. and Mrs. Francis Dominick. So whether South 2nd was the new Mrs. Knapp's home or that of her in laws, where she spent the first years of her marriage, is not of any major consequence. It would be at the corner of Bedford Ave and Ross St. where both she and Joseph Fairchild would leave their domestic, social and historic mark.

Shortly after their marriage Phoebe's mother wrote this letter to her on

June 17, 1855[1]:

I want you my dear Phoebe and Joseph, to be deeply devoted to God, _to resolve, should the Lord spare you to each other, that your lives shall initially flow out upon the world in rich blessings. Do, my dear children, at this early period in your union, resolve not to live for yourselves.

If you will do this, I think the Lord may spare you long to each other. This is being united in the Lord. But if you do not resolve on this, I feel jealous for the Lord of Hosts. He will have no other Gods before Him. I want you to aim at the highest and most extended usefulness, and then will you live happily and God will be glorified.

Eminent holiness, usefulness and happiness are inseparably connected.

A mother's blessing be on my dear son and daughter

O N JUNE 23, 1857, their first child Francis Dominick Knapp was born. Named for Joseph's step father, Frank Dominick, the happiness of a new baby was very short lived, as the infant died just 14 days later. It would be five years before their second child Antoinette was born on March 21, 1862. Like both her grandmother and mother, Antoinette often called "Netty" seemed to not have any recorded middle name until she too would marry. This may of been a 19th century custom. Within two years she would be joined by a brother, born as Joseph Palmer Knapp on May 14, 1864.

As Joseph F. Knapp threw himself deeper into the big business world of both lithography and his new interest of insurance, Phoebe turned to music and started composing it for her mother's lyrics. At first they appeared in her mother and father's monthly publication "The Guide To Holiness". Being a lithographer, it was a natural decision for Joseph to do the printing of these songs. His abilities to make wise business decisions, also guided him in copyrighting his wife's works, while the new copyright laws were still evolving. Most of Phoebe's co written works are copyrighted in her name only. At first, most were published by Phoebe's brother, Walter C. Palmer's Bible House Co. in NY City. Later the general music firm of William A. Pond, for whom Major & Knapp did the printing for, was also engaged as a publisher of her songs. Although about 99% of all Phoebe's published compositions were of religious nature, one secular song stands out, possibly as an insight into how she may of dealt with the death of her firstborn. That song is titled "Watching For Pa" There are two published versions of this song. One attributed to Henry Clay Work in 1863 and one to Mrs. Joseph F. Knapp , obviously adapted from, but copyrighted in 1867. The lyrics to both are nearly identical, but the melodies are distinctly different and melodies were Phoebe's forte. In the 1870 census, there is an older minor child named Charles Warren born about 1854 and living with the Knapps. This would make three children again under their roof. Charles would continue living with them as an adult working as a clerk at Metropolitan Life. The lyrics in Phoebe's version are as follows:

---

1 Memoirs: The Life and Letters Of Mrs. Phoebe Palmer by Richard Wheatley Palmer & Hughes, 1884

Three little forms in the twilight gray
scanning the shadows across the way
six little eyes four black two blue
brimful of love and happiness too
Watching for pa , watching for pa
yes watching , yes watching for pa
Oh how they gaze at the passers by
he's coming at last they gaily cry
try again pets exclaims mama
and nellie says there's the twilight star
Watching for pa ...

Soon joyous shouts from the window seat
and eager patter of childish feet
gay musical chimes ring through the hall
a manly voice responds to the call
Welcome pa -pa, welcome pa-pa
yes welcome , yes welcome pa-pa

Of interest in the H. C. Work lyrics, which have been noted as adapted, he has more verses than Phoebe's and all three children are named, May, Nellie and Willie (who was a real son of Henry's and is described as a bit of a rascal) whereas Phoebe only uses Nellie which is not a far cry from Netty. Some of Work's better known songs were My Grandfather's Clock and Marching Through Georgia.

A unschooled musician (labeled amateur in the 19th century) with a "pleasing but thin soprano-voice[2]," Phoebe's love of music was life long and she shared it with her children, in the form of piano lessons for Antoinette and violin for Joseph. How far Antoinette pursued the piano is not known, as true to Knapp form she stayed well under the radar screen for most of her life. Although she was quite the socialite and co hosted with her mother, many a musicale, little more is known of her musical abilities. In 1883 at age 21, Godey's Ladies Book published two of Antoinette's short poems, "Truth Meeting Falsehood" and "Light". Her brother Joseph, in his reflective latter years, mentioned he knew enough to put the violin down after hearing Fritz Kreisler play. Kreisler born in 1875, more than a decade Knapp's junior, was a renowned virtuoso and did not make his American debut until 1888, at which point Joseph would of been a married man about to start a family. Knowing what Joseph P's lifelong hobbies were, shooting pool, birds, and golf balls, along with fly fishing, he may of abandoned the violin long before he ever heard Kreisler. Or it would not be uncommon, knowing his mothers bent for great music and musicians. to have exposed a young Joe to the child prodigy Kreisler performing in Europe, on one of her many trips abroad. In any event once Kreisler moved to America

---

2 This comment with no direct attribution, has appeared in her biographical materials with enough regularity to give it a modicum of credence.

and started recording, many fledging violinists used the "Kreisler excuse" to put the instrument in it's case for good.

Blessed Assurance & Insurance

Of the over 500 songs, that Phoebe composed in her lifetime, only two are widely remembered. The Easter hymn "Open the Gates Of The Temple" and " Blessed Assurance". Of those two it is "Blessed Assurance" written in 1873 that was her ticket to song-writing immortality. It has been recorded since the days of the Edison wax cylinder and adapted to just about every style of music known. With lyrics by her lifelong friend and frequent co writer, Frances "Fanny" Crosby, Blessed Assurance started out as Phoebe's melody first. The simple story of it's creation was often told and retold by the blind poet "Miss Fanny".

"I was at the Knapp Mansion and we went into the music room. Phoebe asked me to listen to a new tune she had composed, that she thought would be appropriate for a hymn. It was one of the finest hymn tunes I had ever heard and I immediately clapped my hands and said, Why that says Blessed Assurance."

In a very short time Fanny's lyrics would join the melody that has lasted for over one hundred and thirty four years and been recorded both with and without the lyric

Blessed assurance Jesus is mine
Oh what a foretaste of glory divine
Heir of salvation purchased of god
Born in his spirit washed in his blood
(Chorus) This is my story this is my song
Praising my saviour all the day long
This is my story this is my song
Praising my saviour all the day long
Perfect submission perfect delight
Visions of rapture burst on my sight
Angels descending bring from above
Echoes of mercy whispers of love

Chorus

Perfect submission all is at rest
I in my saviour am happy and blest
Watching and waiting looking above
Filled with his goodness lost in his love

Chorus

Blessed Insurance

In April of 1863, New York Governor, Horatio Seymour, signed a bill authorizing an experiment new to the history of life insurance. *"From and after passage of this act—the company hereafter incorporated by the name of the National Union Life and Limb Insurance Company, shall have and possess the power to make insurance on the lives and limbs and health of the officers, soldiers, sailors and marines of the army and navy of the United States."*

The act went on to name twelve men as directors of the new company. Of the twelve, only Simeon Draper, a friend and associate of the Astors and the Belmonts had the prominence, wealth and connections to carry off raising the mandatory $100,000.00 deposit for the State of NY, along with the rest of the capital investment needed to get the company off the ground. The charter limited the company to writing war insurance only and with events like the battle of Chancellorsville, in May of that year, where 17,287 Union soldiers were killed and then General Lee invading the North just six weeks after that battle, investors were gun shy to say the least. That was followed in July by the Draft Riots in NYC and it put National Union Life and Limb on life support. Draper saw the handwriting on the wall and withdrew as head of the company. Two retired army officers, Major General Daniel E. Sickles and Brig. Gen John Cochrane stepped in to take his place. But neither of them ever did anything with it. So with their charter about to expire, a group of Brooklyn and New York businessmen re organized it, naming Orison Blunt, an inventor of an early machine gun known as the Pepper Gun to head it. A man who was held in high public esteem for his honesty Blunt, was vehemently opposed by Tammany hall chieftain and future felon, "Boss" William Tweed, who tried to block his appointment. After two years of false starts and reshuffled presidents, directors and investors, the National Union Life and Limb Insurance Co. opened for business at 243 Broadway in two and a half second floor rooms. But Blunt also proved to be a man of too many occupations and pre occupations with no underwriting experience. The new company received a flattering send off from the trade journals of the day, but by December of 1864, only seventeen life and fifty six accident policies were written. And so once again the company decided to re organize. This time changing it's name to National Life and Travelers Insurance Co. after its first choice, Mutual Life and Travelers was found by the state to be in conflict with Mutual Life ,which happened to be the largest company of it's type in America.

Besides the name change, the biggest change was in the board of directors of very talented and prominent men of the day. But before the newly reorganized company could do anything, the Confederate Army collapsed and cut the ground out from under them. What saved them from folding their tent entirely though, was a revised charter that allowed them to write ordinary casualty as well as war risk business. Business was brisk during the year of 1865 and the company laid out over 23 thousand dollars in printing and advertising. Their printer (perhaps their exclusive one?) was the Major & Knapp Engraving Co. In spite of the brisk business, they still finished at the bottom of the barrel and once again another reorganization was called for at 243 Broadway.

This time they decided to split the company in two, separating the life and casualty business. Several directors withdrew and new ones mainly from Brooklyn were added. One of them was Joseph F. Knapp. Their new president was a retired physician Dr James R. Dow, who was also successful business man . Although he had no insurance experience (that was left to others) Dow's medical judgement proved to be very helpful in settling claims. The year of 1866 finished with the company no longer at the back of the pack. By June of 1867, the company wanted to get out of the casualty business and concentrate solely on life insurance. This took more funds than were available and when they were called on by the state to make an additional deposit of $25,000.00, it was director Knapp, who came forward and made the personal loan. By the end of 1867, National Travelers had done well for itself in the life insurance field . Although the two companies were now separate, they shared many of the same directors and on the casualty side, premium income was nearly eaten up by expenses. By 1868 the American business scene was bizarre. Lincoln's healing plan had been set aside by the carpetbaggers and in New York City "Boss" Tweed owned the government. Average corporations could not operate without greasing the palms of Tweed and his associates. It was in this uncertain climate, that the directors of National Travelers decided to re organize once again. After four major changes of direction, it was now sink or swim time. Joseph F. Knapp moved for the adoption of a resolution to send Dr. Dow to Albany to apply to the Legislature for yet another charter amendment. In the 18 months that he was involved with the company, Knapp had won the approval and respect of his colleagues. It was no small matter either, that he was the major investor in the still ailing company. New York City was now spoken of as The Metropolitan District and the name change chosen was, The Metropolitan Life Insurance Company. Up in Albany, Dow stayed close by and watched the bill make a quick trip through the state house. Then on March 24, 1868, the governor signed the act sending Metropolitan Life out into a very uncertain business world. That year, 19 new companies entered the life insurance field. Eighteen of them would fail within a few years.

Their new chairman of finance for Metropolitan Life was Joseph F. Knapp, who was also now their largest stockholder, having bought up shares from retiring investors to add to his portfolio, representing a personal outlay of $19,000.00. Knapp still had other life insurance connections too. He sat on the board of Security Life and Annuity, a high flying firm with a reputation as a business getter and in 1869 he also became a director of Hope Mutual. So at age 36, Knapp blessed himself with opportunities to acquire a first hand knowledge of all sides of the insurance business. By instinct a learner and a doer, J. F. Knapp took full advantage of it and poured his dynamic energy into steering the Metropolitan Life Insurance Company through many stormy seas yet to come.

Nearer My God To Thee
(Just Up The Street At 47 Bedford And Of Course In The Knapp Mansion, Too)

As if being extremely active in two large companies was not enough to occupy his time, J. F. Knapp may of been one of the original multi taskers. Both he and Phoebe spent a great deal of their time and money at and on a building, just a few hundred feet from their door. That would be the St. John's ME (Methodist Episcopal) Church and Sunday School on the next corner of 47 Bedford Ave and Wilson Street. This huge stone cathedral looking St. John's, was an out growth of the South Second Street ME Church which was the oldest one in Brooklyn. The Second Street church, like the Dominick's home, was just one mile away from the Knapp mansion. It was still his mother's church and the one of his childhood. He helped support it too and gave $35,000 in 1889 to restore the old church in his mothers memory. From the 1860's through the time that Phoebe sold the mansion in 1894, many interconnected events occurred at both places. By 1870, St. John's had over 1000 members and the Sunday School alone of which Knapp was the principal financier and superintendent of, had over 1500 children attending, including of course 8 year old "Netty" and 6 year old J.P. Knapp. From Edith Blumhofer's Fanny Crosby bio comes this reference to the St. John's Sunday school: "The Methodists deemed their St. John's Sunday School "of the very best grade" and opined that it had "no superior in the whole country" It did not hurt of course that the Knapps gave unstintingly to promote its interest, even providing a fine organ to help the music along. The Christian Advocate reported that the Knapps supplied the school with everything which ingenuity could suggest or money procure" It seems Phoebe and Fanny did their best with providing the music too.

One of the true treasures that has physically come my way, due to my pre publishing research via my web site, is a book printed in 1869. A book dealer in Vermont contacted me about it. Titled "The St. John's Methodist Episcopal Sabbath School" it is beautifully autographed no less, by Jos F. Knapp to Anthony Creagh, who was the Treasurer of the School and an employee at Met Life. It is in near pristine condition and contains many facts, illustrations, and for me enlightenments into not only the Knapp family, but how they were perceived by their friends, and neighbors. From this book. I offer a few facts and recollections.

The Sunday School was divided into three departments of Seniors, Juniors, and infants. Phoebe was a teacher in the infants. Each class of which there were many in each division had a name. Morning Rays, Truth Seekers (senior) Snowflakes and Wayside Gatherers juniors, Little Soldiers and Lambs of the Flock (infants).

The new Sabbath school, which was an oblong building 100 feet by 50 feet with a 32 foot high ceiling, was completed in March of 1868 and located on Wilson St., just behind the massive church, which was still under construction. During the Christmas anniversary program on Tuesday Dec. 29, 1868, the school held a unannounced tribute for it's major benefactors Mr. & Mrs. Knapp "Not the least interesting feature of the evenings presentation was the surprise of which the Superintendent of the School was made the subject. When the exercises were about half through and while the organist was playing a beautiful march, suddenly the doors were thrown open and a chariot covered with red velvet and drawn by twelve young ladies in white and two young gentleman, made its appearance, and passed slowly up the aisle to the alter. In it were seated four Misses, holding a beautiful frame, in the shape of the Greek cross, containing the photographs of all the officers and teachers of the School, about eighty in number. Rev Dr. Andrews came forward and after a few appropriate remarks. presented the picture to the Superintendent, who was so much touched at this manifestation of the teachers esteem that he could hardly find the words to respond. When the hour for bringing the entertainment to a close had arrived, the presents were distributed to the children, each one receiving an ornamental box containing fruit and candies; also a neatly printed copy of the "Christmas Hymn" and to many were given beautiful and interesting books. At the close of the public exercises, the officers and teachers accepted the kind invitation of the Committee to assemble in the Church parlor and participate in the distribution of a variety of gifts, which were suspended on a Christmas tree and also to partake of the "good things" of this life, which were spread on the table before them. Here also, the Superintendent's wife, was kindly remembered and presented with a special token of her associates esteem."

Getting Rich Quick...

Although it has been previously stated that J. F Knapp got into the insurance business (probably at the suggestion of his uncle) partly as an investor and partly to provide coverage for his employees at the litho firm, I can honestly say after reading the book "A Metropolitan Life," that his business affairs with Met were in no way whatsoever a get rich quick scheme. Many insurance companies then were for many, fly by nights, with some spare capital. The fact is at the time when Knapp was just an initial investor in the company, he had already made a sizable fortune in the litho business. After the Civil War, Sarony withdrew from the litho firm to pursue photography and it was just Major & Knapp. They grew to become one of the dominant printing firms in the US. However the trials and tribulations of the insurance company were many and the fact that Knapp often seemed to throw good money after bad, to prop up Metropolitan over several decades, tells me a lot about the person and his personality.

Knapp's education in the insurance business, came at a hefty enough expense, even by today's standards that might of sent another person packing it in and cutting their losses. As late as the 1880s, Mr. Knapp recalled times when, " We dreaded opening the morning mail, the only way to meet the day's claims was to go and borrow the money."

I'm not sure what decade in the 20th century that Met Life started using the phrase *"Get Met, It Pays"* but the fact is, at first for Knapp, it cost him dearly. Knowing what I have learned about it, I would venture to say, it is not a stretch that the headaches he encountered with running this company, may of contributed to his early death.

In 1869, there was $614,000,000 worth of life insurance sold in the US. Compare that to $24,000,000 in 1861, however it would take another 17 years until 1886 ,when the $600,000,000 figure was ever reached again. What follows are some of the ups and downs, Knapp encountered for two decades running The Metropolitan Life Insurance Company. Met closed its books that year with a record of encouraging progress and "Hardheaded director Knapp seemed to be directing more than the formal records of the company showed." Several execs, including the vice president Elias H. Jones, resigned from the company. Jones was from the school of when things were good anyone could make a killing in insurance.

In 1870, Chairman Knapp hired a young bookkeeper named John Rogers Hegeman, who was working at Manhattan Life to replace Jones and take the title of Secretary of the Company. Hegeman was given a confidential mandate by Knapp to conduct an exhaustive examination of the company books. At that , insurance companies that seemed solvent in their representations of statements were failing, usually because of managerial incompetence, rather than embezzlement or fraud. Knapp wanted to really know how things were at Metropolitan.

Dr. Dow took seriously ill and Hegeman was raised to Vice President. Together with Knapp they took vigorous control of the company and rounded out the year with the best record yet. Underwriting for $11,078,000, it was also the best record for any company in the entire state of NY. And yet it was tempered by a statement of excess liabilities over assets in the amount of over $94,000. The 1869 figures, that were prepared by Jones, had shown a surplus over $36,000. This mystery whetted both Knapp and Hegeman's interest to look deeper into Metropolitan's affairs. In February of 1871, Knapp laid Hegeman's findings before two of his colleagues in the finance committee. They in turn reported it to the full board with the following opening statement. "This is certainly a startling exhibit! The finance committee were hardly prepared for such a showing."

Hegeman had uncovered more bad news. The shortage was not $94,053 it was $176,107. "The difference owing to a inherited accumulation of doubtful accounts and unrealistic presentation of these financial statements." Knapp's insurance education was making progress. Dr. Dow, who was said to have been a man of high business ideals, never got to hear this news, he went south for his health and died two days after it was presented to the board.

Hegeman's report got action. Stockholder's dividends were discontinued. Funds that were already declared divisible were frozen and placed into credit. The company went on a cash basis by refusing to accept notes as part payments. A move was initiated to shore up the capitalization to $300,000. The directors raised $50,000 themselves with Knapp and his litho partner Mr. Major putting up $25,000. Knapp also bought up shares of stock from disheartened investors. The board issued this statement about Knapp at their meeting. " For the thorough and business like manner that he has come to the aid of the Company in it's hour of Trial , we commend our courageous director. " as if that wasn't enough trouble for one year, George Miller, a henchman of Boss Tweed, had become the state insurance superintendent. Miller shows up and wanted to look at Met's books. By this time his "examinations " were well known throughout the industry. Pay him an exorbitant fee and you got yourself a glowing report. Two of the other companies, in which Knapp sat on the board (National and Hope) had just received visits from Miller, paying out $2,500 and $2,980 to him. Met got off easy paying only $1,350. This time Miller's glowing endorsement was justified. Again the board thanked Knapp "for assistance rendered during the Examination by the New York Insurance Dept, just terminated so favorably."

With all this going on, the board did not get to pick a successor to Doctor Dow until June 3rd of 1871. Knapp was nominated for president and Hegeman Vice

President. The minutes of that meeting said *"Before the balloting commenced ,Mr. Knapp desired to thank the Board and rose to say that he desired them to understand — he did not seek the office—it sought him. Having other and larger interests at stake, he could not devote himself entirely to the service of the Company—although he would pledge himself to give all the attention which his pride in the success of the Co. and his reputation would dictate. Furthermore, he did not propose after bridging over present difficulties—to make way for another. The position must be permanent. More than this he did not propose (as some had intimated) to work for nothing, because he was able to do so, but to be paid liberally. Mr. Knapp requested the Board to consider the matter in all its bearings and have no delicacy regarding him on account of any services he may of rendered. He added that Mr. Hegeman and himself must receive equal compensation".*

And so the balloting began and when it was over, this abrupt stocky little titan who saved the company from the road to ruin, wound up as its president on his terms. The board then voted that his and Hegeman's salary be $4,500 each, with a provision to increase it to $6,000 within 18 months. When the capital of the company should be intact and the stockholders received their 7 percent dividends, Knapp and Hegeman would receive commissions of 1.5 percent of the net premiums, which were premiums minus agents commissions.

Knapp was still the companies largest stockholder and he was in no way what you would call a figurehead president. Because of his other business, it was Hegeman who had day to day direct charge of the company, but the two of them made for a great team and added balance to each other. Hegeman thrived on responsibility and was a pleasant man to both work for and do business with. Knapp was blunt and incisive. Haley Fiske, a company lawyer who would also become the president of Met Life in 1919 after Hegeman, worked for both of them back then and painted this picture of office life in 1872. "In one room a stolid, persevering, stubborn, iron man—and in the other a gentle, persuasive, diplomatic young fellow, able to express himself and to put into language the ideas of the elder. A great pair—a great pair!"

Meanwhile back at the mansion

The 1870 federal census showed the following, about the 8 people living at the Knapp residence on Bedford Av. Joseph, age 38, occupation printer, Phoebe age 30, "Netta" age 7 (and in school) Joseph 6, Charles Warren, age 16 at school (no relationship stated), and servants Delia Maby age 33, Johanna Masker, age 30 and Mary Maler age 18. All three domestics were Irish immigrants. The declared real estate value of the house was $17,000. which does not square with the reported $35,000 purchase price. There was a public school just two blocks away on Wilson St. where the Knapp children went for there primary education. Although Knapp was a strong believer in academics, secondary education was not a priority for young ladies of the 19th century and I have found no evidence that "Netty" was an exception to that norm, though she is listed as at school at age of 18 in the 1880 census. Joseph P. went to Brooklyn Polytech about 2.5 miles away for high school and college prep.

You would think with all he had going on between the business and his active layman's duties at the church, that J. F. Knapp was not at home much. That does not appear to be the case, as he and his wife thoroughly enjoyed their home and used it for many social activities. It seems that every president, from post Abraham Lincoln save for Andrew Johnson, but definitely Grant, Hayes, Arthur, Garfield and Harrison were at one time Knapp mansion visitors. Lincoln may of visited too with Bishop Simpson during his 1860 run for office. Although they were living in Williamsburg, there is no trace of any member of the J. F. Knapp family, nor his mother, step father the Dominicks in Brooklyn or his in laws the Palmers of NYC in the 1860 federal census. Knapp who was 28, when hostilities broke out did not serve during the Civil War. He was however a patriot of high order and a staunch Republican, when both terms carried a very different meaning. His politics and political connections, may of had some significance in Major & Knapp becoming the lithographer for the U. S. Government's geological survey, that covered the country's westward expansion and also for the many editions of D. T. Valentine's Manual of The Corporation Of the City of New York, which was a pictorial record of the city and its changes from the 1840s through the 1870s.

For those who never entered the interior of the original Knapp mansion, the rather austere exterior did little to reveal the splendor that lied within. The exterior blended with most other buildings near it and at three stories tall it was of average height for buildings in that area. It had among its many original rooms, a billiard room, library, a conservatory and art gallery.

Perhaps some of the largest and wildest displays held there were the post Civil War Memorial Day Parades. The mansion was festooned with Red White and Blue bunting and a grandstand was set up in front of it. For those dignitaries inside, it was only accessible by climbing out of the drawing room windows. I would think the sight of Ulysses S. Grant , General Sheridan or Benjamin Harrison, looking like a burglar would of been a photographers prize. When presidents were there in the ballroom, 1000 visitors would pass through the receiving lines, entering on Bedford Ave and exiting on Ross St. The *New York Times* reported a Memorial Day festivity held there this way:

GRANT & SHERIDAN CHEERED
THE DAY CELEBRATED WITH MUCH ENTHUSIASM IN BROOKLYN"

"The principal feature of the day in Brooklyn aside from the parade was the reception given to Generals Grant and Sheridan and Mayor Low at the house of Mr. Joseph Knapp on Bedford Ave. As early as 8 O'clock in the morning people began to gather at the foot of Broadway where it was known the distinguished military guests would land. A salvo of cheers that for a time almost rendered inaudible the booming of the cannons burst from the thousands who thronged the street as the carriages were driven rapidly up Broadway and escorted to Mr, Knapp's house by surviving veterans of the 19th Regiment. It was a triumphal progress. All the houses along the route were decorated with flags, and the cheering was continuous. The front of Mr. Knapp's house was a mass of silken flags and streamers. On a platform just opposite Arbuckle's band played stirring marches. When General Grant (who by now was also an ex president) looking well, but moving rather fee-

bly, was helped down from his carriage and with the aid of his crutch walked up the steps of Mr. Knapp's residence the cheer leading was simply deafening.

The reception took place in the art room, an apartment regal in it's size and was attended with very little ceremony. During the handshaking Gen. Grant became so fatigued that he had to rest himself for a few minutes on the sofa once or twice. Mr. and Mrs. Knapp were assisted in their several duties by Major Corwin and Messrs. H. V. Calvert, George A. Price, G. H. Frankenberg. A. H. Frost ... (it goes on to list a dozen or more names) and many other citizens prominent in both military and civil life. After the handshaking had come to an end, the guests partook of lunch, at the conclusion of which Gens. Grant and Sheridan once more entered their carriages and were driven to a reviewing stand at Washington Park, between Myrtle and DeKalb Avenues –NY Times May 31, 1881

Phoebe continued with her church work, both with her parents in NY City and her friends and neighbors in Brooklyn. In July of 1878, she took her children who were then 16 and 14, to a religious camp meeting on Shelter Island. That island lies in the middle of the Peconic Bay and between the north and south forks of Long Island. It was a camp meeting in name only, as they stayed at the fashionable Manhasset House there. The train route from Brooklyn to Greenport, on the North Fork where they would catch the ferry to the island passed through A. T. Stewart's planned community of Garden City. It may of been J. P.s first look at Garden City, a place where he would make his home for a time, in the beginning of the next century.

The following summer the entire family sailed for Europe. The Brooklyn Eagle reported their send off thusly:

OFF FOR EUROPE
The steamer William Fletcher as it lay at the South Sixth street dock yesterday afternoon attracted general attention on the part of the people about the locality. A profusion of bunting decked the vessel indicating that the boat was on a mission of more than ordinary importance. Such was indeed the fact. Mr. Joseph F. Knapp, his wife and a son and daughter had arranged to sail for Europe and a large number of their friends had determined to accompany them down to the bay. The party had secured the William Fletcher for that purpose embarking on the steamer a few minutes after three o'clock in the afternoon. Members of the St. John's M. E. Sunday School and Young People's Association attached to the church were the principal promoters of the excursion trip. They had also invited several clergymen and other guests well known to Mr and Mrs. Knapp on the trip to the "Hook"

The party included the following named persons. Dr. and Mrs Palmer, the parents of Mrs. Knapp, Rev J. O. Peek, D.D. Pastor at St. Johns, Rev J Hyatt Smith, J. F. Ditmars, Lewis P Nostrand, Job Throckmorton, W. H. Edwards, W. Anderson, W. W. Hanna, W. K. Cort, David Buckman, Aug. H. Marinus, Colonel J. W. Jones and wife, Silas B Dutcher, Dr. Milos Palmer, ... (and the list continues with about twenty more.) Mr. A Jahn the florist was also on board with two beautiful floral pieces, constructed to order by his artist workmen. One design was a min-

iature ship about 30 inches in length sent by the employees of Major & Knapp Lithographing Company. The other a horseshoe with a cross in the center was the gift of St. John's Young Peoples Assn. Mr. Knapp and his party arrived at the steamer Fletcher on time and were greeted with "Hail To The Chief" by Deverell's band, followed by hearty cheering from his friends in waiting. Soon afterward the Fletcher's lines were cast off and the boat's course laid for the Battery. Rounding that, the vessel was pointed up the Hudson to pier 40 at which the ocean liner Germanic of the White Star line lay moored. The Fletcher was soon made fast to. Not as a matter of choice but on compulsion, Mr. Knapp and his family then had to part company with their friends it being absolutely requisite that they go aboard the Germanic so that the steamer not be delayed once under headway. At four o'clock the ocean monster slowly steamed out from the pier to mid stream. Both the steamers decks and the dock were black with humanity, the assemblage onshore as one man cheering the departure of friends with voices and handkerchiefs while those on the vessel returned the compliment in like kind. As the Germanic steamed down the river, the Fletcher with its passengers moved on in the same direction at no great distance. The vessels maintained the same position until Sandy Hook was reached when the order to about ship was given by the captain of the Fletcher. At that juncture Mr. Knapp's friends shouted their last cheers and well wishes for a safe voyage and return. The homeward bound party arrived in Brooklyn about 9 O'clock that evening.—Brooklyn Eagle July 6, 1879

What was most likely a vacation for Phoebe and the children, was actually a four month work trip for J. F. Knapp. It was on that trip that he carefully studied the English system of selling what was called "Industrial Insurance" (low cost life insurance for ordinary working people) and upon his return, he applied it to Metropolitan Life, thereby changing the companies course, fortunes and making himself a multi-millionaire in the process.

CHAPTER
12

A Depressing Idea & A Brighter Day

As the Knapps steamed out of New York harbor, aboard The Germanic on what was probably their first big family adventure in Europe together, I think it is reasonable to speculate that the trip was germinated by Joseph's thoughts as far back as seven years earlier, when he dealt in a newer, slightly larger but still leased office at 319 Broadway, with a national depression that was taking his company two steps backward for every one he took forward.

1872 saw 17 major insurance companies go down the tubes. Public confidence was at a very low point, yet Met was regarded as "The most enthusiastic apostle of the progressive school in life insurance" by The Spectator—an insurance trade paper. In spite of conditions nationwide, Met had finished the year of 1871 as eighth in number of policies written (7,602 for a total of $8,312,000). Wisely using the power of his mighty steam presses on Park Place, Knapp launched The Metropolitan, a free monthly magazine for the policyholders, that was declared by the trade paper Insurance Chronicle as "Typographically and artistically without rival in insurance company publications" More than just lavish graphics, it published confidence building articles and asked its policy holders to alert the main office of any improprieties or misrepresentations both real or perceived by its field agents. In short, Mr. Knapp wanted to know what was going on in the field.

On an even brighter note, 1872 saw the Boss Tweed Ring and his stranglehold on NYC really starting to crumble. Tweed himself was out on a $1,000,000 bail, most of it put up by robber baron and Vanderbilt nemesis Jay Gould. Gould by the way was also aboard the Germanic with the Knapps in July of 1879 One wonders if any conversations or pleasantries were exchanged between Knapp and Gould on that voyage? Tweed's insurance henchman Miller, had resigned in the wake of a legislature investigation into his shakedowns. Knapp retired from the board of Hope Mutual, just before it's questionable mergers came to light, chalking it up to part of his insurance business education and he was able to cherry pick talent from the rapidly folding companies.

By now Knapp was convinced that Hegeman was the man he wanted for the job and sold him 470 shares of his own stock. He also wrote to one of his agents in 1872 that "insurance for the masses is uppermost in my thoughts—I have several think-ers at work, who will no doubt soon produce something." That something was Met's own form of Tontine Insurance, which they launched in September of 1872. Not exactly a new idea, as Tontine was a form of insurance that had been around since mid 1600s. In the simplest form, it was a subscriber deal where the survivors benefit as other subscribers die off, with the whole lot going to the last one stand-ing. It was popular and good move for the times, but not without critics. Nor was it the one that would insure the company's future well past the Knapp years.

In 1873, a pact was renewed with the Hildise Bund, a group of German im-migrants that had been purchasing insurance from Met as a group as far back as 1869. The event was noted in the paper the Brooklyn Times on July 2, 1873 "*Quite an unusual event occurred on Bedford Ave. last evening—the Hildise Maennerchor composed of members of the Hildise Bund, numbering around forty, marched with lighted torches and halting in front of the elegant residence of Joseph F. Knapp be-gan to sing. Mr. Knapp invited the serenaders inside, where a sumptuous repast was partaken of.*" The occasion was Mr. Knapp's 41st Birthday.

The crash of railroad securities in 1873, spread to everything else, taking the good with the bad. Within two months plants and mills were closing down. Any progress amid the mess the country was in was noted and Joseph F. Knapp's name was becoming known beyond the insurance and printing trades. He was mentioned that year, for mayor of Brooklyn. The board at Met voted for new ten year contracts at $6000 plus 1% of the net premium each for him and Hegeman, regardless of the state of capital or if stockholders were in receipt of dividends. In spite of that optimism, things in the country went from bad to worse and 1874 saw a general depression. Thinking that things would soon blow over though, Knapp and Hegeman made future plans. The company had outgrown its new quarters and Knapp was through with renting. He intended that Met should have a home of it's own and with that he picked out a place he wanted to locate it at.

It was a seven story white marble building, at the corner of Park Place and Church Street (pardon the pun but it was just a stones throw from his litho firm) The board authorized an outlay of $350,000 to purchase it. Knapp got to work negotiating and the depression was working in his favor. He got the owners down to $190,000 and they were stuck there, until one of the owners bailed. The final price paid was $165,000 and Met took title to it in December of 1875. They put $100,000 into renovations that included steam heat and an elevator. They were moved in, with a large Pennant that said Metropolitan Life Insurance flying from the roof in early 1876. They rented rooms they did not need and one of their tenants at $40 a month, was none other than Chester A. Arthur, who at that time was the collector for the Port Of New York. Within 5 years, Mr. Arthur had moved out of there and into The White House.

In spite of the rosy new headquarters, and offering several types of insurance, business continued to shrink. Knapp found himself laying off clerks and reducing salaries on those who remained. Although Met was doing fairly well compared to other companies of it's size, rows of empty desks were constant reminders that things were not really very good. In an effort to stop the downward slide, Knapp started thinking again about insurance for the masses. At this point in spite of attention having to be divided by his other business interests, it would be fair to say Mr. Knapp's insurance education had progressed to the point where you could call him a bona fide underwriter and a rather talented one. Unable to get a grip on large policy business, that seemed to be firmly in the control of larger companies, Knapp laid before his board, a plan to tap into a market where competition in the US was nil. It was known in England as the Prudential League and what it was, was simply life insurance for ordinary working men.

I N WHAT MAY SEEM TO SOME AS MICRO MANAGING TODAY, KNAPP ALSO TURNED his attention to scrutinizing miscellaneous expenditures of the company. With money getting scarcer, the name Knapp appears in pencil scrawl on what might seem as trivial bills, like one for office cleaning at $18 that was divided among three women Mrs Morris, Mrs. Daly and Mary Grogan for 6 days work each. Or $8 payable to P. Moran for the carting out of ashes for the month of November 1876. The firm of Shannon, Miller & Crane, dealers in Military, Theatrical Church, Society Goods & All Kinds of Gold, Silver and Tinsel, submitted a bill for "repairing flag" for $4.50 (The Met Pennant On The Roof) it too is signed off by Knapp for payment. The signature though is hastily scrawled and nothing like his flourishing autograph in the St. John's Sabbath School book I possess. But time was money. The year closed with lots more bad news, including the failure of Continental, a large company and victim of "financial buccaneers" Knapp's name had once been linked with them too. He seemed to have a sixth sense to get away from companies that were about to fail, because of shady deals. It was now the fourth year of the worst depression the country had ever seen. He braced himself for repercussions and went before his board and had this to say. "Gentlemen the record of the year 1876, has been fraught with so much disaster to Life Insurance Associations of the country, that it behooves us to take a retrospect of the past and from it and the outlook of the future, draw such conclusions as will able us to protect the interests of our the thousands of policyholders, committed to our care. He then reviewed what had been done to date, since he took control of a company with a failed reputation. Our assets have been raised from $833,000 to $2,291,383. —To this date we have not lost a dollar on a Mortgage and our stocks and bonds, could at anytime be sold for more than they cost. Although business for the past 5 years has been depressed and confidence destroyed in the stability of Life Insurance companies, through failure, mismanagement, and fraud rendering it almost impossible to secure applications, we have steadily improved the standing and reputation of this company as each year has passed by. We firmly believe that Metropolitan will in the not far distant future be the equal in every element of strength with the best institutions of its kind. But we must not fail to take cognizance of the fact that there is a growing disposition on the part of the Insurance departments to favor the older companies. The accumulating evidence of the influence which vast moneyed institutions exert, in the appointment of officials and the manipulation of them and their subordinates and of the procurement of legislation conducing directly and indirectly to their own advancement, is of serious moment to younger corporations and should lead to measures on our part as will place the future of the Company beyond a doubt."

Talk about history repeating itself think about the business world in 2007. The directors got Knapp's message loud and clear. A free for all was raging between the tontine and non tontine companies and the big dogs were doing their best to make it tougher for the small companies to survive. This is what Rockefeller was doing in the oil business and some insurance moguls liked his idea.

"The question naturally arises, what measures can be taken to place the Metropolitan in an impregnable position. " He then proposed this bombshell to the board, "The policy holder should contribute to make the Companies strength beyond question." He then suggested that in case of necessity, that the board be empowered to levy an additional charge or lien of one years whole life premium against policies issued or revived after December 31, 1876. This he said, would be accomplished by inserting a clause permitting such assessments. Aside from the elaborate advertising and promotional claims, Metropolitan at that time was known as pretty straightforward in dealing with their policy holders. In short, it made good on all it promised. Many other companies then were promising the moon and going bust. Knapp's philosophy was, nobody got something for nothing and he asked nothing of his policyholders, that he was not willing to do himself (Of course he was probably in a better financial position to do so than say 98% of his policy holders)

Mr. Knapp then concluded by saying that the requirements of state insurance departments were getting stricter and that a hostile examination might result in a report that would make it impossible to secure new business. The item that worried Mr. Knapp, was balances in the hands of agents, to which he said "It becomes necessary for someone to stand in the breach. Your president is ready to cover the Agents balances." The Agents balances at that time were $96,240.74. The board voted to accept Knapp's offer and on the spot he forked over bonds in the amount of $94,000. (You could say the gentleman had an ace up his sleeve before he spoke) The securities were transferred to Met's safe and a receipt was signed by both Hegeman and Sylvester Beard, who was now Chairman of the Finance Committee (a position Knapp's son, would occupy in the early part of the next century). After some debate, the board also voted to accept Knapp's lien proposal, but at their next meeting added a change that restricted that move to emergency use only.

Nip It In The Bud
But bad news continued in 1877 and it was worse than even Knapp was pre-

pared for. The depression reached its height or you could say low point and ten thousand business firms folded. America's working men roamed the country, there were bread riots and labor union "terrorists". In Pittsburgh, a rail road strike, was at the mercy of a mob for three days. In New York, the senate started to investigate life insurance companies after numerous failures and public outcry of being bilked. Knapp saw all of this as demoralizing. Writings of new business fell to levels they were at in 1864. No company that survived 1877 was as hard hit as Metropolitan, yet Knapp fought on for his company and his policyholders. The biggest defections seemed to come from the German Hildise Bund, who accounted for 80% of Met's policy lapses. The higher rates and bad times were the main reasons the Germans let their policies go. In August of that year Knapp told the board "Every lapsed policy could be replaced by a new one, if we pursued a reckless plan of exorbitant commissions and allowances. The true policy of this company should be one of conservatism. The dishonorable practices brought to light by the failure of so many of our trust institutions could have been NIPPED IN THE BUD if Directors & Trustees had been true to the responsibility they assumed in accepting the trust."

Seven weeks later, he faced his board with even worse news! The lapse rate was alarming and could not be accounted for by the earlier reasons of the German Bund and price increases. It may have been that Met was a victim of rumor mongering started by rival companies. Knapp's solution was another audit by the State, to stem the tide of such rumors. The state sent a crew, but it's report was not finished in time to cushion the worst year end statement yet: 2,405 new policies written against 5,771 lapses. Insurance in force slid from $24,223,000 to $16,536,000. Fully one third of the company he had helped build for the last six years was gone. And that was not his only setback. Three key men of the company left. Mr. Grannis, the secretary, got a better offer from another company. The Actuary, Mr. Stewart's contract was up and although Knapp wanted to keep him, the board overruled him. The third may have hurt the most. Abraham Kaufmann, the head of the German department and the man who set up the Hildise Bund that at one time was extremely beneficial to the company (perhaps to the point of its survival in the early days) found himself in financial difficulty and asked for an advance. Knapp was in favor of it, but the board refused and directed Knapp to terminate Kaufmann. Knapp accepted the reverses by the board with good nature.

Finally in February of 1878, the state insurance commissioner, John McCall issued a report on Met's health. And after turning over ever piece of paper in their office, he concluded that their assets were $2,087,582.47 against liabilities of $1,795,822.26. The comments of the commissioner were as good as anything Knapp could have wrote himself: *"To the present management of the Company the Policy - Holders are indebted for the solvent condition of their corporation. Every step taken by the President and the Vice President, has been to render the security of the insured beyond question. Too much cannot be said in praise of the Company's investments."*

With this report the board voted to endorse a determined effort to halt the exodus of policyholders, but Knapp drew the line at paying the higher commissions other companies were, in the effort to get new business. He also was able to attract to the board a leading financier banker, Charles Curtiss. A number of his stockholders however were looking for exits. Mr. Knapp and his wife obliged them by tying up another $58,570 of his money to purchase their stock. Believe it or not, a good illustration of just how shaky things were, Hegeman himself sold 350 of his shares to Mrs. Knapp. A prime example of the faith Knapp put into this enterprise occurred in 1872 when needing $30,000 probably for his printing firm, he mortgaged his home to Metropolitan to get the money. Not many life insurance executives of that era would have done that.

On a much smaller potato field, but one that illustrates what a grip he held on the day to day goings on at the company, he personally approved a bill $125. It was for the purchase of a newly invented piece of office equipment _ a type-writer. Not only did he approve it, but he took a ten dollar discount by paying it promptly. He was a man who was always in favor of labor saving machinery as his printing plant was full of it. You can probably be assured though, that before he parted with the funds to buy the typewriter, he was fully aware of what it could do and not do for him. In 1877, typewriters were very rare. Almost as rare as women in business offices. A few months before purchasing the typewriter, Knapp had hired Carrie Foster as a clerk in the records department. Like many of his employees, she too attended St. John's Sabbath School of which he was the superintendent. She remained with Metropolitan for 52 years, but never touched a typewriter. Women stenographers did not start to appear until the 1890's and many of the first ones were at Metropolitan.

Before the typewriter turned up at Met's office, the only other piece of office machinery was a letterpress for duplicating correspondence. It was not until 1884, when the company bought more rare specimens of office equipment. This time they got a dozen arithometers. (multiplying & dividing machines) They worked by turning a crank and in time they could cause an occupational com-plaint known as "actuary's wrist"

In 1878, Met checked it's wholesale walkout of policy holders, but Knapp also pursued his policy of downsizing, which may of saved a few more policy holders from leaving had he not. That said, he began to intensify his study on the Pruden-tial Assurance Company of London methods of selling insurance. So Mr. Knapp and Mr. Hegeman commenced to pouring over the fine print of reports and state-ments of the London company, marking passages for each others attention. As for the current state of Met's problems, it was Knapp's idea to shrink them symmetri-cally, to maintain the company's solvency. He seemed to bear his exacting respon-sibilities easily. A reporter from the trade paper Insurance Age visited in 1878 and wrote: *"Mr. Knapp seldom lets anything interfere with a good dinner and bears the reputation as one of "the whitest men in New York" (?) All the same his manner impresses us with the idea that time is money and he has more of the last than the first and intends to keep it—he can decide quicker and safer, stick to it better, and fight for it longer, than any president we know."*

When he reached England, in July of 1879, he spent several weeks studying all phases of Prudential's operations. With him was his longtime friend and lawyer, Stuart Woodford. The officers of Prudential showed Knapp everything he wanted to see. The trip also began a lifelong friendship with Henry Harben, the builder of Prudential. In October of that year, Knapp returned to America and addressed his directors, who were eager to hear what he found. During his absence the wheels at Met had come to a standstill. But thanks to more personal advances from Mr. Knapp of $10,000, the spirits of the directors were ready for fresh adventures. The long depression had finally worn itself out and recovery was on the way. Knapp gave them a picture of enormous success' of Prudential and then laid out his plans to steer Metropolitan on that course. The board deliberated and in the end the ayes had it for Mr. Knapp's new direction.

In the simplest terms what Knapp proposed to do for insurance, was what Frank W. Woolworth did for small dry goods and general merchandise in 1879, when he priced every article he offered at 5 cents. Knapp proposed offering small policies. at small cost and collecting the minute premiums on the spot once a week. You could say he intended to nickel and dime the entire working populous on a weekly basis. To make this work, he would have to issue policies in the tens of thousands and do his own collecting at the policy holders door. The amount of detail and labor intensity in an operation like this is very apparent. Mr Knapp had returned with samples of all of the London company's forms, books, blanks etc. First Met's operating machinery would have to be redesigned from top to bottom. Noting that this would require a considerable outlay of money, the finance committee suggested an outlay of $100,000. That was nearly a third of the company surplus. The board also gave Mr. Knapp the privilege of contributing all or any portion of that amount from his pocket, in exchange for the company's note.

An entire new sales force in the field would have to be built from scratch. Advertisements such as these appeared in the newspapers:

AGENTS WANTED

No necessity for any man to be out of business. The Metropolitan Life Insurance Company of New York is now offering its protection to persons of moderate means in amounts running from $25 to $1000 at payments of five cents per week and upwards. Steady employment; previous experience not necessary. Intelligence and industry all that is essential

As time went on, more emphasis was laid on the experience not necessary feature. Within 60 days he had 124 new agents and 7 superintendents, all working in the NYC area. It was by no means an adequate force, but it was a start. Many of the men were trained on the ground in door to door lessons. Knapp's friend in London, President Harben had told him he devised the training plan by trail and error and that maintaining a field force would be his biggest problem. An annoying percentage of agents were highly unpredictable. The stabler ones became superintendents and assistant superintendents, charged with shaping up the recruits into a viable field force. Knapp thought the supers and their assistants were his key to making this work. *"No army without seasoned sergeants is much good regardless of who the generals are."* Mr. Hegeman, reminiscing of the early days, mentioned that the company was sadly in need of superintendents.

Because speed was essential in Knapp's plan of conquest of this new business, he intended to make Metropolitan the dominating force in the field before the competition knew what happened. He now had four rivals too. Prudential, John Hancock, Provident and Germania. To get his superintendents into shape, he sent his main man, Brice Collard, to England in 1880, to round up as many experienced men as he could induce to emigrate to the U. S. and to embark them and their families at company expense. Instructions sent to a transportation agent in Liverpool were very simple *"Please furnish Mr. Collard passage for as many passengers as he may require"* The first group of one superintendent, three assistants and 13 sailed in April of that year. They were met at the home office by Knapp and Hegeman, then trained for a day or so before setting out to work. More arrivals came promptly and by mid June, they had 22 new superintendents in Connecticut, Rhode Island, Massachusetts, Maine, New Jersey. Pennsylvania, Ohio, Maryland and New York. Things were beginning to move. By now letters from America were arriving to the new transplants friends and family back in England and the "Yankee" Brice Collard, who was an English immigrant himself, was finding his recruiting task in England a lot easier. In all he sent 544 men who were accompanied by 744 dependents across the Atlantic. It was one of the largest importations of skilled labor in American history.

Metropolitan's first policy in Industrial Insurance was written on Nov 17th of 1879. It's first claim was paid less than a month later on Dec 12th. It was for August Pfalzgraf, 2 years old, whose father was a Brooklyn butcher, The policy was in force for four days. The amount was $19.00 of which the company had received one weeks premium of 5 cents for. Mr. Knapp intended to make prompt payment of claims without quibbling.

CHAPTER
13

'80s Ladies...Gentleman Too

The Knapps loved to entertain guests at their mansion on Bedford Ave. By the latter half of the 19th century, it seems their home was almost destined to become the catering hall it would in the 20th. Judging by surviving newspaper accounts I have found, Phoebe seemed to always have something going on there and I can picture her husband Joseph, happy to accommodate her in every way possible and actually beyond her dreams because he could.

In the summer of 1881, Phoebe went to Europe for four months. Her trip was most likely connected with music. Upon her return, there was a little surprise waiting for her. Coming up Bedford Ave from the East River, it would not be visible, as she arrived at her front door, but I would wonder how long she was inside her home before she noticed something had changed radically. It was a "small addition" to the rear. Octagon in shape it measured 40 feet by 80 feet with a skylight stained glass roof. A reportedly famous Italian artist had painted a frieze of hymning, singing, dancing, piping fauns and nymphs around the room. And one side stood a George Jardine, three manual pipe organ, the largest in the NY City area, it cost $3,000 in real 1880s greenbacks. Also near the organ was a grand piano. If it truly was a complete surprise, I can imagine what the look on her face and her husband's was upon his unveiling it to her. There were many musical instruments through out the room, including of course Joseph Palmer's violin which at age 17, he may of still been playing, while attending his freshman year at Columbia University in New York City.

New Years Day, was by tradition a receiving day, by ladies of social prominence. Announcements were published in the papers telling those who would be at home receiving guests and when to call and even what to wear.

Brooklyn Union Argus, 30 December 1882

New Year's Day in the social aspect promises to be more generally observed than usual of late years, providing the weather is propitious. The caterers have had more orders for the arrangement of tables, and the florists have been busier with decoration for the reception parlor than they have been in some years past. Most every lady who opens her house to callers on the 1st of January will receive in full dress attire, and to many of the houses gas will be burned all day for the purpose of showing off the toilets to the best advantage and of giving the scene more striking effect. In the evening, at the houses where a number of young people receive, parties will be given. Gentlemen who pride themselves on etiquette will not begin calling until noon, and then they will not be foolish as to don their full dress suits, but wear either Prince Albert coats or neat cutaways. Pen-tailed coats are made for evening and their use out of place only furnishes amusement for the giddy girls of fashion.

The names of some of Brooklyn's prominent citizens and fair ladies who will receive callers on Monday are given below: Mrs. Joseph F. KNAPP, Miss Emma C. THURSBY, Mrs. J. L. PATTON, Miss STEWARD, Miss RITCH, Miss DRISCOLL and Miss KNAPP at 81 Bedford avenue.

Of the names mentioned to receive gentleman callers, that Monday Jan 1st 1883 at # 81 Bedford Ave, which was the same address as 554 Bedford and used both ways then, Miss Ritch was the daughter of one of Knapp's lawyers, Thomas G. Ritch and Miss Driscoll was a friend of "Netty" . The most notable name mentioned and very famous by that time was, Miss Emma C. Thursby, who Phoebe took credit for as "her discovery." Miss Thursby (1845-1931) was one of the great operatic singing voices of the 19th and early 20th century. While J. F. Knapp pursued a very quiet hobby of giving a leg up to promising young men of business and finance and putting them on the road to success, Phoebe was probably his equal in doing the same with musical talent, although Emma was only 6 years her junior. Exactly how much Phoebe had to do with Emma Thursby's undeniable talent and her rise to international musical fame, might be a subject to debate, but the fact is it certainly did not hurt. Phoebe and Emma remained life long friends. In late September of 1882, Emma returned to America, after a two year absence of doing concerts in Europe. Her fall American concert schedule was immediately packed with about 50 dates, all over the States (think of the traveling time!) in her first two months back, but the Knapps hosted a musicale and reception for her, at their place on November 2nd in which over 800 guests were invited and reportedly nearly everyone showed up, including the Rev. Henry Ward Beecher and Ulysess S. Grant. Of particular note to my eye, was a Mr. Ed Wallace who will become very significant in a few paragraphs and years gone by. By 11 O'clock that evening, which was a Thursday night, there were still 500 folks hanging around. This may of been the first REALLY BIG BASH, that the Knapps threw at the recently remodeled and enlarged mansion. If you'll pardon my pun hostess - organist Phoebe, pulled out all stops for this one and J. F. pulled out his checkbook and perhaps cashed a bond or two. And as the old cliche goes, "a splendid time was had by all" Here is how the Brooklyn Eagle reported it on November 3, 1882. I offer it as written, for the colorful and full description in the language of the day of a major social event, as reported by an eyewitness the morning after, with a minimum of my modern observations in parenthesis.

RECEPTION TO MISS THURSBY: *A Notable Musical and Brilliant Social Event–Mr. and Mrs. Joseph F. Knapp Throw Open their Magnificent Mansion to the Friends and Admirers of Brooklyn's Famous Songstress."*

The most notable musical event which has transpired in Brooklyn in many years took place last evening. The affair socially was also exceptionally brilliant, the participants including many persons of prominent society circles, in art, music, and literature. jurists of eminence, professional men of high degree, and a liberal representation of distinguished clergy. The scene of the affair was the elegant mansion of Mr. and Mrs. Joseph F. Knapp on Bedford avenue : the occasion, a reception extended by that public spirited citizen and his estimable wife on behalf of Miss Emma C. Thursby to the friends and admirers of Brooklyn's famous songstress. Miss Thursby is generally known as a native of this city; her musical career and her growing fame as a cantatrice have been followed with eager interest and noted with gratified pride and general appreciation. Her artistic triumphs abroad, achieved in her recent foreign concert tour in which she laid the art and musical centre of Europe under contribution, have strengthened her position in the affections and esteem of this public. It was to be expected therefore that the opportunity for doing the honor and according her hearty welcome to her native city would be eagerly availed of, as it was; and last night's gathering is to be accepted as a grateful tribute to the worth and ability of one who from small beginnings has attained to a commanding place among the foremost singers of the day. The reception proper extended from eight to eleven o'clock, at which latter hour about five hundred guests were still assembled.

The Magnificent Mansion

The splendors of the Knapp mansion have been made familiar heretofore, but it is safe to assert that never before had it presented so truly a superb a scene as on this occasion. The florist decorations surpassed description, and while the eye was delighted by the rich and costly surroundings. the ear was charmed by the strains of delicious music which floated above the hum of conversation from a full orchestra concealed from view (Hey I thought we were honoring the music here? where are the delegates of AFM Local 802 when you need them) *among the exotics of the conservatory. Miss Thursby assisted by Mrs. Knapp greeted the guests in the spacious parlors, receiving the numerous congratulations which were showered upon her with becoming grace and modesty. She was magnificently attired, her robe being of white satin, trimmed with point lace, and wearing for ornaments diamonds and white roses. From the parlors the guests passed on into the music room of the mansion, an apartment unequalled for the extent and completeness of its appointments in the country. and from thence to the supper room. The program of orchestral music, given under the direction of Mr. Lucien Conterne, was worthy the fullest praise, and led up finely to the musical reception which followed. The latter comprised of an organ solo by Mr. J. M. Loretz Jr, of the "William Tell Overture"* [Hi Yo Silver! The Lone Ranger Rides For The First Time In Williamsburg] *"Twilight" and the "Hussar's Song" by the Dudley Buck Quartet Club; a piano solo by Miss Hoaugh, a bright little lady of 13 and a pupil of Mille: an aria from "Carmen" by Miss Imogene Brown; a Nocturne of Chopin, solo for violin, by Richard Arnold; Cowen's "Better Land" splendidly sung by Miss Emily Wieant: Rubenstein's "Dream" by Mr. Then Toedt; "Robert of Lincoln" a reading by Miss Sattie Blume; an aria from "Poliuto" , by Mr. R. B. Roineyn; the "Rigolletto" quartet, by Mrs. Brown and Mrs. Rice-Knox and Messrs Romeyn and Morwaski. and an aria by the latter gentlemen. all which were rapturously applauded and encores demanded in every instance. Miss Thursby greatly to the regret of this audience, did not sing. pleading fatigue of the reception and her engagement the next evening with the Philharmonic Society*

Emma had just come off a string of 15 dates in October stretching from Boston, Chicago, Washington, Philadelphia, Detroit, Cleveland, Buffalo, Albany, Orange, NJ, New York City and Brooklyn with no real logic to the travel routing and had just sang last on Oct 31. She had to perform with the Brooklyn Philharmonic on Nov 3 & 4 and her concert schedule for the rest of the month was for another 13 concerts all over the east coast (source: The Life of Emma Thursby by Richard Gipson). *"Among the guests who paid their respects last evening to Miss Thursby and enjoyed the hospitality of Mr. and Mrs. Knapp were the following, Hon Seth Low and lady. (The Mayor) Hon Judge and Mrs. George G Reynolds, Colonel J. H. Mapleson, Mr. and Mrs John R. Hegeman, Rev. Bishop. Dr. William R Hurd, Mr. and Mrs. John H. Havemeyer (the Domino Sugar King) Mr. and Mrs. Edward Pierpont, Dr. and Mrs. DeWitt Talmadge..."* and the list goes on and on.

Two years later however the Knapp Place would not be open to any callers for New Years or for sometime before and after. There was quite a hub bub of construction going on next door to it. A new house was going up and would soon be actually connected to the mansion. One minor news account, reported a construction shed there being broken into and tools stolen. In spite of all the pre eminent preachers, politicians, authors and musicians etc that came to call at the Knapps, it was probably this event held in middle February of 1885 that was the biggest and most important for Phoebe and Joseph. That would be the marriage of their daughter Antoinette to Edward Copeland Wallace. It too made the newspapers and is re reported here to demonstrate just how important the media felt it was.

The Account Of The Knapp Wallace Wedding February 15th, 1885
The Marriage will take place on Tuesday evening, in St. John's Methodist Episcopal Church, Bedford Avenue and Wilson street, of Miss Antoinette Knapp, daughter of

Joseph F. Knapp, to Mr.Edward Copeland Wallace. A reception will be held after the ceremony at the residence of the bride's parents, No. 84 Bedford Avenue. At the Altar. Mr. Edward Copeland Wallace and Miss Antoinette Knapp.

A Brilliant Wedding in the Eastern District-Rich Decorations, Costly Gifts and Distinguished Guests-Fashionable Society in Bedford Avenue.

The marriage of Miss Antoinette Knapp, daughter of Mr. Joseph F. Knapp, of No. 84 Bedford avenue, to Mr. Edward Copeland Wallace, of the firm of William H. Wallace & Co. of New York, last evening was a prominent social event. Fashionable society, in the Eastern District especially, had long been preparing for the wedding, and, as a result, those who were favored with invitations appeared in the richest and most costly toilets, with sparkling diamonds for ornaments. The nuptials took place in St. John's M. E. Church, on Bedford Avenue, only a short distance from Mr. Knapp's residence, and the edifice was crowded by brilliant audience in full evening dress. If the scene inside was one of bewildering beauty from pew to pulpit, in front of which the bridal party was arranged, that outside presented many aspects of confusion, for the large gathering of stylishly dressed people crowded each other around the canopy at the opening near the sidewalk to observe the bride and bridegroom and the many guests as they alighted from their carriages and, after the ceremony, re-entered them.

At 8 o'clock the handsome and spacious edifice was crowded with the guests, while ladies and gentlemen who did not attend the reception filled the galleries. The floral decorations were elegant and profuse. When the bridal party entered Professor Arnold struck up a wedding march from, "Lohengrin," and continued playing during the ceremony. the eight ushers, in full evening dress-A. S. Wallace, J. P. Knapp, A. H. Higgins, Frederick Vernon, Harry Cohn*, John A. Taylor, of Philadelphia; Herman December. Selding and Howard Walden-marched up the center aisle,two abreast, arms linked, followed by the bridesmaids-Misses Laura Wallace, Frances Wallace, Kepner, Adams, Craig and Foster-arm in arm, and then came the bride and bridegroom. In front of the railing surrounding the platform the ushers and bridesmaids separated leaving space in the center for the bride and bridegroom elect. Of the ushers young Mr. Knapp, brother of the bride, and Mr. Wallace, brother of the bridegroom acted as best men. The bride elect was attired in cream colored satin, cut in princess style, with an exceedingly long plain train, heavily corded at the edge. The Bishop William L. Harris and the Rev. Watson L. Phillips were at the pulpit to receive the bridal party, and without any unnecessary delay the Bishop performed the marriage ceremony, assisted by Mr. Phillips. After the nuptials the bridal party marched to the vestibule, and thence on rich carpet under a canopy to their carriages. They were driven to Mr. Knapp's residence, where a reception was held. It was half an hour or more before the last of the guests had departed from the church. A canopy covered the carpeted sidewalk in front of Mr. Knapp's large and handsome residence, and the eager gathering who crowded around the church surrounded it. The scene in the interior of the building was beautiful. The broad hall in the center of the house divides the parlors and reception and dinning rooms, and back of them are the spacious music hall, the library and the conservatory. The massive chandeliers in the parlors, music hall, and library were filled with ignited candles, which shed a light as bright as a *noonday sun, while the other rooms were illuminated by gas confined in rich glass globes set in massive glass chandeliers. The floral decorations which like that of the church was by Mr. A. Jahn, lent charm to the scene. In the conservatory off of the parlors, were arranged azaleas and large banks of tulips; the library was decorated with choice roses in vases and cluster; loose hybrid roses and a large bank of many colored hyacinths were placed in the reception room; the dining room was embellished with smilax, tulips and new sparrow grass, which at this season excels the smilax. A piece in one corner of the music hall, comprising Roman hyacinths, carnations, mignonettes and tulips in a basket five feet high and three feet in diameter, was much admired. The chandeliers were decorated with sparrow grass, and three vases were filled with lilac. As the 250 or more guests walked around through the fairy like scene the strains of Professor Lauder's full orchestra-the same one that furnished the music at the Astor wedding in New York not many months since, and at the Schultz-Lawson nuptials-filled the mansion. The bride and bridegroom received congratulations of their friends, standing beneath a Moorish lantern of silver filigree in an alcove in the library, near the conservatory, while behind them was a pyramid of roses and rare exotics eight feet high. The numerous and costly presents were displayed in the billiard room. The company was quite a distinguished one and comprised representatives of almost every profession and business calling.*

Some of the presents included the following: House and lot, No. 80 Bedford Avenue, from Mr. and Mrs. Joseph F. Knapp; Steinway piano, from Mr. C. Wallace; bronze center equestrian place and side figures, from Mr. Richard Major; Parisian vase, ebony pedestal, from Mr.and Mrs. John R. Hegeman; silver full set, from Mr. and Mrs. W. H. Wallace; bronze vase, from Mr. and Mrs. W. F. Hamilton; silver berry set, from Mr. and Mrs. Stewart L. Woodford; large Mexican onyx table, from Mr. John L. Foster; pedestal and vase, from Mr. and Mrs. L. M. Palmer; pair Sevres vases, from Mrs. Kepner; mantel mirror, from Mr. Joseph P. Knapp.

Note: The entire guest list along with a complete list of gifts (that would make the PBS program Antiques Roadshow implode) is online at the Knapps Lived Here website.

Among the names on the guest list are Sophia Kepner and her daughter Sylvia who was a brides maid. By this time Sylvia had been dating young Joseph Palmer for over a year. Joseph, was a guest at Sylvia's sister Clara's wedding to William Orr Barclay in Nov of 1883. In the near future, Sylvia would change her last name too, becoming Mrs. Joseph Palmer Knapp in 1886.

Antoinette's husband Edward, was a guy on his way up in the William H. Wallace Co. of New York. Though it sounds like a brokerage firm, W. H. Wallace Co. actually supplied steel for the early sky scrapers. They had done very well at this business. Steel was almost a precious metal and speaking of precious metals judging by the gift list, silver smiths and their merchants for miles around must of been very happy with the Knapp - Wallace nuptials. Though I have not discovered anything personal about the mother daughter relationship of Phoebe and Antoinette, it seems by all accounts of reported social events they attended, that they were very close. Both enjoyed the whirl of social activity and were almost always in each others company. As for Daddy's little girl, what could be nicer than giving her a house right next door and actually attaching it with a 5 story conservatory to hold the ever growing Knapp art collection? Pause to gaze at a European master or two, as you went from kitchen to kitchen to borrow a cup of sugar. Though the insurance business may of still been shaky, printers ink had long turned to gold for Mr. Knapp

As grand an event as it had to be for the Knapps, it was foreshadowed by a tragedy just a week before, when the Major & Knapp printing firm on Park Place in New York had gone up in flames for the second time in four years. In 1881 there was a blaze that did about $30,000 worth of damage. Both times the fires started in another business, that shared the building. The Knapp plant occupied the third - fifth floors and their people were working beyond the normal 6 PM quitting time when it caught fire on Feb 5, 1885. This time, one fireman died and Henry Welch an 18 year old worker there was severely burned. I do not know what his future held. The damage was estimated to be about a quarter of million dollars. In 1881 Knapp had 30 insurance companies covering his printing business. He probably had more or larger policies in 1885 as he certainly had a lot more employes and equipment by then. 30 some odd steam presses alone and tons of paper stock. Major & Knapp's loss was around $175,000 of the quarter million total estimate. In any event, the wedding,costly as it was, at least provided some distraction for him.

By this time his son Joseph P. was working there full time and perhaps by 1885 fairly high up in the company. But he truly started on the ground floor, no matter that the ground floor at Major & Knapp was three flights up from the Park Place cobblestones. Actually, young Joe had dropped out of Columbia University ,whose campus was just down the block from the printing plant, in 1881 after what he described as "one riotous year." To say that his parents were not pleased at all about this, may be the major understatement of this whole book. J. P.'s father put him to work in probably the lowest and dirtiest position he could find for him, that as a flyboy on the press. The flyboy's job was to literally catch the pages as they flew off the press. Not exactly a glamour job, nor one equated with a suitable position for the typical "bosses son". But in the case of either Joseph Knapp, neither boss nor the son was in anyway typical. For this J. F. paid his son $5.00 per week and his mother promptly took over half of that away from him ($3) to put into St. John's coffers. Of course all of J. P.' s worldly needs at home were more than well provided for, far beyond what most average men his age who were making their way in the world were. However when he wanted to have some folding money, to say date the likes of say Miss Sylvia Kepner, $2 a week was not going to cut it even in 1881. It didn't take J.P. long to figure out how to remedy that little problem. The final outcome of his solution to his having some "folding money" perhaps had as big, if not bigger effect on his father's early demise as all of the headaches of running the Metropolitan Life Insurance Co. ever did.

CHAPTER

14

The Flyboy Takes Flight

In several of the personal reminisces given in the 1930s, by then old "Joe" Knapp and some of his associates, most seem to recall his encounter and early eventual business dealings with James B. Duke of the American Tobacco Co. as one of the major milestones that helped set him out on the path to his own fortunes, independent of those of his father. Knapp recalls and must of relayed this to his friends too, that when he was working at the drudgery of being a flyboy, observing the printing salesmen, made a strong impression on him. They seemed to be the best dressed and highest rollers in the entire company. Two things of natural importance to a 17 year old man on the town. So the son took it upon himself to engage in selling printing for the company on his lunch hour and after hours. It was on one of those early sales calls where he happen to knock on the door of Mr. "Buck" Duke.

Based on his surroundings, James Buchanan "Buck" Duke (1856 - 1925) father of future heiress Doris Duke, might not of appeared to be a true tycoon when young J. P. Knapp came calling to sell him printing services in the early 1880s, but fact is he already was. He and his brother Benjamin had taken over the family tobacco company based in North Carolina in 1880. With Buck's acquisition of the patent on the automatic cigarette rolling machine and the control of its license, it helped seal the deal, as all his competitors would need the machine to stay in business.

* Doris Duke who was a minor child when James died, became known publicly as "The Richest Girl In The World" She would live a life in the media spotlight from that day on.

ONE WOULD NEVER KNOW HOW WELL OFF DUKE WAS THOUGH FROM his bunker like NY office. It was located in the basement of an east side tenement building. Buck was impressed that a young man was taking the initiative of working through his lunch hour and gave him his printing business. It was there J. P. convinced Duke, that by inserting small photo cards into the packs of his cigarettes, he could sell even more of them than he already was. This was the birth of the collector trading card, made popular with subjects like Civil War generals, opera singers, actors and notorious figures and then probably immortal with the inclusion of baseball players.

The Duke printing account alone put a mighty wind into J. P.'s sails. Before long his sales commissions were adding up to a very formidable sum. His father, not wanting him to have that much cash to perhaps spend foolishly, instead offered him stock options in the Knapp litho firm. Young J. P. wisely took his father's offer. At about the same time, J. F.'s longtime partner Major retired and the Major & Knapp company soon became just The Knapp Co. Essentially a father and son business and a very formidable one. That evidence exists by the sheer amount of printed trade card products from that era by Major & Knapp and The Knapp Co. that have survived and show up daily on E Bay.

I would surmise that J. P. absorbed and took business counsel from not only his father, but from most every successful and intelligent person he encountered. Back when J. P. was briefly in college, he would befriend several classmates who would play significant roles in his future business decisions. One classmate, Samuel Untermeyer, would go on to be a world famous lawyer and prosecutor in several future Government anti trust cases. Untermeyer who was brilliant and a friend to people like Albert Einstein, may of unwittingly wielded a dramatic double edge sword in Knapp's personal and business life that was to occur within a very short time after the firm became The Knapp Co.

From the time J.P. was old enough to realize such things, his father was very successful and I'm sure this only emboldened young Joe's confidence in all he would do on his own. In studying J. P.'s business life, there seems to be a consistent thread of his ability to recognize a good idea, no matter who had it, and to act upon it straight away. Probably 90% of the time these decisions worked in his favor. There was also a beneficial fallout of his actions too, which often helped others on their way up. One such person who remembers it well was Edward Bok, who became the editor of Ladies Home Journal in 1889 and wrote of Knapp in his 1920 memoir *The Americanization of Edward Bok*.

Just about a year older than Joe Knapp, Edward Bok came from a vastly different background, arriving in America in 1870 from the Netherlands and speaking only Dutch. He went to school for a few years, but was forced to leave at 13 to help support his family. Bok furthered his quest for self education by writing to and collecting autographs of famous historical people. Within several years he had amassed quite a collection (it was written about in the newspapers of the day) and he actually met many of these people like Mark Twain, Generals Grant and Sherman, Mrs. Abraham Lincoln and Jefferson Davis in New York City, at places they frequented like the grandiose Fifth Avenue Hotel opposite Madison Square.

It was while sitting in a restaurant one day and trying to think of a way to use his collection to help his family financially, that he spotted a man open a pack of cigarettes and throw something from the pack on the floor. Bok speaks of himself in the third person throughout his book: *"Edward picked it up thinking it might be a prospect for his collection of autograph letters. It was a picture of a well known actress. He then recalled an advertisement announcing that this particular brand of cigarettes contained, in each package, a lithographed portrait of some famous actor or actress, and if the purchaser would collect these he would in the end have a valuable album of the greatest actors and actresses of the day. Edward turned the picture over, only to find a blank reverse side. "All very well," he thought , "but what does a purchaser have, after all in the end, but a lot of pictures? Why don't they use the back of each picture and tell what each did: a little biography? Then it would be worth keeping." With his passion for self education, the idea appealed very strongly to him and believing firmly that there were others possessed of the same thirst, he set out the next day, in his luncheon hour to find out who made the picture.*

At the office of the cigarette company he learned that the picture was made by the Knapp Lithographic Company. The following luncheon hour he sought the offices of the company and explained his idea to Mr. Joseph P. Knapp. "I'll give you ten dollars a piece if you will write me a 100 word biography of one hundred famous Americans" was Mr. Knapp's instant reply. "send me a list, and group them as for instance , presidents, vice presidents, famous soldiers, actors, authors etc." And thus," as Mr. Knapp tells the tale today (1920) " I gave Edward Bok his first literary commission, and started hi off on his literary career." The Americanization of Edward Bok *by Edward Bok, Charles Scribner 1920.*

However Edward soon found the Knapp company calling for more copy. Writing as fast as he could, he still could not keep up with the demand. As soon as he finished the first hundred, Knapp asked for a second hundred and then a third. Edward offered his brother 5 dollars a piece to help him and even both of them could not keep up with the demand. Bok found himself employing several other journalists, he could trust and found himself editing the bios which he found to be more profitable than trying to write them himself.

It has been said by several sources that J. F. Knapp had to divert more and more time to the affairs of Metropolitan Life in the mid 1880s, especially with the launching of Met's new direction in industrial insurance and that more of the day to day business decisions at the the litho firm fell to his son J. P. That may or may not be completely true. True J. F. did have over $650,000 of his personal money invested into Met Life and he once waxed philosophically in the mid 80's that he felt that most of that money "has gone up in smoke". (I guess there was plenty more to burn) There was also a major two year trial going on over a policy holders dispute. Therefore he may of been somewhat pre occupied with matters at the insurance company. However J. F. Knapp's attention to very small details, had carried him to great successes all through his life and I can't see him suddenly changing tactics in his 50s. It was also said by his close associates like Fred Ecker, years after J. F. was deceased, that the father was "A REAL DRIVER" in regards to how he instilled his work ethic on his son and accordingly J.P. who was raised in much easier circumstances, did not like being driven.* And then again J. F. may of relaxed his concerns about business affairs at the litho firm to a small degree, because after all it was his own son watching after things there. There just is no way to know for certain.

Fred Ecker to author Marquis James A METROPOLITAN LIFE

I N NOVEMBER OF 1886, 22 YEAR OLD JOSEPH PALMER KNAPP MARRIED 23 year old Sylvia Theresa Kepner of Manhattan, a woman he had been dating for several years. Unlike sister Antoinette's huge wedding, which was one of the society events of 1885, this one was a much lower key affair. The NY times only listed a brief announcement. The Brooklyn Eagle gave it the following paragraph:

Hymnal Knapp-Kepner *Miss Sylvia Theresa Kepner was married last evening to Mr. Joseph Palmer Knapp of this city, at 15 West Fifty Eighth street, New York the home of the bride's mother, Mrs Sophia Kepner. The officiating clergyman was Rev. Dr. Krotel, of the Holy Trinity Lutheran Church. About forty relatives and intimate friends were present. The bride wore a dress of heavy white satin trimmed with point lace and pearl passementerie. She also wore a tule vail and carried a bouquet of orchids and lillies of the valley. The bridesmaids were Miss Beyer and Miss Yuengling. They wore dresses of white silk trimmed with lace and carried large bouquets of pink roses. The ushers were George H. Barnes and Reginald Barclay, of this city and A. V. Williams Jackson and William Yuengling of New York. The couple stood under a floral bell while the ceremony was performed.—Brooklyn Eagle Nov 10th 1886*

As for someone who has been trying to study the life of all three generations of Joseph Knapps, by relying mainly on what was written as public record, I would say this snippet sets the precedent for most personal articles about Joseph Palmer Knapp's entire life. And that precedent keyword is LOW KEY. However it is what it doesn't say, that gives me pause to speculate a bit on what might of been going on in his life at the time.

First off the wedding is held at home in NY City, instead of the Brooklyn M.E. church that J. P. was brought up in and his father and mother were major benefactors and officers of. The ceremony is performed by a Lutheran minister which is understandable as the Kepners were German. With the guest list missing, we can't know who is actually there, but I would think J.P.'s parents and sister were. Sylvia T. Kepner's mother Sophia Betz Kepner, was a longtime divorce.' It doesn't state who the best man was, but as far as the ushers go, George Barnes was a lawyer and golfing pal of J. P. Knapp, who went in with him in 1898 on building the original country club and golf course in Bellport, LI. Reginald Barclay, was the brother in law of the brides sister Clara. The Barclays had the very successful Barclay Soap & Perfume Co. Clara who became a widow in 1900 would wind up successfully suing Reggie in 1915 for defrauding her out of millions. But I'm reasonably sure on Nov 9th of 1886, all was well between them. The Yuenglings who established David G. Yuengling & Sons, America's oldest brewery in 1829, were connected by marriage with the Betz family, with breweries in New York, New Jersey and Philadelphia. So we know they had the wedding refreshments well covered.

Also unlike Antoinette's, no wedding gifts were announced publicly, but it's possible that J.P.'s father thought the added responsibilities of the litho firm management. might be just what a newly wedded executive needed. But to verify this is beyond my scope of research and is no more than pure reasoned speculation on my part, based on memoirs like Bok's that place J. P. Knapp as "The Decider" at the Knapp Co. in the mid 1880s.

The newlyweds took up residence in NY City rather than Knapp's boyhood home city of Williamsburg. The earliest place I can verify ,that J.P. & Sylvia lived at was, 322 West 72nd Street, just off the Hudson River and Riverside Drive. It is 10 miles away from the Knapp mansion in Brooklyn. It is estimated to take an hour to drive the distance in traffic today. In the 1880s with far less traffic, it probably took several hours in a horse drawn carriage. Part of the original brownstones are still there and though far from roughing it or what one would call the country, 322 West 72nd, may of set the table for J.P's lifelong desire to spend as much time as possible far from the madding crowds. Just down the block from the Knapps at Number One, W. 72nd & Central Park West, was the new two year old Dakota Hotel, so named because "it was as far from the center of New York City as the Dakota Territory was from the settled parts of the country"

CHAPTER

15

Politics

"To make things plain at the start put down this fact—I am not a candidate for mayor and I would not allow myself to be nominated under any circumstances"
—JOSEPH F. KNAPP, APRIL 25, 1885

As a man who hosted almost every US President at his home between 1860's - 1880's and probably presidential candidate Abraham Lincoln as well, Joseph F. Knapp was certainly, if not a politician, a man of politics.

How refreshing to read a media statement from someone who was being considered for political office that is brief and rings true from start to finish. Whatever happened to folks like that? The following interview with Joseph Fairchild Knapp, appeared in the Brooklyn Eagle Monday, April 27th, 1885. Although the focus of it is primarily political, because of it's length, several personal glimpses of his thoughts are also revealed as well, plus more observations by the unnamed reporter on Knapp's home that he took great pride in. I offer it here as printed, totally unedited and find that the language of the day makes for quite an interesting read.

POLITICAL - AN INTERVIEW WITH MR. JOSEPH F. KNAPP

Local and State Republican Conditions Discussed by a Representative Republican Citizen - He Will Under no Circumstances, be a Candidate for Any Office.

A reporter of the EAGLE on Saturday night had a conversation with Mr. Joseph F. Knapp, relative to the Mayoralty and to general politics, from a Republican point of view at his spacious residence No 84 Bedford Ave at its junction with Ross Street. Prior and subsequent to the conversation, Mr. Knapp showed the reporter through his picture gallery, which occupies the ground floor of the art annex to the mansion. There are gathered in this large and magnificently decorated gallery the gems of American, English, German and Italian painters of this generation of the first degree of excellence and reputation. Several superb examples of sculpture are also grouped within the enclosure and the apartment has by wealth and taste been made one of the most notable private possessions in either city. Willing often to throw open the resources and accord the hospitality of his mansion to occasions of religion, patriotism and charity, Mr. Knapp has never sought to make a public parade of his rare stores of art treasures, but has been content to share the enjoyment of them with hosts of attached personal friends, and with such distinguished divines and authors from abroad as come to him with letters of credence from his intimate associates sojourning in foreign lands. Amid the pleasures and splendors of a refined home and enjoying the comradeship of a devoted family, of which every member is endowed with some special artistic gifts. Mr. Knapp can easily be believed when he punctuates his remarks on current politics with absolute renunciation of any partisan ambition of his own and with the positive statement that on no account would he accept the nomination to any position. The conversation which occurred is appended, the parts sustained by the reporter and by Mr. Knapp being easily distinguishable.

"I wish to ask you, " said the former. "concerning the Mayoralty and State and national politics, from your view point as a Republican.

"I am glad to see you on that subject." was the rejoinder. "especially as the Eagle has lately named me, along with my neighbors, Eiltor Peters, and ex Alderman Baird as possible Nineteenth Ward Republican candidates for the Mayoralty. To make things plain at the start, put down this fact. I am not a candidate for Mayor. I will not receive the nomination. I would not allow myself to be nominated under any circumstances. I would not accept the nomination if offered or qualify for this office if elected. There is no likelihood of either event occurring, but I wish to use exactly the words which will explicitly take me out the number of those who are discussed for the office."

"What are your reasons for such a premptory declaration?"

"Partly business reasons and partly personal ones. I hold an insurance trust, which with my other business of printing, takes up all the time and thought I wish to spare from the rational enjoyments and home employments of life. To serve the public aright my relations to my business would have to be intermitted, and that I am neither required nor disposed to do. There is no emergency in public affairs making a premptory call on any citizen, and probably if there was, the call would better be made on some other man. Nor do I covet a career of public functions, being entirely content to keep on in my quiet way on the sunny side of *the private station."*

"There are not then, so many candidates for Mayor among the Nineteenth Ward Republicans as the Eagle hinted at?"

"There may be more," replied the gentleman dryly. "but one who was hinted at counts himself out. Of the other two named, Mr. Peters and Mr. Baird, I have a very favorable opinion, but I think Mr. Peters will not find it compatible with his duties as an editor and a publisher to aspire to the nomination. He puts in a great deal of time at his business. That business in its largest respects, involves frequent participation in the councils of his party and to the occasions of his fellow citizens not political. From this he gathers the impressions which tone and color his utterances as a public instructor. He thus catches the aroma and incitement of public life, while escaping its responsibilities. Instead of being a Republican leader, he becomes so to speak the leader of Republican leaders in a large section of our city. He can be the Mentor of all, without being the target of any. Besides this is an important consideration: Were Mr. Peters nominated, the Times would be silenced from advocating him and that would be a loss indeed in the canvas. The paper could not advocate it's owner and editor. The Eagle would while treating him with courtesy. oppose him and support his opponent, if the latter was an acceptable man. I hardly think it would be feasible to expect the Union earnestly to support the editor of a rival contemporary, for the remarks of the two journals toward one another have bordered on asperity and gone to the verge of civility. Both by the preoccupations of his calling and by the accidents of his position. Mr. Peters is I fear dis-enabled from seriously contemplating himself as a candidate, though I must say that his treatment by the Eagle at this early stage of convention canvas has been as chivalrous as it has been suggestive.

"Now as to my neighbor Baird. He is an astute politician and has a fair public record. If he is a candidate, I should favor a delegation from this ward for him, though I guess one would form for him spontaneously without effort. He has however preferred power to place heretofore, and by showing his opponents in the party that they could not down him, while he could down them, he has made them come to him as allies. I think," said Mr Knapp musingly, "that Mr. Baird may labor to give delegations to other people rather than get one for himself."

"For what other people?"

"Well, for General Tracy for Governor, if the latter is a candidate, but I think that Messrs. Dutcher, Baird, Beard, Jourdan, Dady and others could give him the delegation from most , if not all of this county, if he were a candidate. If the General should run for the nomination and Mr. Baird should aid him, the Nineteenth Ward would turn out to be for him in my judgement."

"Let us not go to the Governorship before we reach it," suggested the reporter, looking at his notebook. "What about the Mayoralty?"

"Oh, I see I have been wandering." good naturedlly rejoined Mr. Knapp. "As to the Mayoralty, I want to say this; In my judgement there is no danger of a reversal of the home rule principle. Public opinion will force whoever is elected to stand by it. It is in no danger. It is now a common law, a household sentiment, a city habit in Brooklyn. The men who would like to reverse it are as numerous in one party as in the other and potential in neither. There may be a different standard of honor *among politicians from what there is among private citizens; but self interest is the same and the independent spirit in both parties can at any time combine to beat either party when it menaces the principle of accountable,responsible,and indictable home government.*

The politicians know this. They have to consent to such a curtailment of their ambition or powers as obedience to this principle involves. At heart, I think they like it. It reduces their importance a little. It increases their comfort a great deal. It frees them from obligations to a vast number of unworthy men who make unquestionable service and mythical influence the basis of claims which they urge with a begging power, which would shame a tramp or a Neapolitan mendicaut."

"The city is now in it's fourth year of experience of this system. The administration of Mayor Low reflects credit on the skill and industry with which he has carried out this system. The success of the system in its application to affairs reflects credit and in history will reflect honor, on Frederic A. Schroeder, by whose efforts the system was enacted into a law in the Legislature. He labored and other men entered into his labors. Mayor Low has administered well on ex Senator Schroeder's political estate. That is the exact truth. I know that in its inception the full application of the home rule principle had to be made prospective. That was owing to the political complications in the Legislature at the time. and they were a reflex of divided or imperfectly developed local opinion. But statesman have to concede a little to insure more, and to defer to present susceptibilities in order to attain ultimate ends. Mr. Schroeder did that and had to do it. but when Mr Low came in, he found the matured powers of the perfected charter ready to his hand. I think he himself would acknowledge this fact. I know he ought to acknowledge it, for it is a fact. Mr. Low's administration has been a success of honesty to the public, of conservative common sense in action, and of an attractive participation by himself in the social and civic occasions of the city. Brooklyn has several older men who could of done as well. It has few younger men who could of done so well. It has not many of either age, who could of done much better. But in all he has done or omitted, Mr. Low has had this to favor him: the fact that the way and the powers were all prepared for him, which only required him to maintain their existing situation, and the other fact that whenever he did well, his youth-fullness made his action wear the idea that it was the action not merely of a reformer, who is a frequent character. but of a prodigy, who is a rare character. Add to this the other fact that on every social or civic occasion, Mr. Low has spoken always acceptably and sometimes originally and brilliantly, and you account for the result that his administration has been one which has scored a fair business success along with a genuine sentimental approbation in its favor among the people."

"I want to add this desultory view," continued Mr. Knapp, "these general remarks : the security of the Brooklyn principle of home rule prescribes a type of character for candidates which each party will have to observe, If either party violates or slights this obligation, it will in my judgement, be beaten and it ought to be beaten. With reform conceded, however to be in no danger, the tendency of citizens will be to give a non political character to the local ballots and to vote for the best man , no matter if some of them are to be found on both tickets. Split voting is well understood in

Brooklyn. Should the Republicans nominate a man of commanding capacity and character, and the Democrats one of mediocre capacity and indifferent character — or should be the converse be true — the better man regardless of his Republicanism or Democracy would get more votes. Brooklyn has now a settled preference for edu- cated gentlemen as well as friends of reform, in her chief office and will elect such if they are opposed by boors and dunderheads in the canvass. In local affairs the party poll cannot be depended on as a partisan solid, even if the reform principle be con- ceded to be in no danger. If the contest were limited solely to party lines, by the fact that each candidate was equally capable or equally uncapeable—a contingency not likely to occur—the Democrats would win, for there are more Democrats than Re- publicans in Brooklyn. It would be gratifying to me to see each party at it's best, with it's best men not only at the fore, but in every part of the tickets. I do not forget that might insure Democratic success and I would not care. This city has had good and bad administrations of both parties, and if a result which should insure the reform system, under local Democratic administration should occur, I would be willing to give that party the credit for paying the homage of imitation to its Republican pre- decessor."

"What of the candidates?" Mr. Knapp

"Why, as to them, I have hardly thought, the EAGLE deploys them as well and brings out so many of them that I am willing to let it do my thinking about them, except to take myself off of the list. I am more interested in watching the effect of the reform system on parties than on individuals. I do not suppose Mayor Low will run for a third term. I do not know now, whether he is a candidate for Gover- nor. Whether he is or not, he will hardly get the nomination for State Republican- ism is vivid with the resentments of last year and no man who was not overtly for the Republican candidate for President will likely get the Republican nomination for Governor. Maybe this should not be so, but it is so. Human nature is made up that way and on a scale as large as State politicians have to do with awarding of honors. If Mr. Low was nominated he would make a phenomenal run in Kings, but in the rural counties where Republicanism at large is more realized than a local reform record, he might be badly cut. But before the election is the nomination and politicians have not friendly feelings toward Mr. Low. To become Governor, he would better have contented himself with one term as Mayor. His first term was not perhaps better than his second has been, but it had more novelty and remark- ableness about it, and I must say was, I think freer from some political tendencies which have made him a little more trimming than consistent of late. A suspicion of ambitious hopes, mixing with current actions a little, detracts from his reputa- tion as a reformer, and in the character of a politician. I do not understand that he seeks to be considered at all.

"Had he retired at the end of his first term, he would have retired as a disinter- ested and extraordinary successful prodigy. His party having gone through with its complications and disasters, could then have summoned him from his retire- ment and rallied around him by common consent. As it was. he was himself com- plicated by his being Mayor in time of great partisan contention and he had to bear himself in a way to inspire no faction of his party with a sense of obligation to him. Yet it is just such a positive record, in State politics which counts, while a

sedulous endeavor not to make a record does not often avail, amid the quickened memories following a national contest.

"Now excuse me from saying any more. I do not care to discuss individuals. I am not apt at it. A Republican always, I believe my party is likely to continue to present men whom I can accept, even though I might wish it had presented others. Republicanism has never been so good, as I wish it had been or so bad that I could not reconcile myself to its action. And I take it that is the view of Democrats by conviction concerning their own party too. I would use either party in local affairs to insure the reform system of home rule, but I think that each of the parties in Brooklyn, by education, conviction, interest and experience will pay equal court to that system, and that our local contests will either be determined on party lines or by the patent superiority of one candidate to another in character and in capacity."

This ended an interview which our readers of both parties will, the EAGLE thinks, find of much interest in at this time.

And to which I say *Whew!* Joseph Fairchild Knapp, had quite a vocabulary and a brilliant mind. The praises sung by his boyhood teacher, Lyman Thompson, were not at all overstated

CHAPTER
16

Father & Son Going My Way?
Not Exactly.

From what remains of society columns and public records in the latter 1880s, I was able to learn some things about the personal relations of the Knapp father and son, at the time where both their lives took major turns. Phoebe of course was always a-whirl with her musical, philanthropical and social life and Antoinette Wallace, her daughter and next door neighbor, seemed to always remain at her side. Their homes, like their lives were literally attached. Her new daughter in law Sylvia also seems to be included in many of the Knapp social affairs for the first few years.

From the Brooklyn Eagle Feb 15, 1887:

Mrs. Joseph F. Knapp receives with mesdames Joseph Palmer Knapp and E. C. Wallace

Mrs. Joseph F. Knapp, Mrs. Joseph Palmer Knapp and Mrs. Edward C. Wallace held a reception yesterday afternoon from 4 to 7 O'clock, at the residence of Mrs. Joseph F. Knapp, 554 Bedford Avenue. The dwelling is connected at the first story with that of Mrs. Wallace by a walled and handsomely finished promenade and both residences were thrown open. Mrs. Knapp is known as a charming and accomplished entertainer, who possesses the tact of making her guests feel quite at home without the least show of restraint common at most receptions, while she

*gathers around her the most refined people. She received in the spacious and el-
egantly appointed music hall and was attired in ruby velvet and black thread lace
over yellow satin. She was assisted by her daughter in law, Mrs. Joseph Palmer
Knapp dressed in white satin, with front of imported pearl embroidery, and Mrs.
Wallace who wore white satin and point lace. Miss Wallace and Miss Foster assisted the three ladies in entertaining and dispensing the hospitalities of the house
to the guests. Mrs. Bentley of Albany who has a high sweet soprano voice, rendered
a few solos, as did Mrs. Wilkinson and Mr. Wilbur F. Gunn. Instrumental selec-
tions were performed on the organ, piano and violin. A choice collation was served
by Pinard and Lander furnished the music. Mrs. Knapp will hold another reception next Monday.* The article concluded by listing a long partial guest list.

Sylvia also hosted her own socials and musicales of a similar bent, but
seemed to favor athletic social pursuits like horse shows, perhaps because of
her older sister Clara's strong equestrian interests. She soon followed that with
dog shows, which may of been fueled by her husband's interest in hunting and
his involvement with the sporting dogs and the rapidly expanding Westminster
Kennel Club. Both were strong gilded age, high society interests that helped
fill the newspapers society columns of the day. Westminster Kennel Club was
formed originally in the late 1870s at the Westminster Hotel as a way to earn
bragging rights for country esquires hunting dogs. The first show was held at
Gilmore's Garden in 1877, it soon rapidly expanded with the arrival of Madison Square Garden and has been forever linked with it. A decade later WKC included most all known breeds. Sylvia's dog of choice, was the fashionable Boston Terrier. The Joseph Palmer Knapp silver cup, was soon offered at Madison
Square Garden for Boston Terrier best of breed.

As the 1880's drew to a close, recreationally speaking, twenty something Joseph Palmer Knapp, seems to be pursuing quite the sportsman's life. His reputation was rapidly growing as one of the top wing shots in America in both live
birds and skeet. That reputation, is supported by his numerous tournament
wins reported in the press. He also has taken up yachting and golf. Indoors he
has become one of the top billiard players of the day, according to several daily
newspapers and the Police Gazette, which was mainly a newspaper devoted to
sports and not crime as the title suggests. The sports J. P. Knapp excelled at,
shooting, billiards and golf all required excellent hand and eye co ordination.

In keeping with his Methodist religious teachings, Joseph F.'s chief hobby
seemed to be taking a strong interest in promising young men of modest means
and helping them to succeed in business. At Metropolitan, Fred Ecker was one
perfect and perhaps outstanding example of Joseph's tutelage and help. Fred
started as a clerk with the company at age 16 in 1883, after working as an office
boy for Mr. Knapp's attorneys Woodford & Ritch. When the telephone came
along, he was the only one at Met who knew how to use it. He would eventually
become Met's 4th President in 1929 and its longest employee of all time (and perhaps in the world) staying on well past his retirement age. In 1959, 76 years after
he started, Fred Ecker was still there as Met's Honorary Chairman of the Board
and obviously drawing much more than his 1883 starting salary of $4 a week.

As the 1880's closed in the business world, Metropolitan Life was growing rapidly and as the worlds leading industrial insurer, with over 13 million dollars in assets and two million policies in force, it was larger than its two nearest competitors Prudential & John Hancock combined. One could say Met sat on very solid ground, but also needed more ground to sit upon. The company had outgrown its Park Place building and Knapp set his sights on Madison Square between 23rd & 26th streets for a new home. His choice at the time seemed to astonish most real estate men, who said 23rd Street was too far north from the heart of the city. At the time Knapp was scouting locations, Madison Square was just a quiet tree shaded park with the 5th avenue hotel , a Presbyterian church and several fashionable residences around it. The hotel was a rendezvous for dignitaries from the world over. In 1890 Knapp obviously knew better than the real estate experts and acquired the block on the east side of the park that consisted of four residences. Just north and behind him, land had been razed to make way for another future New York City landmark, Madison Square Garden. But the fight to grow his Life Insurance Company into a world leader, had taken its toll physically over the almost two decades that he was calling the shots. His friends and associates noted he sometimes appeared exhausted. Fred Ecker recalled in an interview in the 1940s, that he often accompanied Mr. Knapp to the vault at National Park Bank where the companies securities were stored. "Mr. Knapp always unlocked and locked the vault and watched carefully as the work was performed there. But one time he told me to lock up. I thought to myself, Mr. Knapp must be very sick, he has never done that before." In 1889, both Knapp children presented their parents, then 57 year old Joseph and 50 year old Phoebe with their first grandchildren. Edward Knapp Wallace was born in January, followed by Claire Antoinette Knapp in October.

In May that year, one of Brooklyn's most prominent citizens, Joseph Fairchild Knapp would host President Benjamin Harrison (the 5th President of the US to sample the Knapp's hospitality) at his Memorial Day extravaganza, that was an annual high water mark event. President Harrison actually stayed at the Knapp mansion overnight, arriving in the afternoon before the parade and having a formal dinner with the Knapps followed by breakfast next door at the Wallaces. After breakfast with a large group, that included Antoinette's brother in law and newly elected Congressman William Wallace, it was back to Knapp's where 1200 guests and dignitaries passed through, most entering the Knapp's front door on Bedford Ave and being announced as they entered the music room, meeting the President who gladly kissed babies, shook hands, signed autographs etc. Then most were shown to the side door on Ross Street. With Brooklyn scooping the Big Apple on hosting the president, the NY Times wrote perhaps with a touch of envy in their report, "Mr. Knapp likes to entertain Presidents, and his modest boast is that he does it well"

Whereas the Eagle reported *"Memorial Day 1889 will ever be remembered as a great day in Brooklyn. A great day for Joseph F. Knapp and a great day for the Grand Army of the Republic. The townsmen of Mr. Knapp are accustomed to something out of the ordinary at his big receptions. They are familiar with the costly paintings and decorations of his parlors, the perfume of his conservatories, and the beauty of his broad halls. They know too, how hearty is the welcome, how genial the hospitality, Mr. Knapp accords to his guests, and therefore when it is said the reception today in favor of the President of the United States and Secretary of the Navy Tracy more than realized of those who were bidden, a great deal is meant.*

At an early hour this morning people began to collect about the entrance to Mr. Knapp's house. They stood outside in the rain and looked wonderingly at the closed curtains that draped the windows of the beautiful Pompenian guest chamber on the first floor, which was occupied by the President. At about 7 o'clock the few guests who had been invited to breakfast with Mr. Knapp's distinguished visitor began to arrive. They were Congressman William Copeland Wallace, Mayor Chapin, and Mr. John A. Nichols. In addition to these Private Secretary Halford, Mr. and Mrs. Edward C. Wallace and Mr. and Mrs. Knapp were at the table. Secretary Tracy joined the party before the breakfast was over. In the reception room, adjoining the dining room a number of well known Republicans stood in groups awaiting the President. The home of Mr. Knapp is particularly well suited for an entertainment such as took place there today, for the arrangements of the rooms afford ample facilities for a great crowd to move comfortably in. Joining the main building that has for many years been occupied by Mr. Knapp is the residence of his daughter. Mrs. Wallace. A spacious hallway connects the two buildings which were thrown open today, giving the appearance of a commodious clubhouse or hotel. At 9' o'clock the hour fixed for the beginning of the reception,the parlors looked brilliant in the extreme. Naval officers in showy uniforms, Grand Army men in silk sashes and shining buttons filled the rooms. Past Commander Henry M. Calvert of Grand Post acted as master of ceremonies and introduced the guests to the President. [About 20 names and titles are then listed here.] *At precisely 9:15 o'clock President Harrison, leaning upon the arm of Joseph F. Knapp, left the dining room. passed into the large picture gallery where the reception took place. The President stood at the north end of the room the light from the skylight above shining down on his pale face, which was illuminated by a pleasant, kindly smile. The Chief Magistrate seemed to be in excellent spirits. He shook hands with everybody in a hearty fashion, as if he was not bored by the presentation.*

Mrs. DeWitt Talmage was the first person introduced to the President and Mrs. Elon Foster (Phoebe Knapp's sister) and Miss Phoebe Foster were also introduced. They together with Mrs. Knapp and Mrs. Edward Wallace, were the only ladies present. [The article then goes on to name many, many more, who shook the Presidents hand and in what order.] *The citizens of Brooklyn owe Mr. Knapp and his son in law Mr. Edward Wallace, a great deal for the enjoyable occasion of today. Notwithstanding the fact that they had but little time in to which to prepare. "I hope, " said Mr. John A. Nichols to the President, in the breakfast room this morning, "that you will not be like one of your predecessors who expressed himself as anxious to get out of Brooklyn." With a twinkle in his eye, President Harrison replied: "On the contrary, I have enjoyed every moment of my visit here."*

Mr. Knapp entertained last night at dinner, the President, Congressman William Copeland Wallace, and the officers of the Grand Post who were on the Reception Committee. The menu of the dinner was as follows: Consomme, Homard a la Newburgh, Mignons filet de beef Montebello, Haricots verts, Ailes de poulet a la Genin, Petit pois a la parisienne, Asperges a la vinaigrette, Beanassines garnies de cresson, Petites torrines de foios gras, Salvie de laitre, Piecus montaues, Glaces, Fantasies, Bonbons, Motious, Fruits, Dessert, Petits fours, Cafe." Brooklyn Eagle May 30,1889.

JOSEPH PALMER AND SYLVIA KNAPP WERE MORE THAN CONSPICUOUSLY absent from this grand affair, where literally hundreds of guest names, some repeatedly, appeared in print, as they moved from reception to reception over the two day period. I also note that J. P. and his wife would remain absent from Knapp Mansion social functions for the next few years. The large fire at the litho firm back in 1885, appeared to have little consequence on the fortunes of that company (they were fully insured) and during the rest of the decade it continued to grow larger. At first it appears there was just a verbal agreement between father and son to take his ever growing sales commissions, fueled mainly by the Duke account in Knapp Co. stock options. J. F.'s objective was a simple one, keep his son from having access to what he considered far too much money for a twenty year old. J. F. kept devising new philanthropic activities that his son may of felt was a bit unfair and that could of hastened what ultimately happened. As J. P.'s printing sales kept growing and growing, J. F. decided it was time to exercise far stronger controls on it. A formal buy and sell agreement was drawn up by their respective lawyers, for control of the Knapp Company, where a price was fixed in which J. F. might offer to purchase his son's stock. As part of the final agreement, J. P. was offered the same deal. What none of the lawyers figured on is, what eventually would happen between the two.

As J.P's business dealings with Buck Duke, who now had one of the largest tobacco companies in the world grew, he expressed interest in the possibility of getting into publishing his own newspaper with Duke as a partner. He presented this idea to his father, as another outlet for their ever growing stock of litho prints. His father was not impressed with this idea at all. Actually he was dead set against it. Perhaps as headstrong as his own father, fueled with a young mans ambition to make his own mark in the world and frustrated by the ever tighter financial controls, J. P. argued back. This no doubt had to shock J. F, and the conversation then got so heated between the two, that he wound up demanding his son sell him back his stock.

J. P. would reveal in his later years, that he felt his father often thought that he was not destined for success anywhere and I suggest that feeling could of played a part in the son's decision. Crestfallen, J.P. told his former Columbia classmate, lawyer Sam Untermeyer of the battle. To which he added that not only was his father not speaking to him, but he was probably going to be out of a job soon too, if he sold his stock back. Untermeyer did some quick investigating and told J. P. based on the stock he already owned, he could borrow enough money from the banks to buy out his father. To what must have been a shock to the entire family, J.P. did just that and his father never forgave him. In the beginning of 1891, the litho firm of which J. F. Knapp had been a part of since he was 16 and made his initial fortune with, became the Joseph P. Knapp Co. There can be little doubt this strain helped aggravate J.F.'s mental fatigue, as it was originally diagnosed, that had been plaguing him for some time. At the age of 58, J.F. Knapp probably suffered a slight stroke around March of 1891. Phoebe booked passage for Europe and took her husband there in April. seeking medical help in several countries for him in hopes he might recover. Her daughter and son in law went with her.

Now in full control of his own destiny, J. P. Knapp, did not let the idea of owning his own newspaper idea die. Along with Buck Duke and other investors, he opened the New York Recorder in the summer of 1891 on NY's famed newspaper row. Innovative in many ways, including the first paper to print in color in 1893, the Recorder struggled to survive for 5 years with Knapp and Duke pouring over a million dollars into it, before they pulled the plug.

CHAPTER
17

A Death In The Family

Death was never a stranger to Joseph Fairchild Knapp, from the day he was old enough to understand that his own father had died just two weeks after he himself was born. He also must of been well steeled for the idea of "death at too soon an age" by losing his first born son at two weeks old and his big brother at age 28, the following year. I'm certain his strong Methodist faith helped shape his ideas about death and we can't forget that one of his main occupations for over half of his life was paying money out for people who had died. He probably personally saw more death certificates during his life than any 100 doctors ever did. With these facts in mind, I would give more than a penny for his thoughts, as he departed for Europe in early April of 1891 and may of wondered if he would ever see his home in Brooklyn again.

There were at least a half dozen close family deaths during J. F. Knapp's lifetime. Starting with William in 1832, his aforementioned father who he never knew, Frances his own infant first born son in 1857, his brother William in 1858, his mother in law Phoebe in 1874 at age 67, his mother Antoinette in 1876 at age of 66, his father in law Dr. Walter Palmer at 79, who's last act on earth that July afternoon in 1883 was, to write a letter to J. F. and last but certainly not least was his step father Frances, who J. F. met at age 16 when he moved back to New York after his schooling. He lived for several years with his mother and "Frank"

Dominick who was in his late 80's when he passed away. Frank's perhaps is the oddest tale of a latter life and demise of anyone in J. F.s immediate family. It also helps lighten somewhat, the somber, sobering, yet natural experience, we all have to face. The full story appears here as written in the Brooklyn Eagle on September 6, 1889

LIKE FICTION: *The Facts About The Life Of Mrs. Dominick How She Married When But Twenty-three Years of Age a Man of Seventy and the Estrangement Which Followed*

A little more than ten years ago Frank Dominick, then more than 70 years old lived on South Second street, between 5th and 6th streets. Eastern District. He was a widower, his wife having died not long before. She was the mother of Joseph F. Knapp, who is one of the wealthiest residents of that part of Brooklyn, and who is well known in business circles in New York owning to his extensive interests.

Mr. Dominick was well to do—exceptionally so. His floors were covered with Axminsters and Wiltons, his walls were hung with tapestries, and costly furniture of antique make fill his rooms. A housekeeper took charge soon after his wife died, but he tired of that mode of life and decided on selling off all but family relics and becoming a hotel boarder. Among the items he determined to dispose of was a piano, and the fact that he wanted to sell it was advertised in the local newspapers.

Among those who saw the announcement was Miss Mary Marshall, who was then about 23 years old. She lived on South Second Street between Fourth and Fifth one block below Mr. Dominick's home with her parents. She was engaged at that time to marry a young man named Lewis., who had given her a number of costly presents and who expected to make her his wife in a few months. Miss Marshall saw the piano, tried it and liked it. She sang several songs while in the house which so pleased the aged owner that he thought she would make a good second wife for him. The idea grew on him and the culmination was an offer of marriage which was not rejected. Then the young lover Lewis was discarded. He demanded that all he had given to Miss Marshall be returned to him. His list included money and household articles. She declined to give them back saying that he had given all of them to her for her own use. He sued for the articles or their value and the case was settled–by Mr. Dominick it was always said.

The marriage of Mr. Dominick and Miss Marshall was celebrated by scores of uninvited guests, consisting of children as well as adults, who gathered in the street in front of their house. They had drums, fifes, wash boilers, tin kettles and fireworks and paraded in front of the house to the din of accompaniments mentioned. The police found it necessary to disperse the crowd. Many claimed that young Lewis was responsible for the demonstration, but he always denied it.

Except as the husband and wife were concerned, the marriage was not one that was acceptable to the two families. Mr. and Mrs. Dominick cared little for that, although the estrangement of the latter and all members of her family was absolute, while matters on her husbands side were not much better. A couple of years ago the couple moved to Hewes Street near Marcy Avenue and were never visited by any member of the wife's family and seldom by any of the husband's.

About four months ago Mr. Dominick was stricken down with illness. Senile debility and general breaking up the physicians said it was. Dr. Creamer was first called and said the patient couldn't live two weeks. He did though and lingered absolutely helpless until two weeks ago when he died. His only nourishment had been port wine, of which he drank large quantities. When he died his wife was the only person in the house with him. She alone had nursed him through his illness. She made the arrangements for the funeral during the day and had a colored woman come in at night to keep her company. They were alone in the big house with the corpse. The colored woman had a strong liking for the wine and indulged it freely, so that finally on Saturday morning succeeding Mr. Dominick's decease she was visibly effected by it. Up until that time. no one had called at the house but the undertaker. Relatives of the dead man were telegraphed, but the reply came, "All Gone To Europe." On the above mentioned Saturday evening a couple of friends of the widow called but no one else.

The funeral was held on the following Sunday and on that day some of Mrs. Dominick's family appeared together with a few friends and Joseph F. Knapp the stepson. The room in which the funeral services were held, was profusely draped in mourning cloth and in accordance with the High Episcopal practice, gas was kept burning throughout. In fact it was not turned off from the time of death until after the burial, and in the interim daylight was religiously kept out of the room where the corpse lay.

Mr. Dominick long ago retired from business and his widow is well provided for. She moved last week to Heyward Street. I would give two pennies for J. F.'s thoughts the day he attended that funeral.

The hope for a cure that Phoebe sought for her husband of thirty six years, must of dimmed somewhat a few months after they arrived in Europe, when he had a second stroke and was paralyzed on one side of his body. At Knapp's orders, the family sent for Joseph P. and Stuart Woodford J. F.'s longtime friend and attorney. Both arrived in August and the news they reported back to the states was not good. For several days, roller coaster like stories about his condition poured across the Atlantic ocean cables.

Joseph F. Knapp's Condition

Many of the friends of Joseph F. Knapp, one of the wealthiest and best known citizens of Brooklyn, have been informed by members of the family that Mr. Knapp, who is now in Paris, is slowly dying of an incurable disease. He realized his critical condition some time ago and sent for his sons [SIC] *both who are now at his side* [SIC] *and Gen. Stewart L Woodford his legal advisor. Gen. Woodford left Brooklyn hurriedly to comply with Mr. Knapp's urgent request for his presence—Mr. Knapp is the president of a starch company* [SIC]*—NY Times Aug 30, 1891*
Note: So much for the slogan "All The News That's Fit To Print." It should also be noted that Niagra Starch, was a big trade card client of Joseph P. Knapp Litho at that time

HOLDING HIS OWN: *Joseph F. Knapp's Condition Has Not Changed for Twenty Four Hours. Paris Aug 20th*

The condition of Joseph F. Knapp, who is lying seriously ill at the Hotel Continental in this city, has remained unchanged since yesterday. A report was started this morning that he was dying, but your correspondent made inquiries at the hotel and found that this report was without foundation. A member of the family said his condition is critical and that great anxiety was felt. It was hoped however that he would recover. The fact that he had grown no worse during the last twenty four hours, was regarded as a favorable indication of his ultimate restoration to health. Many inquiries had been made by the Americans in the city. His son has just arrived from New York.—Brooklyn Eagle Aug 30, 1891

Knowing what I do about Joseph F. Knapp, I would surmise he wanted Stu Woodford there to tell him directly and exactly, what revisions he wanted in his will that Woodford had only just changed in April before Knapp left Brooklyn. Woodford sadly reported back to the states in early September that "he did not expect his old friend to recover." J.F.'s call for his son to come to his side needs no explanation. When Joseph P. arrived, he suggested that perhaps a trip home would rally his father and plans were put into motion straight away. The Knapps left Paris for Havre on a special train and sailed for the states on Saturday September 12th aboard the La Champagne. J. F. made the trip from Paris to Havre fairly well considering his grave condition, but sunk into a coma on Sunday the 13th onboard the ship. He reportedly only rallied once ,when Joseph Palmer entered the room. He brightened up and said "This is Joseph, he's a fine boy, a fine boy" He did not recognize his old friend Stewart Woodford, nor speak with anyone else in the family that day. On Monday morning he died clasping Phoebe's hand and whispering "My Wife."

Expecting the worse, the family had brought a metal coffin along with them and the body was embalmed, and the stateroom cleared quietly, without the knowledge of his death communicated to the passengers. When they arrived in New York City on the 20th, friends had gone to the docks to meet the Knapps, not knowing what had transpired. When the ambulance that had been waiting, drove away empty, news spread quickly. Joseph P. took charge of bringing his father home to Brooklyn on the steamship Rosa. On the 21st, all the major NY Papers and many throughout the nation carried large front page obituaries. However, the funeral service held at his home was according to his wishes and kept as simple and unostentatious as possible. Burial was at Green Wood cemetery on the 23rd with only family and very close friends in attendance. This editorial in the Brooklyn Eagle, perhaps sums up the feeling of his hometown best:

Joseph F. Knapp will be deeply mourned, widely missed and long and lovingly remembered. He was a good man in the manliest meaning of the word. He was an able man in the strongest sense of the word. He was a believer in religion, reared in and attached to a particular form of faith, but un-secraterian in heart, liberal in thought, fragrant in life and broad in example. He was a philanthropist who not only relieved suffering, but who also planted or fostered the seeds of self help in others. The causes he aided were many. The men and women he assisted were many more. His good deeds were self unheralded. They became known at all only because they were constant and because those for whom they were done would not remain quiet about them as he did and would have them do.

His counsel was well nigh the soundest and gentlest of any rendered by any citizen of his standing in Brooklyn. His senses of what should be done was seemingly unerring. He foresaw results and had the insight into forces. Generally nature does not make a man as wise for himself as for others. This man was exceptional in such regard. He was his own best counselor. He was the best counselor of others. His judging faculty could hold even himself in poise and look at himself as another, so to speak. The gift was given to him to see himself, as others saw him.

With this judicial quality was a spirit of local sentiment, patriotic feeling and boundless hospitality. This was so well known, that it was a public possession. If a great cause required an occasion for its needs to be seen and supplied, if a great man or a group of great men, whether great in religion, valor, statesmanship, art, charity, science or in any large field of work or thought desired to meet the best life of Brooklyn or that life desired to meet them, the home of Joseph F. Knapp was recurred to as a matter of course. The office he filled in this respect was unique. His house was capitol of the finer and better forces in Brooklyn. He was the host of all men and women who came here representing those forces, and he was their host by the informal and invariable designation of the people of this great city, who delegated to him the gracious welcome of guests of their own. Wealth, tact, and taste enabled him admirably to fulfill this function, but they were but the exterior aids to what it was in his heart to do.

Other facts should be borne in mind. Riches wrought no essential change in him. They only brought out his qualities into service for others. He was as modest as he was munificent. Although every President since Lincoln has been his guest and great chieftains and statesmen, with kings and queens of art, oratory, song, and philanthropy, Joseph F. Knapp was the least proud or vain man on any of such historical occasions. His elation was solely due to the pleasure he was conferring. His joy was solely in the happiness of others. He would pass congratulations entirely to the credit of others. To try to convert them into compliment or praise did not gratify him. It annoyed him. The ingenuousness of the man in all this was simply beautiful. He absolutely preferred to be taken for a spectator when his house was the scene of its most splendid tributes to genius and when grander characters were his guests than any other man or mansion in the land could claim. Of course he delighted in the society of the great and good as who does not? But beyond the inspiration he drew from their personal influence and beyond the satisfaction he had in bringing Brooklynites and them face to face, his feeling did not go. He was no "lion hunter" no man worshiper, in any sense. Nor as guest or friend did anyone ever cross his sill, no matter how gifted or fortunate or distinguished, whose character was not admirable, whose powers had not been used for good ends and whose influence was not toward such ends, so far as he could learn. He was not superior to imposition. No unsuspecting and generous soul is; but he conceived hospitality, as he did wealth, to be a trust to be employed only for innocent, true and enabling purposes. He held a proxy for the collective heart and for the collective spirit of a community.

IN THE DAYS THAT FOLLOWED THERE WERE MANY MORE RESOLUTIONS from the various companies he was associated with and essays on the life of Joseph F. Knapp, in newspapers and trade journals. Most are relegated to deeply hidden 19th century archives and very little remains of his history in contemporary print. There is one colorful sentence that appeared in several business eulogies that jumped out at me. *"His common sense, was of a sledge hammer nature, when it came in contact with shams and absurdities"*

In October of 1891, some details of his will were made public. Again the Brooklyn Eagle carried the most details and led off with with this headline: **KNAPP'S WILL** *The Estate Left In Trust to Wife and Daughter. No Statement as to the Amount Involved. The Whole Property to Go to Mrs. Wallace on Mrs. Knapp's Death.*

From reading the entire article, I would surmise the deathbed changes he directed Stuart Woodford to make were, from possibly no mention at all of Joseph Palmer in the April 6th 1891 version of it, to a slight change of heart. Most of the story that was reported is directed towards his dealings with his son. *"The Testator says that as he has sold his interests in the business of Knapp & Co to his son, Joseph P. Knapp, on such terms that he should make a large profit, he discharges so much of the debt due from his son as is represented by certain promissory notes and chattel mortgage upon personal property. The amount of the notes is not stated, nor is the amount of the chattel mortgage, So much of this debt as is secured by real estate not occupied by the son in his business as a lithographer and printer which was sold to him by his father, the executors are directed to collect and apply to the trust estate. This mortgage upon real estate is $275,000. The remainder of the estate is left to the executors in trust, who are directed to pay two thirds to the widow. Phoebe P. Knapp and one third to his daughter Antoinette."*

I make no claims at any legal expertise, but what I gather is, J. F. cut his son some slack here by discharging the debt, but still wanted him to know that he was very upset with him and still could call some shots even from the grave. The fortunate son got another break when his sister decided to share her inheritance of Metropolitan Life stock with him.

CHAPTER
18

As The Century Closed

Although the "Gay '90s" started on a rather somber note for the immediate Knapp family, with estrangement, illness and death, the last decade of the 19th century would also be marked with changes in their personal and in the case of J. P. Knapp, his business life, that would effect the lives of millions well into the 20th century, and for this author, most of the first decade of the 21st.

Whether J.P.'s recollection that his father may of thought "he was not destined for success anywhere", was drawn from his J.F.'s actual words or just J. P.'s impressions of his father's feelings towards him, can only be speculated here. It could well of been a combination of both. However the fact remains that the road J.P's ambitions would travel on, was well laid in the beginning of the 1890s. He actually started publishing his NY Recorder newspaper in February of 1891 and even though it would ultimately fail, the groundwork for another of his really big ideas, that would lead him to mega success' in business life, was already well on its way to becoming reality, as they laid his father into the Knapp Family Circle plot at Greenwood.

By the time this brief item rolled off the presses at the New York Times, the first week of the New Year in 1892, probably everything was in place but the drapes and the president's chair behind the desk.

LITHOGRAPHERS TO COMBINE : *Tuesday Jan 5, 1892*

A movement has been afoot for several months to form a combination of all the leading lithographers in this country, and it has now reached a point where success seems assured. A meeting was held in this city Saturday (Jan 2nd) at which the question of forming the American Lithographic Co. with a capitol of $12,000,000 was discussed. A plan of organization was agreed on, but not per-fected. The details have not been made public.

Another meeting will probably be held in a short time, and then the organization will probably be completed. Nearly every firm of repute in this city is interested in this scheme. There are more than 150 individuals and firms engaged in the busi-ness in this city. Among those who were represented at the meeting on Saturday are Giles Co. Schumacher & Ettlinger, G. H. Buek & Co. Joseph P. Knapp, F. Hep-penheimer's Sons, Donaldson Brothers, Leiber & Maass, Klien, Lindler, & Bond Lithographing Company, Manhattan Lithographing Company, Lindler Eddy & Claus. Several out of town firms were also represented.

Three days before the final announcement that American Lithographic Com-pany was born, another big event at 322 West 72nd Street, N Y C, would occur that had Joseph Palmer Knapp filling out a pre printed form from the City of New York. I have a copy of Certificate #5430 and it states thusly that: Joseph F. Knapp, male, white, was born on February 3, 1892 at 322 West 72nd St. New York and the father's name is Joseph P. Knapp, who resides at the same address and that the father was born in Brooklyn and is 27 years old. His occupation is that of a Lithog-rapher. The mothers name is Sylvia T. Knapp and her maiden name is Kepner and that she was born in New York and her age is also 27. The number of previous chil-dren is stated as two and the number of living children is also two. Now whether the number of previous children is a mistake made by an excited and very busy new father, is open to question here. I do know, I have never found any evidence of any other children that Joseph and Sylvia had, other than Claire Antoinette, who was born on October 23, 1889. The certificate is filled out in J. P.'s own hand-writing on Feb 6, 1892, the same day the New York Times and many other papers printed this item about one of Americas first conglomerates:

A NEW TRUST : *The Organization Of The American Lithographic Co.*

An effort which began several months ago to consolidate the larger lithographic establishments of the country was partially consummated yesterday in the orga-nization of the American Lithographic Company. Guggenheimer & Untermeyer, who managed the English brewery syndicate purchase of American breweries, and Oudin & Oakley were the attorneys who negotiated the combination. Although the entire programme was not fulfilled, enough of the larger establishments were united to make a trust which practically controls 90 percent of the lithographing business.

Joseph P. Knapp of the Knapp Lithographing Company is the moving spirit and President of the new company or trust. The other institutions which have attached themselves to the new company are Donaldson Brothers of the Five Points, G. H. Buek & Co. 155 Leonard St., Schumacher & Ettlinger 34 Bleeker St. Lindner , Eddy & Claus 66 Centre St., The Giles Lithographing Co., 30 West Thirteenth St. and Witsch & Schmitt of 94 Bowery; George T. Harris of Phila-

delphia, and F, Heppenheimer & Sons of Jersey City.

The new company was capitalized at $11,500,000 at which $3,500,000 is pre-ferred and $8,000,000 is common stock. and the individual companies sold out to the new company and took their pay in stock. To provide the new establishment with working capital, a first mortgage of $1,000,000 was voted. None of the stock or bonds of the new trust will it said be put on the open market.

The promoters of the new trust have figured out a prospective income of more than 10 percent. The officers of the new trust are: President Joseph P. Knapp, Vice Presidents George Harris, and George W Donaldson, Treasurer Louis Ettlinger Secretary William C. Heppenheimer. The trust is organized under the laws of New Jersey.

Two things jump out at me from this item. One of the attorneys, who put this deal together was Sam Untermeyer, the same pal of J. P.'s ,who advised him on how to buy his father out in the 1880s. Ironically Untermeyer would go to work for the U. S. Government to bust up trusts on the other side of the turn of the century. Among those Untermeyer prosecuted were James B. Duke's and his American Tobacco Co, and the biggest banker of all, J. P. Morgan of which Knapp's crony and sometime business partner Thomas Lamont headed. It seems like the strange bedfellows,politicians are made of, are also made of the big bucks of big tycoons. The other item is: "J. P. Knapp , is the moving spirit of the new company and president"—which I'm sure put a smile on J. P.'s face, whenever he thought of his fathers doubts about him and perhaps it was a salute from under the quiet pines at Green Wood.

Town & Country

Lest you think Joseph Palmer only kept his nose on the business grindstone after his father passed on, think again. Though he seemed to take on multiple business ventures and new responsibilities in the 1890s (like a seat on the board of directors at Metropolitan Life) he did not give up any of his recreational activities, in fact he expanded upon them, especially geographically speaking. As a teen ager in the 1870s, he probably got his first view of eastern Long Island when his mother took him and his sister to Shelter Island for summer religious camp. In the early 1890s he started coming out to Babylon where the Westminster Kennel Club had their clubhouse for bird shooting and field dog trials. The Joseph Palmer Knapps also turn up frequently in society's doings at country clubs in places like, Lakewood, New Jersey, Saratoga Springs and Tuxedo, New York. He was a member of the N Y Yacht Club and in 1890 owned a modest 22 foot catboat named "Petrel." He moored "Petrel" at the very prestigious Larchmont Yacht Club up in Westchester County. He did not keep "Petrel" long though, as it appears in the 1892 Lloyd's Registry of Yachts with a new owner. He also leased larger magnificent steam yachts like Intrepid and the schooner, The Idler that were berthed at the New York Yacht Club's facilities at City Island.

In 1894 he sailed eastward and started summering with his family in Bellport, a unique, artsy, and fashionable summer colony on Long Island's south shore, some 60 some miles east of New York City. Year round it was a fishing village founded in the mid 19th century. The Knapps must of really liked Bellport, as they were season regulars there for almost two decades. They even spent some off season time there. It was most likely while in Bellport, that J. P. discovered the Carman's River, just a few miles east of Bellport village. The Carman's ran all the way across the 16 mile width of Long Island and on the south shore separated the area known as Brookhaven and the peninsula of Mastic. The river was literally owned by the Smith Family of the Manor Of St. George, who traced their massive land holdings back to the King of England. Though hard to believe, but because of colonial land grants, in addition to over 10,000 acres of land, the Smiths owned the bay bottom and the rights to take shellfish in all of Brookhaven Township, all the way eastward to the Southampton Town Line. They also controlled lucrative oyster fishing rights in the 1800s. Because the Carmans River was connected to the bay at Smith's Point, they declared the river theirs too, and won several court challenges to protect their claim.

In the 1890s there remained four brother and sister Smith heirs, living on their colonial manor. They were all unmarried and derived some of their income from leasing their waterways to wealthy sportsmen for hunting and fishing. Sugar baron Harry Havemeyer, who had a large estate in Islip tried to purchase much of their water rights holdings in the 1890s, but it was no sale. There is an 1894 river lease that was drawn up between Joseph P. Knapp and William, Clarence, Martha and Eugenia Smith. It was renewed up until 1898 and included "gunning and fishing privileges on the Carman's River from Squasoxx Landing dock, northward several miles to the 'going over' which was where the South Country Road (Montauk Highway today) crossed the river in the hamlet of Southaven."

I'm not sure when J. P. discovered the game of Golf, but it was probably around the time it started to get popular in America with high society. Like he was with billiards, he seemed to be a natural at golf and quickly rose to be one of the top of amateur golfers in the country. By the end of the century, he was winning many tournaments and that continued into the early 1900s, when he won the Florida State Championship. He also was the spark plug and investor behind the construction of several golf courses, notably the original Bellport course in 1899 which was a 9 hole affair on the bay and Golf Links of America in Shinnecock Hills, Southampton, which is still a major course on the PGA tour today.

The Bellport Golf Course was incorporated in May of 1899 with directors: Joseph Knapp, George Barnes, his lawyer friend from Brooklyn, John Mott, Fred Edey and Frank Otis. In the 1890s the Knapps stayed at The Wyandotte, one of Bellport's fashionable hotels or sometimes rented a summer home. His friends Otis, Edey, (related by marriage) and Mott all had large estates there. Otis' "The Locusts" became the new Bellport Country Club and Golf course in 1917. The Mott's estate "Brook Farm" is still there today but has long been in use as a theatre, known as the Gateway Playhouse. In the 1950s it was used by Columbia Pictures as a talent farm.

The Widow Knapp
Phoebe Palmer Knapp's public life as a widow, was not radically different than it

had been as when Joseph was alive. She continued heavily with presenting and attending concerts and musicales and stayed active with philanthropic work, usually associated with her faith, like The Kings Daughters.

She also ventured to Europe for the summer season again several times in the 1890s and was usually out of the country from May to October. The earliest year I have found a record of, was 1893, when she was accompanied by her daughter, daughter in law and grandchildren Edward, Claire and baby Joseph F.

In the first months of 1894, several newspapers reported that she had vacated the Knapp Mansion in Brooklyn for a home located at 215 W 72nd St. (about a block east of Joseph and Sylvia's residence). Some newspapers reported that the properties were exchanged for each other. Others reported various figures for both houses ranging from selling the Knapp Mansion in Brooklyn for a low figure of $40,000 and paying upwards of $100,000 for the home on Central Park West. I believe somewhere between the two lies the truth. Here are several such reports.

"GOSSIP OF THE REAL ESTATE MEN" *New York Times on Jan 28, 1894*
The handsome four story brick and stone front dwelling 251 West Seventy second street, north side, between the Boulevard (Broadway) and West End Avenue, has been exchanged by messr. Lamb & Rich for the residence of Mrs Joseph F. Knapp at the corner of Bedford & Ross Street, Brooklyn. The latter with grounds measures 50 x 120 feet. The Seventy - second street house is 25 x 90.

Followed by the NY Daily Tribune : Feb 9, 1894
"THE HOUSE OF MRS. JOSEPH F. KNAPP SOLD"
The handsome brownstone of the late Joseph F. Knapp president of Metropolitan Life Insurance Company of this city, who died on a French steamer returning from abroad, has been sold for $40,000 by his widow. The house is at Ross St and Bedford Ave and was purchased years ago for $35,000. Nearly $100,000 was expended on the interior decorations. It has a music room that is regarded as one of the finest in the country. In the lifetime of Mr. Knapp, it was the scene of many notable gatherings. Among those entertained were Presidents Grant, Cleveland and Harrison. United States Senator Hill and many other State officials. Mrs Knapp vacated the mansion after her husbands death and has since then lived in New York where she purchased a home for $100,000.

And again in the NY Times:
"RECORDED REAL ESTATE TRANSFERS": Feb 16, 1894
72nd St 251 West Jasper N. Reymond to Phoebe P. Knapp ...$91,000.

In any event she did not remain on W. 72nd street very long. She then moved into a suite at the new Hotel Savoy, on 5th Ave and Central Park South lock, stock & ORGAN! I wonder what the other hotel guests thought about that or if she played it before 8 AM or after 9 PM? The Wallaces also left their attached home on Bedford Ave, Brooklyn moving to 787 5th Ave, just about a block north of the Savoy. Other than attending many social functions with her mother or hosting her own dinners, at places like Delmonico's, there is not much else written about Antoinette Knapp Wallace in the 1890s. In October of 1900 Phoebe sold the house on W 72 St for $60,000 which is $40,000 less than she had reportedly paid for it.

Although the Knapps had left the building so to speak, their good name would remain with it forever, just like "the mansion" that you were introduced to in the first chapters of this book. The mansion on the corner of Bedford & Ross in Brooklyn would never shake the name Knapp mansion, even when various owners of it, well into the twentieth century, reincarnated it. The first of such transformations was announced nine months after Phoebe sold it. Here is how it was reported by the Eagle on September 24, 1894

"THE OLD KNAPP MANSION" *Has Been Transformed Into A Dancing Academy - It Has Been The Scene Of Glittering Festivities - Two Presidents Having Been Entertained Under It's Hospitable Roof - Some Of Its Associations*

The transformation of the old Knapp mansion at Bedford Ave and Ross Street, into a dancing academy and place for public assemblages, has been completed and on Tuesday "the mansion"* as it is now called, will be formally dedicated. The programme includes a reception, admission which will be by invitation only, and a musicale.

The old Knapp mansion, although not so very old at that** has been one of the best known residences in the elite neighborhood of the eastern district. It was purchased several years ago by the late Joseph F. Knapp, for many years the president of the Metropolitan Life Insurance company. It is said to be the most complete house in Brooklyn, luxury and elegance prevailing in the furnishing and decoration. Adjoining the Knapp mansion was a smaller house, where Mr. Knapp's daughter lived and as the two houses were connected by a conservatory, they were practically one. Both of these buildings are now in the hands of strangers. Mr. Knapp is dead and the other members of his family have moved away.

Mr. Knapp was a royal entertainer, and two Presidents of the United States, Harrison and Cleveland have shared his hospitality, and inspected the beauties of his house.

The mansion has now passed into the possession of William Pitt Rivers[1] the well known professor of dancing, who has secured a five years lease of the property, with the privilege of purchase at the expiration of the term. The building which is a spacious one, will under Mr. Rivers' direction, take on the character of a public hall or place of assembling. In other words, he hopes to have a Pouch mansion in the eastern district, and thinks there is room for it. Already the Amphion Music Society, a well known organization, is discussing the advisability of leaving their present quarters on Clymer street and taking the top floor of the mansion.

During the past week the place has been over run by people who desire to see the beauties of the house about which they have heard so much. The main room on the first floor is the dancing hall, although in case of emergency, the main parlor, the library, and the regular reception room all on the ground floor will also be used for dancing rooms. The dancing hall itself which was the music room when Mr. Knapp was alive, the feature of the house, admittedly one of the finest in the country, and

---

1William Pitt Rivers actually rented it from its new owner Thomas Adams, the chewing gum manufacturer.

the feature the wealthy occupant most admired. It's construction so different from the ordinary hall makes it a unique and pleasant place for dancing.

On the corner with an excellent view of Ross Street and Bedford Avenue is a large reception parlor which will still be kept as such. The parlor across the way, the dining room back, and the billiard room will all be devoted to dancers hereafter, Although the entrance way between the two houses has now been blocked up, one half of the conservatory is now in the mansion and this will be used as a smoking room.

In the basement will be the restaurant and kitchens and there will be plenty of room to accommodate good sized supper parties.

At present the third floor is vacant, but the probabilities are that the Amphion society will take it for themselves. Dr. Darlington, the president of the society, is quite interested in the transformation that is going on. Christ church of which he is rector, will hold its annual fair there, November 19,20,21, and 22.

S OME POINTS ABOUT THAT ARTICLE: IN MASTIC BEACH DURING THE 1950's "the mansion" only meant one place, even though there were five of them still standing then. Manor Of St. George, Bayview, Knapp, Floyd and Dana The Old Knapp mansion in Mastic Beach, was not that old either in the 1950's, most likely it was built circa 1900. It neglects to recall that General Grant a frequent visitor, was also President Grant and it was written once that Abraham Lincoln was a guest there, but I have found nothing concrete to support that other than the connection to Bishop Simpson, who was a close friend of Lincoln and the Palmer family. Simpson married Phoebe and Joseph in 1855. Lincoln was in Brooklyn in 1859, campaigning for president, so it would make perfect sense he would be a guest of the Knapps. President William McKinley was Phoebe Knapp's guest at her Savoy Hotel Suite. In 1894, Phoebe returned to Europe for the season, but took seriously ill in Rome, sought treatment in Paris and then actually sent for Dr. Fiske, her physician from Bedford Ave. Now that is some house call! I wonder what the doctor's bill was? While they were dancing up a storm in her home in Brooklyn, she was sailing back to the states. I would surmise her voyage, probably held more than a few memories of her trip in September of 1891. On a somewhat lighter note, while Phoebe was away in Europe during the summer of '94, this item appeared in the Brooklyn Eagle.

"THE KNAPP MONUMENT RAN AWAY"

A flat car containing the big granite monument to Joseph F. Knapp got away at Greenwood Saturday afternoon and ran all the way into the main yard of the old Culver depot at Coney Island. There the superintendent piled lumber enough on the tracks to check the speed, and climbed aboard and shut down the brakes. Although Saturday was a rush day, the car ran the full length of the line, seven or eight miles without a collision or accident___ Brooklyn Eagle July 16, 1894

In 2005 for J. F.'s 173rd birthday, I ran a photo, on The Knapps Lived Here website of that monument, that I took in 2002 . (it's about a 25 foot tall obelisk that looks just like the Washington Monument) In the spirit of the Eagle article I added this musing: " All the way to Coney Island it went. But who could blame J. F. for not wanting to go see the Elephant, one more time before it burned down in 1896, or anything else at Coney Island for that matter?" I also have the photo of "The

Elephant" hotel on there. It was a wild and wooly place, located on Surf Ave. It was built in 1884 in the shape of the huge pachyderm complete with tusks and howdah (riding chair) on it's back. At 122 Feet tall, it towered over the rest of Brighton Beach and was Coney Island's very first tourist attraction.

Going Full Tilt

Joseph Palmer Knapp was a very busy man in the 1890's in the world of business. He was sitting on the finance board of directors at Met Life and getting ALCO (American Lithographic Company) up and running strong. He was also on the board of directors for the Worlds Fair aka 1892 -93 Chicago Exposition and did most of the fair's printing, hundreds of fair items still survive today; postcards, trade card ads, souvenir albums etc. His lifelong printers desire to always use as much color as possible, sometimes in spite of the costs, saw another advance with using his new color presses to print the Recorder, before any of his competitors did. Hearst soon followed suit with The Journal, as did Pulitzer with The World. In spite of Knapp's innovations and even with promotions like customer coupons and free art prints, suitable for framing (many too still survive) on Sundays, the Recorder struggled for circulation. Several managing editor changes were also made and it was an expensive lesson in becoming a publishing printer.

In mid decade he acquired property on the corner of 19th street and 4th Avenue to erect the American Lithographic Company office building. Twelve stories tall, it was finished in 1897 and still stands proudly today with an unchanged exterior and the name AMERICAN LITHOGRAPHIC CO, chiseled in stone above the entrance. However I doubt that J. P. would care for how they chopped up the interior of his printing palace into tiny cubicle offices.

While he was multi tasking, the summer of 1895 found his wife, children and mother in law along with a maid and governess in Europe returning in early October aboard the brand new steamer St. Louis.

The Partial Truth

In his reminisces printed in the late 1930's , J . P. Knapp told reporters he always considered himself just a printer. That said, along with owning a newspaper, he also had his first taste of magazine publishing in the 1890's. Truth Magazine was around for a quarter of a century starting in 1881. It changed style, content and ownership multiple times until it finally disappeared for good in 1905. It started quite plainly, with no real distinct market or mission and then in the mid '80's became a gossip mag along the lines of "Town Topics" which was considered the first of its kind to chronicle the lives of "NY's 400" aka the very rich. It declined in readership until backers were obtained in 1891 and it re emerged along the lines of the political humor mag Puck and the comic weekly Life, but with higher quality printing (courtesy of American Lithograpic's state of the art presses) It had cartoonists like Richard F. Outcault, (creator of the Yellow Kid) Archie Gunn, Hy Mayer and more and writers like Stephen Crane before Red Badge Of Courage made him famous. The new incarnation was a success with a circulation of near 50,000 but it also was very expensive to produce. It soon found itself in deep debt to American

Lithographic Co and ALCO successfully petitioned the courts to declare the magazine bankrupt and award them controlling interest. I would like to think this was mainly a tactic by Buck Duke, but I doubt it could be proven today. In 1894, ALCO gave the editor of Truth a nice severance package. Of ALCO's time running things, the assistant editor James Ford would write in his memoirs "American Lithographic knew how to print pretty pictures, but they had no idea on how to run a humor magazine" That said, Truth soldiered on under a constant parade of changing management in the editors chair, but had the finest covers and most sophisticated centerfolds of any magazine in print.

By appearances alone, it looked like Truth was thriving, but perhaps the red ink at the Recorder's misfortunes may have spilled onto the books for Truth also. In 1897, it changed again with every fourth issue being entirely devoted to a serious subject similar to Harper's monthly. With the close of 1897, Truth reduced its cover price from ten cents to a nickel. It's contents became very indistinguishable and contained mostly bland non fiction.

When the Spanish American war broke out, Truth focused heavily on it and circulation soared to over 300,000, but soon dropped with the wars end. Then in 1899 ALCO totally revamped it, making it a showcase for the printing arts. Illustrators like Mucha and William de Leftwich Dodge were commissioned for the covers (Dodge by the way also would paint Sylvia Knapp's portrait in the early 1900's, most likely at his estate in St. James, Long Island) They also raised the price to 25 cents, but it is widely acknowledged that there was no finer graphic publication in America and possibly the world at that time.

Although it is said J. P. Knapp knew enough to not interfere with the editorial decisions (at least publicly) in any of his publishing ventures, he did pay a high price to learn about the business. Truth continued halfway into the first decade of the twentieth century, but on October 11, 1896, many of New York Recorder's competitors carried stories like this one in the New York Times.

"END OF THE RECORDER : *Morning Edition's Evening Successor Suspends - A Costly Venture"*

The Evening Recorder appeared for the last time yesterday afternoon. The suspension of the paper had been expected for some time. It was the short lived successor of the morning Recorder, which had been in difficulty for several years, and had been losing money with magnificent lavishness that portended early disaster.

The evening venture was a last desperate effort to save something from the wreckage, but yesterday the enterprise went out with a gasp.

In 1891 W. Duke the cigarette manufacturer, the Knapp Company, lithographers, and Howard Carroll conceived the idea of establishing a great newspaper. They had plenty of money, millions to expend in founding a great metropolitan daily, and they began to spend it freely on The Recorder, which they launched under particularly favorable auspices, so far as newspaper talent was concerned. Some of the best journalists of New York were engaged and no expense spared. The lithographers strewed the elevated stations and plastered the walls and fences with costly pictures calling attention to The Recorder and a Sunday supplement resplendent with chromos was issued at a tremendous outlay.

Finally in 1893, the enterprise began to pay. The profit for one year amounted to

$50,000.00 The proprietors thought that they could now reduce the value of the paper and keep up the subscription list. This policy, together with other ill-judged plans, soon brought the paper into trouble, and it never again recovered the ground it lost.

About this time George W. Turner of The World left that journal and went to the rescue of The Recorder. He introduced a great many novelties and devices for selling the paper. Catch-penny schemes of all kinds were tried. One of them consisted of a sort of lottery. Red numbers were printed on the paper, and the person who got a certain number was to receive a prize. This scheme got into the courts, but was declared to be in no violation of the law against lotteries.

Advertising rates were cut, in the hope of drawing a large patronage to the paper;but this plan also failed, and matters grew worse and worse. Beside these money troubles, there was dissension among the members of the staff. In September of this year C. N. Greig succeeded Mr. Turner as publisher and announced that Mr. Turner had nothing further to do with The Recorder.

Mr. Duke it is understood withdrew from the paper about a week ago, and it became known that the suspension of The Evening Recorder was just a matter of only a few days.

After the last edition came out yesterday afternoon, a notice was pasted on the bulletin board of the editorial rooms announcing that the services of the employees were no longer required.

The suspension of the the evening paper also involves The Sunday Recorder, which will not be issued after today.

It was proposed to issue today only, the Sunday supplement without the news matter, as the Sunday part of the paper had been prepared before it was determined to discontinue publication with yesterday's issue.

Mr. Turner when asked about the reasons for the suspension said: "At the present time it is impossible for me to make a statement." It is estimated that The Recorder in it's life of five years lost more than $1,000,000.

The Beat Goes On

The last years of the century, finds many items regarding Joseph P. Knapp's hobbies of trap shooting, golf and billiard expertise in the social and sporting columns. As the curtain slowly rang down on the gay nineties and the City of Brooklyn was about to be absorbed into the City Of New York, we find that his mother was still very active in all sorts of social affairs, but centered mainly on music. This article from January 1898 finds her in her element at her new location

"MRS. KNAPP'S MUSICALES : *A Former Brooklynite Who Has Been Giving a Series of Unusual Importance at the Hotel Savoy"*

Mrs. Joseph F. Knapp has been giving a series of delightful musicales this season in her apartments in the Hotel Savoy, Fifty ninth street and Fifth Avenue. Borough of Manhattan and a particularly fine programme has been arranged for Tuesday evening next, when it expected that some Brooklynites will be among the guests.

Mrs. Knapp it will be remembered, is the widow of Joseph F. Knapp and during her residence in Brooklyn, she was a prominent figure in the social world, as was her husband in business and club circles, and both were particularly identi-

fied with the life and interests in the Eastern District. The family occupied the handsome residence at the corner of Bedford avenue and Ross Street, which is still termed the Knapp Mansion, and here were entertained during a long period of years many of the distinguished visitors to Brooklyn, including Presidents Grant, Arthur and Cleveland. After her husband's death in 1891. Mrs. Knapp's health failed and she went abroad to recuperate. On her return to this country, she took up her residence in New York. At the Savoy she occupies a large suite facing Fifth avenue, and the artistic taste and culture which were the distinguishing characteristics of her Brooklyn residence are observed in her present quarters, and the homelike air which pervades them is seldom met within hotel apartments.

The music room is in many respects the gem of the suite and a beautiful piano occupies a central position surrounded by rare specimens of bric - a - brac and art souvenirs from many lands. The furnishings are all of a delicate tint. The large organ which was a special attraction in the Brooklyn home, has recently been placed in position in this room and will be used at a musicale to be given in the near future. A sweet toned orchestration and other musical instruments are also in evidence. The reception rooms are fitted up in the most artistic manner.

Mrs. Knapp has a host of friends in musical circles and the formal entertainments where leading musicians of the metropolis are present either in the capacity of performers or auditors are interspersed with impromptu affairs at which delightful programmes are rendered by those already known to fame and by others whose talents have not been so fully recognized. Occasionally the hostess contributes to the attractiveness of these impromptu musicales by her own playing and singing, as she is a musician of unusual ability.

Mrs. Knapp devotes the larger part of her time to church work and almost every day finds her assisting at some religious service or Bible talk and her leisure is given to musical compositions. She has written the music for a number of compositions of a sacred character, which have been sung by many well known church and concert soloists. Her latest work is entitled "The New Leaf" and is likely to be widely sung as both the words and music are beautiful.

For sometime it has been rumored in the Eastern District that Mrs. Knapp contemplated marriage with a well known young pianist, but there is no foundation for the story. Brooklyn Eagle Jan 09, 1898

As the century closed, the affairs held at the Knapp Mansion in Brooklyn were numerous and varied. From 1888 - 1889, the Eagle reported over 300 events of dances, musicales, card parties, revivals and religious activities of all denominations of churches, civic, sports clubs and music school recitals . You could say it was one big cultural tent, similar to the vision Father Skelly would hold for the Knapp Mansion that he would purchase in Mastic Beach, some 60 miles down the block and 50 years down the road. The last article I found for the 19th century was dated December 31,1899

KNAPP SUBSCRIPTION DANCE *The December subscription dance took place last night. The subscribers, nearly all of whom were present were: It then lists over 80 people by name, a mixture of couples and singles*

CHAPTER
19

Turn of the Century &
A Turn of the Tide

*N*inety pages into "Her Heart Can See", Edith Blumhofer's 21st century and well researched biography of Fanny Crosby, we meet for the first time in some detail one of Fanny's co-writers and friends, Phoebe Knapp. After the standard background bio on Phoebe and her husband Joseph, Ms. Blumhofer writes:

> *"Mrs. Knapp was what would now be called a social activist and she claimed to 'care more for the active movements of the world of society than for spiritual abstraction'. Her understanding of Christianity was to aid the poor and foster social reform. By the time she was thirty and Fanny met her, she was actively involved in many political and social activities and had already given away large sums of money to the poor.*
>
> *Phoebe Knapp was an attractive woman, tall, slim, with fine, regular features, intense eyes, and dark, curling hair. Although she was deeply concerned about the plight of the poor, she did not by any means disdain the life of the rich. She was a lavish dresser, given to wearing elaborate gowns and diamond tiaras. The "Knapp Mansion," a palatial residence on the corner of Bedford Avenue and Ross Street in Brooklyn, was a New York institution. There she held a European-style salon in which she entertained most of the prominent people of the day... [THEN SOME*

OF THOSE WHOM I HAVE ALREADY WRITTEN ABOUT ARE NAMED]...*in her music room was one of the finest collections of musical instruments in the country, and well known artists and performers were from time to time her guests. Phoebe Knapp was not liked by many people. Very talkative, she had the reputation of being a smothering, possessive, strong willed woman, and a bizarre eccentric. She considered herself a better musician than she actually was and gave vocal recitals, despite the fact that her soprano voice was thin and weak."*

I MUST SAY WHEN I FIRST READ THAT IMPRESSION OF PHOEBE KNAPP, I was taken back a bit, because heretofore I had not read anything negative about her personality, although I had seen similar comments about her musicianship and voice almost always within the confines of commentary from a religious source rather than a musical one. Speaking as a professional musician with some notable awards and credits as I mentioned in chapter 5, I can authoritatively say as a composer, Phoebe Knapp demonstrated a high degree of musical ability with her religious composition "Blessed Assurance" and secular one "Watching For Pa". As for how well she could actually play or the quality of her voice, since it was never recorded, we can only rely on with what has been said, but must be mindful of the source and credentials of who said it. Talent evaluation in any field is sometimes more of a human failing of envy rather than an actual fact. Couple that with Phoebe's highly visible good fortune and you do have a recipe for perhaps highly biased criticism. From my correspondence with Dr. Blumhofer regarding her sources, I have learned where they came from: "The sentences about her unpopularity, are based on letters from the William Doane Papers in the American Baptist Archives. It is evident from their correspondence that Doane and the owners and hymnal editors at Bigelow and Main considered Phoebe Knapp officious, interfering, and overbearing."

Well that certainly cleared some of it up for me, as you too will soon read about regarding Phoebe Knapp and her feud with competing music publishers Bigelow & Main, over the welfare of Fanny Crosby, with poor Fanny caught in the middle of it all. On this matter Dr. Blumhofer has done a very fine job of research and it is quite an interesting curtain lifter on early copyright and music business practices of which much is still unchanged. Now with that said, it does not define one way or another what Phoebe Knapp's true personality was like and can't we all be that way at times especially when provoked? I have found in my experience of being around musicians for over 50 years, that many do think of their abilities as sometimes far greater than they technically are. I have also found myself fortunate to have been in the company of several true virtuosos (some world famous and some unknown) but they all seem to be extremely humble in my humble opinion. So what does that tell us about one Phoebe Palmer Knapp? Well she was a fine looking woman, who composed some beautiful songs, she was a excellent hostess and fancy dresser, a friend to the needy, a lifelong champion of the arts and culture. Could she take requests for "Melancholy Baby" or fake her way through it? No! Why? Because it had not been written yet! As for what her voice was like, we have no recordings to judge it by. I do have the first recording on an Edison wax cylinder of "Blessed Assurance" by the "

Edison Mixed Quartet " though. It is dated 1908, but Edison historians tell me it could have been recorded as early as 1905-06. When I listen to it, I like to think that Phoebe Knapp heard this same recording of her "big hit".

Phoebe was not the only member of her family riding some stormy seas in the first few years of the new century. Her son in law, Edward C. Wallace found himself in a bit of a legal fix thanks partly to that new fangled machine some thought was the work of the Devil himself. I'm talking about the horseless carriage and the general publics perception of it and of those who used them, the first few years they started to appear on the roads. Prior to Henry Ford's assembly line and the Model T, early automobiles were toys of the wealthy. They were considered nothing more than a passing fad by those who would curse at them or yell out "Get A Horse" when they noxiously and noisily sputtered down the public right away, upsetting many a man and beast.

In late May of 1902, there was an incident about 40 miles north of the city in upstate Nyack, NY. involving Mr. Wallace, his son Edward, the bright red Wallace automobile, and a horse and wagon. It made many of the papers in New York City and in Brooklyn where the Wallaces once resided. In Brooklyn this "editorial" ran on Memorial Day in the Eagle. It shows the general publics prevailing attitude about the automobile at this time. It's not a news story his deceased father in law, who was used to being toasted as he held his annual Memorial Day extravaganzas, would of approved of, that's for sure. It's also way over the top considering the trial was still a week away from starting.

AUTOMOBILES AND PEOPLE

The case of Edward Copeland Wallace, well known in Brooklyn from the long residence of his family here, is a sample of the sort of trouble which men who drive automobiles at railroad speed over highways are going to get into. Some of these reckless riders have been fortunate enough only to kill or injure children, so that they have escaped with merely showers of stones. Mr. Wallace was unlucky enough to injure a Republican leader in Rockland County, who knew what his rights were and the automobile owner will have to pay the piper. If the damages which the injured man collects, are heavy enough to be punitive, the defendant will find no sympathy outside of the men who own automobiles and are afraid of facing his punishment for similar recklessness. The injured man Mr. Lovatt, was driving a mettlesome horse which is not a crime, and in the country is not even an impudence. He saw Wallace's automobile coming at a great speed under the control of a boy of fourteen. Mr Lovatt signaled him to slow up, but the signal was unheeded. As the automobile passed the horse bolted and threw Mr. Lovatt and his wife out, injuring the latter seriously. There is no indication that Wallace stopped his automobile, then made any inquiries or expressed any regrets. Indeed there is indication that he tried to escape, and would of done so had not Mr. Lovatt telephoned his son far ahead on the road, who built a barricade on the turnpike which stopped the man. The son attacked Wallace on the machine, dragged him before a justice and had him held for trial. Beside this prosecution, Wallace will have to face suits for damages to the occupants of the carriage and injuries to the horse.

If this were the first case of the kind it would not be occasion for alarm or feel-

ing. But this sort of "accident" happens so frequently as to convey the impression that automobilists think they own the highways outside of the large cities and sometimes in them. They will find out presently that they do not own the right to run their machines at any rate of speed which endangers the safety of other people. They will face not only bridges, but missiles and ultimately shotguns, if neither their own sense nor the punishments inflicted by courts bring them to a serious consideration of the rights of other people of which they now show a cynical and reckless disregard. This country is not going to be turned into a vast racing track nor a slaughter house merely because a new vehicle has been invented.

A justice in Flushing recently held that a man was justified in throwing missiles into the face of an automobile driver when the latter endangered a child by his recklessness. This is not a new law, but merely an application of the fundamental doctrine of self defense to new conditions created by the automobile. It will be reaffirmed wherever the occasion arises ,because it both common law and common sense. The matter will become of even greater consequence than it is now., if as Mr. Edison announces he has so perfected and cheapened the storage battery that automobiles will be placed in the reach of every man who has been able to own a horse and buggy. This may be merely an Edison dream or it may be true. Many electricians have been working on the problem for a long time and it is one of the difficulties whose ultimate solution is confidently expected. When that time comes the preponderance of automobiles near cities will make over the laws of the road to some extent in their favor. But no law will ever take away the right of a man to walk or ride or drive a horse on any public highway. So long as that right remains people who run powerful engines of destruction in public thoroughfares will be forced to regulate their speed with regard to the safety of others, rather than with an eye single to their own pleasure. It is to be hoped that Mr. Lovatt, who is a man of wealth and position, will not attempt a settlement out of court of this case. He ought to insist on the last ounce of punishment and all the incidental publicity which the law provides for the sake of the many obscure persons injured who have neither the means nor the influence to take the men who run into them into court.

Some mighty strong opinions there and some interesting insights into early thoughts on the automobile, but could they have not waited, at least till the trial started? Also if these were the sentiments of the hometown paper of the defendant, one wonders what was being said closer to the scene of the crime? Could a lawyer today get it moved on the basis of pre trial publicity. The New York Times reported on the trial the following week

NEW YORK AUTOMOBILIST ON TRIAL IN NYACK

June 7 - The trial of Edward Copeland Wallace of New York, who while speeding through Rockland County with his automobile last week, frightened the horse of Edward G. Lovatt, a lawyer of Spring Valley and caused serious injury to Mr. Lovatt and his wife, was begun before Justice Charles H. Fisher in Nyack today.

Mr. Lovatt limped painfully when he appeared as the principal witness. His wife who has a broken arm and many painful bruises, was unable to leave her

house. Mr. Lovatt has his interests looked after by Congressman A. S. Tompkins.

Mr. Wallace who arrived in his automobile was accompanied by his young son. and C. N. Bovee of New York is his lawyer. As soon as Mr. Wallace arrived in court he was served with papers in a suit brought by Mrs. Lovatt for $25,000 damages. Mr. Wallace did not appear to be surprised.

Mr. Lovatt testified that on the afternoon of May 29, with a horse and buggy accompanied by his wife, he left his residence at Spring Valley to drive to Nyack, where his daughter and son in law live. While driving up a long hill about a mile west of this town, he sighted an automobile, he said coming over a hill and rushing at a rapid rate of speed down toward him. As the auto approached he saw his danger and rising to his feet in the wagon, he held the reigns in his left hand and waved his right hand above his head, at the same time shouting to the people in the automobile to stop.

No attention was paid to his cry, he said and he arose again, waved his hand and shouted "For God's sake, stop!" That, said Mr. Lovatt, did not have any effect and he cried "Please stop." but the automobile hurried on. Mr, Lovatt said that the horse started to run up an embankment at the side of the road, that the wagon was overturned, and that he said his wife was thrown out. Mr. Lovatt testified that the automobile was running at the rate of fully thirty miles an hour, and that it did not slacken it's speed, but sped on. The automobile was stopped at Spring Valley. David Summer a grocer of Central Nyack and his wife, who live near the scene of the accident, corroborated the testimony of Mr. Lovatt regarding his waving a hand and crying to the automobilists to stop. The defense is to be heard two weeks from today.

I take it it wasn't a jury trial, as two weeks seems to be a long time between sides. Again the former Wallace hometown paper some 50 miles away, took a hard line in reporting the goings on. CROWD JEERS E. C. WALLACE was the headline in the Eagle on June 7th 1902—along with the same facts of the case that were in the Times The Eagle added some color:

"Ever since the accident the feeling against Mr. Wallace has been growing in intensity This feeling found expression today during the trial which was held at the local clubhouse. On the way to the trial Mr. Wallace was hooted and jeered as he passed through the streets. In the courthouse there was evidence of marked hostility, which broke forth in exclamations of anger at all points where Mr. Wallace's part in the accident were brought out. It was clear that all present wished to see Mr. Wallace punished. After the morning session of the trial the throng of townspeople, who had crowded the room used for the trial to suffocation, filed out and lined up along the walk that leads to the street. As Mr. Wallace passed down this walk he was hooted and jeered and insulting epithets were hurled at him from all sides.

The principal witness against Wallace was David Sommers, who saw the accident. He swore the automobile was going at the rate of least thirty miles an hour at the time Lovatt's horse was frightened. When this testimony was brought out everyone cheered wildly. Somers said he knew on good authority that Mr. Wallace's automobile had been sent on trials of sixty miles an hour.

The article then goes on for several paragraphs to present the facts of the case as presented by the plaintiff's attorney and states that Mr. Wallace was "speeding through Nyack with his fourteen year old son on his way with his son to his home in Tuxedo, a very fashionable resort area for High Society. It also does not state who was driving—*It is alleged that even after he had seen the accident, Mr. Wallace did not slacken his speed, but continued on his way. The accident occurred on the Nyack Turnpike just outside the village. The farmers who live along this road have provided themselves with double-barreled shotguns,which they threaten to turn on to automobilists if the occasion arises. They say they will try to stop the automobiles by puncturing the tires. The County Board of Supervisors will meet on Monday and it is believed will sanction this course.*

So much for Law & Order and responsible journalism! The article then goes on for several paragraphs giving extensive and totally irrelevant background information on the entire Knapp family and the Wallaces, stating he is a wealthy manufacturer, where he works, but it mainly focuses on the Knapps, including the deceased Joseph, Phoebes music, the Wallace wedding , descriptions of the Knapp mansion, where Phoebe lives currently, her son Joseph P. Knapp etc. It does not do the same for Mr. Lovatt . I have to wonder did the fact that the Knapps moved from Brooklyn to Manhattan weigh in with the editors at the Eagle?

When the trial resumed two weeks later, the Eagle appears silent but the NY Times said:

TWO VERSIONS OF ACCIDENT
E. C. Wallace Denies that His Machine Was Speeding at Nyack June 21. - "The automobile was going eight miles an hour and did stop." testified Edward Copeland Wallace of New York before Justice Fisher in Nyack today—The defense was heard today and Mr. Wallace and his son were the principal witnesses. They agreed in their testimony that the machine was stopped as soon as Mr. Lovatt was seen waving his hand, and this testimony was in direct contradiction of that given by witnesses for the prosecution two weeks ago, who swore that the automobile was going thirty miles an hour and did not stop. Counsel will argue the case next Saturday.

Once again the Eagle appears to be silent on the trials conclusion, but the NY Times reported:

AUTOMOBILE OWNER FINED *Edward C. Wallace of New York Adjudged Guilty of Running His Machine Too Fast June 28- Justice Fisher in Nyack today decided against Edward Copeland Wallace of New York in the suit against him for violation of the law governing the running of automobiles—Justice Fisher adjudged Mr. Wallace guilty as charged and fined him $25.00. Mr. Wallace paid the fine out of the $200.00 which he had deposited as bail for his attendance. It is said he will appeal—Mr. E. T. Lovatt will press his suit for $25,000.00 damages instituted against Mr. Wallace in the Rockland County Supreme Court.*

And with that Edward Copeland, master Edward Knapp Wallace and C. N.

Bovee their attorney, got in their machine and probably drove very carefully out of town back to Manhattan. The Wallaces would not drive through Nyack on their way to Tuxedo for some time, if perhaps ever again, as they rented out their summer cottage "Tanglewood" and sailed for Europe for the season. They would have to return to Nyack however, for a civil trial scheduled for November.

A more positive spin on the delights of happy motoring was reported in The Brooklyn Eagle on July 27, 1902 when it noted *"Mr. Joseph P. Knapp of Manhattan, a member of The Automobile Club of America, took lunch at the Garden City Hotel during the early part of the week. Mr. Knapp was making a tour of Long Island by automobile and expressed himself as delighted with the manifold beauties of the Island."* This could well be the visit to the Garden City area that convinced J. P. Knapp to buy a home there or it could of been the golfing. In the early 1900's he owned a "farm" in Sands Point (Great Gatsby land) located near the Gould, Morgan and Guggenheim estates, which is considered part of Garden City. Knapp was a member of the Garden City and Metropolitan Golf Clubs during this era and his son Joe went to St. Paul's a prep school there.

Legal problems large and small nipped at J. P. Knapp too during the first decade of the Twentieth Century. Knowing his lifelong penchant for privacy, I'm sure some of them never made the papers, but this one did in early 1902 and is a bit of a puzzle to me. The headline read: **"WOULD BE SWINDLER FOILED. JAN 4 — PUZZLING ELEMENTS ENTER IN AN ATTEMPT TO DEFRAUD MRS. J. P. KNAPP, OF THE HOTEL MARIE ANTOINETTE AT BROADWAY AND SIXTY SIXTH STREET."** The first thing that puzzled me right off the bat was What is Sylvia doing living in a hotel in 1902? Her home is just a few short blocks away. It goes on: *"out of $50 for which Frederick Belleck of 378 Second Avenue who says he is the son of a master plumber, is held pending further examination in West Side Court.*

Mrs. Knapp with her husband, who is President of the American Lithographic Co. at Fourth and Nineteenth St., recently attended an evening performance at Weber & Fields[1] On their way home in a carriage Mrs. Knapp dropped a chain of diamonds and pearls valued at $1,200. It was found by George Dickerson a broker of 122 East Thirty fourth street, who happened to be in the next fare. Mr. Knapp offered a $100 reward for it's recovery in an advertisement printed Monday, and the same day received the jewel from Mr. Dickerson who refused the reward. Both regarded the incident as closed until on New Years Day Belleck called on Mrs. Knapp at her home and presented a letter written on Waldorf - Astoria paper and signed with Mr. Dickerson's name, which stated that the bearer was a worthy young man from a respectable family, but in very poor circumstances, and that if Mrs. Knapp would care to give him one half of the reward which she had offered for the recovery of her gems she might do so. She became suspicious and told Belleck to come back the next day.

In the meantime she communicated with Mr. Dickerson who had no knowledge of the note, and so when the young man kept the appointment, he walked into the arms of Detective Fitsgibbon of the West Sixty eighth Street Station. Belleck said

---

1 Weber & Fields were headline comics and burlesque performers of that era with their own Music Hall on Broadway ... The show the Knapps attended was called "The Hoity-Toity"

he received the letter from a man whose name he did not know, but whom he had met casually, who simply asked him to deliver the note and get a reply.

Mrs. Knapp and Mr. Dickerson appeared in court yesterday and said they had no idea of how any knowledge of the loss and recovery of the jewel could of reached beyond their intimate friends. Magistrate Meade adjourned the case to give detectives a chance to look up Belleck's antecedents and see if he could point out to them the mysterious man to whom he says he was to give the money.

I TRIED TO FOLLOW UP ON THIS STORY, BUT WAS NEVER ABLE TO FIND another thing in print. It must of been an inside job though from an "intimate friend" The question of what Mrs. Knapp was doing "living at the Hotel Antoinette" at that time initialy puzzled me, until I found years later that they were seperated for quite some time before their divorce? She eventually would move back to 322 W 72nd breifly and JP would move out. I never found any reward printed in the New York Times, but it could of been printed in other papers and certainly on an unlimited amount of handbills. I also have often thought about how many of the Knapps may of encountered con men or women in their life and always thought that might of been why Knapp heirs were so skeptical about my intentions when I encountered them in 2001. But I have always slept well, knowing I never wanted anything from any of them, other than to view photographs of the Mastic Beach mansion and the folks who lived and worked there, providing of course they even had any. That too unfortunately, I would never be able to find out the answer to.

A far bigger problem, was dropped on J. P. in July of 1902, when Benjamin Hilton, a minor stockholder of American Lithographic Company, instituted an action to dissolve the company ,charging that it was insolvent. In his application that was made to the Attorney General, Hilton asserted that American Litho has capital of $3,783,000 and that much money has been wasted in experimenting. His petition alleged that the company lost $194,914 in 1900 and $155,789 in 1901 in the publication of the magazine Truth and that another large loss was sustained by publishing the Recorder. It also stated that president Knapp receives a salary of $22,500 a year and the treasurer Ettlinger $15,000 with liabilities totaling $3,093,339 the petition said it had deficit of $580,842.

Louis Marshall of the firm Gugenheimer, Untermeyer & Marshall, who represented the majority of stockholders blasted back "Mr. Hilton's allegations were made entirely on belief and hearsay. He did not advance any solid facts and figures to uphold his statements. Auditors reports and volumes of facts and figures which I advanced show his charges to be ill-founded" Marshall then said the assets of ALCO, included modern machinery, valuable patents destined to revolutionize lithographing outside and above the stock amount to $2,600,000 and that the company was paid up in full on the interest on it's indebted stock. He further added that sales for 1901 amounted to $2,300,000 and projected it will amount to $400,000 more. Wages paid last year amounted to $700,000. The company owns real estate in New York City and Buffalo, which is increasing in value. The headquarters building on 4th avenue and 19th street alone, gives them an income of $48,000 per annum with a 57 year lease. They have 150 patents covering new methods of operation which will enable them to enter larger fields of work and therefore tend to increase their earnings. No objection to, has ever been made to the salaries of the officers of the company, by the Directors. Their salaries have steadily increased over the past ten years. No man in the company receives a greater salary than he would receive a commission, were he paid on that basis.

Mr. Hilton last October bought fifty shares of the 26,000. His affidavit now is made out in favor of George W. Donaldson, the ex vice president and director who was forced to resign. Mr. Donaldson is now in Europe. The men in charge represent $2,300,000 of the $2,600,000 in common stock and $1,800,000 of $2,500,000 debenture. The loss on Truth, which was counted out, was greatly exaggerated by Mr. Hilton. In fact that publication will realize a profit which will cover all indebtedness. The debt of The Recorder was also counted out. That paper failed about eight years ago and this company was organized in 1896 so that it is not held for that debt."

Louis Marshall seemed to certainly have a lot more ammo and facts at his disposal than Hilton did, but the truth is, he played a little fast and loose with a few of them. The Recorder went belly up in 1896 and American Litho which was initially organized in 1892, re-organized in 1896, following the Recorder closing up. Marshall did clarify that fact though a few days later. He also stated that among other items regarding executive salaries that Mr. Knapp had made valuable inventions (actually he bought the patents) which he turned over to corporation without further compensation. But Marshall's "snake in the bag" probably occurred when he presented facts to the Attorney General that George Donaldson, who was now residing in England, was forced to resign from the company two years prior and ever since has been an avowed enemy of American Lithographic. Donaldson had assigned 50 of his shares to Hilton for the sole purpose of qualifying him to take this action. The attorney general reserved judgement and gave both sides two additional weeks to present further evidence. On September 5th, 1902, he ruled in favor of American Lithographic.

Not long after that Edward C, Antoinette K, and their teenage son Edward K. Wallace would board the White Star Liner "Oceanic" for their trip back to the states and day in court, reaching New York on Sept 18th which at 5 days and 16 hours broke trans Atlantic records. A notable passenger on that trip was J. Bruce Ismay, head of the White Star Line, who would become somewhat notorious for his seemingly cowardly behavior, sneaking aboard a lifeboat dressed as a woman as the Titanic sunk. Ismay had come to NY to meet with J. P. Morgan, probably to get some financing to build the Olympic & Titanic. Morgan, who just by going to the pier to meet the Oceanic, aroused much curiosity of the press. In November again, the Eagle printed a rather long rambling article about The Wallace - Lovatt case, held 50 some miles away from Brooklyn and with no current Brooklynites involved, demonstrating to me that the press following the lives of the wealthy is far from a recent phenomena. Of the sixth paragraphs only two actually reported on the case itself and the rest was Knapp family history. The headline of the story read :

HORSELESS VEHICLE TRUSTED

Millionaire Takes Wife and Son To Court in It - He's a Son-in-Law of Late Joseph F. Knapp

Nov 14 -Edward C. Wallace succeeded yesterday in closing up the complications that resulted from a runaway accident in West Nyack on May 29, which was said to have been caused by his automobile. Mr. Wallace was first summoned to police court on the allegation of carelessness. This charge did not hold. [APPARENTLY THE EAGLE DIDN'T READ THE TIMES STORY ON THE WALLACE BEING FOUND GUILTY AND FINED $25 OR I NEVER SAW IT PRINTED ANYPLACE IF WALLACE GOT THAT JUDGEMENT OVERTURNED?] *Then suits were brought against him by the Lovatt family of West Nyack who were in the vehicle whose horse the automobile was charged with scaring. The first of these to come to trial was that of Mrs Sarah T. Lovatt who had an arm hurt. She was demanding $20,000.*

Justice Maddox was on the bench when the case came on at Nyack yesterday. The plaintiffs side was partially presented before recess. During lunch hour the lawyers got the principals together and a compromise was effected. Mr. Wallace agreed to pay $8,750.00 on the condition that all other suits should be withdrawn and the case closed. This was agreed to. Mr Wallace as if to indicate his faith in the accused automobile, took his wife and son in that vehicle to the court room and returned in it, with them to New York.

One wonders how you could accuse the automobile itself of the crime and I wonder if Edward took Antoinette along thinking she might keep the jeerers at bay? The article then goes on for four paragraphs of Knapp-Wallace history and their current activities, residences, etc. It also notes that the Knapp Wallace wedding was one of the biggest social events in the history of Brooklyn.

Two years later and many miles away in a courtroom in Colorado, a seemingly non related divorce case was heard involving an insurance executive and his wife. It might not of had a Knapp connection then, but it would not be long before it did.

CHAPTER

20

Shades of Evening Envelope Us
& I Withdraw

Although her children were experiencing some of lives ups and downs, that were not immune to economic insulation in the first decade of the twentieth century, Phoebe Knapp seemed to be having a swell time, at least during the first half of it. She may of been entertaining at her Savoy hotel suite, even more frequently and in bigger numbers (upwards of 1500 persons at a time) than she had at the Knapp Mansion.

Seven years had past since Phoebe left her former Brooklyn palace, when it was reported in early December of 1900 as destined to become a "high class" vaudeville theatre. However by December 14th, Thomas Adams, the chewing gum manufacturer who owned it, reported that the deal between himself and a Mr. Huber of the Museum of 14th St in NYC had fell through. "Does Your Chewing Gum Loose It's Flavor On The Bedpost Overnight?" Adams then revealed his new plans to enlarge the building further, adding more studios, bachelor apartments and offices, keeping William Pitt Rivers the "Dancing Master" as the manager of it. I can only wonder which plan was more distasteful to Phoebe Knapp.

At the Savoy on Central Park South and 5th Avenue, it was reported Phoebe entertained both William McKinley and Theodore Roosevelt and seemed on her way to hosting as many US presidents and future presidents there, as she had hosted with her late husband back in Brooklyn. She supported, belonged and was an officer in many cultural, civic and religious organizations like The Kings Daughters. The one she seemed to be most remembered for, at least in print, was the International Sunshine Society. It was an organization founded by Cynthia Alden in 1896. Cynthia was a member of the editorial staff of the New York Recorder. The Sunshine Society was incorporated on Phoebe's birthday March 8, 1900. With over 250,000 members, it was the largest club in the United States at the time with international chapters too. Phoebe was the president of the New York Chapter. The main mission of the club was quite simple " To incite it's members to the performance of kind and helpful deeds, and to thus bring the sunshine of happiness into the greatest possible number of hearts and homes" In short it may of been thought of as Phoebe being on the same mission her mother was on, just far less mystical and abstract and perhaps somewhat ironically, by her secular practical deeds, able to reach out and touch even more mortal souls? Using the one million readers per month of yet another loose Knapp connection, editor Edward Bok's *Ladies Home Journal* to report on the activities of the society and the good deeds of its members, she may of also inadvertently planted some seeds in her sons mind. Seeds that would lead him to grow and expand his publishing empire over the next 4 decades. She also wrote the music for "Scatter Sunshine" the Society's theme song. The Sunshine Society was all so positive as the name itself implies and she must of felt great helping to scatter sunshine into lives, where many times it seemed only misfortune had cast dark shadows.

"Uncle Dan" was an early member of the Sunshine Society and the founder of Colorado branch. He was bee keeper and well up in his seventh decade of life when in 1899 he paid his dues to the society by sending them 24 combs of honey to distribute. When Phoebe became aware that "Uncle Dan" had become an invalid and was still tending to his bees, she sent him the most comfortable wheel chair obtainable at that time. This was in the summer of 1900, just before she took off for Europe and while over there, sent him a letter that might be in the Guinness book of records, if such a record was ever even recorded. The letter was reported about by the Eagle on August 11, 1900. I for one would love to find out if it still exists someplace.

A UNIQUE LETTER - *Illustrated Account of a Trip by Mrs. Joseph Knapp*

A letter which is undoubtedly one of the most unique and interesting ever received from a foreign land, arrived at No. 96 Fifth avenue, Manhattan, the headquarters of International Sunshine Society, a few days ago. The letter is six and a half yards long by actual measurement. It is written on ordinary letter sheets pasted together. It came from Mrs. Joseph Knapp, New York State President of the society and is addressed to "Uncle Dan" of Evans, Colorado, in care of the Sunshine Society.

The letter is a cleverly written description of all that its writer has seen since she left this country for her trip abroad. Not only is every place accurately described, but pasted irregularly all through it are prints and photographic views illustrating the places described. The letter contains at least a hundred of these illustrations. It also has several portraits, one of Mrs. Alden, the society's president general and one of Mrs. Knapp herself.

In one place there is a collection of small silk flags representing the national flag of every country visited and described. There is a souvenir of the steamship *Oceanic* in which Mrs. Knapp crossed the ocean and another of the Paris Exposition. The letter was sent from Paris and the postage on it was the equivalent of $1.50 in American money.

The letter will be forwarded to Uncle Dan very soon and it is likely that it will likely go the rounds of a large circle of Sunshine friends.

In The Good Old Summertime

As previously mentioned,the Knapps first came to the quaint yet somewhat high society summer community of Bellport, as early as 1894. It may of been the lower profile of Bellport, as say compared to places like Newport that drew the J. P. Knapp there and in keeping with what seemed to be his lifelong desire to remain low key. Not that the Knapps didn't also visit and vacation at probably every well known eastern seaboard society summer colony from Newport to Miami. How they spent as much time traveling and vacationing, could be a tribute to what had to be some very wise business decisions by J. P. in regards to whom he left minding his increasingly varied and growing "stores"

By the mid 1900s, the Knapps were Bellport regulars, at least for part of the season and as I stated previously even in the off season. J.P. Knapp by 1900 was considered one of the best "wing shots" in the country, certified as America's amateur billiard champion, and now in the hunt to become one it's amateur golf champions too. To do that though required him to travel much further and wider distances from New York, though it seemed he was almost always on the links at Bellport, Southampton, Islip and Garden City. He would also frequently turn up in press reports as scoring well on the courses at Lakewood, NJ, Hot Springs, Va, Pinewoods, NC. and Palm Beach, Fla. including being the Florida state champion. I'm sure all this golfing required him to be away from home for large chunks of time, just owing to travel time required alone. I'm also sure his family couldn't be with him all the time (school etc,) and lots of separation can lead to marital problems.

In 1904 the New York Times ran this small item of the charms of Bellport in the where to summer for the season suggestions.

WHAT BELLPORT OFFERS - *Special to the New York Times July 24,1904*

Yachting is ranking precedent above all other outdoor sports at this resort, among the clever handlers of yachts being many young women. Among some of the yachtsmen are J. P. Knapp, R. G. Rowley, A. B. Boyd, and George Droste. The links of the Bellport Golf Club continue to be crowded on Saturday afternoons __ The idea of uniting the golf and yachting clubs and bringing them under a country club is finding favor here. At the Goldwaithe House this week there has been a bewildering succession of dances, dinners and card parties. Tuesday evenings have been reserved for dances by the little folk.

Note : J. P. was of one of the movers and shakers in combining the Bellport Yacht Club with the golf club he helped found in 1899. Prior to constructing the course at Bellport, it was reported in the Brooklyn Eagle that J. P. Knapp of Bellport was a "fiend for golf" traveling daily from Bellport to Oakdale to play the game. Oakdale is about 13 miles west of Bellport and even with his fast horses, J. P. would have to ride through 5 villages including about two miles of Patchogue to get there. In short, quite a daily 26 mile roundtrip. Two of the dancing "little folk" were Claire, who was 14 in '04 and her 12 year old kid brother Dodi. Both probably learned to sail at Bellport. By 1908-09 Claire was racing her "Lady Claire," a 26 foot cat boat at Bellport and other fashionable South Shore resorts.

According to all other biographies, Joseph Palmer and Sylvia Theresa Knapp got divorced in 1904. The first detail I have ever found about it, was in a story the Washington Post ran on Sylvia's fashion setting fashion trends in NYC in 1913. That article states the Knapp divorce took place in Georgia. That seemed an odd place for a divorce for the wealthy back then. My main curiosity was the reason stated, though I'm fully cognizant the stated reasons for divorces can be far from the truth. The fact is they did divorce, but news items show they stayed in touch with each other, at least while the children were still minors. J. P. was stated by the Patchogue Advance, as seen driving around in Bellport in a new automobile in 1906. Sylvia and Claire and occasionally Dodi Knapp were known to have lived in Bellport seasonally as late as 1912. It would be years later and only through the digital revolution, that I was able to find some definite details on the Knapp divorce.

In May of 1903 The Brooklyn Eagle reported that Sylvia had moved to Sioux Falls, South Dakota for the express purpose of obtaining a divorce. It turns out that Sioux Falls was the predecessor to Reno, Nevada for such actions Both Sylvia and J. P. refused to comment on it to the press, and the Eagle reported when they contacted J. P. at his office he said, "You must excuse me from discussing the matter, and I would much rather the papers would say nothing about it." A little over a year later this seemingly unrelated item appeared in the NY Times:

MRS. A. G. McILWAINE DIVORCED - *Will Have Custody of Child and Annual Allowance of $5,000 Colorado Springs, Colo June 29 - Mrs. Elizabeth L. McIlwaine formerly of New York, secured a divorce from Archibald G. McIlwaine, a prominent insurance man of that city, in the District Court this afternoon. In addition Mrs. McIlwaine secured an order for heavy alimony for the remainder of her life and custody of their child Archibald, together with sufficient money to rear it (sic) properly. Desertion was the ground for divorce. They were married in New York in January 1895 and lived together until 1903 when the defendant ceased to live with her.*

The order of the court called for divorce, a permanent alimony of $1,300 with $5,000 yearly allowance and $83.34 monthly allowance for the child. In case plaintiff remarries the custody of the child passes to the husband and the allowance is cut off. The child cannot be taken outside the limits of the United States without written consent of both parties.

Elizabeth Laing McIlwaine, never really lived in Colorado, other than the usual time western states require to obtain a divorce back then. She was born in New Jersey, either about 1863 or 1871 (she changes her age on many official documents) and lived much of her life based in New York City, which was where her son Archibald was born on November 20, 1895. One of New York area places the newly divorced Mrs. McIlwaine did live at for eighteen summers, starting in 1904, was Southampton, Long Island. The Hamptons would be my best guess as to where she may of met Joseph Palmer Knapp, as he played a lot of golf out there. Elizabeth would become the second Mrs. Joseph Palmer Knapp on October 16, 1905 in what I am sure had to be a very private affair. They were married by judge H. P. Bailey, far from the madding crowds of NY City, in Sioux Falls, South Dakota. Oddly, the Eagle reported on the reasons for J. P.'s now two year old divorce from Sylvia in his new marriage story. They said it was because Sylvia took up Christian Science and J. P. offered her no sympathy. When the newly weds returned to New York in 1906, they first took an apartment at the Beaux Arts, before moving into the The Knickerbocker, the city's first co-op just a few blocks north of the Met Life company at 247 5th Avenue. The Knapps remained at 247 until the early 1920s.

Other endings and beginnings
One effect that having to fold the Recorder, had on J. P. Knapp was, that although he called himself "a printer first" he would never again be content to be anything but a publishing - printer. By 1904, Truth magazine, in spite of all the variations of format, personnel changes and money invested, was breathing it's last. He folded it for good in 1905. In '04 Knapp started Associated Sunday Magazine, which was the first syndicated Sunday News Magazine available to major newspapers through out the country. American Lithographic would print the same content, changing only the name of the newspaper at the top of the cover. Associated Sunday Magazine would continue until WWI when extreme paper shortages made it totally economically impractical to print. Associated Sunday Magazine was the forerunner of "This Week" also from Knapp's presses and Parade Sunday news magazines.

In 1906, an old time Kentucky printer named John S. Crowell, had been producing two monthly magazines out of his plant in Springfield, Ohio. Both titles "Farm and Fireside" and "Woman's Home Companion" were self explanatory. Crowell became overwhelmed by his own success and when circulation reached a half million copies per month, decided the only solution to keeping his health was to sell the business. Along came Joseph P. Knapp with $750,000 and he now had himself a printing plant in the middle of the country and two magazines to get out. What overwhelmed the elder Mr. Crowell only whetted 42 year old Knapp's appetite to expand it. Before very long he was looking for more titles to round out his fresh approach at becoming a major periodical publisher.

Throughout this study of the Knapps, I have relied heavily on their interaction with others to learn more about them. To do so led me to read as many books as I could find, to gather a snippet here and there on any and all of them and in turn also learn something new. Probably the greatest amount of biographical material available in print on any of the Knapps, is that which was generated by Phoebe's relationship with hymn writer/poet Fanny Crosby. As I discussed briefly in Chapter 20, I discovered things about Phoebe Knapp in the previously mentioned book *Her Heart Can See—The Life & Hymns of Fanny Crosby*, by Edith Blumhofer published in 2005 by Wm B. Erdmans Co.

Besides the brief musical critique from what amounted to some people who were in competition with her to sell sheet music & hymnals, there are some glimpses into Phoebe's somewhat enigmatic personality, that reveal the interesting and sometimes bizarre eccentricity that makes all of us what we truly are—uniquely human—nothing more, nothing less. Sometimes that personality can be enhanced or diminished by one's station in life, but my main interest in studying the Knapp family has always been what made them tick, not how many mansions they had. I also have read Bernard Ruffin's bio of Crosby simply titled Fanny Crosby and published by United Church Press 1976 in which this letter appears, written by Phoebe to Carrie Ryder also spelled Rider, who was Fanny's sister and caregiver in Connecticut. At the time Fanny was in NY city at the Savoy, working with Phoebe and Carrie simply wanted to know when her sister might be coming back home:

Dear Mrs Ryder:
I am taking the best care of our dear Fanny – whom we both love. Each time that she comes to me I am so satisfied (and as never before)–that someone in Bridgeport cares for the personal interest of the dear one–and I am happy indeed!
*I cannot possibly let her go home until Friday next in the afternoon–just now I need her and she is having a good time. Sincerely hoping that you are well, Fanny sends lots of love and says that for just once she is going to try and commence to be good. That is going to be hard work as we all know. For she has been keeping bad company of late and I hear nothing but Mr. Dooly and upon mention of his name she begins a wild dance–and I, awe stricken, say **"Shades of night envelope us"** and withdraw.*
Your friend,
Mrs. J. F. Knapp

You got to love the colorful language of the 19th century. I for one miss it. What information follows here regarding Phoebe and Fanny is gleaned mainly from the two aforementioned books blended in with my irreverence. I am however respectfully in the debt of both religious scholars Dr. Blumhofer and Mr. Ruffin.

There were probably no two songwriters further apart in economic status and life's circumstances than Phoebe Palmer Knapp and Frances Jane Crosby. That they collaborated to create a work like "Blessed Assurance" which has endured world wide over a century, past their days of popularity, says much of the creation itself and the unique talents both women had. It seems though that the differences, caused by their life's economic circumstances of which neither really had that much control over, allowed me to gain some insight about Phoebe Palmer Knapp that none of her many other activities would. Most of these revelations seem to occur around the idea of Phoebe wanting to be a major benefactor of Miss Fanny's welfare and well being. Her efforts would be met often with strong opposition from Fanny's music publisher Bigelow & Main and some of Fanny's other wealthy collaborators, like Ira D. Sankey and the other millionaire co writer William H. Doane. You may recall it was in the Doane papers that the rather strong statement is found: "Many people did not like Phoebe Knapp"

In 1858, Fanny Crosby married blind songwriter Alexander Van Alstine, who she first met at the New York Institution for The Blind that she attended in the 1830s. "Miss Fanny" and "Van" wrote several songs for Phoebe's "Notes Of Joy" hymnal published in 1869. Her marriage and daily life was very different from Phoebe Knapp's. Fanny and Van moved very frequently and lived separately since the 1880s for reasons Fanny kept very private. In 1902, Fanny was living in Bridgeport, CT and was at Baptist William Doane's Watch Hill, Rhode Island estate working with him, when Doane received a telegram from his publisher Bigelow & Main that Van had passed away in New York from a massive stroke. At first he did not want to tell Fanny, as he was concerned for her health and well being, but realized she of all people had the right to know. When he did tell her, she excused herself, went to her room and emerged several hours later with a new lyric. Titled "I Am Satisfied," a 4 verse text of deep praise of the Lord, it is only in the third verse that it possibly reveals her thoughts on her life with Van: *"And tho' at times, the things I ask, In love are oft denied, I know He gives me what is best, And I am satisfied.*

Because he felt it might be too much of a strain on the frail 82 year old, Doane and other friends did talk her out of going to New York for a funeral. Bigelow & Main arranged for Van's body to be placed in a vault until some final arrangements could be made. Fanny had always wanted to be buried side by side with Van, but her own family, for reasons not disclosed, did not want that either. Finally after a few weeks of limbo, Phoebe stepped in took full control. She paid for Van's burial in an unmarked grave at Mt. Olivet cemetery in Queens, near the home where Fanny and Van first lived together when they married. This probably further annoyed other friends of Fanny. Phoebe's reasons for not marking the grave have never been explained (certainly not financial). But they were certainly pointed out by others who had said repeatedly that Phoebe Knapp was far too meddlesome in Miss Fanny's affairs. That said, at least Alexander van Alstine was finally laid in a grave, though Mt. Olivet was far away from any convenient transportation for Fanny to visit the gravesite. In spite of all these hurdles, Fanny managed to visit it anyway and only once said of their relationship "He had his faults—and so I have mine." Born long before most of her collaborators and concerned friends, Fanny would also out live most all of them passing away in 1915 at the age of 95.

The really big brouhaha, that probably caused Fanny Crosby more pain than the fight her friends and family had over what to do about Vans death, was over the welfare of Fanny herself. Phoebe Knapp had always thought that Bigelow & Main, did not treat Fanny fairly in regards to royalty payments. Bigelow & Main took much offense at Phoebe's public assertions. However Fanny herself also refused Knapp's attempts to copyright their compositions jointly and even though Phoebe gave Fanny all of the money both would earn from their songs, along with a great deal more too, Fanny gave much of that money away, content to live a very simple life. Phoebe thought that because of Fanny's world wide acclaim, she was entitled to a much better domestic situation than she had. Many times after Phoebe became a widow, she asked Fanny to move in with her. Fanny however preferred her independence and enjoyed the company of other collaborators too, that possibly didn't care for Phoebe Knapp and vice versa. Speaking as one who has written with my share of co-writers in Nashville, I can well see Fanny's point and have experienced being in the middle of a similar type of friction.

Things really came to a head in the early 1900s when Will Carleton, one of

Fanny's newer friends found an ally with Phoebe Knapp. Carleton was a very popular poet of his era and lived in an affluent section of Brooklyn. He also served as president of the American Society of Authors founded in 1891 which was an advocacy group and sort of a foundation for the future American Society of Authors, Composers and Publishers, founded by Irving Berlin and known as ASCAP. Carleton had written a series of magazine articles about the life of Fanny Crosby and he and Knapp arranged a series of schemes to combine them into a book they felt would alert the public to what they had both felt and spoke about in public. Fanny's poverty in spite of her then world wide acclaim and poor financial treatment by Bigelow and Main.

Fanny agreed to allowing Carleton to compile her life stories into a book titled *Fanny Crosby's Life-Story by Herself*. She still was not interested in any money, but probably did not grasp what her publisher's reaction would be. They not only disapproved of Fanny allowing Carleton to do this, they also felt it would hurt their sales of a new collection of Crosby's poems titled "Bells Of Evening" that they now had promised to donate all royalties from to Fanny. Prior to this, Bigelow & Main never paid Fanny any royalties, just a straight salary.

Always frustrated by this arrangement, Phoebe felt based on Fanny's popularity and amount of money she generated for Bigelow and Main, that they should of also provided Fanny with a home and servants to run it. Phoebe now went into high gear and threw her tremendous energy (as a woman then of 64, it has been said by many that Phoebe seemed more like a 40 year old in both energy and appearance) and her influence to resolve this to her satisfaction.

She enlisted the help of Methodist Bishop Charles McCabe to launch a campaign to provide for Miss Fanny's needs. McCabe got Fanny's permission to raise a testimonial for her and by placing notices in religious publications invited the public at large to donate to the cause. McCabe's request published in mid 1904 carried the heading "Fanny Crosby In Need" stating that her hymns had never been copyrighted in her own name, but sold for small sums to publishers who have profited handsomely from it. Phoebe then arranged a note to be placed in Carleton's book that the sale of it would "add substantially to a fund intended for the comfort of this grand woman, who has been singing in such far reaching tones the praise of her God and her Christ for sixty years." The note promised that profits from the book would enable Fanny to "have a house of her own in which to pass the remainder of her days."

This Ain't My Story–This Ain't My Song

Letters started to come to Fanny's attention and she was understandably somewhat embarrassed by all fuss. If Fanny was embarrassed, Bigelow and Main was furious and took actions to put a halt to it. They contacted the Bishop and he complied to issue a retraction, stating that previous notices were based on mis information. They got Doane to ask Fanny to take legal action against Carleton to stop the sale of that book. She would not do that, but did issue a fairly lengthy statement to the religious press saying among other things that: she was in good health, and had a comfortable home, "wished to say that the book being sold to buy me a home" was never authorized by her to do so, and that through legal counsel, she has asked it not be advertised that way. Nor was it written by herself, but rather based on a series of articles about her first published four years ago and really only tolerated by her rather than consented to. It goes on further to state that the book was not an adequate biography and that her royalty payments have only amounted to $325.

"Furthermore I wish it known that Bigelow & Main, as publishers of my hymns, have dealt with me in a manner wholly satisfactory to myself. I regard them highly as among my truest and oldest friends and have considered them so for almost forty years."

In reading the entire statement or just what I have paraphrased here, I think I can assuredly state that if Fanny dictated it in those very words, then I'm the third writer on "Blessed Assurance." And if that wasn't enough blowback, Bigelow & Main also issued their own statement.

"We desire to state positively that Fanny Crosby does not need help, nor is she the object of charity which the article implies. She is receiving from us, and will continue to do so as long as she lives, a regular weekly salary amounting to the average amount which she received per week for hymns sold to us during her prime. In return for this we ask nothing of her except to be happy and live as long as she possibly can. We wish Fanny Crosby all the riches of this world (she is sure of those in the next) but please do not make her out as an object of charity—for she is not."

Although this controversy would eventually pass, before it did, Phoebe went up to Bridgeport to talk with Fanny under the premise of discussing hymns. She may have done that, but she also blew up at Fanny and that "blowing up caused Fanny to be put flat on her back." She followed that outburst, with two letters threatening heavy damages if Crosby sued her or Carleton. (Which I'm sure never entered Crosby's mind).

On the other side, Hubert Main wrote to Doane that Carleton was "trying to cut us out" and that Carleton and Knapp just wanted to "Take Over Fanny Crosby." Ira Sankey went as far as to say that Knapp & Carleton were ploys of Satan! Crosby didn't believe any of it and just felt they all wanted to do well by her, and remained on good terms with everyone. Will Carleton stopped advocating for Fanny, based on what he felt was Fanny's wishes, and of course Fanny and Phoebe stayed friends for life. Her affection for all at Bigelow & Main never waivered either and they continued to send her $8 a week. In February of 1904, Bigelow & Main planned a big 40th anniversary celebration of their relationship with Miss Fanny by holding a big reception at the 5th Avenue hotel. Again 84 year old Fanny stayed with Phoebe at the Savoy and ironically Phoebe financed the party, though wisely did not attend it.

Phoebe's problems with Fanny all seems so trivial, compared to a far more serious event that would effect the Knapp family in 1906. On the last Sunday of April that year, 18 year old Edward Knapp Wallace was riding his motorcycle on Jerome Ave. in the Bronx. According to a witness and classmate Caleb Bragg who was driving his touring car, Wallace passed him at a high rate of speed and was about 100 yards ahead of him when the motorcycle bucked and threw the rider over the handle bars. Edward landed on his head about about thirty feet from where the cycle continued to run on its side. Bragg and his passenger put the unconscious boy into their car and rushed him to Fordham hospital. It would later come out that Wallace and Bragg were racing each other. After about an hour doctors revived him briefly, just long enough for him to whisper his name and address. His father was summoned and a operation on his fractured skull was performed, with doctors predicting very little hope of any success. His family was at his bedside where Edward remained in a coma until he died on Thursday May 3rd. He was buried in the Knapp circle at Greenwood.

I am of the opinion that not only did Antoinette's son die that May day, but it also marked the beginning of the end of her marriage to Edward C. Wallace. Even long past the accepted period of mourning, very little was seen of her in the society circles the Wallaces frequented, nor do I find her hosting anything. It probably took a heavy toll on his grandmother Phoebe too, as her social activities seem to greatly diminish coinciding with her grandsons death.

On May 27th of 1908 this ad appeared in the Situations Wanted section of the New York Times Classified

Coachman : *Lady giving up horses wishes to secure a position for her coachman, who has served faithfully many years, is a careful driver, honest, sober, reliable in every particular. Mrs. J. F. Knapp Hotel Savoy*

The fact that the ad only appeared once, I trust good results were had. In early July, Phoebe went north to the Mansion House, a huge sprawling Victorian Hotel resort in Poland Springs, Maine. She was not there but a day or so when she succumbed to a massive stroke on Friday July 10, 1908. Her obituary that would appear in the New York Times the next day was quite brief and contained several errors re the names of her grown children.

PHOEBE PALMER KNAPP *widow of the late Joseph Fairchild Knapp once President of the Metropolitan Life Insurance Company, died at Poland Springs, Maine yesterday morning. The Knapps were well known in Brooklyn society at one time, and the family home was at Bedford Avenue and Ross Street. Mrs. Knapp leaves two children Mrs. William* [sic] *C. Wallace and Joseph F. Knapp Jr.* [sic]

Phoebe was buried at Greenwood of course, in the growing Knapp circle family plot, next to her husband Joseph and first born child Frances D., Also in the circle was her mother in law Antoinette Knapp Dominick, brother in law, William Timothy Knapp, grandson Edward Knapp Wallace , and day old infant, Frederick Edward Ballard

CHAPTER

21

The Knapps Lived Here, Too

"Joseph Knapp Jr. has a sure enough wireless apparatus. Edward Boynton is building an airship at the Wyandotte Garage."

—PATCHOGUE ADVANCE, SEPTEMBER 24, 1909

Those were the lead items in the twice weekly column that "W. F. G." an ace Bellport village reporter, had for that Friday's edition of the Patchogue Advance. "Gee" or "W. F." to his (or was it her?) friends, may of been touched with bit of Jules Verne's or H. G. Well's literary prophecy, just by listing those big story items adjacently. As you may recall way back in beginning of chapter 3, "The Seven Year Itch," the first two dots I connected in this Knapp story, were the wireless radio equipment and airplane parts, I discovered as a 6 year old, lying alongside of each other right in front of me in the hayloft of an abandoned barn in Mastic Beach in the 1950s. So just imagine my delight when a seemingly innocuous item like the one above, would appear right in front of me on a scratchy, faded page, as I slowly scrolled the Patchogue library micro-film screen reader a half a century later. It was a plethora of little one and two liners, that appeared in both local papers, like the Advance (which published it's first issue in 1871 and is still printing a weekly 136 years later) along with journalistic giants like the New York Times and Washington Post, that would cause me to say Eureka! more than once, if only silently, each time a snippet about the Knapps would appear. They are some of the real building blocks in which I have reconstructed where the Knapps lived, what they did and also left behind for me to ponder and have as much fun now as I think I had then, playing with the neat stuff they left in their barns.

So here are a few more little gems from The Patchogue Advance, The Brooklyn Eagle, New York Times and more, that have given me something to go on as I would learn about other places that the Knapps lived at, besides in that big place in my backyard.

THE JOYS OF BELLPORT

This pretty town is almost crowded with Brooklyn and New York people. In fact it is the most prosperous season we have ever had. The class of people summering here are of the sort calculated to benefit the town. Nearly all the cottagers have arrived. Senator Otis is at his cottage "Near The Bay" He is taking great comfort with his yacht The Climax which is a fast racer. Frank Otis his brother is showing off his fine horses to good advantage. He has several that are hard to beat. He is now at The Locusts. Joseph Knapp who is summering here takes his daily drives behind a team of elegant horses. J. B. Mott who drives a Tally- Ho is now entertaining several friends. He has the only private banquet hall in Bellport—Brooklyn Eagle, July 21, 1894

SPORTS IN FAVOR AT BELLPORT

Life at this charming resort has been gay during the past week. The principal attractions are now sailing and fishing and these are thoroughly enjoyed. Bellport prides itself upon the number of pretty yachts that dot it's harbor. The harbor is without exception the prettiest along the south side. Yachting is followed by everybody. Among those who own yachts are Captain Oscar Dole, The Edith S, General Varian, The J. A. King, Steven Van Rensellar, The Brandy & Soda, Doctor Mandeville the steam yacht Magnetcia, Joseph Knapp ,The Idler, Senator James Otis, The Climax, F. A. Otis, The No Name — Brooklyn Eagle, August 11, 1894

BUSY BELLPORT

a column by "W.F.G."

Joseph P. Knapp has been seen skimming around the village recently in a new automobile —Patchogue Advance, April 6, 1906

At the Sayville races last Saturday in the one design class, Miss Knapp's Lady Claire won first prize.—Patchogue Advance, July 1909

Mrs. Sylvia Knapp has opened her cottage for the Summer months _Lead item in Busy Bellport column_ Patchogue Advance April 2, 1910

Saturday's race at Babylon resulted in a victory for Mr. Meserole's one designer Miss Knapp's "Lady Claire" was second —Patchogue Advance, Sept 2, 1910

Miss Claire Knapp recently entertained a large company at a birthday celebration —Patchogue Advance, Nov 10, 1910 (This would've been her 21st birthday)

Mrs. Sylvia Knapp and Miss Claire Knapp have closed their cottage here for a few weeks. —*Patchogue Advance, Jan 14, 1910* (for a trip to Paris perhaps, as Sylvia did take at least one trip there, listing Bellport as her home address on the ship's passenger list.)

Guess not this time—back so soon? *The slush, mud. rain,wind, sleet and snow of last Saturday, did not deter Miss Rich and Miss Knapp from their daily horseback rides—Patchogue Advance, Feb 4, 1910*

Miss Knapp has some fine horses out on the roads these days.—Patchogue Advance, May 19, 1911

MINEOLA HORSE SHOW BRINGS OUT SOCIETY
Thomas Hitchcock's Stable Wins Chief Honors In First Days Judging Note: Hitchcock was a famous polo player.

The ideal weather yesterday served to make this first day's judging of the Mineola Horse Show which was held at the Fair Grounds, Mineola L.I., one of the greatest opening days in the history of the Long Island Association — In the harness horse class the entries proved the best of the afternoon and competition was exceedingly keen. Seven teams were driven to appropriate traps, with Miss Claire A. Knapp the only woman driver —NY Times, Sept 29, 1911

As I said in an earlier chapter, the Knapps, may have used one of the Bellport hotels like the Wyandotte, when they first summered in Bellport, but I'm sure they were living in a home there in the later 1900s. What was referred to as "cottage" among the wealthy in those days, could be considered a very large home today. As to where it was located, my best guess was ascertained by the 1910 Federal Census when Sylvia and Claire along with their household staff were enumerated between the J. B. Mott estate "Brook Farm" (The Gateway Playhouse today) on the north side of South Country Road and Major William Langley's huge estate known as Ol' Kentuck on the south side. Ol' Kentuck with it's landmark postcard windmill, was leveled around 1950 and became Bellport's first housing development. Claire Knapp owned several fine horses then including her prize winning Zulal purchased at an auction held at Durland's Riding Academy in New York City. Zulal would travel far and wide with Claire in horse shows all over on Long Island, Madison Square Garden, and the mid Atlantic states. When a passing locomotive spooked Zulal at a show in Long Branch, New Jersey in July of 1911, he threw Claire in the air off his back. She picked herself up, dusted her self off and got right back on him. Realizing had I known what I do now, when I was walking around in her empty Mastic Beach mansion, I would of looked her up out east. I regret knowing that I could of possibly actually met Claire Antoinette Knapp in person, even though I would of only been a young boy

"The Traitor" is a thrilling story of Reconstruction days, now furnished by the library. Now who will donate "The Clansman" by the same author?
—*Patchogue Advance, Jan 17, 1908*

Now this one is very interesting! Owing to who the "same author" was and from where this item may of generated itself into this particular newspaper. The Traitor, was written by Thomas Dixon of North Carolina, New York and Virginia. It was published in Garden City in 1907. The Traitor was advertised as the concluding trilogy to Dixon's former novels, "The Leopard's Spots," (1902) and his really big one, 1905's "The Clansman." "The Clansmen" which was also produced as a stage play, would propel Dixon into worldwide notoriety, when it was transformed into the historic film "Birth Of A Nation" in 1915 by D. W. Griffith.

Now this little item would of certainly passed me by without a second thought, if not for what I had already knew about Thomas Dixon Jr. and his Knapp connection and why some biographer or J. P. Knapp himself, at one time had made a point of, stating how and when he first became acquainted with Dixon. The story that is in the Knapp's bios, is that he and the former Reverend Thomas Dixon Jr. first met on a duck hunting trip about 1918. When Dixon found himself in financial difficulty, thanks to some bad Wall Street advice and slow royalty payments from Hollywood, he would sell his 2,500 acre Mackey Island, duck hunting paradise located near the Virginia state line in Currituck, North Carolina to Knapp around 1920. When Knapp bought the island, a bunch of North Carolina history was made. History that would provide some great benefits to the state, thereby linking forever J. P. Knapp's name to it all.

Now that information of course could not be refuted by this little anonymous plug to add "The Clansman" to the shelves of the Bellport Library. Nor could any facts be gleaned that Dixon himself was in Bellport at this time either. But thanks to both the Advance and The New York Times, I know that Thomas Dixon Jr's son Thomas "Spot" Dixon III, who was 18, when this story unfolded, and who often also called himself Jr. further adding to the confusion, vacationed in Bellport, "Spot" was well acquainted with the Knapp family and would stay well acquainted with them on and off for decades to come. This story appeared in the Advance, which published then twice a week, on Monday June 23, 1911

Bellport - Saturday afternoon Do-do (sic) Knapp and his friend Mr. Dixen (sic) of Virginia went over to Smith's Point in Mr. Knapp's motor boat. The engine refusing to work, a small sailboat was borrowed for the return trip home. When in the middle of the bay, the boat capsized. The young men clung to the boat and called for help as long as their strength lasted. Their calling was heard by Mr. Stack in Brookhaven who telephoned the Wyandotte. Capt. Charles Rice went out in his power boat and after searching in the dark, finally found them. Having been in the water from five-thirty until nine -thirty they were exhausted. The friend of Mr. Knapp was revived with difficulty as he had been unconscious sometime before the rescue.

What's In A Name?

The name Dodi or was it Doty? Knapp rarely appeared in print, but seemed to be the name everyone who knew him in the Long Island area called him by. Same rarity for Joseph Knapp Jr. as he wasn't a junior, but rather the namesake of Joseph F. Knapp his grandfather. He was also sometimes referred to as just Joe, as was his father, which has confused many more than once over the years about which Joe Knapp they meant. That usually could be ascertained by activities involved or subject of the story. Doty usually means to dote on and that could well be true in his economic situation and of growing up when he did. How it was spelled exactly is any ones guess, as I have seen it written as Doty in the UK, Dodi, and Dodie (usually associated as a feminine name) However I have only seen it printed as Do-do once and that would be in the above Advance story. There was no correction printed to that story by the way.

And from "The Paper Of Record," the NY Times on Sunday June 22, 1911:

CLING TO BOAT FIVE HOURS

Two Princeton Youths Exhausted When Rescued in Great South Bay

Thomas Dixon Jr., son of the Southern writer and Joseph F. Knapp were rescued from the Great South Bay yesterday morning after they had been clinging to the keel of a capsized catboat for five hours. When their cries were heard they were on the verge of exhaustion, and could have held on only a few minutes longer, they said.

Knapp has been entertaining Dixon, a classmate in Princeton in his parent's summer home. On Tuesday evening the two went out on Great South Bay in Knapp's motor boat, the Lady Dixon[1] The two had dinner at Smith's Point, but when they started home about 8 o'clock in the evening, they found the engine would not run, so they hired a small catboat, in which they started home.

Two miles off of Bellport a squall struck the small craft and over it went. The shore was too far away for either youth to attempt to swim to it, so they clung to the boat. Frequently they tried to climb upon it, but their clothing caused them to slip back.

The water was cold, and the young men soon became numb with the cold. Their fingers became cramped, and they feared they would lose their hold upon the boat. The wind blew them slowly toward Bellport, and at intervals they shouted for help. Shortly after midnight Capt. Charles Rice, a life saver at the Wyandotte Hotel, Bellport, heard the shouts and putting out in his motor boat, rescued the boys. Both fainted from exhaustion after being pulled into his boat.

It was the Times' report that both Knapp and Dixon went to Princeton University. I kept looking for articles, photos etc of Dodi Knapp's days at Princeton hoping to catch a glimpse of what he looked like. After a thorough search by the Princeton Alumni association, they reported back to me that Thomas Dixon III was in the class of 1914, which means he was a college freshman there in 1911, but that they had no record of a Joseph F. Knapp ever having been enrolled there. This was further reinforced by a Knapp family member years later who told me unlike his father, that Joe Knapp did not go to any college. Big Joe or J. P. you may recall by his own words put in "one riotous year" at Columbia in 1880-81. Instead young Joe probably went directly into his father's firm, the American Lithographic Company, after attending St. Paul's prep school in Garden City during the early 1900s.

---

1 A few differences in the Times and the Advance's local story and perhaps a typo or two. Although Tom Dixon had a younger sister named Louise, who may or may not also visited in Bellport and may or may not of dated then 18 year old Dodi Knapp, I would bet the name of the boat was not the Lady Dixon, but rather The Lady Claire. And if it happened according to the Times on a Tuesday instead of a Saturday as the Advance reported it, why would the Times take a week to run it and then say it happened yesterday? Minor points indeed, but there was one that sent me on a wild goose chase for some months.

Greener Pastures

Arthur Penney, one of Claire Knapp's nephews (see chpt 6), once said "I don't think Aunt Claire could ever be happy staying in one place for very long." This impression he probably first got from his mother Edith or father Clarence, who would know more about some of Claire Knapp's earlier moves for greener pastures long before Arthur was born in the 1920s. Now Bellport (at least in the area the Knapps lived in) wasn't then. nor is it now, a place one needs to leave for something better. Unless you want to totally change your setting from a quaint pastoral seaside country village to say the big city life. The thing is, Claire who lived with her mother Sylvia had both. When in Manhattan they remained at the fashionable house on W 72nd Street and Riverside Drive well after Sylvia and J. P. divorced. They traveled to Europe together, and I know that Sylvia at least frequented other society vacation spots like Newport and Claire could of well went with her.

Named for Sylvia's older sister Clara aka Mrs. William Orr Barclay, and her father's big sister "Netty," Claire Antoinette Knapp, most likely inherited her aunt Clara's love of horses and taste for the horse show society set from her. Though her father was quite the horseman also.

Sylvia who attended many horse shows was also sometimes a competitor, but seemed to be more a spectator, while making fashion statements. Traveling all over the eastern seaboard with the horses, just may of whetted Claire's appetite for a horse farm of her own. As a young girl, she was in the Garden City Riding Club when the Knapps had their Sands Point "farm" fox hunting at places like Meadowbrook which held a huge annual society event. As I said earlier, I do not know how much land the Knapps had during their 18 odd years at Bellport. I am sort of puzzled for that as prominent as they were in making Bellport, a desirable summer destination, with creating a golf course and yacht club, and the fact they also were there in the off season too, it should of familiarized them with the locals. Yet today, no one in the Bellport Historical Society, (they have a building and a charter) seems to of heard or know anything about them.

In 1912, Claire Knapp bought a nice little 12 acre farm, 30 miles north west of Bellport in the Greenlawn-Centerport area near Huntington on LI's north shore, complete with an early 1800s 2 story farm house. Although the January 26th 1912 deed transfers the property from Harrison and Ida Gilmore of Oneida, NY to Claire A. Knapp of Bellport Village, I doubt that she and her mother moved there right away, as it was greatly improved upon to the tune of $75,000 in 1912 dollars, above the purchase price, by adding a wing to the house some twice the size, plus riding stables, corrals, servants quarters and a beautiful landmark water tower not unlike the one that adorned Ol' Kentuck in Bellport. Although the restoration, layout and improvements were most likely Claire's vision, I know that it was her father who actually put the money up for all this and the finished product that appears in December 30, 1914 issue of The American Architect is titled *"Alterations to a house of Mr. Joseph P. Knapp Esq. Huntington, LI, NY"*

Although I was aware of the Greenlawn Knapp home from the early days of my research, I had no idea if it was still standing. If it was like most Knapp residences on Long Island I had learned about, it would be long gone without a trace. It was not until August of 2004, when attending my 40th High School reunion, that I decided to use some free time and a 1920's property map that marked it and take a trip to Greenlawn to see where it probably once stood. As I drove down a heavily forested road, imagine my surprise when I saw the remains of a mysterious looking water tower poking above the tree tops! It was on the opposite side of the road that Knapp estate was marked on my map, but the tower intrigued me as much as the much plainer one, I first saw in my backyard in Mastic Beach in 1950 did. The more I investigated, the more things rapidly unfolded when I saw myself actually standing not 30 feet in front of the eyebrowed window original farmhouse. What happened next, is a major story stranger than fiction in itself—I was invited inside! My visit is completely documented with many photos of the entire place inside and out on my website. It is still furnished and decorated as it would of been when the Knapp's lived there, who also were unknown to the current occupants (who are also horse people) and who have owned it for over 50 years. Although there are some photos of it in this book you can really enhance the experience seeing all of it and getting the rest of the story by visiting it directly online at: *http://www.spoonercentral.com/ Greenlawn/visit.html*

So while Claire was probably supervising the alterations to her new place in Greenlawn, she may of still spent some time in Bellport. If she did, she along with everyone in the village and many newspaper readers through out the country would know about this national story that appeared in The Times and Washington Post, Chicago Tribune and probably every major paper in the US.

If the name Knapp is a stranger to todays Bellport historians, the name Edey certainly isn't. Banker Frederick Edey and Frank Otis were two of the original investors with Claire's father, who built the Bellport Golf Club. Fred Edey married Birdsall Otis and the two had tremendous influence on the recreational, civic and cultural life in Bellport. They built a summer playhouse on their "Near The Bay" estate and they even had the state divert the main east west route now known as part of Montauk Highway several miles north of the village to reduce summer city traffic heading for points east like the Hamptons. "Birdie" was the national leader of the Girl Scouts of America and there is still a camp Edey located in Bayport on Long Island's South Shore.

Fred Edey's brother Henry, a stock broker and his wife Katherine also summered in Bellport. In the summer of 1912, Fred Edey gave his sister in law a horse that proved to be quite frisky and Henry employed local liveryman Gardner Murdock to give his wife riding lessons. Besides the riding lessons, Katherine and Gardner were seen taking long buggy rides and it did not take long before rumors started flying all around the village from both the society people and the locals. In August of that year Mrs. Edey left home. Gardner followed the next day. Rumors evolved into press articles and the stories about the Edeys and the Murdocks in the respectable national papers, read like ones you would find in supermarket tabloids. The Murdocks, who were fisherman, hunting guides, and inn keepers also had deep Bellport connections. Gardner's wife Nellie, was a Corwin, another old Bellport family and her father was the village post master. When Gardner left in August of 1912, his wife and young son Milton moved in with her parents.

Just before Christmas of 1912, Katherine Edey reconciled with her husband and the scandal seemed to die down, but then the story gets very complicated. Mrs. Murdock did not return to her home and Gardner Murdock served papers on Henry Edey claiming damages of $100,000 for alienation of affection. On the morning of January 2, 1913 Henry Edey shot his wife in their Bellport home and then turned the gun on himself. This double murder suicide would fill pages of the national papers for days with all sorts of salacious details about the relationship between all four. At the coroners inquest there was extensive testimony given by both Nellie and Gardner Murdock with their son Milton, probably hearing things about his parents no child should have to. Add to that the national media circus it attracted and to have to live in a small town like Bellport, could only make what had to be a terrible time for young Milton that much worse. At one point, a concerned person took the boy out of the courtroom.

Now what does this all have to do with Claire Knapp you ask ? other than that the Knapps and Edeys undoubtedly knew each other well in Bellport and that a horse was somewhat involved? It probably had little to do personally with Claire. Undoubtably all the Knapps heard all about this incident. Both Claire and her father were in Europe in January of 1913, when the murder took place returning to the states in early February. However twenty years later, there would be another marital scandal in the Bellport area, though a much quieter one and thankfully without a homicide. Like the one in 1912, it involved two families from two distinct economic classes and one was from the same family as before. This time it was Milton Murdock and Dodi Knapp.

In June of 1916 for reasons unknown to me, J. P. would lease Claire's Greenlawn place for the summer season to Baron de Stackelberg of Russia. Where she and Sylvia went is unknown—perhaps to Europe. With the war going on there for two years though, that doesn't seem logical. In October of 1916, Claire A. Knapp, would leave her finished twelve acre horse farm in Greenlawn and head south east across Long Island for the South Shore again. This time it was for the very place that started everything you have read about so far and will continue to stand as the framework for the rest of the story, a 24 room mansion on about 200 acres of waterfront property that her kid brother had just bought in the middle of the wilds of Mastic.

CHAPTER
22

Mastic, Next Stop...
All Aboard For Mastic

If you were sitting in a Long Island Railroad car at the Brookhaven Station, perhaps taking on water for the steam engine and you heard the conductor announce "Mastic, next stop Mastic, all aboard!" say around 1906-1916 or so, you might start to gather your things. For the train would be rolling eastward on the Montauk line into the tiny Mastic. formerly Forge station, in just about ten minutes or less. That is you would, if say your name was Smith, Robert, Lawrence, Floyd or Dana, otherwise there is little chance you would be getting off there, unless perhaps you may of been an invited guest. Though you could also have been a Dysart, Johnson, Penney or Clune and were returning from a visit to relatives "up the Island" or say a real special trip to New York city and were heading back to work on the vast estates of the first group of names.

Mastic is a squarish peninsula, about 4 miles across at its widest point, where it is bordered on the west by the Connecticut or Carmen's River, that separates it from Brookhaven and the Mastik (original spelling) or Forge River, that separates its eastern shore from Moriches. Then from Narrow Bay on its south shore, that connects Bellport Bay to Moriches Bay, Mastik Neck as it was sometimes called, extended north about 4 miles as the crow flies, up to the South Country Road, known today as Montauk Highway. Exact boundaries were somewhat vague and existed on hand drawn maps and deeds that were kept private in Chippendale desk drawers of the stately manor houses, only to be rewritten slightly over hundreds of years, when someone married into the family or died or worse yet, lost their vast land holdings, because they unwisely bet against those rag a muffin rebels in the Revolutionary War. An 1815 map show 7 homes on some 7,000 plus acres there and has "FLOYDS" in much larger print than Mastic on it.

Mastic, circa 1910 was still true blue blood country, with proud membership in the DAR. Inhabited with historic colonial patriots like the Woodhulls, Floyds, and Lawrences, from the French and Indian, Revolution, and War of 1812. Nathaniel Woodhull, who fought in the French & Indian conflict, was the first American General to die in a war that was partly started, when his brother in law and Mastic neighbor William Floyd, put his "John Hancock" on that Declaration, Thomas Jefferson would write in 1776. Jefferson and his pal Madison would both visit with Floyd in Mastik after the war. I wonder if he put them to work, helping fix up his house, that the British army had trashed, when they occupied it for the entire wars duration. I don't know if Tom and Jim played home improvement with Will or not, but Madison made his move and proposed to Will's daughter Kitty. She turned him down. Jefferson claimed he was only along for the ride to *"study the Indians." "INDIANS! WHAT INDIANS? I don't see any Indians"*—George Armstrong Custer—just kidding there— Custer was further west of Patchogue and not even a gleam in his fathers eye yet. But seriously *"Don't Give Up The Ship!"* was indeed Captain James Lawrence's last words, as the British blasted and then boarded the USS Chesapeake on June 4, 1813. Fresh out of Annapolis, it was Lawrence's first and last Naval battle. The Lawrences would marry into the Woodhull family and get about 500 acres out that deal. Then one of the Woodhulls would marry a Smith and well you get the picture, before long cousins were marrying cousins.

Mastic was the wild woods too, with thousands of acres of woodlands, salt meadows, creeks, and yes Virginia, Indians! The largest landholders of all, the Tangier Smiths, living on their Manor of St. George, had given about 150 acres of land on the Mastik River, as far northeast of their manor house as possible, to the Poosepatuck Indians in the 1600s "to have and to hold forever." Swindled over the years out of much of it, by 1916 the tiny tribe was holding on to about one third of the original grant.

Doctor, Lawyer & An Indian Chief
(a hit song from the 1940s movie *The Stork Club*)
According to the 1900 Federal census of the 100 or so "Capitalists and Indians", living in Mastic Hamlet, I found these statistics. 2 of the 5 families that owned 99% of all the land listed their occupations as capitalists and of those 5 capitalists families, two had lawyers among them, one had a doctor, others listed Landlord as their occupation. Spinster sisters or widowed sister in laws of the capitalists of course have no occupation, nor need one. The rest of the population is comprised of household servants and caretakers aka as "men of all work". They are usually Irish, German or eastern European. The rest of the occupations

listed are mainly fisherman and day laborers and most of them were Indians. Indians were not enumerated as Indians however, but rather just as "B" for black. You see slaves from the nearby colonial plantation of William Floyd had long ago mingled with the small Poosepatuck tribe, changing their complexion dramatically over the centuries. Among the five land owning families: Smith, Robert (Smith in laws), Floyd, Dana (Floyd in-laws), and Lawrence (Woodhull and Smith in laws), there was Landlord, Frank Mauran Lawrence, born in Mastic in 1862. Frankie in 1900 was still single and living with his two spinster sisters Elizabeth and Emma on several hundred acres on narrow bay, right in the middle of the peninsula.

In 1907 Frank (who's mother was Sarah Mauran of Rhode Island), married his cousin Louise Mauran from Providence. The Maurans are a Providence shipping family, who trace their lineage back to Carlo Mauran 1779-1844. Carlo came to America from Italy, as a shanghai victim. He escaped and turned to privateering (running enemy blockades during the war of 1812) and became very wealthy by later managing clipper ship fleets and sitting on bank boards. Louise had come to Moriches for the summers and boarded with the Edith & Bartlett Ross family of Moriches. The Ross' had a son in law named Clarence G. Penney, whose family also held a long heritage on Long Island. The Penneys of Moriches were mainly self employed trades people. Some also worked on the private estates in bordering Mastic. It is said at the Ross and Penney homes is where Frank first courted Louise. Marrying fairly late in life at the age of 45, I think Frank may of possibly remodeled the Lawrence mansion that would become forever known as the Knapp mansion, as a wedding gift for Louise. Funny thing about those Knapps though, when they moved into a place or left one, it always seemed it was their name that remained associated with it. Property maps of the late 1800s and the very early 1900s do not show a building in that vicinity, just others nearby, but after 1905 there is a fairly large mark on the map indicating a larger than average building there. It is also noted in the Woodhull farm journals that Miss Emma Lawrence resided in a splendid home there at the turn of the century. I also came to this conclusion from studying the architecture of it, and comparing it to the other surviving 19th century Smith-Lawrence houses in Mastic. Frank Mauran Lawrence was related to renowned architect John Lawrence Mauran, who I believe may of been the one who designed the home that looked like no others in Mastic.

Still with me? Good — In 1912 a similar styled new home would be built nearby in Tangier, the ill fated million dollar boondoggle, stillborn development on 7,000 acres of the Tangier Smith's property, just across some creeks and meadows, a mile or so west of the impressive three story Frank and Louise Lawrence residence. By 1915 the Tangier development was belly up, with it's fly by night developer F. J. Quinby, literally flying out of town in his own plane, along with the investors dough. His model manor home, known as the Island View Manor, that still stands today, along with all the property he never built on, reverted back to the Smiths. An interesting side note about the Island View Manor house occurred in the 1950's, when it was a nightclub and Tony Bennett would often sing there. Did Quinby have his personal architect look over the Lawrence place to kind of copy it? Or was it just the style of a particular manor home of the day ? The major difference that set the

Lawrence place apart from Island View Manor though, was it's asymmetrical towers on the north and southeast corners, reminiscent of the earlier victorian round towers. These were squared and capped with gabled hip roofs. It gave the place a very distinctive look.

By 1916 with his two spinster sisters now dead, and finding himself spending most of his time in Providence running the Mauran coal company with its large coal barges, towboats and tugboats, Frank decided to sell the family estate in Mastic, which had been truck farming mainly salt hay in its last years. On October 2, 1916, the purchaser according to the deed was a none other than 24 year old Joseph F. Knapp. Two days later, the brand new 180 some acre Knapp estate with a 24 room residence, all sorts of barns, outbuildings, caretaker houses etc was sold again. This time the purchaser was Joseph's sister, Claire Antoinette Knapp! Did Dodi Knapp flip this house? Probably not, but his father Joseph P. Knapp, may of flipped when he learned what his young son had done and decided that an estate of that size would be in safer hands in the name of his older sister, who seemed to want to stay in the country anyway. Dodi still worked for his father at American Lithographic in New York City then. The initial P in Joseph P. Knapp's name could of also stood for purse strings and it was undoubtedly his purse that still controlled the strings of the big ticket items his son and daughter would have and hold in their own names. When their Greenlawn estate was sold in 1917, it is Joseph P and Elizabeth's name on the top of the deed. They listed their address then as Town of Hardenburgh (upstate in the Catskill mountain area). J. P. & Elizabeth had a Thomas Jefferson styled Monticello home up there that burned down. However J. P. would maintain his trout fishing camp there along the 4 miles of Beaverkill River that he leased, for most of his life. Also listed on that deed as owners of the Greenlawn estate are Claire and her brother Joseph. That could of been for inheritance reasons.

I can only speculate here, but it's fun to do so and it relieved some of my tediousness searching and reading legal documents. One of the other theories I have is, that Sylvia Knapp may not of moved to Mastic with Claire in 1916, but rather someplace else, as she eventually would when she moved to France. If she did move away in 1916 or early '17, Joseph P may of felt his unmarried daughter would be safer moving to Mastic with her brother. There was more than enough land and house for Claire to have her horse farm and whatever else she wanted out in Mastic. The only thing that may of prevented Sylvia from moving overseas at that time was, the war to end all wars, that had been raging in Europe for two years already. With it looking like America might get into it at any day, she may of decided not to leave the states (she kept her US Citizenship even after she eventually did) until after it was over "over there". That said I have only found one reference to Mrs. Joseph Palmer Knapp and the Knapp estate at Mastic. That is when she came from France to visit with her son and daughter in November of 1924.

Mastic Goes To The Dogs While Taking To The Air

In November of 2003, I visited with two of three homeowners, who have built very nice and large homes on the three and a half acres the Mastic Beach Knapp mansion actually foot-printed it self upon. Ed and Marilyn Albano, who spent summers in Mastic Beach since the early '60s, have owned a large split level high ranch on the west side of where the mansion sat (the ballroom entrance) since the 1980s, They told me that when they first moved to Monroe Drive, they were told by some older Mastic Beach pioneers, that back in the 1940s a large arched sign, hung over the driveway that led to the Knapp house on the what is now the curved corner where Dogwood Road meets Monroe Drive. I don't know what the sign might of said in the WWII era, which was just after the Knapp's left, but probably the first sign, if indeed one went up after the first World War, would of said Clairedale Farm. Although Claire was still involved with her show horses then, she was also trying her hand at raising show dogs, rather than just buying them from other breeders. Her mother as you may recall, had Boston Terriers at the turn of the century, but not her own kennel. Claire's first breed was the Airedale around 1911, hence the name she would eventually use, but she soon switched her attention to Chow-Chows. By 1922 Clairedale Farm had simply become Clairedale, a name she would register with the AKC and keep as her kennel name the rest of her life. Her first print ads appear in 1922, advertising chow puppies for sale at $75-$150 they simply said Clairedale Chows, Miss C. A. Knapp, Mastic, NY.. Whether or not Clairedale Farm or just plain Clairedale was still hanging up on the driveway arch in 1940's is highly doubtful, especially with all the changes that would occur at the Knapp estate in Mastic from 1916-1940.

Another sign that could of gone up within months of the Knapp's owning the estate, could have said "Aerial Coast Patrol, US Naval Reserve, Unit 3." However that sign would not of even stood hanging through the duration of America's 18 month involvement in the war, much less the roaring twenties and the great depression. Unit Three was so low profile, that US Naval records of it are almost non existent. I know I have more info about them than the Navy does. They were one of the first things I would discover, besides the Buck Rogers style helicopter landing on the Knapp estate in the 1930s, about what happened out in Mastic when the Knapps lived there (it's still a decade from being named Mastic Beach). The time that Unit 3 was keeping em' flying over the bay was colorful indeed.

As early as 1915, a Yale college student named Frederick Trubee Davison and his brother Harry were trying to organize a group of their fellow students into what they hoped would be a Navy flying unit, to protect our shores from German U Boats and eventually go "over there" and fight the Huns. Airpower then was just basically no power, even as America got into the conflict. Very little interest was expressed by the powers that be in Washington. The first people Trubee, who was the driving force in this idea, had to convince though, were much closer to "Peacock Point" the Davison family estate on Long Island's north shore. That would be his parents Kate and Henry P. Davison. Trubee actually won over his mother first because Henry P. Davison was away on a salmon fishing trip in Canada in 1916 at (surprise!) J. P. Knapp's remote lodge on the Natashaquan River in Quebec and could not be contacted. When they did get a message to him that they wanted to fly aero planes, he wired back "DO NOTHING TILL I GET HOME!" The Davison brothers, once they won

over their father and aided by his strong contacts he had as a Wall street banker, pursued their dream. Unit One of the Aerial Coast Patrol was up and flying
on Long Island's gold coast area of the north shore by March of 1917. That is
the same month that US severed diplomatic ties with Germany. Among the
earliest members of the First Yale Unit, often called The Millionaires Unit
in the press, was none other than Archibald G. McIlwaine. On April 5th 1917,
President Wilson went before congress and asked for them to declare war on
Germany. A few days later there was no less than an Admiral of the US Navy
traipsing around on the shoreline of the Knapp Estate in Mastic. surveying
it for a seaplane base. Talk about cutting through red tape, with a blue torch!
Here is what the NY Times said about it on April 15, 1917:

AIRPLANE STATION TO NAVY
James [SIC] *P. Knapp Gives Land and Will Build Hangers and Wireless*
*James P. Knapp, President of the American Lithographic Company has pre-
sented to the navy through Rear Admiral Nathaniel R. Usher commanding the
Third Naval District, an airplane station to be equipped with three hangers and a
wireless station on his property at Mastic, on the south shore of Long Island. The
offer was made through the Advisory Committee on Aeronautics of which Allan R.
Hawley, President of the Aero Club is chairman.*

*The property was inspected yesterday by a committee made up of Mr. Hawley,
Rear Admiral Bradley A. Flake, Clinton Davis Backus, organizer of Aerial Coast
Patrol Unit 3; Warren S. Eaton, Henry Woodhouse, David Dunlap, W. Hagsom,
H. M. Fraduenthal, and E. K. Jaquith, the aviator who recently flew from Atlan-
tic City to Miami, Fla. The committee was conducted over the property by Mr.
Knapp and his son J. F. Knapp. The station was was found to be ideally situated
strategically being halfway between New York City and Montauk Point, which
would allow aviators from the station to patrol the whole Third District.*

*The station has been accepted by Rear Admiral Usher and the hangers will be
put up at once. It will be used as soon as possible as a training station for one of the
units of the aerial coast patrol.*

Again when I first read that and a similar article in the Patchogue Advance,
I could see the old airplane and radio parts that we found in the barn as a kids
flashing past my eyes. It was not the first time that Joseph P. Knapp would be
called James by the newspapers. nor would it be the last.

Aviator E. K. Jaquith was Edwin Kenneth Jaquith (1893-1984) and he was to
be Unit Three's flight instructor. Jaquith was the son of a Chicago banker, held
aviators license # 40 and had been flying since about 1912. Before getting hired
by Knapp, he was running a sight seeing flying service in Atlantic City, New Jersey. From what I have read about Jaquith both before, during and after the war,
he must of been a real character. In 1913 he was arrested by a game warden in
Rochester, NY for hunting ducks from his hydro-airplane. That didn't stop him
from his self pro claimed bright idea and he continued doing it. He even had
a recipe in Ladies Home Journal for cooking 5 minute duck! Other states and
other counties in NY even, thought his antics made for a novel news item. You

can tell just from looking at his photos, that there was some excitement to be had while learning to fly with E. Kenneth Jaquith.

The planes they used for these aerial coast patrols were hydro-aeroplanes, also known as Flying Boats. Most were built by the Curtiss Airplane Company on Long Island and in Hammondsport, New York. Costing about 10 to 12 thousand a piece, they actually were flying boats with fuselages made from mahogany and large double wings of canvas. Mounted above the pilot's head and under top wing was an engine of the pusher type, not to mention radiator as they were still water cooled. The propeller faced the rear of the plane. They could cruise anywhere from 65-100 mph. It was thought that they were far safer than land aero-planes because when the engine quit, as it often would, or you found yourself in other difficulty, you could just glide down (volplane) onto the waters surface for a nice soft landing. There was very little truth to that selling point. Trubee Davison while soloing for his license in the summer of 1917, corkscrewed into the Long Island Sound and was basically crippled for life. Although he went on to a long and highly distinguished career in both aviation (he was secretary of the Navy in WWII) and was in on the ground floor of the CIA, as well as president of The Museum of Natural History. Trubee was just one of many that were hurt or killed in aviation training accidents. They took a bigger toll, than actual combat did.

The original flyers of Unit Three of the Aerial Coast Patrol that were sworn in by the Navy in May 1917 were: Clinton D. Backus, Harold A. Pumpelly, William J. Connors, Harold Howe, Irving Paris, Leslie MacNaughton, Duncan Forbes, William Hamilton Gardner, Austin Feuchtwanger, Stewart Johnson, John Laird, Thomas Dixon Jr. and Joseph F. Knapp. Most were either from Yale or Princeton. If the proximity of the last two names does not ring your bell, you need to stop skipping around the book and go back and read Chapter 22.

The unit's ranks started to swell quickly and considering you had to buy your own plane and pay for your own expenses (the Navy paid for nothing at first) within two months there were 36 members in Unit three. That also explains why they all probably couldn't stay bunked on the Knapp Estate. The mansion only had 4 bedrooms, not counting the servants rooms. The two other 1850s houses on the estate property, could of been converted into some type of barracks, but its more likely that the bulk of the flyboys moved over into the Hedges hotel, just across the Narrow Bay at Smith's Point. That would explain why many of the publicity pictures taken of the unit were taken over there and why there were large hanger buildings remaining there until the early 1920s.

Of course that many flyboys would also prove to be far too many for one teacher and another early Wright flyer, Leonard W. Bonney, license #47 joined in to instruct. Although Bonney's license number was issued six numbers higher than Jaquith's , it was for Aviator rather than the restricted Hydro-Aeroplane aviator. Bonney had been flying since 1911. He had dropped bombs on Pancho Villa in the Texas and Mexico desert, courtesy of General Pershing. He also flew the earliest flight across Tampa Bay in Florida, taught flying in Garden CIty and gave exhibitions all over the country. He and Dodi Knapp would remain friends long after the war ended and he returned to the Knapp Estate in the early 1920s, building a highly futuristic experimental plane there. His future wife would become a close friend of Claire Knapp. Flora Bonney raised Dalmations at her Tally-Ho Kennel in Flushing Queens, but more about the dogs later. For now its Dog Fights.

One of the first items in the newspapers,regarding the new Unit Three, besides the preliminary press photos of them making front page news, was a flying record set by E. K. Jaquith and his passenger, student Harold Pumpelly on June 2, 1917. They flew from Atlantic City to Mastic, a distance of 225 miles in one hour and 55 minutes. From Mastic they filed this news dispatch over the Knapp wireless station.

WEDDING NEWS BY AIRMAN
J. W. Mott Atlantic CIty Hotel Owner, Married in a Rustic Place
Amid the quaintly romantic rustic setting at Buck Hill Falls in the Pocono district, Miss Lucille Gawthrop, daughter of Evan B. Gawthrop, of West Grove Pa. and Joseph Walton Mott, owner of the Hotel Traymore, in Atlantic City were married today. The announcement of the marriage was carried by E. Kenneth Jacwith (sic) aviator now instructing the aerial coast patrol, who flew from the scene of the ceremony to Mastic, L. I. to file the dispatch —Washington Post June 2, 1917

Not exactly strategic stuff or of any importance to military matters whatsoever. Mott owned the hotel that Jaquith flew sight seeing trips out of. I have several press photos from the summer of 1917, taken at or around the Knapp Seaplane Base as it was also called by the press and although some newspapers and magazines reported it's location, other times the photos were marked as "an undisclosed location" or "somewhere in America". It's somewhat ironic and typical of how silly the government can be. Some photos appeared in French newsmagazines, that could of easily be obtained by spies. There was also a Unit 2 of the Aerial Coast Patrol, which was much larger. located at Bay Shore, Long Island about 15 miles west of Mastic and a US Naval air station near the city at Rockaway, Queens. German submarines in WWII actually got into the New York and Long Island area attacking several cargo ships. Aero patrols fought back too. Harry Davison on his very first patrol with Unit One shot his propellor off going after a sub and had to be towed in off of Fire Island near Bay Shore.

In August of 1917, Jaquith, Bonney, Dixon and Knapp , flew east out of Mastic and gave an exhibition at the Devon Yacht Club near Amagansett. Each one had his own Curtiss flying machine. Among the spectators that day were Mr. and Mrs. Joseph P. Knapp, who frequently summered at Southampton and entertained the flyers afterwards. Elizabeth's son Archie would also fly out there from Huntington to see his mother and play golf. Also in August that year, back in Mastic, Harold Howe's flying machine on takeoff, was carried by a gust of wind, smack into the wooden Smith Point bridge, totally destroying his air craft. Howe escaped unhurt.

I have a photo taken at what had to be a public airshow of sorts at Smithpoint. It is labled "Fleet of US Flying Boats" "passed by the censor, Washington, DC" and shows ladies, gentleman and little kids in their finery looking at an assortment of seaplanes on the beach with the very identifiable Smith Point bridge in the background. About a week later, Lenoard Bonney was returning to Mastic from New Jersey with student Austin Feuchtwanger aboard, when the engine quit over Long Beach. Bonney tried to volplane his craft down, but it fell rapidly a 1,000 feet and crashed into the sea. Reports varied from no harm done to both men being injured, Feuchtwanger seriously, and nearly drowned because he was caught in the wreckage.

In October that year, Lawrence "Gyro" Sperry, who's family summered in Bellport, dropped by the Mastic base in his own seaplane. By far the most experienced and talented pilot around then, not to mention inventor of many aviation firsts like the auto pilot and gyro stabilizer that made flying much safer, "Gyro" asked who had the fastest flying boat in the unit. It turns out it was Tom Dixon's and Sperry took Dixon up with him doing a Loop to Loop 1 mile over Pattersquash Island. They too nearly crashed. This was a first for a flying boat and it made national news complete with photos. From the aviators I have spoke with, it is almost impossible to Loop the Loop in a flying boat. But then there really was only one Gyro Sperry. One of the many benefits I have enjoyed from studying the Knapps, has been learning about folks like Lawrence Burst Sperry.

Also in the fall of 1917, some of the members of unit 3, Knapp included, went to ground school at MIT in Boston. After that onto the Naval Base at Pensacola, Fla for further training. It was there that J. F. Knapp became an Ensign and a Navy flight instructor. He spent the duration of the war at Pensacola and was a Lt jg when he resigned in July of 1919. If you think that not going "over there" was really that much safer, think again. Although your method of getting killed was reduced by not dying in a dog fight or being picked off from German ground-fire, the fact remains that there were more pilots killed in training accidents and routine patrols than actual combat in the Great War. Another charter member of Unit 3, Ensign Leslie MacNaughton went through advanced training with Knapp at Pensacola and was then assigned to train flyers at Hampton Roads, Va. In March of 1918 he was in the rear seat of Seaplane #426, instructing fellow Ensign M. Stevensen, when their plane crashed into water from an altitude of 300 feet. Ensign Stevensen was able to extricate himself, but the upper wing had buckled trapping MacNaughton in the plane. Unit 1 flyer, Bob Ireland saw it happen and put his plane down, swimming to the wreckage in the icy water, but he was unable to save MacNaughton.

In the fall of 1917 "Chip" McIlwaine shipped over seas to France. Elizabeth soon followed and stayed in Paris to be near her son. Chip flew 28 missions over enemy lines, including bombing raids while stationed at Moutchic and Orly. He made it back ok, but three of his friends from the First Yale Unit, Albert Sturtevant, Kenny Macleish (brother of poet Archibald MacLeish) and Curtis Read did not return. After the war, Archibald Graham MacIlwaine Jr. would marry Curt's sister, Miss Caroline Hicks Read. They named one of their sons, John Curtis McIlwaine.

M EANWHILE BACK IN MASTIC IN THE FALL OF **1917**, rumors were circulating that Unit 3 had fallen apart because the Navy just forgot about them. Jaquith kind of drifted off somewhere leaving Bonney to try and keep it together. In January of 1918, Jaquith was interviewed in a hotel in Washington, DC, downplaying a story in the press that he was killed in combat overseas. He said he was still awaiting his orders to report to duty from the Navy. He must of forgot he never joined the Navy and his WWI draft card claims exemption on his reason that "he was more valuable as a private citizen flight instructor." Unit Three's spokesman, Eugene Untermeyer, a son or nephew of Knapp lawyer Sam Untermeyer, issued a denial to the press saying that " Unit 3 was still very active, had more flying boats than ever and was in good hands under Bonney's leadership." By the first of the year, the remaining members of Unit 3 who stayed on, had transfered up the island to Bay Shore and the Knapp Seaplane Base of Mastic, Long Island, NY, became a footnote in Naval aviation history. The Navy's official note on it is : "The members of Unit Three failed to complete their training before the wars end" By 1920 there was only a trace of a partially demolished hanger in a photo taken during winter at Smith Point. But thankfully there was all that neat stuff in the Knapp barn hayloft that provided hours of fun for me and my friends to haul away in our wagons and play airport with, safely in my backyard in the summer of 1953.

CHAPTER
23

"Will the Real Mrs. Joseph Palmer Knapp Please Stand Up?"

*I*f that good old TV quiz show, *To Tell The Truth*, could of been played at a vaudeville theatre say between 1906-1916 and both Sylvia and Elizabeth were contestants, both would naturally rise at the games conclusion, when bow tied quiz-master Bud Collyer spoke that familiar phrase that concluded each game. It was a no brainer when a Mr. & Mrs. J. P Knapp were mentioned often in the circa 1910 era of Palm Beach society, but with Sylvia often using the name, Mrs. Joseph Palmer Knapp after her divorce, it is somewhat difficult to distinguish which Mrs. Joseph P. Knapp the society columns were referring to unless, other members of the family were mentioned along with it. e.g. when Mrs J. P. Knapp and Miss Knapp were mentioned together at say a horse or dog show. Then you could bet it was Sylvia and Claire. When Master Knapp might be mentioned along with Master McIlwaine as summering together (as they did as teenagers in '07) or traveling abroad with Mrs. Joseph P. Knapp. Then that Mrs J. P. Knapp, was obviously Archie's mother Elizabeth.

Elizabeth seemed very close to her son Archibald. When she re-married, Archie (I have no idea if he was ever called Archie, but we can hope he was) did move to Connecticut to live with his father per the divorce agreement. But judging by the society columns, he spent a good deal of time with his mother too. She would furnish items to the papers on most all of his activities, well being etc.

even when he was in college at Yale. Archie was a golf prodigy at 17 and I'm sure that caught the undivided attention of his step father and perhaps set up a bit of natural rivalry with his step brother who also enjoyed the game. In the 1920s Dodi Knapp had Clarence Penney construct a golf course on the Mastic estate.

In Oct of 1905 J. P. Knapp before a justice of the peace, married Elizabeth Laing McIlwaine in Sioux Falls, South Dakota, They returned to NY City in December and took an apartment at the Beaux Arts for a time before moving into their co - op apartment at 247 5th avenue. So if that address was included in the copy with a Mrs Joseph P. Knapp, in her many travels, often alone, then I also knew it was Elizabeth. Minor details to some, but when you are trying your best to be accurate and write a story out of hundreds of snippets—well you get the picture.

Here are a few examples of what I mean:

SNAPSHOTS AT SOCIAL LEADERS
Washington Post Nov 26, 1911: A mild sensation was caused at the horse show in New York Friday night, by the remarkable costume of Mrs. Joseph Palmer Knapp. Mrs. Knapp has always been known for her strikingly becoming gowns, but the one she wore Friday night surpassed all her former achievements in originality.

The skirt of white chiffon was close fitting. It was crossed diagonally with bands of white satin, but below the knees in the intervals of satin it was quite transparent. The diaphanous material showed the absence of lining. The waist was cut low and draped with tulle. It was trimmed with bands of purple velvet. Mrs. Knapp wore a large diamond brooch at the bodice and a chain of diamonds. A black satin hat completed the striking costume.

My humble opinion? This was Sylvia and not just because it was a horse show either. Now here is one that is a true classic, leaves no doubt and was obviously written by a true student of journalism who knew the basics. The same ones I first learned from Mr. Norman Bessette, my 7th grade Social Studies teacher at William Floyd in 1958: Who, What, When, Where, and Why.

TROUSERETTES FROM PARIS
New York Society Leader Imports Creations of Gold Lace Over Chiffon special to the Washington Post, New York Nov 15, 1913: No longer will the skirts of tradition encumber. Freedom has arrived in the form of the daintiest creation of trousers from "gay Paree" "They" have been specially imported for Mrs. Sylvia T. Knapp, society leader of this city.

"They" are real harem style and the technical description of them reads as follows: "Regular Turkish negligee trouserettes of woven gold lace over accordion-pleated black chiffon, with a border of gold Spanish lace, and black chiffon sleeves. The bottoms of the trouserettes are shirred with elastic."

Mrs. Knapp who is introducing the innovation on this side of the Atlantic, was the first wife of Joseph F. Knapp (SIC; oh well real close just not minding their Ps & Fs) *son of the founder of The Metropolitan Life Insurance Company. She was divorced from her husband in Georgia in 1903.*

(Was she now? In Georgia? That was a wild goose chase for me and a long way from Sioux Falls, South Dakota which before Reno, Nevada, was the divorce capital of the US. Sylvia went to Sioux Falls in May of 1903 for hers)

NEWS OF NEWPORT
May 28, 1912, Mrs. Joseph Knapp of New York has rented the Pinard cottage No. 1 for the summer.

I assume this is Sylvia again, because Elizabeth normally went to Southampton in the summer. From around 1910-1920 or so the J. P. Knapps, rented a Southampton estate known as "Tenacre" for most of the summer seasons. Elizabeth was very active with the Southampton Street Festival, the annual premiere society event held there, that raised money for the local hospital. When the Knapps built a $125,000 summer home near Tenacre in 1921 on twelve acres along Ox Plains Road, they named it Cherry Creek Farm. However the name Tenacre stuck and remained with the, James Russell Pope designed home. It was advertised in 2003 by the realtors as Tenacre, the former home of publisher J. P. Knapp. The asking price was 12.5 million dollars.

At their apartment on 247 5th Avenue, Elizabeth entertained frequently and quite royally. She hosted dinners for the likes of people like Sir Arthur Conan Doyle (author of Sherlock Holmes) whose stories and articles were featured in Knapp magazines. The Knickerbocker apartment was New York City's first duplex built in the late 1880s. Located on the south east corner of 28th Street, it is still there in a greatly remodeled form, just a pleasant stroll two blocks north of Madison Square. At 11 stories tall, families rented entire floors at $4000 per year in 1913. Among the Knapp neighbors in that building were; Major Jack Bouvier (Jackie Kennedy's father) The Edeys of Bellport, and inventor Edward Rogers and author Aline Gorren Tolfree, who became Knapp neighbors in Mastic too, when they purchased the "Island View Manor" in Tangier.

SIDELIGHTS OF THE SMART SET
Interesting Events and Gossip Both at Home and Abroad as Chronicled in the Posts Exchanges Washington Post Feb 4, 1912—They say that Mrs. Joseph Palmer Knapp has had a combination billiard and ball room added to her big apartment on Fifth avenue, New York, so that she may have ample room for a number of entertainments on a large scale she is planning in honor of her son, Archibald G. McIlwaine 2nd when he comes home from college. He has been ill of late, but is now rapidly recovering his health.

And how big was that apartment you ask? Well a about a year later, Elizabeth hosted a 21st birthday party there for her step son Dodi Knapp. They held it a month early of his actual Feb 3rd birthday on January 2, because one: everyone was still in town and perhaps partly recovered from New Years Eve and two: his father and sister had a trip to Europe booked leaving soon after, as you might recall from the Edey coroners inquest in Chapter 22. J. P. and Claire sailed for the French Riviera right after the party. The Carmania carried them both back along with perhaps Claire's first Chow puppy on January 25th, docking in New York on Feb 2nd and they might of had a quiet birthday welcome home celebration on Feb 3rd ? But here is what the New York Times reported on Jan 3, 1913 of Dodi Knapp's 21st birthday blowout held the evening before.

DINNERS AND DANCES ARE SOCIETY'S LURE - MRS J. P. KNAPP HOSTESS
Mrs. Joseph Palmer Knapp gave a dinner dance last evening at her home 247 5th Ave for her stepson Joseph Fairchild Knapp, to celebrate his coming of age. There was a dinner for fifty guests and later one hundred additional guests came in for dancing. The decorations included baskets of pansies and orchids and Mrs. Knapp and Miss Claire Knapp received.

The dinner guests included Misses Margaret Trevor, Edith Logan, Angelica Brown, Margaret Andrews, Genevieve Sanford, Katherine Baldwin, Pauline Clarkson, Adelaide and Viola Townsend, Audrey Osborn, Claire Knapp, Justin Smith, Helen Underwood, Evelyn Childs, Rosalie and Estelle O'Brien, Mr and Mrs Judith Sears, Mr, and Mrs Arthur Carroll, Mr. and Mrs. Albert Gallatin, Miss Elsie de Wolfe, Mr. and Mrs. Henry Whigham, Felix Doubleday, Edward S. Knapp Jr., Frank V. Burton Jr. Robert Winmill, Francis Roche, Moncure Robinson, Archibald G. McIlwaine, Count Andrew de Fouquieres, F. Townsend Martin, Howard Martin, Harrison Rhodes, and Harry Sproul.

Among the guests who came in later for the dance were many college men and young girls.

150 and with room to dance around—that is a pretty big apartment. There were some big names there too; Doubleday, Roche, Underwood, the O'Brien sisters (father Morgan was a supreme court justice) Edward Spring Knapp Jr. was of the Long Island Knapps, who go back to Shepherd Knapp the NY CIty retailer. They were related somehow, but I've never been able to pin it down exactly. The Islip - Bayshore Knapp family put out a private published book in the 1940's titled "We Knapp's Thought It Was Nice" about there lives of horses, golf and sailing along the south shore.

I have way too many one and two line society items about the two Mrs. Joseph Palmer Knapp's activities from 1906-1914, to put in this book or bore the reader with, but all of them as innocuous as they seem, helped me form an impression of who both ladies were. This one however from the Southampton Press a weekly in June of 1922, needs to be included here.

MRS. J.P. KNAPP DIES AT HER COTTAGE
Collapses After Motor Trip From New York to Summer Home Here.
Mrs. Elizabeth Laing Knapp, wife of Joseph Palmer Knapp of 247 Fifth Avenue, died suddenly Friday at her home Cherry Creek Farm, which was recently completed. Mrs. Knapp had not been in good health for more than a year. She left her home in New York by motor Thursday, accompanied by her nurse and collapsed soon after reaching Southampton. Her son Archibald G. McIlwaine Jr. arrived with his wife by motor when Mrs. Knapp was in a coma.

Mrs. Knapp had been known here for eighteen years and previous to building a residence had leased a place known as Tenacre from the estate of the late Mrs. Charles Gouvenuer Weir of New York.

Mrs. Knapp was the daughter of the late Eugene Laing of Plainfield N.J. During the war she did much relief work and was in Paris with the Mayfair Relief Unit. At the same time, her son by a former marriage Archibald G. McIlwaine Jr. was with the naval air service in France. He was a member of the Trubee Davison unit. Mr. Knapp is in Canada on a fishing trip and could not be notified immediately of Mrs. Knapp's death. Mrs. Knapp leaves her husband and son who three years ago married Miss Caroline Read daughter of the late William Augustus Read of New York, and of Mrs. Read.

Funeral services were held Monday afternoon at 3 o'clock at Cherry Creek Farm.

The New York Times obituary of June 24th, was unusually brief considering how well known she was at the time.

Mrs. Elizabeth Lang Knapp wife of Joseph Palmer Knapp of 247 Fifth Avenue, died yesterday at her Summer residence in Southampton in her fifty-ninth year. For the last two years she had been ill with diabetes. Funeral arrangements to be announced.

If funeral arrangements were announced, they did not make it into the papers. Neither obit mentioned where she was buried, but I would find out later from reading her son Archibald's Navy records. When they said he was buried Southampton, it was a no brainer why he would be there. I visited the McIlwaine family plot in 2005. A long black granite tombstone is simply inscribed Elizabeth Laing Knapp Wife Of Joseph Palmer Knapp Died June 23, 1922. Along side her are the headstones of her son Archibald, daughter in law Caroline, and her first born grandson Archibald III, who was a Naval Aviator in WWII. He went missing in action in the Pacific in 1943 and was never found. Not 50 yards away is the Knapp family plot that I discovered in 2001 of Joseph F. and Claire A. Knapp.

On August 17th 1922 the Southampton press printed this story regarding the Elizabeth's will

MRS JOSEPH P. KNAPP'S ESTATE GIVEN TO HER SON

The will of the late Mrs. Elizabeth L. Knapp, who died on June 23 at her summer home Southampton, has been filed for probate in the New York County Surrogates Court. The will bequeaths all decedents, stocks, bonds, her home in Southampton, and the contents of her residence at 247 5th Ave, Manhattan to her son Archibald G. McIlwaine of Glen Cove, The decedents daughter in law Caroline McIlwaine also of Glen Cove is left Mrs. Knapp's diamonds. The document discloses the decedents husband Joseph P. Knapp resides at Mackay Island, Currituck County North Carolina. There is no reference to him in the will except to say the deceased "hopes he will carry out the original clause in his will by which one third of what was my share in the husbands estate shall go to her son which the testatrix says was under the agreement made years ago.

The accompanying petition filed with the will gives the value of the estate as $30,000 in real and $40,000 in personal property. The petition also states that

the son's share of the will amounts to $60,000.

Note that a later probate announcement says her sons share of the will amounts to $90,000.

I have a copy of the actual will, and not because I searched for it either. I discovered it a year or so after I found the newspaper, in what I thought was a very unusual place. I was curious to who else may of owned the Southampton house through the years and lo and behold Elizabeth's will is used for the actual deed to the home. A copy of it is in the Register of Deeds in Suffolk county.

I was taken back a little, when I read the newspaper account of how they mentioned Joseph P. Knapp is not mentioned in the will at all, other than to say she hopes he will live up to his agreement from years ago. The way it is presented in the press, suggests perhaps that they were estranged at the time of her death? This is very possible, as she did announce she was not returning to her 247 5th Ave for winter season in 1921, but rather moving to a new place on the west side of Manhattan. I know that they pursued separate interests over the course of their 16 years together with regards to vacations and leisure activities. Elizabeth seemed to prefer society gatherings over the call of the wild of fishing and hunting. She entertained a great deal at Southampton home. Rockefellers, Morgans and European counts were all guests there. Joseph P. was away fishing in Canada when she died, but he had been doing a whole lot of fishing and duck hunting in remote places, long before he married Elizabeth. I read some articles where in the earlier days she had traveled to meet J. P, at far away destinations and vice versa. They even took separate trips to Europe, with her taking the children to France or England and J. P. going Germany on business, but would rendezvous at places like Switzerland. Here is an example from the Southampton Press June 1, 1917: Mrs. Joseph Palmer Knapp closed her home at No. 247 Fifth avenue last week and came to her residence at Southampton for the summer. Mr. Knapp started last week for Labrador and will be absent until the autumn.

I'm assuming that he made it back for the funeral or that they at least waited until he did. It seems the Southampton Press implied something they may of thought was true or heard rumors of around the village? Southampton, for as sophisticated as its reputation is, was always a very gossipy town and still is to a large degree, if only fueled today by press agents rather than towns folk. That said, the actual wording and typing errors in the will says the following:

"I desire that my husband Joseph P. Knapp & my son Archibald G. McIlwaine act as co-executors. I hope that my husband will carry out the original clause in his will where he gives to my son 1/3 of what was my share. that was an agreement he made years ago and I know his fairness & justice in all things."

SOUTHAMPTON, LONG ISLAND OCT 24 /21

She asks that both JP & Archie act as co-executors. The only contest I found to this will I found years before I stumbled onto the will itself. That was a court decision about bequeathing her diamonds. Seeing that it does not name who brought the contest, I am assuming it was Archibald himself and used more as a clarification rather than a challenge. Small detail, but then remember it was small kid who started playing with all that airplane and radio junk! Notice the will was made out just 8 months before she died, which suggests to me that there was a earlier version and there were probably to borrow from that old song, "some changes made" Some other interesting points not mentioned in the Southampton press are the following instructions and bequeathments:

$1000.00 to George for his long & faithful service as my butler & $1000 to Agnes Swanson for her long and faithful service as maid - $300 to Emily Berger for her devotion & care during my illness—Elizabeth L. Knapp
  Peter my gardner $500
  All real laces to Needle & Bobbin Club, if there are any they desire. To my former maid Agnes Swanson, I give a set of fine dinner plates. Any one's she may select, except the gold one I give to Helen.

I don't know about you, but I am touched by the tiny and specific details Elizabeth laid out.

"I give and bequeath to my to my son Archibald G. McIlwaine Jr. all stocks, bonds Life insurance <u>*my home at Southampton, complete with furnishings.*</u> [EMPHASIS ADDED—THERE'S YOUR DEED!] *Together with all household furniture at 247 Fifth Avenue New York. To my daughter in law Carol Read McIlwaine, my diamond chain - I give to my first born grand daughter born to Archibald G. McIlwaine Jr. my string of pearls, all bracelets and small diamond ring. In case of no grand-daughter then to my eldest son's wife provided she meets the approval of my son Archibald G. McIlwaine Jr.* [OBVIOUSLY A SLIGHT TYPO OR MISUNDERSTANDING HERE AS ARCHIBALD WAS HER ONLY SON] *Automobiles to Archibald Southampton Long Island.* [AUTOMOBILES! Ok got my attention, wonder what kind? and where they might be?] *In case she does not meet his approval, it is to be given wisely at his discretion to whom he sees fit. My diamond wrist watch to Helen Harmon. My large diamond cluster ring to my cousin Laura Randolph Weber, at her death it is to go back to my son Archibald G. McIlwaine. Sable coat to Caroline W. Zeagler, all other furs wrist watch, pearl earrings, and pearl & jade necklace to Helen Harmon. Clothes to be equally divided between my sister and Helen Harmon.*
  Elizabeth Laing Knapp (L.S)
  Witness Edward H. Howell — Southampton, N.Y.
    Katherine M. Robinson — Southampton, NY

As for Sylvia, I'm not sure of when she sailed away for France, and perhaps other places in Europe. I would later find out she moved to Los Angeles for a few years after WWI and into early 1920s and had extended visits to Europe. Her younger brother moved to Germany, possibly to brew beer. Her sister Clara was a world traveler too, but kept a hotel suite on Park Avenue for years. I know that Sylvia returned to the US from France in November of 1924, to visit with her children. What put me onto that, was this story I found in NY Times in 1929 regarding that visit which might of been the one that soured her from ever coming back to the US.

WINS HER CUSTOMS CASE
Divorced Wife of J. P. Knapp Upheld in Foreign Residence Claim.

Claims to foreign residence, made by Mrs, Sylvia T. Knapp formerly of New York, in contesting the payment of duties on personal effects brought here on a visit in 1925 are sustained by the United States Customs in a decision made public yesterday. Mrs. Knapp who was divorced from Joseph Palmer Knapp in 1904, brought her protest in 1925 through William E. (Big Bill) Edwards, former Collector of Internal Revenue.

Mrs. Knapp said she was a citizen of the United States, but maintained her residence in France. Her trip here she said was to visit her daughter, Mrs. Claire Knapp Penney of St. Johns Island and Joseph Fairchild Knapp of Mastick, L.I.

Whew, four years to decide a customs case. In the official deposition in her tax case, it mentions she left the US because of disagreements with her children. She must have returned with some mighty fine stuff! In fact some of it was most likely left in Mastic after Dodi Knapp sold the place. According to Claire Knapp's nephew, Arthur Penney , who visited the Mastic Beach mansion with his father Clarence in 1939, "It was full of fine antiques, music boxes, a piano, organ, artwork etc."

The last visit I have ever found that Sylvia Knapp made to the US was in November of 1925. That's not to say she never came back, However a news report five years later in 1929, could of well scrambled a few facts here. Her daughter Claire was still Claire Knapp up until September 12, 1925 and she had just set up housekeeping in Yaphank, LI. I am reasonably sure Claire did not move to John's Island where she lived part time until sometime in 1926. Another small detail, but worth pointing out. As for what happened to Sylvia, who had been divorced now for a quarter century, you will notice she is now using Mrs. Sylvia T. Knapp rather than her former married name. I also can tell you that as late as post WWII, she was still alive and well and "living overseas" according to a very reliable source: Mr. Joseph Palmer Knapp

Business As Unusual

From the early 1900s, until he retired as Chairman of the Board of Crowell-Collier and it's big umbrella, lower profile Publication Corp. at age 81, which was in his owns words "a proper time to retire" Joseph Palmer Knapp's business interests were so varied, that to try and keep them interwoven with the personal stories of himself, and his family would just cause too much confusion for you and far too much work for me. So for the sake of the sanity of all, I have decided to put a fork into Knapp Road and deal with the business stuff from here on out as linear and separate as possible. Because there might be as many different reasons for you dear reader to have opened this book and look around, I will not drone on too much with too may bored meetings, if you will pardon the pun. Over the years when people have asked what the book I was writing was all about, I found I could not describe it totally with out having them sitting down for a minute or two.

When some pilgrim would ask me *"How did the Knapps make their money?"* my wise crack answer would usually be something like "They printed it!" but I found that only took longer for me to explain. Or if they asked *"How rich were they?"* I would quip, *"Well J. P. Knapp loaned Rockefeller the dough to build Rockefeller Center."* If that didn't raise a eyebrow, I'd counter it with *"He also loaned the money to build the Empire State Building at the same time."* If that still didn't get a response, I'd go for my Snake In The Bag — *"He also loaned the Uncle Sam half a million, interest free during the great depression, to undo some environmental damage that was destroying the salinity and fishing of North Carolina's waters."* If you're saying, So?—or thinking, Well, The Donald Had His Own TV Show and I Use To Watch It Faithfully, 'til NBC Said "Your Fired"—then there's no need to read this Chapter or any other one that may appear with the heading *"Business as Unusual"* Part II or III.

I think when we last left the board room (Chapter 21) it was 1906 and Joseph P. had just bought himself a printing plant in Springfield, Ohio along with two magazines, Farm & Fireside and Ladies Home Companion from John Crowell for $750,000. With the various plants he had operating under the American Lithographic umbrella and now this new facility, he needed plenty of work to keep those presses busy all the time.

In 1907 J. P. went to Washington to try and negotiate a contract with the postal service to provide preprinted postage stamps on envelopes that the post office could sell. The government specs were written in a way that Knapp and many other large printers could not make it worthwhile to bid. He got very frustrated with the red tape over envelope sizes and bureaucratic nonsense and perhaps some gate keeper looking for a kick back or two? However he also met Mr. Myron C. Taylor there in the Postmaster Generals office. Taylor a textile manufacturer, was negotiating for a contract to provide canvas sacks for letter carriers. Taylor got with Knapp and told him he thought he might be able to get the PG to change the specs. The two of them hand wrote out (described as scribbled) a contract on a 50/50 basis. It worked and that contract was framed and hanging on the wall behind Chairman Knapp's desk 'til he retired. An Ohio statistical journal from 1908 had the production figures for envelopes in it that were produced in Knapp's Springfield Plant. It may have been a typo, but it was several million envelopes per week. That's a lot mail to fill those letter carrier sacks with.

Myron Charles Taylor (1874 - 1959) would go on from making canvas sacks, to become among other things, a major financier and head of US Steel Corp in the 1930's and FDR's ambassador to the Vatican in WWII. He remained a life-long friend and fishing buddy of JP's. "Underhill Farm," the Taylor estate in Lattingtown, Long Island, was literally next door to "Borogrove Farm" Archibald and Caroline McIlwaine's estate in Locust Valley, giving J.P. double reason to darken the doors in Gatsby Ville on his drives out on eastern Long Island to Mastic and Southampton.

By the end of the first decade I am reasonably assured that J.P. Knapp saw the future of printing for the masses lie in the roto gravure process. American Litho then was using all forms of state of the art printing processes. He may of come to that conclusion by his producing the Recorder and Associated Sunday Magazine. Basically roto gravure is printing on a rotating copper cylinder verses a flat press and it allowed for being able to transfer quality photo images onto newsprint. In the 1890s -1900s J.P. was making frequent business trips to Germany which was a mecca of sorts for graphic arts. I am fairly assured that is where he invested in the development of the 6 Cylinder multicolor press that he has often been mistakenly credited as the inventor of. He knew a good idea when he saw or heard it and had the capital and contacts to move on it quickly. He also purchased the Corkett-Intaglio printing house at this time and applied to change it's name to American Lithographic, pulling it into his big printing tent.

This reputation that if "J.P. Knapp is interested in it" caused competitors sometimes to get reckless and make mistakes, mainly in errors of judgement, None can be more clearly demonstrated than by this item that appeared in the NY Times on April 3, 1912

$100,000 SWINDLERS SOUGHT IN LONDON-William Ottmann Declares They Defrauded Him Over Lithographic Process-TO REVOLUTIONIZE TRADE-The Professed to Produce Prints in 15 Minutes-Their Extradition Is Demanded—District Attorney Whitman, on the complaint of William Ottmann, President of the United Stated Lithograph Company of 1261 Broadway, has cabled to the authorities of Scotland Yard, requesting the arrest of Alfred Henry Motley and Clark A. Miller for swindling the United States Lithographing Company out of $100,000 in February and May 1911. They are said to be conducting business at 19 Cursitor Street, Chancery Lane, London and to be living at the Sterling Hotel in the same city.

Could these guys, Motley and Miller, be the original Motley Crew? The article goes on to say they approached Ottmann and his partners stating they had perfected a method of making lithographic plates in both B&W and Color at one tenth of the cost of the current process. They also said they could "do prints in any size from the smallest label up to the largest poster" Now perhaps when Ottmann and his associates said, we will think it over , Motley & Miller reached for their "snake in the bag" and closed the deal with this one. "J. P. Knapp has already offered us $100,000 for the rights to our invention, but we refused because "we do not desire to subject ourselves to Mr. Knapp's concern"

They said they had $500,000 thousand invested in the development of their process, but would sell cheaply. Ottmann gave them $50,000 as a binder and when they asked for $50,000 more three months later, he wanted to see their process demonstrated. Unbelievably the two said "We can make you this label in minutes that would normally take you all morning." They left the room and returned with a still damp label in 15 minutes, and repeated this demonstration several times until Ottmann forked over another $50,000. Soon hearing that his new "partners" left the country and were somewhere in the Mediterranean, Ottmann investigated further and found there was no such "process" as Motley & Miller described. I would not be surprised, if he learned that indirectly from Knapp or someone at American Lithographic Co.

In 1911 J. P. looked for a magazine with a more masculine appeal to add into the mix and with more general interest than Farm & Fireside had. He found it in American Magazine which was on shaky financial ground, just down the block from the Crowell NY Office. American had begun in 1876 as Frank Leslie's Popular Monthly and had it's own large city block 5 story building situated at Park and College Place, almost next door to the Major & Knapp Litho plant. I'm sure it did not go unnoticed when J P went to Columbia in 1880 and started his apprenticeship at M&K in '81. In 1906 Leslie's Mag was taken over by a lively group of muckrakers such as: Ida Tarbell. Lincoln Steffens, with John

S. Phillips as editor. Phillips knew that with America's thin resources, the future looked dark, so when Knapp offered him $334,000 in Crowell Stock and $40,000 cash, he moved his staff up the block to the Crowell offices. However it was not a marriage made in heaven or anywhere else for that matter and as for as hands off the editors chair as Knapp reportedly was, one by one the staff drifted away leaving just Phillips and one profane fellow named Sid Siddall, who the world would hear a great deal from in the future.

The Feeling Was Mutual or Was It?

This is another J. P. Knapp business decision story that I have read several variations of.[1] Regardless of exactly how it all came down, nothing else he ever did would effect as a great a many people as this one did. It was the fall of 1914 and the "great war" was already going on for several months in Europe. This has nothing to do with that war, but rather the secret ones that go on down on Wall Street and in the board rooms of major companies, that are ripe with capital for corporate take overs.

In 1914 Metropolitan Life was running as strong as any company in America or the world could be. Big J. F.'s old side kick John Hegeman, was still its president, as he had been since 1891 when big Joseph Fairchild Knapp had passed away. Hegeman had been with the company now for 44 years since 1870 when J. P.'s father had hired him as a book keeper and he had seen more than his share of Wall Street's ups and downs, competition wars, recessions, depressions and political investigations like the Armstrong hearings. In October 1914, John Rogers Hegeman was over 70 years old and a very tired man, as he had a every right to be. Ironically it seems that Met Life's unwritten contracts with all of its first four presidents was till "Death Do Us Part" Hegeman who was the third one, would still be president until April 6, 1919 when he died at age 75. Hegeman's number two man in 1914 was Haley Fiske who also had been with the company for years, first as legal consul in the days of Knapp and then as vice president since Knapp's death. Fiske was really the one running things at Met in 1914 along with Fred Ecker the former office boy wonder from the 1880s, who was now the companies long time treasurer.

In Good Hands

It is really a tribute however to the Joseph Fairchild's judge of character into his hires of a trusted trail of successors that Met was still in such "good hands" in 1914, if I may borrow the slogan from Allstate, which was still over a quarter of century from even being founded by Sears Roebuck. I'm sure that by 1914 if you could ask him, J. F. would also of been very proud with his son sitting on Met's Board of Directors, as he had for well over a decade. Not only was J. P. long

---

1 The variation I have heard was told by J. P. himself to Fortune Magazine in 1937 and involved a showdown between himself and John Hegeman over the decision to mutualize Met that was only resolved when J. P. threatened to resign from the board of directors at which would put the brakes on completely at the company, because by it's charter the company could not operate without the principal stockholder on board.

ensconced on the Board and helping to make very sound and wise business decisions for the company. but he and his sister controlled the largest amount of Met's stock. In short Met was still very much a Knapp family company in many ways. In actual practice though, it had long been operating as a mutual company for the benefit of all of its policyholders for decades, which also was just the way Big J. F. wanted it to be. In 1902, Hegeman had started to initiate official mutualization of the company, but it was abandoned in the face of opposition by two unnamed "ultra conservative" corporate attorneys. Long a leader in progressive reforms that benefited all its policyholders, it was what happened in 1914 that Haley Fiske called "the crowning act" in the evolution of Metropolitan into a nonprofit corporation for the sale of life insurance.

In 1914 Hegeman was a shadow of his former self, who along with J. F. Knapp had saved Metropolitan from bankruptcy in the 1870s. Under Hegeman's steady hand, Met became the worlds largest insurance company. He was still a very flamboyant and vital man, as he held the rivet gun and drove home the last rivets (perhaps one for Big Joseph Fairchild?) into the framework at the top of worlds tallest office building[2] at 1 Madison Ave in 1908. His unique wide brim floppy hat blowing nonchalantly in the breeze, while many of his board members looked on admiringly, but nervously with one hand on a girder and the other on the brims of Derbies and Straw Boaters to keep them from sailing out 700 feet above the tree tops of Madison Square Park. However for the last few years, 62 year old vice president Fiske was the man the takeover sharks would have to deal with when they came swimming around that landmark tower, Hegeman had built. Still a NYC landmark and a Registered National Historic Place, today Met Tower is no longer the company headquarters. "The Light That Never Fails "at the very top of the gilded cupola and the entire tower below it that held its torch high over the NYC landscape for nearly a century was purchased in 2005 by S L Green Realty Trust (obviously an oxymoron) who "flipped it" to a company called Africa Israel Investments for 200 million in 2007. I thoroughly enjoyed visiting both the freshly restored tower and the original 1890s Met Boardroom and looking at that very rivet gun Hegeman held, when I was a guest of Met's company historian Dan May in January of 2002. That it has been registered since 1989 as a National Historic Place is small comfort though, knowing how the US government and the financial world now acts so recklessly in most matters. I would not be surprised for the "right price" if it could possibly fall off the register.

And speaking of falling, it was Fiske who happily, if only figuratively threw the sharks out the tower windows, when they would make offers like the following one in 1913, when Met Stock had a par value of $25 a share and would often sell as high as $45. Fred Ecker told this somewhat amusing tale in 1947 to Marquis James who authored the book "The Metropolitan Life" : Fiske asked the representative of group of English financiers what they were paying. "As Little As We Can," said the bargainer. "Five Hundred?" asked Fiske (mean-

---

2   From Our Numerology Dept: I don't think I am the only one who sees the irony in the fact that Old Nickel & Dimer, Frank W. Woolworth, who built the Woolworth building during the skyscraper wars at the start of the 20th century, replacing Met Life Tower as The Worlds Tallest building in 1913, would die the very same day as Hegeman on April 8. 1919.

ing five times par or $125 a share). "Possibly," said the negotiator. Mr. Fiske pointed out the stock could pay no more than $7 on the hundred and at 5 times par the yield would be 1 & $^2/_5$ percent. Then bluntly said "Do you suppose that you are going to buy that stock and come in and handle these assets?" "Go ahead and buy it and the take a seat on a bench in Madison Square, you'll never get in the front door." "Well you know, really," replied the visitor, "I just came in to talk this over with you to see how you felt."

An emissary of a Canadian group, who also made an offer of $125, was more candid. "We like the way this company is run and we want the insurance business run as it always has been; only you know, when we buy the stock, why of course we control the finances. "What I told him," Fiske said, "cannot be repeated in polite society."

Fiske could speak that way because he had the full backing of the Knapp heirs who also had refused tempting offers for their stock. Met's surplus at the time exceeded $33,000,000 and although the management had said over and over money belonged to Mets policyholders, the charter of the company gave it's stockholders a proprietary interest in the surplus. The exact amount would of most likely taken a court to decide. That said the stockholders clearly held an interest in it and it was all that dough naturally that was fueling these wild offers of $125 for $25 par value stock.

Fiske wanted to take action and stop this speculation by retiring Met's capital stock of which he only held a small amount of 1,185 shares. Hegeman held just under 12, 000 shares which was still a drop in the bucket compared to J. P. and Netty's 30,562 shares. He was further spurred into action by Prudential, who had just begun formalities to mutualize itself. At this point Hegeman neither endorsed the idea or supported it. But the times had moved past John R. Hegeman. Fiske asked Fred Ecker who had always been on great terms with J. P. to intervene, as he knew without J.P.'s approval the idea of mutualization was dead in the water. After several initial talks J. P. invited Fred to dinner at Delmonico's. At the end of a very leisurely meal Ecker brought up the subject that was foremost on his mind by saying "What a tribute to your father this move would be." further adding in that he thought "It would a tragedy not to insure the permanence of his life's work." J. P, thought that it was a very appealing idea, but he also thought that Met was secure with the stock in control of his family.

Now I'm speculating here, but it would not be surprised that some thoughts along these lines also crossed J. P.s sharp mind that evening. One: that his sisters only boy was already in the grave at Greenwood now for 8 years and she was not going to have any more children at age 53. Two: His own children were 25 and 22, with neither one even close to being married. "Spinster" Claire was still over a decade away from marrying and would be the only one to have children. So just who would be the Knapp heirs that would insure his fathers lifetime legacy? Percy Rockefeller had recently offered J. P. $150.00 a share, but as much as he enjoyed making money, he was now in position to weigh all sides, and it is not what he saw as the best future for the company that his father and so many good men had put their life's work into. Fred Ecker talked on and at one in the morning Knapp finally asked him " What will you pay?" Ecker who himself had around 500 shares knew about the Rockefeller offer to J P, but also knew what was really on the line here, the perpetuation of a family trust of a man who had given Fred Ecker a reason to get up in the morning now for over 35 years[3] and after a moments hesitation he said "Seventy Five dollars a share." "It's a deal" said Joe Knapp Then the old friends ordered a bottle of wine to seal the agreement. I wonder what the bottle of wine cost? J. P. walked away from the table with close to 6 million dollars[4] for his sister and himself. He continued on of course as one of the most active directors of finance committee at Met.

Pressing On

It was also in 1914 or early '15, that J.P. got a weekly called *Every Week* up and running. This was a completely in house project, unlike Associated Sunday Magazine that relied on national newspapers signing on to carry it. At three cents a copy, *Every Week* was a large 14x11 mag, with color and provided national news coverage. Though it soon climbed to 500,000 copies circulation with major national advertising, the "great war" took it's toll directly on Knapp with disruption of freight services and paper shortages. With three other monthly magazines to feed a limited amount of paper to, his stockholders got very nervous and they say J. P. reluctantly and tearfully folded *Every Week*'s tent.

In 1917 American Lithographic was doing its fair share in the war effort by contributing to relief funds, printing millions of recruitment, Red Cross and morale boosting, home front posters like they were going out of style. Many originals are still in circulation and there are also untold amounts of repros offered on auction sites daily today. Of all of them, the most famous is without a doubt James Montgomery Flagg's iconic Uncle Sam "I Want You" posters. Flagg was a regular contributor to the stock images of American Litho for years before and after the war. Much closer to his wallet, JP had donated the waterfront of his son and daughters Mastic estate for a seaplane base and paid for the erection of hangers, housing, supplies, private instructors and probably his son's Curtiss F-5 Flying Boat if not all three of the first planes there. Though there was a lot at stake for everyone in the outcome of the war to end all wars, it was probably a drop in the bucket compared to what he would sink into his next big venture.

In 1866 when Joseph Palmer Knapp was just two years old, Peter Fenlon Collier migrated to the US from Ireland. He studied to be a priest, but did so well selling Bibles door to door he followed the path of book salesman instead. With $300 he bought printing plates for a Bible from a bankrupt publisher and set up the very first installment book selling business in America. It flourished and in 1888 he started a little magazine called "Once A Week" changing it to Col-

---

3 Fred Hudson Ecker may hold the distinction of being the longest employee of any company in the entire world. He was with Met Life for 80 years. He started at age 15 in 1883 and retired as honorary Chairman of the Board in 1963.

4 Six Million Dollars is what Met Paid to buy the controlling stock of the Knapp family, according to Louis I. Dublin's book *A Family of 30 Million*. In 1943, Dublin was Met's 3rd Vice president and company statistician. I'm sure attorneys' fees took up more than a few dollars. Met's assets at that time were 40,000,000.

lier's Weekly about 8 years down the road. It did very well and part of the reason he kept it going was to provide a future job for his son Robert, who seemed to be taking his sweet time completing his college education in such stellar places at Georgetown, Oxford, and Harvard. Peter died in 1909 and when Robert J. Collier finally settled down into the publishers chair at Collier's in 1912, he turned out a brilliant and widely acclaimed weekly crusading magazine that exposed the frauds of big business, adulterated foods, snake oil patent medicines, and the politicians who were lining their own pockets, while protecting their corporate fat cats, all the while selling out and endangering the lives of the very people who gave them their livelihood. But unfortunately light and truth is never that profitable is it? Collier's got hit with lawsuits left and right that had to have took a big bite out of their bottom line. Robert won his share, but many were settled out of court. William Randolph Hearst alone sued him for $500,000 (not sure who prevailed). In spite of all that, circulation still soared and advertising under Bob's old college pal, Condé Nast eventually doubled, putting the magazine into the black again. Circulation climbed from 220,000 to 840,000 per week. Bob started to really roar five years before the '20s would start. During the war, three of his friends, who had a stake in Colliers financial well being, saw their investment going into the dumpster via Bob's fast living with aero planes, big game hunting etc and intervened, wresting control of it from him in 1917. When 42 year old Bob Collier collapsed at his 5th Avenue dining room table in November of 1918, just two days before the Armistice, he had just returned from the front in France, where he had gone to write a story on the war. A heart attack was the cause of death. Although he was married, there were no children and the trustees of the Collier Estate went looking for a buyer for the P. F. Collier Co. They soon found one in J. P. Knapp

Knapp was persuaded to buy it by several of the young turks he had hired to run his Crowell Company. Thomas Hembly Beck (who would become J.P.'s true blue business protege) Bruce Barton and "Cap" Winger. All of these fellows had worked at Collier's before and were shown the door there over editorial differences. You will learn more about them as we travel further down Knapp Road. Along with a small handful of others, they would make up the nucleus of the men J. P. trusted over his lifetime to mind the store, while he was away hunting, fishing, and golfing and generally enjoying the fruits of his business and character judgement, he most likely inherited from his father.

One more small item before we adjourn this first board meeting. I want to briefly talk about a business decision J. P. made during this time, that also illustrates a side of him that was not just all business, but rather something else entirely. In 1912, a group of what might be thought of as intellectuals, artists and specialists, formed the Mentor Association with the sole purpose that a " Worthy Person Might Learn One Thing Every Day" Among it's founding members were William David Moffatt of Scribners. Moffatt with his journal background, proposed they put out a small publication. He drew from a pool of charter member experts like Luthar Burbank, plants, August Thomas, plays and Fritz Kreisler music. Kreisler was the violin virtuoso who J.P. upon first hearing him as a boy, wisely decided to put his violin back in it's case and stick with the pool cue, golf club and shotgun. The little publication was simply called The Mentor and by 1915 it was a full fledged monthly magazine similar in size of the National Geographic. Though wide circulation was never it's goal (circulation was 100,000 at its peak), Moffatt saw an opportunity to insure The Mentor's continued existence, by aligning himself with J. P. Knapp. Knapp thought it was a splendid idea and he partially funded The Mentor out of his own pocket, keeping it going at times over his stock holders objections, because he too believed in the idea of "Learning Something New Everyday." Like he was when he folded Every Week, they say Knapp was in tears when he finally had to pull the plug on The Mentor after the Great Depression wreaked more havoc on the little magazine, that even a big tycoon could not save.

CHAPTER
25

Meanwhile...Mainly
Out in Mastic

It may seem a bit strange that I am starting to write a chapter with this title on the very day in October 2007 they are laying Mildred Agnes Clune Skolnick Mitchell to rest at Mt. Pleasant, Center Moriches, NY about 1000 miles away from my home in Nashville, Tennessee. Not strange though that Mildred is buried in one of the older public cemeteries around my home town. (it opened in 1850) Mildred's parents and many of her family are there, as are so many people connected to this story in various degrees, including my grandparents Walter and Julia Joseph, who were instrumental in my family moving to Mastic Beach. And true it's really not any stranger than the manner in which I became involved in this story by living there too. I consider myself very fortunate to have been able to ask someone like Mildred, about what went on in Mastic, long before I and even people like my grandparents lived there.

Actually the sequence and title for this chapter, I decided upon just a few days ago and as I was writing the last paragraph of the chapter that precedes it, my e mail light came on. It was from Kathy Clune with the subject "Sad News" It was a brief note: "Ken: Aunt Mildred passed away last night in her sleep. I thought you would like to know, K."

Just like Darby Penney, the help and interest I received from Kathy Clune over the years has made a tremendous difference in filling out the meat and bones of this Knapp story, as it applied to Mastic.

Back in early May of 2005, I had just returned from a trip to Washington, DC. I was there primarily for a family Easter visit with my in laws. While there I took advantage of the vast resources of the Smithsonian and Library of Congress and found some interesting stuff on both the Knapps, e.g. Lt. Knapp's WWI Navy records, articles of Knapp seaplane base and of Dodi Knapp's step brother "Chip" McIlwaine, in the Aviation Library at the Smithsonian Aerospace museum. Over at The Library Of Congress,I found a beautiful photo of The Idler in full sail. She was the schooner J. P. Knapp sailed into Bellport with, in the 1890's. I also found a table top sized 1934 map of The Mastics, that showed the private estates that were still existing there.

I don't think I was home a day or so when I got an e mail from a Kathy Clune in California. I'm paraphrasing, but the gist of it said " I really enjoy all the work you have obviously put into your web site and I think you should speak with my Aunt Mildred, as she might be able to help you"

Who Is Aunt Mildred?

Well I sent off a fast response asking Kathy, Who Is Your Aunt Mildred? because I recognized the Clune name immediately. There has been an Arthur Clune American Legion Post in Mastic Beach since the late 1940s. I also knew of the Clune association to pre Mastic Beach as the caretakers of the Richard Floyd homestead known as "Patterquas" since the 1920s. I was told that early on, by my childhood pal Larry Schulz's mom Estelle, that the Clunes ran "Pattersquas" when it was known as the Lawson Estate in the 1930s. Estelle Parr Schulz who came to Mastic in the mid 1920s, as a young girl, is another person I would learn a great deal about Mastic and Mastic Beach from.

Kathy wrote back "You have a picture on your website of my Aunt Mildred, with her brothers standing on a dirt road in the 1920s and that's their house in the woods. I knew exactly which photo she meant. It was a copy of a copy, undated but from the 1920's and taken at the future crossroads of what would become known as the 5 Corners of Mastic Beach. Though my copy was not perfectly clear, the house in the woods identified it. That house remained there until 1956, even as a gas station and stores were built around it. The girl in it looked to me to be about 8 years old. My guess turned out to be mighty close, as I would later learn the photo was taken on March 8, 1923 and Mildred Clune's birthday was May 10, 1916.

Kathy also filled me in a bit on her family. It turns out I actually knew Mildred's son, Jack Skolnick, from my school days. Jack was 4 years ahead of me, but I was always aware of the older kids in the small school we went to, as I had an older brother there myself. She told me that although Mildred was well up in her 80's, she saw her recently and she was sharp as a tack and could probably tell me a thing or two about Mastic Beach history.

It wasn't a day or so later that I found myself speaking with Mildred on the phone. We talked for quite a spell. I had looked at my files and notes before I called, and had a list of questions to ask her. There was a 1920s census that I always wondered about, because the Clune family was enumerated right next to Knapps. With no address or house numbers listed back then, just the nearest main road, I knew they had to be in close proximity. William Clune's occupation was listed as that of caretaker for a private estate and I had originally thought that he may of worked for the Knapp Estate. I was put off of that trail because Estelle Schulz had told me the Clunes worked for the Lawsons, just across the Pattersquash creek. Well it turned out, we both were right. That was revealed when I asked Mildred if she knew a Japanese man in Mastic there named Mac Sayama. Mac was listed with the Knapps as a "houseman" and I figured he would certainly get noticed in a town of less than twenty people.

She didn't even hesitate and said, "Of course I do! He was the Knapp's butler"— "SO," I said anxiously, "Then you knew the Knapps," like I was afraid to hear that phrase I had heard so often in the past: Knapps? Never heard of them. Mildred's answer again: "Of course I did! My Mother and Father worked for them. We lived on the Knapp estate in a nice two story house." Well, after I picked the phone off the floor, our conversation continued, and much was learned that day my friends, much was learned. And it will all be interwoven for you supporting the story in the proper places of course.

It turns out Mildred's parents were professional caretakers for most of their lives, up until the end of the private estate era in the Mastics. Her step father William D. Clune was born in 1878. He was a hostler for the Coney Island Jockey Club at Sheepshead Bay in 1900. He then moved further east out on Long Island working with millionaire August Belmont's stable in Babylon. Then further east still, working for The Robert family and also the Lawrence sisters in Mastic, but for only a short time as he said "the Lawrences were not very nice." He also worked on and off for the Smiths at the Manor of St. George, and the Floyds for a time. In December of 1917, he married Mildred's mother at St. Johns in Center Moriches. Leroy Ross another man of all work was their witness. William Denis Clune then became estate superintendent for the Knapps. It's possible through his horse expertise, that he was introduced to Claire Knapp. Mildred's mother Loretta, was Knapp's cook . William's brother Henry who was described as a free spirit, also worked there off and on as a grounds keeper. Loretta who was a very strong woman, would run Henry off the estate when he drank too much and he would go back home to his parents place in Huntington. The draft registration cards of William and Henry from 1917, list their employer as Claire A. Knapp, Mastic NY. William and Loretta Clune lived at the Knapp Estate from the time Mildred was a baby in 1917 up until the early 1920s. Two sons Bill and Arthur were born there. Then the Clunes moved just across the creek working for the Laniers at Pattersquash about 1923 and finally for the NY playwright and Hollywood screenwriter John Howard Lawson in 1930s & '40s. Lawson purchased the Lanier estate, when the Laniers divorced. Mildred's parents stayed working for the Lawson family until they sold the estate in 1946. Her father semi retired and her mother continued working as cook for the St. John's convent and school in Center Moriches, but only after a Poosepatuck Indian taught her how to drive a car as transportation out there was difficult without one. William, a horseman all his life probably didn't think a woman should drive a car. By this time Mildred was married to David Skolnick, a fellow from the city who originally had stopped in at Loretta's pie stand on the 5 corners, asking about the young girl who sometimes worked there.

Of course although I was eager to hear everything, you have to know by now, what was primarily on my mind, and so I asked the million dollar question. "Mildred, do you remember much about Dodi Knapp?" She remembered quite a bit, even though she would qualify it by saying "I was just a little girl then, but yes I remember Mr. Knapp." And in one short reminiscence, she spoke volumes. based on what I now knew as facts and what I had heard or was implied by others. She said this *"My mother used to watch him walk around outside the mansion from the kitchen window and say out loud, What In The World Kind Of Trouble, Will That Damn Fool Get Into Today."*

Again picking up the phone off the floor and hoping it still worked, I asked, "Just what kind of trouble did he get into? "—From 2005 - 2007, Mildred and I exchanged several letters and phone calls. When I first spoke with her, she had just turned 89 and was still living on her own. I found her to be, just as Kathy had told me she was, "Spirited and Sharp As A Tack". I had planned to visit with Mildred in late Autumn of 2005, but she took a fall and was hospitalized. About a year or so later, she moved into an assisted living facility. Her last letter to me was quite brief and she was not remembering things like once she had. However I was very glad to have been able to meet someone who was actually there when The Knapps Lived Here , or as the late great guitarist Carl Perkins used to sing,"I was there when it happened, don't you think I ought to know?"

As The Twenties Began To Roar

The great war was over and Knapps had only owned their Mastic place for about 5 years, when things started to change fairly rapidly. Income taxes, prohibition, the jazz age , all had effects on the society in general. Several other estate owners started selling off pieces of their land holdings to developers. Probably to reduce their tax bill, the Danas, Floyds and Smiths sold small sections of their vast property around the Montauk Highway area.

Buying up some of the Dana and Floyd land on and near the Forge River, Warren and Arthur Smadbeck's, Home Guardian Company created "Mastic Park." The brothers (who were considered the Henry Fords of real estate across the United States) erected a huge billboard at the Mastic train station and advertised in all the major NY newspapers, targeting the working class. Unlike the Tangier Development Company in 1910, that aimed higher for the privileged class and found itself with few takers for land out in the sticks, the Smadbecks soon found themselves with the first modestly successful development in the Mastic area. Home Guardian sold Mastic Park like silver dollar hot cakes in small lots of 20' x 100'. By subscribing to the Brooklyn Citizen Newspaper (their sales gimmick) you could buy a $55 lot for only $10 down and $3 a month interest free. Usually a minimum of three lots was required to build a bungalow on it, but some people would just buy one or two lots and pitch a tent in the woods or put up a shack. Some bought lumber or surplus buildings from the now useless Camp Upton Army base in nearby Yaphank. The "War

To End All Wars" had been successful and the government auctioned off the camp. Between 1922 and '25, Home Guardian sold most of the initial land they had purchased and then started looking to buy some more. Along with that first development, came the first official town of Mastic. It was now more than just a whistle stop, and was designated with a Post Office and a few years later a Fire Department.

One of the earliest customers the Smadbecks had for their land, was a fellow named Paul Schulte. Schulte was a German immigrant who had worked at the India Wharf Brewery in Brooklyn. When prohibition put a halt to that, he opened a delicatessen. In 1923 his wife died and although he had a family to provide for, a life change loomed on his horizon. A fan of boxing, he followed pro boxer Vince "Pepper" Martin out to Mastic to watch him train at the middle-weight's gym. The wilds of Mastic may of reminded him of the Bavarian forest and Schulte bought some land out there. In May of 1926, the Smadbeck's expanded on their Mastic Park development. Paul would make a major move, just south of Mastic Park and become a pioneering businessman of varied interests in a brand new town the Smadbecks called Mastic Beach

IN THE '20S DODI KNAPP WAS WORKING AT AMERICAN LITHOGRAPHIC, where he claimed in later life to have been the chairman of the board. The only official title for him at ALCO, I have ever seen in print was that in a New York state government publication on industrial safety published in 1927 where it lists Joseph F. Knapp "Manufacturing Director" of American Lithographic Co. NYC and Buffalo. Regardless of what his official designation was or wasn't, he WAS the owner of ALCO's son. Mildred Clune recalls that "He had a newspaper in NY City" (That would most likely have been Associated Sunday Magazine) which would of been all a little girl would have to know about what the man who lived in the great big house, across the field from her did. At least that was when he wasn't wandering around the estate grounds causing her mother anxiety, as she watched probably standing on a chair at the kitchen window, shaking her head. Dodi was staying at the 247 5th Ave apartment on weekdays and most likely coming out to Mastic on weekends and holidays, just like some of his new neighbors in Mastic Park would, although I'm sure in a very different style. There was no electricity in Mastic yet, but the Knapp estate had generators. I'm quite sure if Dodi wanted to take a few extra days or weeks off for duck hunting, no one at the NY office was going to say no.

For a year or so after the war, Dodi and his step brother Chip McIlwaine had that huge NYC apartment to themselves at times, (remember how many guests were there for his 21st Birthday Party?) possibly because J. P. and Elizabeth, had a new huge estate in North Carolina that J. P. bought in 1918 J. P. was building a new home there, plus I believe the Catskill place was still standing. Then Chip moved out of 247, when he married Caroline Hicks Read at her Westchester estate in June of 1920. It was a lavish affair with over 600 guests. 18 ushers alone of which Dodi Knapp was one, and umpteen bridesmaids too. Just about every surviving flyer from the First Yale Unit was there including William Rockefeller and a few from Aerial Coast Patrol Unit's 2 & 3. The guest list was a who's who of eastern society. with a special train hired to bring them up from the city to Westchester.

By 1922 Clairedale kennel originally called Clairedale Farm was up and running strong on the Mastic Knapp Estate. Between her natural talent, her mentors and ability to devote unlimited time and money to her kennel program, Claire Knapp found her dogs winning shows early on. With her dogs priced between $75 - $150, she didn't rely on local folks for customers, just for estate labor. Just like the horse show rings had in the early 1900s, the dog business show circuit would soon take her all over the eastern half of the country. The show circuit didn't seem to have any order to it's routing. I would imagine transportation logistics and expenses was not a large consideration though. One day they would be in Boston, next in Chicago, then Rochester etc and other than it's super bowl held every February at Madison Square Garden in NYC, it seemed to run fairly helter skelter.

Also around 1922, an old flyer and barnstormer pal of Dodi's returned to Mastic to live on the Knapp Estate for a time. Leonard Warden Bonney, the second and last flight instructor of Unit 3, came out there to study seagulls. Actually his study of them involved getting caretakers and hunting guides like Dodi's pal Leroy Ross to trap gulls for him. When Bonney found what he considered to be his perfect specimen, he had a taxidermist stuff it. With that stuffed gull and some experiments at MIT's wind tunnel, he started construction of his dream plane, the Bonney Gull. The pale yellow fuselage of this futuristic and strange looking flying machine with huge bird like wings, was most likely originally fashioned in a barn known as the Knapp machine shop, located just to the east of the mansion. This is the barn I refer to as Mr. Clark's place in chapter 1. In a very early interview I did with Terry Hooper, who is a grandson of Willis O. Penney, by his first marriage, I first learned a little about the existence of this plane. Terry told me that he learned from his grandfather, that Dodi was a silent investor in the development of the Bonney Gull. Because of it's strange appearance I asked Mildred if she recalled this plane, and she only said, "My God, he had all sorts of airplanes, all over the property. Half the barns were full of them and they were taking off and landing all over the place, at all hours. In any open field of which there were many, and sometimes right on the roads". Magazines like Popular Science and Popular Mechanics, took an interest in Bonney's new plane and photographs of a engine-less aluminum bird appeared that look like they were taken in the wilds of Mastic. An illustration of it actually flying, wound up on the cover of Popular Science in December of 1926, but it's real maiden voyage would have to wait for almost two more years.

In 1925 Bonney married Flora McDonald, a wealthy mining heiress that had her own dog kennel called Tally-Ho in, Queens. Naturally she and Claire Knapp became friends and it could well of been that Claire met Flora first, via the dog shows and introduced Flora to her brothers flying friend. In any event Bonney moved his unpowered yellow bird to Garden City's, Roosevelt Field, for engine development and final fitting out. Roosevelt Field, which is considered to be the cradle of aviation, is where Lindberg took off on his historic flight.

Changing Times and Caretakers

In January of 2002, I interviewed Roland Penney, who I first saw in a photo as a very young boy. The photo was taken the late 1930s and standing in the pic along with Roland are his father Lloyd, Lloyd's father Clarence and Clarence's father Merritt. Four Generations of Penneys. Roland provided me with a many tips and names of people to talk with to help answer the questions he couldn't about what life was like in the era of the great estates. Knowing I am repeating some of the information and stories that originally captivated me and were mentioned very early on in Chapters 5, 6 & 7, I offer a few of them again here. But in the new light that they had now become more than just stories, but rather substantiated facts of record and paint a picture of what was going on in the roaring twenties out in sleepy Mastic.

Merritt Cash Penney, 1854-1941 of Moriches, who was first mentioned briefly in Chapter 5, was like many natives of the area. He was a jack of all trades, who did what they had to get buy and support his family. Merritt was a fisherman, farmer, did a stint in the US Life Saving Service (the fore runner of the Coast Guard) and in the 1920s, he found himself as the superintendent of the Dana Estate and "Moss Lots" Moss Lots was the large victorian home built in the 1880's on the Forge River by the publisher of the Financial Chronicle, William "Buck" Dana, brother in law to John G. Floyd. The Dana estate had been inherited in 1910 by William Shepherd Dana, who was born in 1892. "Shep" or Bill was Buck's grandson. Raised in the woods and wilds Mastic, Bill Dana preferred the leisurely life of a country esquire over working in the New York office at the Chronicle and that is just what he did. He was an expert sailor, and devoted outdoorsman and some sort of banjo player. He installed oarlocks into the wood door trim of one of his Rolls Royce Silver Ghosts touring cars, to hold the shotguns as he and his friends, who were mainly locals, rode through the woods and marshes shooting at deer, ducks and trees. Being the same age as Dodi Knapp, I had heard from several caretaker family members that he and Dodi had a lot in common as far as recreational interests and work ethics. They also were great rivals especially with their speedboats.

Bill Dana had Clarence Penney along with Clarence Ross, who also worked on the Dana estate, build an island just for duck hunting with their "sand sucker" dredge, just south of the mouth of Forge River on the bay. Clarence Penney, a trained carpenter by trade, followed somewhat in his fathers footsteps becoming a man of all work in the Moriches, Mastic area. He also was a house mover. Most all work was provided by the estate owners and according to Clarence's son Arthur, the Knapp's alone kept his father very busy. Mildred Clune said most everyone she knew back then, worked at all the different estates at one time or another.

Clarence Penney's younger brothers were both private chauffeurs, The middle brother Leonard worked in New Jersey and Willis was driving then for envelope manufacturer Henry Trinchard. Living with Willis at the Trinchard residence on fashionable Ocean Parkway in Brooklyn was his wife, the former Dorothy Terry of Moriches, whom he married in 1917 and their first daughter. It may of been during this time that Clarence, who was building roads in Mastic Park for the Home Guardian Company, was also hired to build the Knapp golf course and had his brother Willis come there to help out? Claire Knapp who was as interested in landscaping and plants. as she was in horses and dogs, most likely took a hand in making sure the golf course was lavishly landscaped, with a man made pond, and nursery grown trees perfectly planted and aligned all along the road that bordered the fairways and led to the dock of the bay.

Exactly when or why Willis O. Penney turned up again in Mastic, is not known by me. But he was back in Moriches area with his wife and now two daughters when his marriage of seven years ended. Arthur Penney said, "Aunt Dorothy was known to have quite a temper," but that could of been due to Willis' new relationship with Claire Knapp, which reportedly was met with much disapproval by Dodi and possibly from a distance, her father. Arthur, who was born in 1923, would of course have heard these stories second hand his mother, father or other locals, but the octogenarian still tells tales of Claire Knapp hiding Willis in closets and secret passageways of the mansion and of Willis climbing out of second story windows and making his escape leaping off the terraces and onto the trees that bordered the residence whenever Dodi came home. Dorothy Penney retained county judge John Vunk and filed two lawsuits against Willis and Claire in December of 1924 The Suffolk County News carried this headline, WEALTHY YOUNG WOMAN OF MASTIC, FIGURES IN TWO SENSATIONAL SUITS. Willis was sued for divorce and Claire for alienation of affection. There was little follow up in the papers and I assume it was settled quite privately

Now Terry Hooper, Willis' grandson by his marriage to Dorothy, told me a different tale about the relationship between Willis and Dodi Knapp. Willis told Terry that Dana, Dodi and himself were "like the three musketeers back then", but Terry had never met his grandfather, until he visited with him in Florida in the mid 1960's and Willis may of been referring to his relationship with the two millionaire playboys, post September 1925. Both could be true, because if there's two things Dodi Knapp could be is, sociable with all, regardless of status and yet a very obnoxious to all, especially when he was drinking, which according to everyone I spoke with who knew him, was quite often. Mildred Clune, was just one of many who mentioned that to me. She flat out said "He could be quite nasty and my mother would not tolerate him at all when he was drinking". She said , "He would change his tune pronto when my mother (who was quite short but very feisty) stood up to him."

The Summer and Fall Of 1925

After the Clunes moved on to the Lanier estate in the mid '20s, another Penney family member, Charles E. Penney, who was a grocery salesman for the Grand Union Company, along his wife Grace and three daughters Alice, Claire and Grace came to Mastic from Patchogue to run things at the Knapp estate. The girls all went to the little Moriches Elementary School, although I heard one of them died before graduation from cancer, The Charles Penney family were still at the Knapps in 1930s and I always held out hope I might of found one of the other two sisters or relatives of same, but it never happened. The Clunes may of partly left the Knapp place to get away from the turbulence of the Willis and Claire affair, but they soon found themselves in a similar situation with their new employer because author and editor, Henry Wysham Lanier and his wife Josephine Stevens Lanier,split up. Josephine put the 212 acre Pattersquash estate on the market in 1925, calling it "Mastic On The Sea." The Clunes however stayed put and would end up taking care of the place for the eventual new owners Susan and John Howard Lawson in 1929, until after WW 2, when screenwriter Lawson (one of the Hollywood Ten) found himself in trouble with the US Congress House Un American Activities Commission. Looking at a prison term, he put the estate on the market.

In late August of 1925, according to the Patchogue Advance, Dorothy Penney and her two children moved from Moriches to Patchogue to live with relatives. Then in the first week of September it reported that "Mr. Penney, the recent purchaser of the Oleson Property, has taken possession, his goods arriving last week". The Oleson property was 12 acres with a colonial home built circa 1776 and out buildings in Yaphank, which is about 15 miles north west of the Knapp Estate. The purchase price was a bargain at $7,500. Then a week later in the Advance's Nuptials column this appeared :

PENNEY - KNAPP: *Willis O. Penney, son of Mr. and Mrs. Merritt C. Penney of Mastic was married Saturday to Miss Claire Antoinette Knapp, daughter of Mr. and Mrs. Joseph P. Knapp of Mastic. The ceremony was performed by Arthur Griffith Justice of the Peace, East Islip, and the only witness was Mrs. Griffith. The couple plan to make their home in Yaphank.*

Well that kind of tells you a great deal more about what the situation for Claire back in Mastic was on the estate that had been in her name since October 5, 1917. She eloped plain and simple, leaving behind a 200 acre paradise for a modest little old colonial farm house and peace of mind. Islip is quite a distance away from Mastic and it sounds like this decision was made to avoid notice, as there are other towns much closer to Mastic, like Patchogue where if they only wanted to get with a Justice of The Peace, they could of. For the record, other than when he donated the land for the air-base in 1917, Joseph P. Knapp never listed his address as Mastic. Nor did his name ever appear on the deed there, though I'm sure he paid for it. In 1925 his addresses were 330 Park Ave., NYC and Mackey Island, North Carolina. Claire's mother, Sylvia, was now living in France. There was however a new Mrs. Joseph P. Knapp replacing the late Elizabeth Laing Knapp, for J. P. had married for the third time to Margaret E. Rutledge at his Mackey Island estate in 1923.

In mid October of 1925, Dodi Knapp and Leroy Ross departed for a hunting trip in the Adirondack mountains. When they returned, two more real estate transactions would occur, that effected Dodi's future.

In Patchogue four businessmen had a formed a little real estate investment group called the C. S. R. V. Corporation to cash in on the real estate boom that was happening all over Long Island in the '20s. They were George R. Carlton, Charles W, Raynor, Samuel A. Smith and John R. Vunk (the lawyer - judge Dorothy Penney retained to sue Claire. The access to legal matters C. S. R. V. had, especially in the areas of probate and estate settlements, might of gave them an edge over some others as far as knowing when a certain estate was about to be sold off. As I mentioned earlier in this chapter, the Smadbecks of NY City were actively looking to expand on their Mastic holdings and it could well be that these local boys beat them to it when the 355 acre J. B. Lawrence estate came up for sale. This was originally the property of General Nathaniel Woodhull also known as the Woodhull Farm. Fact is it may never of even been listed, as C. S. R. V. could well of handled legal matters for the Lawrence family. who had not any physical presence in Mastic for almost a decade. The Lawrence family, as I mentioned in Chapter 23, had married into the Woodhull and Smith family back in the 1700s. The exact price paid for the land was not disclosed, but it was reported in November of '25 as being close to $75,000. That included the Wood-hull mansion and one other residence, plus farm buildings. This land adjoined the entire eastern border of the Knapp estate from the bay up to the northern boundary line. Slightly wider than Knapp's land, it proceeded eastward till it touched the western border of the Floyd Estate. Certainly enough land to make a small town out of and with 3,000 feet of it right on the bay, it would be very marketable if developed wisely. Shortly after that, in December of 1925, Claire Knapp sold her estate once known as "Clairedale Farm" back to her brother for the original 1916 price of $35,000. This was a real bargain, as they had made many improvements to it since 1916. The '20s were roaring and 1925 made quite a racket in sleepy little Mastic, with even more changes soon to come.

CHAPTER
26

The Four Rs: Redin, Romance,
Redskins & Rum-running

T*wo* of the names Roland Penney gave me to contact, were Terry Hooper and "Cut" Redin. He said Cut's family went way back as caretakers in Moriches and that I would find him to be helpful. Terry Hooper who is Willis Penney's grandson and mentioned in the previous chapter also mentioned Cut to me and gave me his phone number. I called Bill "Cut" Redin in South Carolina, where he had retired to. And yes he sure let me know that he knew stuff, but he was very cautious about telling me too much and declared several topics at the outset "off limits" including the subjects of Dodi Knapp and Rum Running! I thought it was a pretty strange way to start a phone interview, but it already told me volumes if only by innuendo.

"The Code"
When I spoke to Cut in 2002 and told him who I was, he said he already knew all about me and "Knew What I Was Up To !"—I was taken aback for a bit with his blunt statement, and tone, but knew what ever impression he already had of me, did not come from his old friends Terry Hooper or Roland Penney, who had prior conversations with me. It had to have come from one or both of Dodi Knapp's two nieces; one who never spoke to me except through her attorney and the other who only told me on the phone "I don't want to talk to you about

anything." I then realized, they really had been circling the Knapp wagons on me probably since September of 2001 and again it raised the question, what in the world are they so touchy about? I did not know at the outset of the call, that Cut too was related to one of them by a marriage - divorce. If I had, I would of never called him, as the last thing I needed was another letter from a Knapp heir lawyer. So this was one of the many times my early initial ignorance of the Knapp line paid off.

At least he didn't hang up on me, and after a few tense minutes, of which I still find to be so weird, he started to tell me some details about his life as a boy following his father around on several estates in Moriches and Mastic in the 1930s and '40s. He mentioned more than once "The Code" of the caretakers, that I obviously was not adhering to in his judgement. But I wasn't a caretaker, nor a reporter for the Enquirer or any other tabloid. I was just a historian.

THE REDINS WERE AN OLD MORICHES FAMILY and William "Cut" Redin's father, Bill was the superintendent for the Mark estate located on Senix Creek in Center Moriches during the 1920s-40s. Lawyer Henry Mark died in the 1930s and Bill Redin continued at the estate working for his widow. Bill has a very interesting and highly detailed account of surviving nearly drowning and of daring rescues during the hurricane of 1938 there. It is published in The Illustrated History of The Moriches by Van & Mary Field. I mentioned I read that to Cut. That coupled with the fact I already had spoke with both Terry Hooper and Roland Penny, seemed to have broken a little bit of initial ice.

He spoke quite a bit about the Danas and what a super person Bill Dana was. He was the first to tell me that Dana had two Rolls - Royces and his father was offered one of them by Ella.(Bill's widow) His father didn't take her up on that offer, much to Cut's regret, but he did on a 1915 Gil Smith catboat named The Lorelei. Cut told me that Lorelei was now in the Suffolk Marine Museum and I should visit there when I'm back on the Island. He also gave me the names of two people to speak with on Long Island about estates and related era stuff. He said one, Johnny LiBaire was way up there in his years and I should talk with him ASAP before as he so colorfully put it "another library burns down." He said the Libaires had large homes in the Moriches and Oakdale since before the turn of the 20th century and were very active in the Great South Bay yachting scene.

The other fellow was Dan Acernio, who lived in Sayville. Dan was a marine mechanic and boat restorer, that had Dana's old Elco speedboat the "Wha Hite" from the 1920s. I owned a 1929 Elco cabin cruiser myself once, so I sort of knew what he was talking about. Cut seemed to really enjoy talking about old boats with me and he did mention that Bill Dana and Dodi Knapp were sailing rivals especially over their speedboats. I dared ask him if he knew what kind of speedboat Knapp had. He said a sea sled, a really fast one. I had never heard of a sea sled before and underlined it in my notes and planned to look into it.

He told me of trips as a boy to Mastic and Mastic Beach during duck hunting season and how long it seemed to take just to drive there from Center Moriches (about 6 miles away) once they pulled off Montauk Highway and rode down endless dirt roads lined with nothing but trees. He said after winter storms there would be firewood to cut for days on end from all the downed trees. He also said some of the estate duck blinds on the shoreline were more like small cabins, fully furnished with stoves and the property owners like Dana even left their shotguns in them ready for action.

Not knowing just how old he was, I asked Cut if he followed in his fathers footsteps as a caretaker too. He said no, that he worked most of his life after high school for the NY Telephone Company. When I mentioned my Dad worked his entire life there, he asked me for his name. I said Wally Joseph— "I thought your name was Spooner—Your Dad Was A Great Guy! A PEACH! I worked with him in his last years with company. He was always telling us in the office about tales of how it was outside in the pioneer days." (My father started with NY Telephone when installers and repairmen still rode bicycles, retired about 1974 after 50+ years with the company).

True my father was very personable with most people outside the family, especially his co-workers. I made a mental note that Cut's judgement of people was obviously based on his own unique perspective. I also thought that he didn't ask me why I didn't have the same last name as my father. For several good reasons, I changed it to my mothers maiden name in the 1970s. Thinking I was on even safer ground, now that Cut knew I was a real "son of a peach," I mentioned to him that Terry Hooper had told me Cut's grandfather had been Dodi Knapp's plumber and replaced the coal furnace by installing an oil burner in the Knapp mansion. It seemed a totally innocuous thing to say, but good grief did he get agitated again. I found it to be very odd. Again he mentioned "the code," which I had now figured out meant something along the lines of, we caretakers just don't talk about what went on at the private estates or what we did for them. Ok — Ok!— then we had some general chit chat, coupled with a bit more history and a total out of the blue statement from him about how he became distantly related by marriage to one of Claire Knapp's daughters. For the genealogists out there, Cut is married to the first wife of the second husband of Claire's second daughter. What are the odds? But it serves no purpose to get into more details here, other than it perhaps explains some of his peculiar caution in talking with me and why he was in on the circling of the wagons.

I did get another Knapp related question in, when I asked him if he knew anything about an experimental airplane built in Mastic that Terry Hooper told me about. I mentioned Terry said the wings fell off of it (I did not mention that Terry told me Knapp was involved with the plane). He said yes he knew something about it. The plane was built out there in the 1920s and the guy who built it was named Bunny. I asked him if he knew how that was spelled? He didn't, just that his name was Bunny and that it might of been his nickname, but he thought it was his real last name. He did break his own code a little and told me that one of the care taking Ross fellows (possibly Clarence but I now think it was more likely Lee Roy Ross), had trapped seagulls for Bunny to fashion the plane from. Other than that and saying that it crashed, he didn't know anything else about it. Knowing about the WWI air base and my own childhood discovery of busted up airplane parts in a barn, I had searched for months after our phone call, for an airplane designer from the 1920s named Bunny or Bunnie and hit nothing but dead ends.

I eventually would accidentally discover a photo on the front page of the New York Times of May 5, 1928, For there and on many other newspapers across America. were photos of the remains of The Bonney Sea Gull Bird Plane, all smashed up. Bunny turned out to be, the former flight instructor of Aerial Coast Patrol #3. Leonard Warden Bonney, the man whom taught Dodi Knapp how to fly. Leonard was killed on the maiden flight of a his controversial flying machine on May 4. 1928. A plane that initially was built on one of my boyhood playgrounds, "Mr. Clarks Barn" aka the former Knapp machine shop. Now that I had his real name, I wanted to learn as much as I could about the plane, Highly unorthodox in design, with wings that indeed resembled those of a prehistoric bird, I discovered it had taken years to build and was initially featured on the cover of Popular Science magazine two years before the crash. As late as a few years ago, flying magazines still run stories on the Tragedy of the Bonney Gull. There is now even the original newsreel footage of it's very short flight online.

But I would further discover a second tragedy associated with it. A week after Bonney got killed trying to prove his airplane could really fly (many of his friends said it couldn't and tried to dissuade him from trying it) his mistress, a singer named Jean Le Brun, whom she initially had met on a trip to Florida, killed herself after an unsuccessful attempt, in her Manhattan apartment, with a faulty pistol. She succeeded finally by turning on the gas. Her body was found surrounded by photos of Leonard and newspaper clippings about the crash. This tragedy was even further compounded when the press arrived at widow Flora Bonney's door in Flushing, Queens. Obviously overcome by the now double shock and discovery, Flora reacted with this statement. "My husband didn't know this woman, and I never have heard of her either. This unfortunate woman must've been of the type that kill themselves when matinee idols like Rudolph Valentino die." Now—I have seen many photos of Leonard Warden Bonney, some taken the very day he crashed and he was no matinee idol, unless your idea of one was say Wally Cox or Woody Allen. Flora soon moved to a beautiful estate on Oyster Bay, Long Island. She continued with her famed show dogs, lived very well until 1965 and never remarried. Her chauffeur driven 1931 Cadillac touring car, was recently auctioned off in London for about $100,000. I was contacted by the grandson of her private chauffeur. who offered me Bonney's flight suit and a scale model prototype that Leonard had built of his Gull. I tried to mediate a purchase of them for the Cradle of Aviation museum ,which is located at the site of the very short flight Leonard took at Roosevelt Field. The grandson offered the items to me, but then told me there was family dispute over ownership of them. He also would never even name a price. All further attempts to contact him and follow up on it were unsuccessful.

Cut asked me where I grew up and I told him, Mastic Beach. He did not have very nice things to say about my town. That came as no surprise because many old timers from Center Moriches ever did. I defended Mastic Beach quite nobly I felt and mentioned I don't think I would of cared to have grown up anyplace else. He then asked me, what I did for a living? I told him I was a musician for most of my life and had started out playing as a very young teenager in the taverns in our town like Schulte's Stable. Well that just set him off again and he went into a tirade about about Paul Schulte (Chapter 26), which again made me think to myself— what is this man's problem? He then blurted out: "I KNEW ALL OF THEM, YES I DID!—I KNEW WHO ALL THE BOOTLEGGERS WERE._WE JUST DIDN'T TALK ABOUT IT!—BECAUSE IT'S THE CODE. Sensing we needed to end our conversation on a high note, I thanked him for his time and got off the line. I had one more phone conversation with Cut months later after I discovered who Bunny really was. It was not very productive.

Following up on leads

I decided not to waste any time following up on the two leads Cut had given me, especially after telling me that he wasn't sure if Johnny Libaire was even still alive. Cut's own colorful phrase was still ringing in my ear and I of all people, could not afford to lose a single book much less have "another library burn down." First I called Terry Hooper again to thank him for putting me in touch Cut. When I mentioned to Terry how cautious Cut had been about discussing very much me, he explained to me that he was also told not to talk with me, but he did so because Roland Penney, who actually sat down with me in his home had vouched for me. I asked Terry, if he had any inkling what the nieces problem with me was? He opened up a bit about the whole Knapp - Penney thing. He told me they were extremely upset with the fact I was putting their family history on the internet and that both of them were from a very different era. I knew that, but still did not quite comprehend why they should be so concerned about what was ancient history and as far as I knew all true. The only thing I ever put online with a big disclaimer was, the *alleged* rum running of Dodi Knapp, that I was initially told about by one of his own Mastic neighbors from 1930.

Terry said he felt for me a bit, as he knew both nieces probably could have helped me with photos and such. He said he had seen scrapbooks of theirs at one time. He also said they were always used to getting their own way about most everything and they had decided I was to become persona non grata with them. He also told me a story his mother told him that shed a little light on the personality of the two nieces. When they were teenagers, they used to give his mother (their step sister) some of their clothes, after they had worn them just a few times. His mother one time mentioned that her own sister could also benefit some from their generosity and suggested they send some clothes to her too. One or perhaps both of them said, "You Don't You Tell Us Who To Give Our Clothes To!" and that was the end of any contact my mother had with them ever again.

Ok—moving right along. I mentioned Knapp's sea sled and names Dan Acernio and Johnny LiBaire. Terry said I might have my best luck contacting Dan Acernio, as he was around my age and knew a lot about antique boats. Taking his advice I called Dan, introduced myself and told him I had been talking some with Cut Redin. Dan knew the name Knapp and told me his story of rescuing Dana's Elco express cruiser from virtually becoming firewood some years back. Though he no longer owned it, (it now was out in Lake Tahoe) when he did and restored it, he had learned some of the history of the Dana family. He had plenty of photos of the Wha Hite, including one that was in a 1920s catalog when it was new. I mentioned that Cut also had told me about a sailor named Johnny LiBaire, who it turned out Dan also knew very well and for a long time. He told me the LiBaire's owned Dana's Wha Hite long before he got hold of it, then he filled me in some about the LiBaire family who were a new name to me. Johnny LiBaire was now in his late '80s and was in and out of poor health, but still visited with his son at Dan's shop from time to time.

Dan had heard several stories about Dodi Knapp through Johnny and many stories over the years about most all the estate and speedboat owners along the south shore. It seems they all were a wild and wooly bunch. As for rum running and Cut's touchiness with the subject, Dan said Cut was always that way. He added in that Johnny said, "We all were involved in rum running at times back then. It was something you just did, if only to supply ourselves and our guests with quality Scotch and Rum from the countries of origin, rather than risk drinking the homemade stuff, that could be hazardous to your health. It was no big deal. Guys would go off shore past the three mile limit where the supply ships legally dropped anchor, load up their speed boats and bring it on back." Johnny, as a young boy, got to hang around with most of these people, because his stock broker father had sailed and raced with many of them since the turn of the century. Dan mentioned the Libaires also had another one of Dana's speedboats. It was a Hacker design hull, with a Liberty V-12 Aircraft engine in it. With it's straight exhaust pipes sticking up in the air, Johnny said "You could hear it coming down the bay from over twelve miles away, but the Coast Guard had nothing that could catch it."

Dan invited me to stop by his shop and visit, next time I was in New York. I certainly put him on my list of people to see. I debated calling Johnny LiBaire and put that on my back burner for a while. In August of 2002, I found myself in New York, as I had gone there to help my son get moved into his college apartment. He was to start at Pratt University in the fall semester, his original college of choice, we visited in March of 2001. You may recall that is when he found the name of Joseph F. Knapp in the Mastic - Shirley Library (Chapter 5).

Kenny Vitellaro,was with me the day we stopped in at Dan Acernio's shop. Dan had some fascinating marine engines in there as that is his area of speciality. One of them was the Liberty V-12 Aircraft- Gar Wood Marine conversion that was originally in Dana's speedboat. Dan was busy with some customers via the phone, but took some photos down off his wall of Dana's boats, so I could photograph them along with the original Elco Factory Blue Prints stamped CONFIDENTIAL for the 37 feet long Express Cruiser. Bill Dana originally christened her the Alberta B in 1925 for his first wife, but he changed the name when they divorced in 1928. I would later find out the new name of her, Wha-Hight meant Up Yours. After some searching Dan found the Hall-Scott marine engine catalog he told me about. It was full of different makes of 1920s boats along with their owners. He opened it to Dana's Elco and I photographed it while he was on the phone. Waiting for Dan to finish the call, I looked through the rest of catalog. As I closed it, there on the back cover I noticed this strange looking boat with a squared off bow. Two men were sitting in it. The caption said: *"MISS DEMURE" - A beautiful Sea Sled owned by Mr. Joseph F. Knapp of New York City and Mastic, Long Island. Designed and built by the Sea Sled Company Ltd. of West Mystic, Connecticut. Length 30' Beam 7' 9', Draft 18" Powered with twin Type LM-6 200 HP Hall Scott Marine Engines, turning two 29" diameter. 31" pitch Hyde surface propellers at 1675 R. P. M. Speed 45 miles per hour.*

"Holy Cow!" I said, and almost dropped the catalog on the floor. Kenny who was wandering around the shop checking out everything, came over to look. We both agreed Dodi Knapp was obviously the guy behind the wheel, sporting a captains hat that shielded most of his face. Nonetheless, I was looking at Mr. Joseph F. Knapp of Mastic for the very first time, albeit from a distance. His passenger was not mentioned, but over the years I have come to think he is possibly Leroy Ross. The shore is too far away to tell if the photo was taken in Mastic, or Mystic, but at least I finally had an small idea of what Dodi Knapp looked like. I showed it to Dan, who had never taken notice of it before or had long forgotten about it. He filled us in a bit on the revolutionary boats that were known as Sea Sleds. Their surface props actually were half out of the water at all times, which is why they were great in shallow water. They had an overhang over the stern to protect you a little from the props exposure and to jettison the spray to the rear. Dan said Sea Sleds normally came with a single engine and with twin engines it was probably a factory custom job. He estimated that Miss Demure probably threw a rooster tail about 30 feet behind her. He also said that 45 MPH for a 30 foot pleasure boat in 1925 was extraordinary. Gold Cup race boats didn't go much faster than that. I now had a boat name and manufacturer to do some research with.

Miss Demure & Miss Gertrude

In several newspapers I found Miss Demure and Miss Demur [SIC] entered in races with the Great South Bay Yacht Racing Association from 1925 - 27 from Babylon to Westhampton. In early August of 1926, the NY Times reported that Capt. Knapp in Miss Demure won a 13.5 mile race in Bayshore with Capt, Dana in the Alberta G [SIC] coming in second place. It also mentions in one of race results Miss Demure was piloted by a G. Knapp. Gee Whiz I thought, could that be a typo? It wasn't a typo, it was just a little half truth or an assumption from the reporter. The "G" was for Gertrude O'Brien. That was a whole truth, I would discover in a year or so, but changing her last name to Knapp, would have to wait for another year to become official. For that is when this little item would appear in the June 14th, 1927 issue of Patchogue Advance. *A notable event was the wedding at his home in Mastic of Mr. Joseph F. Knapp of New York and Mastic (Moriches) to Miss Gertrude O'Brien of Brooklyn. The ceremony was performed by Rev, Herbert Crosier of Center Moriches. Only immediate friends of the family were present. Mr. and Mrs. Knapp expect to sail on the 28th for Europe and to be absent for about two months.*

And sail for Europe they did. Then Mr. & Mrs. Knapp sailed on home from Southampton, England aboard the Mauretania, docking in NY City on August 6th 1927. Of interest to me. from reading the passenger list was, that one of J.

P.s main business partners, Thomas W. Lamont of the J. P. Morgan Co. and his family was sailing along with them. Now whether or not that was just a co incidence can't be stated, but the Lamonts also left for 2 months in Europe on June 25th according to the Times. The J. F. Knapps took a large apartment in New York city at Gramercy Place near 23rd St and Park Ave. At a rent of $400 per month, when NYC average rents were probably $30-50 per month, it was most likely quite luxurious. Their neighbor was Henry Cabot Lodge, who would run for Vice President with Nixon in 1960. And so in 1927, the newlyweds obviously started out enjoying the best of both in Town and Country living.

Circling The Wagons Around The Knapp Estate

When I had interviewed "Aunt Mildred" in 2005, she mentioned how isolated it was growing up where she did. "We were like pioneers out here in the 1920s— there were no other children around other than my two younger brothers. At first we didn't go to school everyday, because it was too far away and there was no way for us to get there everyday. It would be a few years before a bus started to come down our way to take us to school, (That would probably be after the new Moriches Grammar school was built in 1923) When I asked her about the photo of the three of them standing at the cross roads, she said "A man from the real estate company took that because they wanted to show people Mastic was safe for children." It seems Home Guardian Co. had gotten wind about an early negative image of their Mastic Park development. They thought they might be losing prospective customers because of the fact there was an Indian Reservation there. Apparently some of the good people of Brooklyn and the other territories of NYC were saying. "You don't want to buy land in Mastic— it's not safe for your children because there's Indians out there!" Home Guardian had to come all the way south to the shore to even find some children to take a photo of to nip it in the bud.

In Chapter 26, I mentioned the Smadbecks wanted to expand their Mastic Park development and although Smith land was up for grabs to the north of them, the logical way for them to go was south, as that's where the waterfront was. They were marketing their property out there as vacation land and it had no practical amenities not even electricity, so it was the only way they could sell it. That may of been the incentive for the Patchogue speculators C. S. R. V. Corp to spring for the initial $75, 000, they paid in mid November for the 355 acres of the Lawrence property on the Knapp's eastern border. It was a very safe bet and they didn't have to wait long for a buyer to come along. He was Ludwig Freudenthal, a decoy buyer that the Smadbecks used several times, probably to avoid paying too much. Just as many others like Walt Disney would do years later when he bought property for his Disneyland theme parks. None the less C. S. R. V. made about $35,000 profit because Freudenthal spent $110,000 of Smadbeck's money for that property in January of 1926, just sixty days later. The Smadbecks in turn would wait a few months more, before revealing to the press that Home Guardian was the new owner of the old Woodhull Farm, but probably sent their surveyors in right away to start dividing it up into hundreds of 20x100 lots. I wonder what Gertrude & Dodi Knapp thought about that?

Speaking of wondering, I still wondered if my early writings about Dodi

Knapp's alleged rum running was what had really set off his nieces into circling their wagons and declaring me historian *non grata*. I mentioned it to Mildred and she roared with laughter. "What do you mean alleged rum running?!—Do you want to know the routes the trucks ran on carrying the liquor up from the bay, out of town and into the city?"

My poor phone was taking some real abuse from me dropping it at Mildred's stories.

"Sometimes those trucks ran day and night, and they would go right past our house." If I had some of Dodi Knapp's dough, I would've booked a flight to NY the next day just to kiss her.

CHAPTER
27

Catching Up With the Family

*N*ow that we are into the first two decades of 20th Century, I think this is a good time to catch up a bit with the mostly personal lives of the Knapps. I find their lives remind me of the lead up to the intermission of my favorite film, *It's A Mad, Mad, Mad, Mad World*, which if you become a student of (e.g. see it at least 12 times) you realize is far more than just a comedy. It's a great study in human behavior. In the film, you have characters all over the map, in all sorts of situations, that rapidly flash on the screen as the midway point approaches. Though now farther along than midway in our Knapp story, and far less in numbers, the Knapps by this time were all over the map too, and because of their resources, found themselves in all sorts of interesting situations—in other words they were living it up and the next thirty years gets somewhat intense.

Antoinette (nmi)

I haven't mentioned "Netty," J.P.'s big sister since chapter 20, where it was 1906 and she had just buried her son Edward. A quieter Knapp, who seemed to be in her mother's shadow, Antoinette seems to have stepped out a bit after her mother passed away in 1908. By 1910 her marriage to Edward C. Wallace, which I previously stated seemed to unravel with their sons death, appeared to be over with. In 1910 Antoinette was primarily living alone in the Germantown section of Philadelphia, PA although her longtime companion and dressmaker, Josephine Ballard might of spent sometime there with her.

You might recall from her big wedding in 1885 (Chapter 14), that Antoinette's husband's family the Wallaces, had a steel construction company. In 1906 a competing company, the Milliken Brothers of Staten Island went belly up and was taken over by the Wallace company. The Washington Post reported on April 23, 1911:

Foster Milliken, the contractor whose father Samuel Milliken was the founder of Milliken Bros, one of the largest steel firms in the east, was married today at City Hall in Jersey City to Mrs A. Knapp Wallace, daughter of the late Joseph P. [SIC] *Knapp[1], the founder of the Metropolitan Life Insurance Co. Mrs. Wallace was divorced in Philadelphia on March 28, 1911 from Edward C. Wallace, who has been president of Milliken Bros. since the reorganization in 1909 and the company had been in receivers hands for two years.*

The Millikens got into a motor car and headed south for their honeymoon. I don't know how long the honeymoon lasted, but Antoinette would also divorce Foster Milliken after a few years.

In 1912 Edward C. Wallace was engaged to be married again, but I do not know if he ever returned to the alter, because he seems to appear at most social functions after the engagement announcement alone. When he passed away in November of 1915, at age 56, there was no mention of a widow. At the time of his death, his entire estate including some patents he held on motion picture exhibition equipment, was passed onto his sister.

Antoinette would marry for the third time in the 1924 to Paul Goodwin Brown. Brown was a civil engineer, who supervised major construction projects like NY city's tunnels and bridges. I think they met in Philadelphia where Brown ran an engineering firm the Keystone Company. Antoinette and Paul G. Brown had a home there with a large household staff according to the 1930 census, They then moved circa 1933, back to NY City, settling in at 250 Park Avenue, just about a block south of J. P.'s apartment. As Mrs. Paul G. Brown, Antoinette became very active in society again, especially during the 1930s. The P. G. Browns stayed married, dividing their time between Manhattan, Palm Beach, Fla and mid atlantic resorts like Hot Springs, Va. Of a curiosity to me, was the fact that Paul G. Brown took over all of his wife's financial affairs from her brother, who had set up and always handled her family trusts. This would lead to tax problems with the IRS and over a decade long court battle. Also Paul was soon elected to the board of directors at Universal Pictures in California. This gives rise to the speculation that Antoinette, may of purchased the motion picture patents from her ex sister in law, as that business seems far removed from Paul Brown's area of expertise or interests (He thoroughly enjoyed the hobby of horse racing and there was a race horse named for him). One area that Paul's expertise really may of been a help to one of the Knapps, was the construction of several underground tunnels at his new nephew's Mastic Beach mansion. The fact that most of Mastic Beach is just barely above sea level, would of required a certain knowledge on how to

---

1 Newspapers relentlessly seemed to get confused with the middle initials of all three Joseph Knapps.

build tunnels, that were still dry a quarter century later. One tunnel ran a short distance between the residence's pantry and garage, but the other one was over a $^1/_4$ mile long between the residence and the gatehouse on Neighborhood Rd. Security may of been a motivating factor for their construction, though Mastic was 100 fold more secure then, than it is today, and the Knapp mansion held a cache of firearms. I rather think the tunnels were built to accommodate the ultimate privacy in movement, even though the residence was sitting on almost 200 acres of private property. Perhaps to escape the prying eyes of over zealous revenue agents? Many private Long Island estates were raided in the 1920s due to observing their rum running activities. Knapp's place would not be one of them.

Claire Antoinette

When we last left Claire A. Knapp, it was 1925 and she had eloped with chauffeur Willis Oliver Penney, and sold the Mastic estate back to her brother. At Yaphank, she set up a model kennel that was probably second to none as far as efficiency goes and it was featured in a large story in the AKC Gazette in 1926. It seemed her dogs were winning shows with great regularity and Clairedale was established as one of the leading bloodlines in Chows. She also had second estate (perhaps a wedding present from her father?) at St. John's Island near Charleston, South Carolina. As nice as it looked, for some reason she did not stay at Yaphank very long and moved her northern operation to Stony Brook on Long Island's north shore about 1928. Perhaps just to be on the water again? The Penneys kept a large cabin cruiser on the sound. Willis also took a position managing the Stony Brook Hotel for a time. I first went there on a school field trip with my 5th grade class in 1956 (Chapter 2). When the 19th century landmark hotel became the site of the Suffolk County Carriage House museum. Claire and Willis Penney started a family in the '20s and two daughters (whom I was sort of introduced to in 2001) were born during the the the first three years of the marriage.

Joseph Palmer "Joe"

I briefly mentioned in chpt 25 that J. P. had remarried again and like his older sister, for him the third time was the charm too. That is not to say it wasn't charming the first two times either. Margaret Easterling Rutledge, was twenty three years younger than J. P. Knapp (and just two years older than his daughter Claire) when they got married at his Mackey Island estate in North Carolina in 1923, about a year after Elizabeth died. It's been said by those who knew Margaret, that she learned to share J.P.'s love of outdoors and was an avid fly caster and duck hunter. Margaret was born in Mississippi in May of 1886, and still had some family there (a sister Dr. Elise Rutledge Lockwood) when she passed away in 1960. Other than that, I do not know too much of Margaret's background. She was an actress who most likely came to NYC with her reported cousin Amber Lawlor from Louisiana about 1904-05. From 1908-1911 Margaret appeared in several musical-comedy theatrical productions in NY City and Washington, D.C., including ones titled "Funbashi" and "Peggy".

Forever Amber

Both Margaret and Amber were in their early '20s, when they accompanied Mr. Ogden Mills Reid, the wealthy publisher of the NY Herald Tribune as he returned from Southampton, England aboard the Kronprinz Wilhelm in 1905. Amber Lawlor was then Amber Lawlor Morgan and would cause major society headlines a few years later when she declared she was the bride of multi million-aire Mr. Samuel Willets, one of the most eligible and wealthy bachelors on Long Island A town is named for his family. As Master of the Hounds at the Meadowbrook Hunt Club, headlines about the Willets nuptials raged for months over this controversy,with Willets mother and father (who were staunch colonial era Quakers) claiming it was all gossip and nonsense. Samuel's mother seemed to scream to the press the loudest "MY SON WOULD'VE TOLD ME IF HE WAS MARRIED" and his father Edward who almost had a nervous breakdown according to accounts said "I will pay One Million Dollars to anyone who could provide information that this marriage was legal".

As Amber checked out of a fashionable Larchmont hotel, she told the press " I am willing to tack my marriage certificate up on the wall of this hotel lobby,where every one may see that I am the wife of Samuel Willets. Furthermore, I am going down to Roslyn to see Mr. Willets's father and claim that check for $1,000,000 which he offered for information regarding his son's marriage to me." Samuel seemed to vacillate on his statements, first he denied it, then admitted it. His mother seemed to always play a dominant role in his life according to all the press reports.

He was seen in the company Amber and her two young daughters by a previous marriage dining with her at the Larchmont hotel. The press had a field day with this story for weeks on end. Lots of negative information was fed to them from both sides. The daughters who first appeared at the hotel with their governess exclaimed "Mama has just married a very rich man" Amber would later sail for Europe as "Miss Lawlor," leaving her daughters in care of their nurse Delia Murphy. Samuel Willets sailed for Europe a week or two later. No public proof was ever presented of the Willets marriage, suggesting Amber was well compensated for. Sam Willetts would officially marry for the first time a twice divorced Mrs. Hastings Arnold in 1910. Two weeks before Valentines day in 1914, the society headlines in NY Times were

MRS. WILLETS, TWICE DIVORCED, IS HAPPY

She Has $20,000 a Year and Ambitions, and Has Ten Dogs Entered for New York Show.- Westbury was Dull and she could not live with her mother in law

Samuel Willets would continued to live with his widowed mother on a large estate in Roslyn, LI. He would marry another multiple divorce again in 1917! As for cousin Amber Lawlor Morgan Willets_she returned to the states and married Gilbert Allis son of the founder of Allis-Chambers motors in 1910.

Perhaps learning from her cousin's notoriety of getting involved with high society old money, Margaret Easterling Rutledge, seemed to take a much lower profile in regards to her early relationship with the still married J. P. Knapp. I say that, as much evidence points to my assumption that Margaret and J. P. knew each other for quite sometime before they eventually married. Although J. P. Knapp certainly knew publisher Ogden M. Reid both socially and professionally, who may of introduced her to him, he could of well first met Margaret aboard the Carmania on an ocean voyage in late January of 1913, that he and his daughter Claire took back to the states. A Margaret Rutledge of the right age and living in NYC, is the next passenger on Carmania's first class list. Most first class passenger lists of that era are either in alphabetical order or by cabin or boarding proximity. Then the fact that both Margaret Rutledge, born May 4, 1886, in Mississippi and living at Gramercy Square in NY City turns up aboard the Lusitania, the very next year along with one J. P. Knapp also a passanger, leaves far less to coincidence and more to the future plot line of playwright Neil Simon's "Same Time Next Year". Public documents eg passport applications, travel plans, ship manifests and a character reference letter dated 1917 from Walter Solinger, J. P.'s personal lawyer stating he was well acquainted with Margaret Rutledge for over 6 years, give further strong, albeit circumstantial evidence that Margaret and JP were more than acquaintances for over a decade before they married. As does the fact that Elizabeth Knapp moved out of the Knapps 247 5th Ave Apartment in 1920 and stated in her will that she "hoped JP would live up to his word in regards to her son's inheritance." He did.

Finally In 1921, a Margaret Rutledge would purchase a large home next door to the Jacob Rupert Mansion in NYC. There is no evidence to support that she had that kind of money to do so. Rupert was the brewing family of Knickerbocker Beer. The longer separations in the last years of JP's marriage to Elizabeth and her wording of her will gives creedence that she was well aware that something was going on. Claire Antoinette Knapp Penney, would name her firstborn daughter Margaret in 1926.

Sylvia Theresa

Lest we forget the original Mrs. J. P. Knapp, we know for sure that Sylvia Theresa Kepner Knapp was living on and off in Europe in both Germany and France since during the outbreak of WWI and returned to France in 1919 according to a court affidavit involving her 1925 customs case. In 1920 she was living in Los Angeles according to her passport application to visit Paris again for a year. Of interest in the application is an affadavit attesting to knowing J. P. Knapp as an American citizen for over 20 years from her future son in law Thomas Dixon Jr. who was also living Los Angeles at that time. On October 29, 1925, Sylvia boarded the S. S. Paris in La Havre, France and arrived in America seven days later. She had a big hassle with US customs over items she brought with her, that wound up in the courts and took several years to settle. Court papers include her testimony that she left the US over strong disagreements with her children, which is somewhat ironic because visiting with her children is the reason she listed for her return. Nonetheless she won her case (Sylvia T. Knapp vs The United States) by proving she remained an American citizen living abroad. However, I do not know, if she ever returned to America again. She very well likely stayed the epitome of a gay divorcé her entire life, of which I do know was still going strong in Post WWII Europe.

Archibald G. "Chip"

I do not know if any personal contact was maintained with the Knapp family, after his mother Elizabeth passed away in 1922. It seems that the step brothers were somewhat social up until that point with Dodi attending Chip's wedding in 1920. "Chip" and Caroline McIlwaine, lived on a large horse farm estate in Locust Valley, just next to JP's old friend and business associate Myron C Taylor. They had two sons during their first few years of marriage. A. G. III and John Read. Chip inherited the new Southampton residence his mother died in, known as Cherry Creek Farm and put it up for sale in April of 1923, at $30,000 below the $125,000 it had cost J. P. to build it in 1921. In December of 1928, "Chip" retired from his Wall Street brokerage house and was pursuing life as a golf pro, something he could of been at age 17, but went to Yale and then became a Naval aviator instead. He was playing in a golf tournament in Biarritz, France in August of 1929, when he suddenly took ill. An emergency operation to save him was performed. Archibald Graham McIlwaine II, who had survived multiple combat flights in the skies of France in the great war, was buried next to his mother Elizabeth Laing Knapp that September in Southampton. He was just three months shy of his 34th birthday.

Joseph Fairchild "Dodi"

In taking a cue from his father, at staying ever low profile, Dodi Knapp's personal activities in the 1920s, seemed to revolve around improving his estate in Mastic, enjoying the good life and going into the office in the city at American Lithographic. In May of 1926, he may of been caught slightly off guard and found his extreme privacy in the country somewhat diminished, For it was then, that a new town called Mastic Beach was about to be built out of 300 some acres of the Lawrence estate upon his eastern border. A month later the developers acquired a second parcel and opened Section Two adjoining their original acreage to the north of it. Rapidly following that just six months later, Home Guardian had purchased the other Lawrence estate, of the late Hannah Lawrence Sherman, on Knapp's western border right within eyesight of his residence. Dodi could see the new road named Locust Drive from his master bedroom balcony running all along the border.

As previously mentioned in chapter 27, Dodi would marry a Miss Gertrude O'Brien of Brooklyn at his Mastic Beach estate in June of '27. I know nothing concrete about her background, other than she may of been related to Judge Morgan O'Brien, an old Knapp friend. Two of the judges daughters, Rosalie and Estelle had attended Dodi's 21st birthday bash in 1913.

Since colonial days, the Neighborhood trail that ran east and west across Knapp's property was an open public thoroughfare, albeit with very little public faring through it. As the town started to grow in the summer seasons (10,000 lots were sold in 1926 according to claims made by Home Guardian Co.) Dodi would soon close the road off, leaving Home Guardian in a bit of an access predicament to travel from sections One and Two over to Three and vice versa. A deal was struck by 1929, where in exchange for some additional land along his now named Knapp Road, he granted access to Home Guardian to construct a new connecting road (Aspen Road) on his northern border in return for them giving up all rights to Neighborhood Road and removing the utility poles they had installed in a prior agreement they reached with him in 1928, preparing for the coming of electricity and telephones. The deed with a hand drawn map is dated August 21, 1929 and is the first I have found in the names of both Joseph F and Gertrude Knapp. For the duration of the time he would live there, Dodi Knapp would never use the name Mastic Beach for his address. It was always Mastic or Mastic in care of Moriches Post Office. Aspen Road was completely fenced off on the northern border of Knapp's estate and passageway on the Neighborhood Road, that had been open since before the USA existed, was now stopped entirely by fences and no trespassing signs at Locust Drive on the west and Alder Drive on the east. Even though the new Aspen road was cut through,having the old familiar Neighborhood trail blocked off partly contributed to the split personality and two commercial districts' developments of early Mastic Beach, eventually requiring two fire departments to protect them.

Some major developments in the Knapp's business life, would also occur in the 1920s that I will discuss in the next "Business as Unusual and Somewhat Personal: Part 2". One major event occurred in September of 1929, when Dodi Knapp "retired" from American Lithographic Co. at age 37. His father would also make a major decision public in September of '29 about American Lithographic's future, just weeks before Black Friday.

CHAPTER

28

Business As Unusual Part II:
Sinking Sea Sleds and More

Here's another look at some of the business decisions J. P. Knapp made and some of the core business people that he surrounded himself with in the early 20th century, that helped me to draw impressions of who this very private man was.

One of J. P. Knapp's business ventures that in his own words "was one of the old man's ideas, that didn't turn out so well", started out as no more than a fishing trip. As he headed up the St. Lawrence Seaway in his new Sea Sled around 1922, with several of his old business pals aboard, on their way to his salmon fishing camp way up on the Natashquan River near Labrador, Canada, the engine died. The Sea Sled was considered the state of the art in pleasure boats then and the engine conking out was not supposed to happen to a boat of this calibre. J. P. decided to look into the affairs of the Sea Sled Company ASAP and see where the problems lie. He found most were tied to lack of an organized sales force, a strong dealer network and under capitalization. Sea Sled like almost every other boat manufacturer,did not produce its own engines. It just used the standards of the day like Hall-Scott, Chrysler, Lathrop, Sterling etc. Knapp wound up buying a license to reorganize and run the company from Albert Hickman, who although he was the inventor of this revolutionary inverted hull boat, was not a people person by any means. Sea Sleds had set all sorts of records from

1916-1919. The Navy used large 45 footers to launch airplanes from their deck. They actually went fast enough to get a 10,000 pound bomber into the air.

Raising the money in 1924-25 was no problem. Not with friends and business partners like Thomas Lamont (head of J P Morgan & Co). Three million dollars was raised almost the first year and an additional million in 1925. For the first time, Sea Sled enjoyed a professional sales force, organized dealer networks, elaborate printed catalogs, and additional unlimited advertising in Knapp magazines like Colliers, which though really not geared to the boating market, it's full page ads could not be ignored. In spite of the odd look of Sea Sleds, with a squared off bow and inverted V hull, that many boat owners could not warm up to, sales grew dramatically under Knapp's below sea level ownership. Only people inside the boating industry or wall street, probably knew Knapp owned Sea Sled. The only public hint, might of been the moving of the main NY City showroom into the ground floor of the American Lithographic Building. Business took off and $800,000 worth of orders were written the first year. The boats were advertised in a price range from $95 for an 8 foot pram up to $50,000 (though its doubtful if a $50,000 Sea Sled was ever produced). Most standard production boats ranged from 13-26 feet. They employed 125 skilled boat builders, as building the complex inverted hull was very labor intensive. A second factory was opened at Groton to add to the production at West Mystic, Connecticut. The boat ads showed people in full business attire using them to commute. All sorts of publicity attesting to the speed and safety of the Sea Sled regularly appeared in newspapers. Doctors were saving lives, in stormy seas where other craft could not venture out in. Court cases regarding rum running were being decided based only upon the speed of the craft. The Coast Guard then ordered fleets of them to catch rum runners, who had been consistently out running them in the sea sleds. A jewel heist at a Vanderbilt mansion resulted in the thieves making their escape across the Long Island sound in a Sea Sled.

The person Knapp put in charge at Sea Sled was Clarence E. Stouch, a member of his inner circle of trusted employees that remained with him forever. Although Knapp would cryptically say the failure of his Sea Sled venture lie in the fact that "no one wanted a 45 MPH boat you couldn't use at night", the truth was, even he with all his business savvy and high level wall street resources, didn't see how much of the ice-burg known as the great depression lied under the surface. In spite of all the money invested, business expertise and the actual fine product itself, nothing could save Knapp from eventually having to pull the plug at Sea Sled once the depression hit full force. They certainly tried everything too. Traditional shaped hulls were added to the line in 1931 to help bolster sales. Their lowest priced boats, they made in 1933 and priced at $290 were given away below cost for $60. Many wound up as firewood. Like Duesenburgs, and Cords were to automobiles, Sea Sleds were to boats, luxury items at a time when a hot meal was a luxury for many people. From 1924-1933, under Knapp's ownership 6,000 Sea Sleds were produced. Today only a handful of exist. Of that handful most survivors are the 13-16 foot outboard models. A standard production 27 foot single engine inboard "Miss Lakeside" was on the market in 2004 at $125,000. If it were to exist, Dodi Knapp's custom 30 foot, triple cockpit, twin engine "Miss Demure," the 1927 speedboat champion of the GSBYR club, would probably fetch a quarter of a million dollars at auction today.

In 1934, Hickman took his company back and resurrected it somewhat as the depression eased up. In spite of his arrogant and sometimes paranoid personality, he kept it going until the 1950s. For a man who once kept company with giants like Alexander Graham Bell and Henry Ford, Hickman was relegated to a mere footnote in marine history. The ultimate death knell for Hickman's 1900 patent, came when Dick Fisher and Ray Hunt appeared as new saviors for the company arriving with plans to build Sea Sleds from fiberglass. Negotiations broke down and Hickman was still in court fighting with them when he died in 1957. It was probably for the best as Hunt and Fisher's "revolutionary" new boat appeared on the market soon after and the success of their Boston Whaler would of killed him.

After Knapp scuttled his Sea Sled venture, Clarence Stouch returned to the home umbrella office known as Publication Corporation. This was a separate company that oversaw ultimate financial control of everything J. P. was involved in publishing and Wall street securities. Besides Stouch, Knapp's closest inner circle were mainly connected to his magazine publishing ventures. Some worked at Publication Corp and the others at Colliers, Woman's Home Companion, American & Farm & Fireside magazine or Crowell-Collier offices. Besides his lawyer and sometimes business partner Samuel Untermeyer, were lawyers Walter Solinger and Irving Miller, others of his inner circle were Lee Maxwell, Albert "Cap" Winger, Gertrude Lane, Sumner Blossom, William Chenery, and Thomas Beck. Of this group, probably the one he regarded closest as a protege was Thomas Hembly Beck (1881-1951). It's a safe bet that most all of the above mentioned were members of the Joe Knapp Club, regardless of whether or not they were hunters and fisherman. It was a very exclusive private club where Joe Knapp handed out Gold Plated membership cards and expensive shotguns with a small gold oval bearing his profile in the gunstock. Today only a handfull of Joe Knapp club shotguns are known to exist and I have never seen nor heard of a membership card that is still in existence.

There was also a group of old time printers at American Lithographic Co. that had been with J. P. since the formation of the company in 1892. As the new year unfolded in 1927, two of his key men, Gustave Buek and Louis Ettlinger passed away within weeks of each other, Buek was president of ALCO at the time and Ettlinger the treasurer. Knapp relied heavily on both of these men and they in turn were very well compensated for it. In February of 1927, Ettlinger who also did a lot of real estate investing and art collecting for both Knapp and himself, left an estate of over 5 million dollars to his family. Buek left among other things, his historic Easthampton colonial saltbox house, that was once the domicile and inspiration for poet John Howard Payne to write "Home Sweet Home". The architect of my own saltbox house in Mastic, built in 1973, was inspired by Payne's home. The deaths of Buek and Ettlinger may of played a part in placing in motion, the decision Knapp would make before the decade ended to sell American Lithographic, which was by then the largest printing conglomerate in America. His son may of been on track at one time to replace Buek, as Dodi Knapp had always said publicly that he was the retired head of American Lithographic Co. Whatever actually happened, it was never publicly announced. J.F. Knapp's permanent retirement, at a youthful 37, I have been told on excellent authority it was brought about by "him quitting after a big fight with his father."[1] The fact that his retirement coincided with the sale of the company in 1929, might just be only that—a coincidence.

Another major factor of JP's decision to sell, would of come from a technology standpoint, as he well knew the 19th century lithographic printing process , that made millionaires of both his father and himself, was now very antiquated. Gravure printing was the newest and fastest method and one in which Knapp wisely held several patents on and would still acquire even more.[2] When he did announce the sale of American Lithographic to United States Printing in September of 1929, he also announced that ALCO - GRAVURE, a reorganized version of his Corkett - Intaglio Co, which he had acquired in 1911, was not part of the deal. Another interesting side note is that William Ottmann, may of still been the head of United States Printing (formerly US Litho) at the time of the sale. If indeed he was, it would be very ironic, because other than the good name of American Lithographic, United States Printing was really buying not much more than a lot of ALCO'S stock old lithos and lithographic equipment. You might recall Ottmann was the gullible printing executive in chapter 25, who in an effort to beat Knapp to the punch two decades earlier, let two con-men reach in his pockets to the tune of over $100,000, just because they told him that J. P. Knapp had offered to buy their "miracle printing process." That $100,000 was mere chump change for what soon would happen to one and all in America. The ink was probably not even dry on the contracts for the sale of American Lithographic, when the stock market crashed in October of 1929 and many fortunes vanished as fast as disappearing ink.

---

1 Phone conversation 12/07 with Joan Kiely O'Connell, daughter of J.F. Knapp's personal secretary Ed Kiely.

2 The Speed Dri Press process, using highly volatile, ultra quick drying inks in sealed containers, was purchased from it's inventor Adolph Weiss in Germany and patented by Knapp in 1932.

CHAPTER
29

R & R & R

Retirement, Recreation and Reeling

The 1930 census has the Joseph F. Knapp's still living at 45 Gramercy Park North, the NY city address they had when they were first married in 1927. Although he now had more time to be social, J. F. Knapp's name rarely appeared in the society columns. The NY Times had one item in August of 1932, when they reported "Mr. & Mrs. Joseph F. Knapp of Mastic are at The Vanderbilt," a NY City hotel. In the 1933 Manhattan phone directory Joseph F. Knapp is listed at 75 Perry St. which is in Greenwich Village. It also lists him as President of The Knapp Foundation (a philanthropic foundation his father founded in 1929) Heading the foundation probably did not take up too much of his time and was probably only brought about by the death in July of 1932 of lawyer Josephine McFadden, who was the foundation's president. Josephine's father was Louis Ettlinger, a long time J. P. Knapp crony from before the beginning days of American Lithographic. With J. F. Knapp the sole short interim exception, Knapp Foundation presidents, during J.P.'s lifetime and for many years after. were always people outside of the Knapp family. Mainly they were members of J.P.'s Crowell-Collier inner circle like Thomas Beck, "Cap" Winger, and Clarence Stouch.

In the 1930 Peninsular & Occidental Steamship Line brochure, the S. S. Northland is described thusly—Single screw, oil burner. Length 328 feet width

48 feet. Speed 17 knots per hour. Passenger capacity 675. Two hundred and thirty - six first cabin rooms, many deluxe rooms with large double beds, private toilet facilities, running water and every convenience.

Joseph F. Knapp and party of New York, arrived today from over the highway and boarded the Northland for an extended visit to Havana. —Key West Citizen, Feb 21, 1931

At 17 knots full speed ahead,it probably took the Northland around 5 to 6 hours to sail the 82 nautical miles from Key West to Havana. While J. F. & Gertrude Knapp and their party were getting comfortable and enjoying a day cruise to Cuba, some 1100 miles north of where they set sail in Key West, boat craftsmen were busy building a exceptionally comfortable trunk cabin custom cruiser on the banks of the Delaware River. The March 1931 issue of The Rudder magazine printed architectural drawings of it and described the yet unnamed craft this way.

"Exceptional Comfort in 53 Feet" This cruiser is now building by Marine Construction Co. Wilmington, Delaware for Joseph F. Knapp from designs by William J. Deed, naval architect of New York City. She offers unusual comfort and convenience. She is 53 feet long and 12 feet 4 inches beam and 3 feet 3 inches draft. Two Lathrop 100 Mystic model engines will drive this boat about 14 miles an hour and there are two gasoline tanks in separate compartments of 180 gallons each. Fresh water tanks are aft and hot and cold water pressure system is installed. The headroom is 6 feet 5 inches, the ice box holding 450 pounds exceptional and the galley layout is especially good. Attention is called to the size and number of full height clothes closets, one of them as large as a toilet room. Comfortable accommodation is planned for a few people rather than trying to get a number of small uncomfortable rooms. In each stateroom there is a bureau and full height closet for each person, as well as a great number of drawers and lockers.

Her form is the accepted Deed round bottom model with a beautiful flaring bow and neatly rounded sides, there not being a flat spot in the whole model. She has a deadrise sufficient to make her an easy sea boat and will be used for many coastwise cruises and fishing trips. Construction is of the very best type.

ONE THING THAT CAUGHT MY EYE WAS RUDDER POINTING OUT "exceptional ice box" and I immediately flashed back to the wall of refrigerators in the Knapp mansion kitchen. Probably by the time the J. F. Knapp party sailed out of Havana to return to the states, the new cruiser was nearing completion and ready for christening. Knapp christened her "Storm King", and although I do not know for certain the course her first cruise took, I can make a reasonable guess. "Storm King" headed south down the Delaware River into Delaware Bay and out into the Atlantic, then she probably rounded Cape May, New Jersey and headed north east following the Jersey coastline, perhaps even stopping at Atlantic City? From that point she sailed another 100 miles or so into New York waters with The Statue Of Liberty being tall enough to admire her port side as she cruised on by. She would of then proceeded easterly along Long Island's Atlantic coastline, probably entering the Great South Bay either at Fire Island inlet in Bay Shore or Old Inlet in Bellport. From there it was just a short trip a few more miles to the east. At Smith's Point she entered Narrow Bay past the remains of Knapp's old Aerial Coast patrol hanger off her Starboard bow and down the channel (which I doubt was even marked then) a short distance before turning hard to port and being eased into the newly dredged, cut out and constructed 60' x 25' foot bulkhead (the one I talk about first discovering in Chapter 3) on the edge of Knapp's Mastic Beach estate. As Mastic was where the trunk cruiser, "Storm King" was home ported according to the entry that appears in the Lloyd's Register Of Yachts for 1932. In keeping with a Knapp tradition, the word Beach was never attached to his Mastic address.

Knowing the bay as it was in the 1950s, through the present day, I have to wonder if "Storm King" ran aground often out there as she drew over 3 feet. When she did, getting a 20 ton 53 foot cruiser off a sand bar would not be a picnic. Arguments against it happening too often, would be that Dodi Knapp had been sailing in those waters since he was a boy and the Moriches inlet did not break through until a bad storm hit that year, so it would be a while yet before the sands came washing in as they did, making Narrow Bay also shallow bay. Dodi also employed a yacht captain (name unknown) who lived on his estate in the 1930s of whom I would imagine also had to be familiar with the Narrow Bay. That said, running aground just once with a boat like that might be enough and by 1934 the home port of Storm King was Fort Lauderdale, Fla. A boat of that size seemed impractical in Mastic Beach anyway, (largest boat I ever saw moored in the lagoon was about 30 some feet) especially with the sands being washed into the bay bottom from the now three year old Moriches Inlet.

I first spoke about Knapp's big dock and what he may of moored there in 2001 with Estelle Schulz, whose father Bill Parr worked on Dodi's boat. She remembered a cabin cruiser of smaller dimensions than the Storm King, in the mid 1930s being docked there. As a girl she used to accompany her father, as he made house calls at all the area estates servicing both boats and cars. She vividly recalled when she was around 12 years old being aboard Knapp's cabin cruiser while her father worked on the engine, and also of meeting First Lady Eleanor Roosevelt at the nearby Dana estate while her Dad serviced Bill Dana's Rolls Royce.

I got two words for you ...

Although I knew early on that Joseph F. Knapp had a boat or two moored at his private dock in Mastic Beach, I would of never learned too much more about it, nor discovered the name Storm King or the Rudder article, had I not first discovered a 1980's travel magazine article, that was posted on the internet back in 2001. Using alta-vista, the pre-Google standard search engine of the day, several groups of two words emerged along with Joseph Knapp's name—big slob, fist fight and Ernest Hemingway—Now I'm sure the only reason the article was ever written,was the mystique of Hemingway name, who unlike Knapp was certainly never publicity shy. That article then led me to the biography "Ernest Hemingway—a life story" by Carlos Baker and lo and behold in the book's index was the none other than the name Joseph Knapp! Baker includes a short passage that starts out with "He was immensely proud of his quick victory over a wealthy publisher named Joseph Knapp who had come to Bimini aboard his yacht STORM KING"—and then Baker goes on to describe the details of the fight in which he says, Knapp started, Hemingway finished and a song was written about! *The members of a Negro calypso band celebrated Ernest's victory with an extemporaneous song about the "big slob" from Key West.*

Got a whale of tale to tell you lads ...

Well like a great blue marlin or giant tuna, that sports fishermen and women of the day, e.g. clothing store magnates Michael and Helen Lerner (Lerner Shops), western adventure author Zane Gray, stock broker turned author Kip Farrington were all reeling in back then, I was hooked. I spent months, actually years investigating this story. It was the very first story, I encountered to shed any light at all for me on the personality of the very private Mr. Knapp. It was also the first thing actually in print, other than the few news stories I found about his capsized sailboat in Bellport from 1911, the flying boat Aero Squadron during WW1, some race results in the 1920s of his Sea Sled "Miss Demure", or a handful of society columns that briefly mentioned his name now and then. I would also learn more about Hemingway (I had read Old Man & The Sea and saw the film) who spent years in Cuba and Bimini fishing from his famous "Pilar", a 1934 Wheeler Playmate 38 foot cruiser. The austere looking Pilar was often described by Hemingway as a fishing machine. With it's black hull, it was in sharp contrast with the luxurious white yachts of the millionaires, Baker described, that populated Bimini, Cuba and the Miami waters, fishing in friendly competition with Hemingway in the 1930s. Carlos Baker also wrote a second book, "Ernest Hemingway Selected Letters 1917 - 1961" This is part of the text from a letter from Hemingway dated June 4th 1935 to Arnold Gingrich, his editor at Esquire magazine . Three paragraphs in, Ernest writes: *Would it interest you to know that I knocked cold after cutting up badly one Joe Knapp who afterwards found out owns or is alleged to own Colliers, McCall's etc. It was after dark and with bare hands on the dock at Bimini. Witness some 60 including Ben Finney (of 21) Howard Lance, Bill Fagan and plenty others. I think he had read in (Gertrude) Stein that I was a phony and picked the fight. I told him he didn't know what he was getting into and that he was talking so that he could repeat what he had said to me in NY. Anyway clipped him three times with left hooks didn't understand why he didn't go down, on the next he fell forward and grabbed, hit him twice hard, clubbing behind the ear with right, backed away and landed Sunday punch making him hit ass and head at almost same time on the planks. When he got onto the dock to fight I believe he thought it was going to be one of those where you fade right swings and then someone grabs you. But his crew never made a move. He left at 4 AM next day on his yacht the Storm King for Miami for doctorage. In Miami he told Fagan that he was sorry that he had spoken out of turn and had gotten what was coming to him. On the other hand it is called limiting one's market. Still the son of a bitch never touched me once and he started it and weighed 200 lbs, had shoes on and I was barefoot. Lost 2 toenails. If you have any curiosity about this thing it is very easily verified. The nigger band that sings was on the dock, saw it all and have a fine song now that you can hear if you will come to Bimini. I wish the hell you would come. I will be fishing alone there from June 7 to June 25. My wife has to go to St. Louis to get Bumby (His son from his first marriage) who is being shipped there from Chicago. I wish the hell you would come down. It is really a fine place and that kind of fishing is a hell of lot better with two guys than one.*

Anyway write me, care of Capt. George D. Kreidt. 1437 S.W. 5th St, Miami, Fla For E. Hemingway Capt "Pilar" Bimini. He runs the pilot boat and will bring it over — So long Arnold. Will try to write you a good piece. If you have any suggestions sing out.

Well I was off and humming, wanting find out more after reading that and within a short time I started to find some other versions on the same story. The first person I spoke directly about it to, was author Ashley B. Saunders who wrote the book "History of Bimini" in 1989. Ashley is the nephew of Nat Saunders leader of the band "Piccolo Pete and The Buccaneers". Nat Saunders was standing on the dock in Alice Town on Queen Victoria Day in May of 1935, when Hemingway and Knapp slugged it out and it was Nat who actually wrote the song "Big Fat Slob" Uncle Natty, whose age is unknown, but is around 90 something years old, was still around in 2002. I had several phone conversations with Ashley and soon found there were several variations to story depending on whom you talked to or what variation of the Big Fat Slob song they knew. (Nat changes it slightly in the his recollections of the lyric over the years) Here is Nat's story and a version of his song lyrics as they appeared in his nephew Ashley's book taken from an interview he did with his uncle in 1980. (some 55 years after the fight) I noticed right away discrepancies in Nat's tale of how the fight started with Hemingway's account to his editor. These would be the fuel to inspire me to start looking deep as I could at the "Big Fat Slob " story that they still talk, write and sing about in Bimini today.

"This Is The Night We Have Fun"

Q. What can you tell us about Ernest Hemingway?

N.S. Papa Hemingway was a kind hearted man, but he used to like to fight. He like action all the time.

Q. Did he stir up any fight?

N. S. No, he never stir up none. He always like to see boxing going on. This is it. He don't want nobody to hurt each other, and he don't want nobody to take advantage of anybody. Have a good time and go on.

Q. But suppose someone else wanted to start a fight?

N. S. Well then Papa Hemingway would fight the fella. The fella that want to fight, well let Papa Hemingway fight him.

Q. If someone start a fight in a bar and Ernest Hemingway was not around would you or someone else go and call him.

N. S. Yeah, man. He use to tell me whenever any fight or anything start come on up there by the Compleat Angler and call him and let him come down. One night we was playing aboard a yacht and a fella started a fight. He fired off a pistol and wanted to be bad and so forth like that. So I went up to the Compleat Angler and called Papa Hemingway. He say "Who's there?" I say this me, I say "A fella down by the dock wants to fight. So when Papa Hemingway got there he said, " Who is here wants to fight?"And you couldn't hear a pin drop (sic) , You couldn't hear a sound. As much loud mouth as this guy had. You couldn't hear a sound. Nobody say nothing because that was Papa Hemingway.

Q. Did Ernest Hemingway inspire you to write any songs?

N.S. Yeah , I wrote a song called the "Big Fat Slob". There was this very rich man by the name of Mr. Knapp. It was on the Government Dock. Papa Hemingway was there with his straw hat on. So Papa Hemingway said something ordinarily. No harsh words. So Mr. Knapp called Mr. Hemingway a "big fat slob". And Mr. Hemingway ball his fist and pow! Hit him and put him to sleep. All of that is in the song.

Mr. Knapp Called Mr . Ernest Hemingway A Big Fat Slob
Mr. Ernest Hemingway Balled His Fist And Gave Him The Knob
Big Fat Slob In Bimini This Is The Night We Have Fun
Oh The Big Fat Slob In Bimini This Is The Night We Got Fun
Mr. Knapp Look At Him And Try To Mock And From The Blow Mr. Knapp Couldn't Talk
At First Mr. Knapp Thought He Had His Bills In A Stalk And When Mr. Ernest Hemingway Walk The Dock Rocked
Mr. Knapp Couldn't Laugh, Mr. Ernest Hemingway Grin
Put Him To Sleep With A Knob On His Chin.
Boy Papa Hemingway use to like me for that song
From Interview with Nathainel Saunders September 25, 1980 History Of Bimini by Ashley Saunders New World Press 1989

After reading other eyewitness accounts of the Hemingway Knapp fight and then listening to a recorded interview that Nat did in 2002, I believe this first recollection is a mixture of two separate Hemingway fights; one with Knapp and one with somebody else. I also am suspect, of these being all of the original lyrics to the song. There seems to be some parts missing. This is totally understandable for anyone of Saunders age and with that much passage of time. Speaking as a songwriter, from my initial look at this lyric without hearing the actual melody, I feel that Saunders is mixing part of the tale here in with his lyric as some of this lyric just would not sing very rhythmically. Getting to hear Nat perform his song later on bears this out

I brought up to Ashley what I thought were some interesting points in the Hemingway letter versus his Uncle's version and told Ashley I was very interested in learning anything at all about Mr. Knapp and his yacht. I think he sensed I was much more than a curious tourist or Hemingway student. As a lifelong Bimini resident and historian of the place, Ashley relayed to me the Big Fat Slob story the way he first heard it and some of his insights over the years about it that seemed to make a lot of sense to me. It appears the trouble actually started brewing during that afternoon, when Mr. Knapp caught what was probably the largest fish in the tournament and brought it in to the dock to be weighed and entered in the contest. The problem was the fish was mutilated by sharks and

Hemingway protested it. (not to mention it was said to probably be the biggest fish ever caught in Bimini at that time, a record that Hemingway would claim a few months later) It seems the rules then were not quite as clear as they would become, after this incident. Many of the large fish caught there were actually "corkscrewed" that is picked almost clean by sharks. Some heated words were exchanged that afternoon and the obvious resentment between Knapp and Hemingway built up by the time evening rolled around and their boats were tied up at the dock. Ashley added in that the fight was probably fueled further by the consumption of lots of alcohol (no surprise there for either party) which was substantiated by another eyewitness Ben Finney.

The very first time I saw the name Ben Finney, it triggered a distant bell in my memory. rung by Hemingway's notation of Club 21 by Finney's name. Club 21 was like the more famous Stork Club, part of the small handful of NY City night clubs in the 1930's that gave rise to the term Cafe Society. A society that my grandfather Jack Spooner was certainly no stranger to. Spooner aka "The Old Marine" as he was sometimes called by NY newspaper columnists of the day, was in the Marines from 1900 at the age of 15 (he lied about his age) and then as a recruiter in both world wars. For decades New York's Cafe Society was his world and he was it's most famous waiter. When he became Maitre D at the Stork Club's exclusive Cub Room (it was off limits to the general public) in the 1930's - 1940's his reputation grew even further. He had many friends in Hollywood and around the world, who would always ask for his tables at the Stork. His hospitality career began well before "Cafe Society" term was coined by the media. Starting at the Waldorf around 1905 by taking care of clients like Diamond Jim Brady and Harry K. Thaw. Then LaHiff's Tavern (Broadway's in spot) during the Roaring '20's. He also was a partner with world heavyweight champion Jack Dempsy at Dempsy's across from Madison Square Garden. Like Ben Finney, it turns out my grandfather seemed to know everyone that was anyone in the world of sports, radio, stage, screen, politics and media. He also knew Ben Finney very well. I looked and sure enough Finney is listed in Grandpa's personal address book along with many famous names from that era, Cary Grant, Bob Hope, Barbara Stanwyk, Joe Kennedy, J. Edgar Hoover, Walter Winchell, Ed Sullivan, etc.

Well as it turns out Ben Finney also wrote a book "Feet First" (he had a fascinating varied and high adventure life, that spanned the entire world) and Finney was actually on board the boat drinking with Ernest the night of the Knapp fight. His 1970 description of what happened 35 years earlier is highly detailed. Of curious interest is for reasons unknown, he avoids mentioning the name of Hemingway's opponent, long after both parties were deceased.

"We were knocking back a few on the stern of Woolie's fishing boat[1] to celebrate Queen Victoria's birthday. The natives were whooping it up with roman candles, and to demonstrate our friendly feelings toward the good queen, Julio Sanchez[2] dug

---

1 "Woolie" owner of the yacht Popeye, was Jessie Woolworth Donahue, grandson of F. W. Woolworth and heir to his 5 &10 fortune. A Very pistol is a flare gun.

2 Julio Sanchez, was a wealthy sugar cane plantation owner from Cuba , a reknowned sports fisherman and inventor of fishing equipment like the fighting chair.

out the Popeye's Very pistol and started topping the roman candles with flares.

Tied up with her stern to ours was a large houseboat cruiser with the publisher-owner aboard. This gentleman, well known in intellectual New York book-publishing circles, suddenly materialized on his quarterdeck and shouted down at us: "Why the hell don't you bastards knock off shooting that Very pistol?" Before we could kick around just what we should do about his language, Julio let go with another flare BANG!

"You big fat slob, meet me on the dock and I'll ram that Very pistol down your throat!" roared the publisher. Julio who weighed about 130 wringing wet, asked: "You think he means me?" I know damn well who he meant, " said Ernest, as he climbed onto the dock, I followed him.

Down the dock came the publisher hoping, I'm sure, to be able to take home a story of how he had talked down Ernest Hemingway. He didn't have a chance. BAM! Ernest hit him. Although stunned, the big man did not go down. POW! Ernest let him have it again. Still the man was on his feet. Turning to me Ernest asked:"What's holding the bastard up?" The third time Ernest really poleaxed the publisher, who literally bounced along the dock and then lay still. On our way back to the Popeye Ernest muttered: "I had to hit that bum three times,[3] maybe I'm not as tough as I pretend."

Within an hour the publisher's boat cast off her lines and got under way. Julio fired a parting shot from the Very pistol while the local boys serenaded us with Bimini's newest song: "Big Fat Slob in the Harbor"

In July and August of 2001, Tony Brummel of Victory World records, a label based in Chicago, was vacationing in Bimini and got wind of the legendary Nat Saunders. He then brought in a crew with some audio and video equipment, and recorded Nat Saunders and his band live in Nat's funky little bar . The resulting CD and DVD is titled "Bimini Nights" and was released in 2002. All songs are written by Nat and of course his "local big crowd pleasing hit "Big Fat Slob" is on it. The lyrics from that session go like this and are quite different than the previous set of Nat recited to his nephew in 1980. It also gives much credence to both Ashley's and my opinion that the trouble between Hemingway and Knapp started brewing that day of the fishing tournament long before it came to blows.

THE BIG FAT SLOB

By Nat Saunders
Sung: The Big Fat Slob In Bimini, Is The Night We Had Fun / The Big Fat Slob In Bimini, Is The Night We Had Fun
Spoken: Mr. Knapp called Mr. Hemingway a Big Fat Slob / Mr. Hemingway balled his fist and give him a knob
The Big Fat Slob In Bimini, Is The Night We Had Fun

---

3 Here Finney's memory might be off by several punches as Hemingway and most other eyewitness said it took 5 to 6 punches to knock out Knapp. It was the fourth one where Knapp staggered forward and grabbed onto Hemingway. Hemingway's letter which is the earliest written account, just days after the fight, points this out.

There was a dispute about a fish cause it was mutilated by shark / But you know It just couldn't go

The Big Fat Slob In Bimini, Is The Night We Had Fun

Yeah when Mr. Knapp called Mr. Hemingway a Big Fat Slob / Papa Hemingway balled his fist and give him a knob, cause—

The Big Fat Slob In Bimini, Is The Night We Had Fun / The Big Fat Slob In Bimini, Is The Night We Had Fun

Brothers and neighbors come down to look and to see / He was there down as he could be / Most all the boys come to take a little peep / When Papa Hemingway hit him hit him to sleep

The Big Fat Slob In Bimini, Is The Night We Had Fun

Lauderdale captain didn't know what to do / 'Cause he went in and couldn't get to / Now they couldn't enter the fish at all / When papa hit him down he fall

The Big Fat Slob In Bimini, Is The Night We Had Fun / The Big Fat Slob In Bimini, Is The Night We Had Fun

Yeah Mr. Knapp wanted to enter that fish to be a world record / but it just couldn't⁴

The Big Fat Slob In Bimini, Is The Night We Had Fun

When Mr. Knapp got up like a man / He went and shake Papa Hemingway's hand / Folks all of this story really is true / But thats the way the Americans do

The Big Fat Slob In Bimini, Is The Night We Had Fun

One thing for sure was, Knapp did not get up and shake hands with Hemingway that night. Also of interest to me as a songwriter is the opening melody line of Harry Woods' song, " Side By Side "that was first recorded by Kay Starr in 1948 "Oh We Ain't Got A Barrel Of Money" is nearly identical to Nat's melody on his line The Big Fat Slob In Bimini only difference being the syllables. However "Side By Side" is far more sophisticated melodically. Of interest too is the fact that Woods a piano player, only had fingers on his right hand!.Woods a self described amateur songwriter also wrote the standards, When The Red Red Robin, I'm Looking Over A 4 Leaf Clover and Try A Little Tenderness.

Tony Brummel also filmed a fairly lengthy filmed interview with Nat on his life, which eventually got around to the main topic here.

Q: What about the song Big Fat Slob

N.S. I was just gonna tell you about this thing that happened, I was right there, right on the scene. A fella by the name of ... Mister Knapp ... he wanted to enter the fish for a record, 'cause it was big enough for a record. But the fish was cut by a shark, and any fish be cut by a shark, you can not enter it, It is what we call mutilated. And Mister Knapp wanted to enter it and Papa Hemingway got up to protest, and he tell him that you cannot do it, you cannot take that, and there's no use to weighing it because it's not gonna be qualified. ...and he called Mister Knapp a big fat slob—uh Mister Knapp called Papa Hemingway a big fat slob —Papa Hemingway balled his fist and give him a knob — big knob was on his

---

4 From this point on it is obvious that Nat is mixing the lyric with the story as he re told it over the years.

forehead... and he hit him so hard it put him to sleep. You know all of this is in the song...and they take him and carry him below, you know everybody on his boat. his boat was right there, he's a millionaire, and has his captain and so forth. And everybody come to see. ... Mister Knapp didn't come to for a loooong time! They come and look at him. Lilly O'Reid (audio unintelligible) the nurse check his pulse and finally —I wrote the song—Big Fat Slob In Bimini This Is The Night We Had Fun, and we had a ball with it too... 'cause you know Papa Hemingway was a man who like a lot of fun.

Once again more credence to support the fact the trouble didn't just erupt because of Julio Sanchez shooting off a Very pistol in the midst of all the other fireworks and Queen Victoria Day the British Empires version of our Fourth Of July celebrations that night.

It was a fight that probably lasted less than half a minute, and yet it remains talked and written about in certain circles for over 70 some years. Hemingway himself wrote about it again in a 1949 letter. The Big Fat Slob story, like much of history has changed a bit through the years with many of the facts seemingly lost. Biggest error I have seen repeated over and over again, was the fact of just which Mister Knapp it was duking it out that May evening of 1935 with Hemingway. Not that many probably care, but if the story as it has appeared in the last few decades was to be taken as gospel, it would have then 35 year old Ernest beating up J. P. Knapp, a 71 year old man (no bragging rights there) rather than his 43 year old son. There are several books by Hemingway relatives e.g. his brother Leicester and niece Hilary that play pretty fast and loose with the what may or may not of been said between Knapp and Hemingway, that led to the actual fight. Of course Leicester may have heard the story from his brother himself. Hilary's version published in her book "Hemingway In Cuba" seems to be the most embellished and contains more " quoted dialogue " than all the other versions combined. Perhaps it was a combination of the real story and the fiction her Uncle actually wrote about the fight in his novel "Island's In The Stream"? :

"Stranger In The Fight"
Hilary says her uncle had bid good evening to his guests on the Pilar after it was washed down after a day of fishing when a total stranger called out of the darkness and said "Say aren't you guy who claims he catches all the fish around here? she then says the stranger whose voice her uncle didn't recognize was about 20 yards away in the dark and although Ernest couldn't see his face, he noticed he was wearing a nice shirt and pressed white shorts. She says the stranger repeated himself and that her uncle detected a slur in voice (I would maintain that if Dodi Knapp said this taunt, as he well might of, it was more likely said from off the stern of the Storm King during the day while they were both out fishing) Ernest reportedly said " I catch my share" (once again very plausible, but most likely shouted back from the Pilar, that day in which Ernest had come up empty handed). She then continues with the strangers taunts "Where's the proof? or I suppose we are going to have to read about some monster you almost brought in — or will you stand next to some fish and get your picture taken." "Look,"

said Ernest, "I don't even know your name" — You slob, you filthy slob let's just find out if..." she then says some of the boat captains and crews came out on the dock to investigate what the shouting was all about. Ernest then said "Maybe you just need one more drink, why don't you run along and get one." "Oh No you lousy writer, I want satisfaction or I'll shame you off this dock. Are you yellow Hemingway? and then as the stranger set himself into a boxing stance (he uttered the three words that made Ernest see red) Show me what you got—You BIG FAT SLOB! Hilary then said several more boat captains like Howard Lance and Ernest's friend Ben Finney along with a dozen locals stepped onto the dock and as the crowd gathered, the stranger seemed to gather more courage. She said Ernest tried one more time to talk the stranger out of it with. "You don't know what your getting into, your just talking big so you can repeat what you've said to your New York friends and that's horseshit! — AHA GOTCHA! — if he was a total stranger, how come Ernest knew at that point where he was from? Again, I maintain the trouble started in the daytime— and the "Stranger" continued with— "Trying to get out of it, that's just what I figured" Ernest was up on the dock with three barefoot leaps.

Well something is wrong with Hilary's continuity here. Was Ernest down on the boat when all of the previous verbal exchanges were tossed back and forth and why would a crowd gather to see one stranger standing on a dock yelling into the night? She then goes on to describe the actual fight that seems to jive with all other versions. Hilary says Ernest threw 5 punches before delivering his "Sunday Punch" that turned out the "massive bodied " strangers lights. She then said it was Captain Bill Fagen, (who also ran a charter vessel out of Montauk, Long Island and obviously knew Knapp personally), who asked Ernest "Do you know who that guy is?" "Nope," said Ernest. "That's Joseph Knapp. He owns Collier's, McCall's and American Magazines"..."No Kidding! ...well that's what I call limiting your markets," Hemingway said.

Just The Facts

Fact is Knapp's father owned 2 of three magazines Fagen mentioned; Colliers & American and Hemingway was hired by Collier's to be a war correspondent in both the Spanish Civil War and WWII. Another fact is Dodi Knapp was no where near the physical size that he was described as by all who have written and rewritten this tale. Hemingway himself said he was 6' 2" and 200 some pounds. Fact is he was about 5' 8" and perhaps 175 at his heaviest in the 1940s. I used to get frustrated by all these loose facts and fiction, until I contrasted it with the big significant whoppers (like the reason for the War in Iraq) that have negatively effected the entire world and it quickly put things in perspective for me. It is only in the last few years, I have noticed that my take on the whole affair that I have posted on the web site, has been cited by the N. Y. Times. Amazon and others. as a correction to what others have previously written. That I find somewhat reassuring. The most personally rewarding thing came from a phone call I received in Jan. of 2008, from author Paul Hendrickson, a retired Washington Post reporter, who teaches journalism at University Of Pennsylvania.

Mr. Hendrickson interviewed me for his own forthcoming book about Hemingway's boat the Pilar and told me my research was the most unique he had ever read about the matter. I can't claim any credit for the uniqueness, other than to say I grew up in the shadow of the Knapp mansion and just got a little curious a few years ago about who the Knapps were.

"The Rest Of The Story"

Friends I'm now going to tell you a little postscript to all this, that is truly an exclusive, I never even posted this on my web site, because I figured I needed a few gems just for the book, and this one is a real diamond. I have a piece of the Big Fat Slob story to tell you from a very reliable inside source. My source will be revealed in a much broader and I think bigger Knapp story in a later chapter, but trust me you can't get more inside than this. With that said, let it be known that Dodi Knapp claimed he evened the score by knocking out Hemingway at a later date. He did not mention if there were any witness to it, or how it was done, (Many pro boxers of that era Tunney, Dempsy, Baer, all claim Hemingway was not nearly as good a boxer, as he thought himself to be) However what weighs in the strongest for me that this story could be true is, Knapp revealed it in a one on one conversation with my source, who had never heard of the big fat slob incident,until Dodi told him about how Hemingway had knocked him out once and he eventually returned the favor!

CHAPTER

30

Currituck:

Moving To The Country

"Whether life is really worth living depends largely on where you try to live it. One great passion of my life was the dream of a beautiful home. Another passion of my boyhood was the hope of life in a great city... I dreamed of its boulevards, its parks, its palatial homes and its gleaming lights. The only thing that makes New York impossible for a real home is the certainty that sooner or later a hotel, a flat, a store, a church, a factory, a stable or a saloon will be located near you ... The man who does not know salt water is lopsided and underdeveloped" —**THOMAS DIXON, JR.**

W*hen* Thomas Dixon wrote those words for his book *The Life Worth Living: A Personal Experience,* in the early 1900s, his friend J.P. Knapp, although born and raised in the city, had certainly long known about the good life and beautiful homes surrounded by both tall buildings and salt water. Tom and Joe who were the same age, had a far different upbringings. Tom's was in rural Shelby, North Carolina coming of age during the reconstruction of Civil War, while Joe's was in his fathers palatial Williamsburg mansion that hosted people like Civil War victor General Grant. I tell you this, because the Thomas Dixon family was far closer and far longer associated with that of the J.P. Knapp family than any other bio on Knapp has ever mentioned it to be. And because of that interaction, one of the benefits to my research was gathering a bit more insight into the life and times of some of my central characters. And as for J. P. Knapp's time spent in Dixon's Dixie backyard, it just might be safe to say it had the greatest direct effect on people than anything else J. P. Knapp ever did in his entire 86 years on earth.

It was in NY city where the enigmatic and now long forgotten Dixon, found some of his first really strong successes in his multi faceted public adult life as a lawyer, politician, clergyman, author, lecturer and screenwriter. At the time he moved with his family into New York from Boston around 1886, he was a give them fire and brimstone preacher and huge crowd drawing controversial lecturer. An educated man with very strong and controversial opinions who graduated with honors from Wake Forest University, it was while living in NYC that he had his first great financial success while toughing it out mentally at 12 different locations (some quite desirable by NY City standards both then and now) over the 11 years the Dixon family first tried living there, When the Dixons moved out to the wilds of suburban Staten Island, because urban city life was killing him, his oldest son Jordan was bitten so badly by mosquitoes that his legs were paralyzed for the rest of his short life (Jordan passed away at age 32 from polio complications in 1919). His youngest son Thomas III was born in NY City, one week after Dodi Knapp was in Feb. 1892. It is possible his public notoriety as an orator and preacher may of been what first brought Thomas to J. P. s attention, but it may also have been his sharing hours in a humble duck blind on the banks of the Carman's River in Brookhaven, Long Island in the 1890s. It should also be noted the last Dixon residence on Riverside Drive was just a few blocks away from the J. P. Knapp home at Central Park west on 72nd street.

But the country beckoned again and now being able to really afford the good life of a gentry, the Dixon family moved out of NY in 1897 to Elmington Manor, a fine colonial, 500 acre estate smack on Chesapeake Bay in Virginia close to the North Carolina border, complete with an 80 foot yacht. While there he found even greater success as an author and playwright. His first two novels The Leopards Spots and The Clansman, really caught fire and brought him greater notoriety and larger fortunes with it. When D. W. Griffith turned Dixon's The Clansman into Hollywood's first epic blockbuster film "Birth Of A Nation" Dixon reportably became a millionaire almost overnight. All because Griffith who could not fully afford the $10,000 he originally agreed upon for the book rights (itself a record for a novel) instead gave Dixon $2,000 cash and 25% of the films gross profits. The audience for history's first feature length film wildly exceeded any ones guesses and the overall fallout to all who were ever involved with the film,turned exhibitor Louis B. Mayer into a bonafide movie mogul. Mayer is often credited with establishing Hollywood as the mecca for movie making.

Well if that's true, around the same time North Carolina was rapidly becoming the mecca for duck hunting for millionaires. Since the mid 19th century Long Island had long been considered the duck hunters paradise and in the later 1800's, the amount of private gunning clubs located there was actually giving the gilded age sportsman the delirious predicament of too many choices. Dixon who had hunted with Knapp out on Long Island, invited him down to Currituck "where ducks and geese were so thick the sky often turned black with them" [1]

Quack Quack Quack—Duck Hunting Is Just Like Crack

Now hold on a second all you Ducks Unlimited folks out there! Before you come gunning for me, I'm not comparing the millionaire sportsman with his private hunting lodge, hired hunting guides and custom engraved French made 12 gauge to the hopped up crack addict, with a 357 magnum with the serial numbers filed off stuck in his pants, about to knock off a 7-11, while his equally fix craving lookout keeps the motor running on a stolen car. No sir—not one bit! The only reason your humble scribe and curious observer of human behavior has come up with that rhyming sub head here, is my take on the word addiction and because I am a wordsmith, I can. The same way a new millionaire like Dixon could afford to buy an island just to support his duck hunting addiction. And although far from the madding crowd, Dixon was soon not alone as word got around and soon many a tycoon - sportsman flocked to North Carolina and Virginia via yacht and rail, spending small fortunes of their huge ones, just to shoot ducks. And most likely, by using some of the additional riches brought in from the success of Birth Of Nation, Dixon did just that too. In 1916 he bought MacKay Island in Currituck, North Carolina, solely for the purpose of duck hunting.

Mackay Island is actually part of the larger Knotts Island. But for one hunter or an army of them, Mackay was certainly big enough. It reportably covers an area between 5,000 to 7,000 thousand acres. (I have seen both figures) Located on the Currituck Sound on the Virginia - North Carolina line, Mackay Island was just a very short boat trip across the North River from Dixon's Elmington Manor estate. It is reported that J. P. Knapp visited on several occasions and somehow convinced Dixon to sell him Mackay Island just two years later. Perhaps because Dixon fell victim to a cash flow problem brought on by his mistake of self financing the sequel to "Birth Of A Nation," the totally obscure "Fall Of A Nation"?

So by 1918 J.P. Knapp now had himself three distinct recreational play-grounds on the North American continent. In the far north of Canada, there was his salmon fishing lodge on the Natasqhaun River, where he probably only saw the people he brought up there with him to fish and no one minded if Knapp sang to the fish as he reeled them in, not even the moose. Then there was Lew Beach in the Catskill's, where his Beaverkill trout fishing lodge was located. There he at least had a few local townsfolk in nearby Livingston Manor to interact with. But it would be in Currituck, North Carolina where his interactions would be greatly felt by the locals for over the two decades he lived there and it still continued for years after.

---

1 I believe the Dixons may of held onto their last home in New York city, or purchased another home there again, because in 1910 the entire family was enumerated as living there at 867 Riverside Dr. The same address that Tommy Dixon used on his 1917 Draft registration card. The 1920 census finds them living in Currituck, NC. In 1930 the Dixons Thomas, Harriet and Thomas Jr., are all back at Riverside Dr. NY

Knapp Lodge

When Knapp bought Mackay island, it included a large two story house that a lumber company who owned it before Dixon, used for their employees to board at while they were cutting down huge tracts of oak and pine there. Though large, strong and sturdy looking, with a very nice upper and lower level verandah, the place would of more than sufficed quite nicely to house a group of guys who didn't want to really rough it in a tent. However it obviously didn't suit what J. P. had in mind for a proper place for the kind of entertaining he planned to do there and he had it torn down about 1920[2]. In it's place he erected a 37 room mansion syled like George Washington's Mount Vernon, and situated it right near the waters edge on Live Oak point. I guess he was on quite a building boom then, because at the same time he was also having the big summer house Tenacre built in Southampton, LI. I'm not sure if architect James Pope who designed the Southampton house designed the one in Currituck or not. Pope would also create the Jefferson memorial in Washington, DC. I recently read a letter J. P. Knapp wrote in 1930s singing the praises of Jefferson, which not that many Republicans do these days.

Word got around locally about a new millionaire owner of Mackay Island who was spending money hand over fist making improvements and it wasn't long before possibly smelling a story, that news reporters came calling to see what was going on over there. One of those reporters was W. O. Saunders, a fellow who wrote and published his own weekly newspaper called The Independant in a tiny town with the big name of Elizabeth City, NC (Story goes that Elizabeth town was already taken so the founding father and son in law had to call it Elizabeth City) It seems that W.O. Saunders was quite the character with a nose for different kind of stories. In the 1960s his son Keith published a book, now long out of print, about his Dad's human interest stories and of course I found this one to be quite human and interesting too. NO BULL!

I'm paraphrasing Keith Saunders here except for the quotes; my comments are in italics .

Mackay Island was only about 25 miles away from Elizabeth city, so when my Dad heard about this new millionaire owner buying about 5000 acres of it, he wandered over there looking for a story. The owner wasn't there and no one seemed to know much about him. They just told my Dad his name was "Mister Knapp" and they had an idea that he was in the calendar business. (*once low profile, always low profile*) Some called him "Knapp The Calendar Man"

As my Dad roamed about the island he took note of the beautiful home, boats, the shooting equipment, (*I guess someone let him in the door?*) and that about 50 acres was freshly cleared and put in condition for farming. There was a new very fine dairy barn, piggery, and poultry house but no pigs, poultry or cows to speak of.

One of the caretakers who was showing Dad around said "Mr. Knapp was going to buy some thoroughbred cows up north and ship them down later" He went on to say they had a lot cattle on the land right now, but they are all scrubs and mostly bulls. "I believe actually we got 42 head in all, but there ain't but two cows in the lot." "For Gosh Sake!" Dad said "What is this man doing with a herd of forty bulls and two cows?"

"Well he doesn't know they're mostly all bulls, you see it was this way. There's a lot of underbrush on this here island and Mr. Knapp had the idea that a lot of cattle turned loose on the place would clear up the underbrush. He told us to go over to the mainland and buy some scrub cattle and turn 'em loose over here. It seems that the folks on the mainland who had scrubs to sell, didn't want to sell anything but bulls. We see now that we made a mistake. Those forty bulls spend all their time fighting over the two cows; the bulls are fighting all day and night back up in the woods."

Now W. O. found this merely to be amusing and he didn't think too much more about it until he got back to his office and reached for his Who's Who In America. There he found some enlightning basics about the "calendar man" Who's who very complete listing told him this new farmer Mister Knapp was the son of Joseph F. Knapp founder and former president of Metropolitan Life Insurance Co. and that he himself was chairman of the board of Metropolitan, which was at that time probably the greatest financial institution on earth. He also found that the calendar business was just an incidental part of the American Lithographic Co of who his new found farmer - islander was also the head of. It went on to tell him that the calendar man was also the principal owner of P. F. Collier & Son inc publishers of American Magazine, Woman's Home Companion, Farm & Fireside and Collier's Weekly.

Keith goes on to say, even all that didn't mean any more to my father than any other very rich man who happened upon an out of the way place where the shooting was good and was spending barrels of money trying to make it livable. (Saunders description of Knapps place sounded a little more than "livable" to me.) It was the fact that Mr. Knapp was incidentally identified with *Farm & Fireside*, one of the oldest farm journals in America, that inspired W. O. to write this story:

NEW YORK MILLIONAIRE BUILDS HIMSELF A HOUSE ON MACKEYS ISLAND

Sept. 23, 1921 — Who is Joseph Palmer Knapp? he is a native of Brooklyn, NY born May 14, 1864, chairman of the board of Metropolitan Life Insurance Co. a member of Columbia University Club, The Players Club, The Bankers Club, New York Yacht Club, The Links and Westmister Kennel clubs and active president of American Lithographing (sic) Co. —

Also as the head of the big magazine publishing house of P. F. Collier and Son, he is incidentally principal owner of Farm & Fireside, one of the oldest and most widely read farm journals in America. Mr. Knapp contemplates an experiment on Mackay Island that will enable him to put into practice some of the fine theories that his Farm & Fireside editors have been trying to drum into the heads of American yokelry for many years. Mr. Knapp is planning a model farm on Mackay Island, in the heart of Currituck sound. He will engage in mixed farming, producing both field crops and livestock,

But his initial herd, consisting of forty bulls and two cows is causing his retainers on the island much loss of sleep. The ratio of cows to bulls being only one to twenty, the bulls are fighting day and night for the possession of each cow. The pawings, snortings and bellowings of two score bulls on that otherwise peaceful island makes the night hideous. And the small human population that Mr. Knapp has domiciled on the island is fearful that the sex crazy bulls. tired of fighting among themselves, will turn upon them and rend them with horns and hooves. But the principal owner of Farm & Fireside, the great American farm monthly is proceeding blithely with his plans to become a gentleman farmer."

That was all of the article Keith reprinted in his book[3], but he went on to say there was at least another columns worth of foolishness lampooning the adventures of a fine gentleman who really was only casually interested in his farm publication. After reading his own proofs W. O. had second thoughts about printing it, thinking he might offend Mr. Knapp who would then never subscribe to the Independent. But Saunders went ahead and not only did he find out that Mr. Knapp was a good sport, he also found that Joe Knapp had a fine sense of humor and thoroughly enjoyed it. He even bought extra copies of the paper to send to his friends back in New York so they could also enjoy the laugh at his own expense.

J. P. Knapp not only became a regular reader of the Independent, he appreciated, clipped and filed many of Dad's editorials because he was not afraid to call a spade a spade or an outhouse an outhouse. One day back in New York Joe Knapp passed his file of Dad's writings to "Sid" Siddall. his editor at The American Magazine. Siddall read them and wrote to Saunders for more. Dad wrote back that he was coming to New York next week!. The two men had lunch together and Siddall told him " I feel there is good copy in you, but I don't know just where to peg you." He then said "If you will attempt a piece of about 5,000 words for me and call it Autobiography of a Crank, I'll pay you four hundred dollars for it if I can print it." Four hundred dollars was a fortune to my father back then and Autobiography of a Crank appeared in the June 1922 issue of The American Magazine.

That led to numerous pieces in not only American, but Collier's and Country Home (the revamped Farm & Fireside) and The Nations Business as well. Years later Dad would write " I would perhaps of been an obscure country editor unknown to millions of magazine readers throughout the length and breadth of the United States, but for my stumbling upon the fact of Mr. Joe Knapp's herd of forty bulls and two cows on Mackay Island in 1921. (and that's no bull)

---

3 Postscript: I have also read the actual news story as it was printed in 1921 and that Saunders included to mention that of the local folks who only heard about Knapp, they regarded him as just another Northern millionaire sportsman who had taken up another portion of their hunting grounds, but that of those who had actually met 'the calendar man", found him to be plain, lovable, generous, hearty, democratic and a neighborly fellow who had not been dehumanized by reason of his great wealth. He makes the humblest citizen feel at home in his presence or on his estate and many of the neighboring people are often guests at his home. His neighborliness and generosity have made fast friends for him. One of his neighbors had to go into the hospital for an expensive operation and left the hospital to find that his bill had been paid by Mr. Knapp. A woman whose husband was injured while working on his island received a Christmas present of a check for $500.00 He also pointed out that Mr. Knapp had a payroll to the locals of $2,000.00 per month, paid $15.000.00 a year in local property taxes, and that the amount of ducks Mr. Knapp and his guests will kill in a season could not diminish the supply very much in over a 100 years. And they do say he pours the largest glass of genuinely good whiskey to be found in all of Currituck County.

At the same time that Knapp was "fixing up" his farm, another NY publishing tycoon was doing likewise. That would be Ogden M. Reid the publisher of the NY Herald Tribune, who would carry Knapp's Sunday News Magazine "This Week" from beginning to end. Reid built his elaborate European styled hunting lodge known as "Flyaway" in 1920 on 350 acres directly across Currituck sound from what was now known as the Knapp Lodge. If his name rings a small bell may I refer you to chapter 28 in the sub title section "Forever Amber" where in 1905 Ogden returns from Southampton, England in the company of two young ladies. Amber Lawlor and her cousin Margaret Rutledge. Reid seemed to be a colorful character and there are several amusing anecdotes about him in Archie Johnson and Bud Coppedge's book "Gunning Clubs and Decoys of Back Bay and Currituck Sound " first published in 1991 CurBak Press. The story about Garland Bright, a church committee man who came to call on Reid at Flyaway one morning in late 1920s caught my eye. It seems the church needed a new Delco system (generator for its lights) After hearing him out Reid excused himself and returned with a bottle of fine whiskey and offered his guest a "morning toddy" Garland respectively declined and the conversation continued for a bit longer while Reid enjoyed his drink. Not sure if his mission was going to have any success or not Bright said as he prepared to leave that Ogden could contact either him or anyone at the Oak Grove Baptist Church, if he decided to make a donation. Ogden replied "Mr. Bright , I have already decided , you tell your committee to go ahead and have the Delco system installed and just send me the bill. I will be glad to take care of it for the church. However had you taken a drink with me I wouldn't of given you one red cent."

I have long thought that it could well have been Reid who introduced Margaret Rutledge to J. P. Knapp at least a decade before they were married. Drinks are on me if Ogden was not a guest. just across bay at the Knapp estate. when the widower J. P. Knapp married Margaret Easterling Rutledge in 1923.

CHAPTER
31

The Bumpy Road to Knowledge
& the Education of Joe Knapp

I have heard several slight variations to this next story of just how Joe Knapp first got involved in a long and highly beneficial association with the education system of Currituck, but basically what happened was this:

It was circa 1920 and his fairly new acquisition, Collier's magazine was running a series on the educational needs of all American schools. J. P. was in Currituck corresponding with his Collier people back in New York, perhaps even writing an article or two (if not making a few suggestions on what to aim at) and he took a drive to the post office to mail something to them. Knott's Island did not have its own post office at that time, and Knapp's PO address there was over the state line in Munden, Va. about 15 miles from his home. It was a very cold and rainy day when he came upon some children of school age walking and stopped to give them a ride. Asking them about their school life revealed that, they only went to school 3 months out of the year, the schoolhouse itself was just one room without heat, lights or running water and they had one teacher for all grades. Well judging by what happened next, he may of thought why not start my magazines crusade for improving education right here in my own backyard? And it may of also been an epiphany for 57 year old J. P. Knapp, to begin to really grasp the full depth of what his mother was trying to instill in him, when he was a young man of 17 and dropped out of college.

I am indebted to Gordon C. Jones, a Grad Student, of Old Dominion University, whose 1971 research paper titled "The Introduction Of Modern Education Into Currituck County, NC" supplied me with many of the finer details and documents of just how J. P. Knapp left his mark on Currituck's schools and explains why to this day, Currituck school children still hold wreath laying ceremonies at his grave site during Christmas and on his birthday in May.

Jones suggests that Knapp probably wasted no time in urging the board of education to participate in a 1921 US Govt. Dept. Of Interior survey titled "Suggestions for the Reorganization of the Schools in Currituck, NC." But alas we all know government moves at glacier like speeds, which might explain why the first documents presented in his paper were three letters from J. P. Knapp to a Mr. W. D. Cox superintendent of schools, all dated October 23, 1922 Mr. Jones presents all three letters in their entirety in his paper to " illustrate the prophetic importance of J.P. Knapp's own words, the kind of man he was and how his mind worked " which is why I am adding them in here too.

Dear Mr Cox:

At the informal conference held at Mr. M. R. Johnson's house, with members of the School Board, you and I were appointed to a committee to make suggestions that would be helpful in educational matters to Currituck County. As I understand it, you think the following plan a wise one to follow and we jointly place these suggestions before the Board.

> A.   *1. The general plan towards which it is desired to work as described in the bulletin prepared by Mrs. Katherine M. Cook* DIAGRAM 1
>
> *2. For these people we will endeavor to obtain the best teachers, paying to secure them, whatever salaries may be necessary; employing them year by year and providing them with teacher's homes, with the idea that the teacher will* KNOW *his or her community and be an all year helpful resident of it.*
>
> *3. In these schools Primary grades shall be of greatest importance, Junior grades of next importance, High School grades of last but still great importance.*
>
> *4.* HOME ECONOMICS *shall be considered of utmost importance, as shall agricultural instruction. Our* AIM *is to teach* CLEAN HOMES, GOOD FOOD, *and* GOOD HEALTH *on prosperous farms for the well-being of Currituck County.*
>
> *5. Transportation shall be provided where necessary and possible because of road conditions.*
>
> *6. Our schools shall differ from the general run in following the most advanced schools as now being successfully conducted in various parts of the country. At this writing you and I believe there is much to be learned from studying the methods employed at: Porter, Mo. - Mrs. Harvey. A one room country school system with an* INTERNATIONAL *reputation, which has given high community service and has adopted educational methods to local needs in a farming district Fairhope, Ala.- Mrs. Johnson. A consolidated country school system, tax sup-*

ported, Celebrated. Columbus, Mo.-Prof. T. L. Meriam. Much in common with Mrs. Johnson's school (see above) Indianapolis, Ind. -Public School No 45 where "learning by doing" is the basis of all teaching. The Bronx, New York City -Public School 45 conducted by Dr. Patri as described in the Collier articles sent to members of the school board.

Among other schools following similar methods are Francis W. Parker School, San Diego, California, Casey, New York, regarded as a great school, Merame Park, Dayton Ohio, Reported to have achieved remarkable results. Gary, Illinois Quite worth of study. In addition to the above, there many more Consolidated, Elementary and One - Room schools which are noted for producing fine results. The names will be supplied to the Board on request.

B. To accomplish these results, it is thought essential:

> *1. That there be a uniform special school tax throughout the county.*
>
> *2. That the tax rate be sufficient to accomplish the results outlined above in providing for annual expenditure.*
>
> *3. That bond issues be made from time to time to provide for permanent improvements. The above correctly expresses, as I understand, our views which we wish to lay before the School Board.*

Yours very truly,
Joseph P. Knapp

In letter No. 2, J. P. offers a little incentive to get things moving! For those of us whose eyes glaze over in legalese, let me just say there are some very generous offerings in the context of this letter.

Dear Mr. Cox:

If the plans described in my letter of the same date be approved by the Board and if earnest effort be made to put them into effect with a reasonable time, it will give me the greatest pleasure to be of financial assistance along the following lines:

Until the time that funds are provided as suggested in paragraph B of that letter I will, up to $20,000 loan to the Board or County any amount expended for Currituck or Knott's Island schools or for extraordinary or desirable expenditures such as any deficit in primary supervisor's salary, the erection of a teacher's home at Currituck or Knott's Island etc.

When 1 and 2 in paragraph B have been accomplished I will, on request of the Board, loan additional amounts up to an additional $30,000 These loans are to be made without interest: are to be repayable one sixteenth each year and are to be so worded as attorneys agree, as to be free from state and county taxes, as are state and county bonds.

Should bonds be issued, as per paragraph B, Section 3, I will buy at par one half of any issue up to a total of $50,000 and as interest is paid each year I will return to the county an amount of bonds equal to the interest so received by me. Should 6% be paid each year on the bonds so bought by me and bonds in that amount be each year returned to the county for cancellation, such bonds will all have been retired within 16 ⅔ years.

I reserve the right to withdraw this offer on due notice to your board, but intend *to do so only if the residents of the county show they will not CO-OPERATE in bringing about the better education and happiness of our children and the future prosperity of our county. If, however, this cooperation be evidenced I will take great pleasure in making the carrying out of the above financial provisions binding on my heirs and executors so that in the event of my death the good work will go forward. **

Sincerely, Joseph P. Knapp Oct 23, 1922

I would not be surprised if the recent death of his wife just four months earlier, played a role in the inclusion of his last sentence in that second letter. And Gordon Jones weighs in with this observation "Although the board members must of had some fore-knowledge of Mr. Knapp's intention to assist them in reorganizing their schools, no evidence has been found to indicate they had any idea that a sum as large as $100,000 would be offered for their use on such favorable terms. They were well intentioned farmers with less than high school educations, who probably never thought in terms of so much money."

Furthermore, J. P. was really burning up the ribbon on his Underwood that October day, as he gets into more details in implementing a plan for success.

Dear Mr. Cox:

Assuming that it is decided to improve the schools along the lines of my letter of even date, it would next seem to me of utmost importance to put down in black and white the CURRICULUM *for every grade, stating plainly what each grade is to do with its school hours and other hours. Unless this is done we have no definite instructions to issue to the teachers, no method of determining their suitability for the positions when engaging them. As I understand our new plans their acquaintance with Porter, Fairhope, Columbia, Indianapolis, Patri methods is of more importance to us than their scholastic attainment.*

We cannot have forty or more teachers following their own ideas or old teaching methods if we intend to have our schools run on advanced methods. Therefore, our new methods must be correctly, exactly expressed in black and white.

(1) Suggest that the Board relieve you now from all clerical and all possible other work. (2) That you visit, soon, four or five of these advanced schools. (3) That calling in people to help you, people who understand thoroughly the operation of these schools, that you with them prepare explicit, written instructions for the guidance of teachers in Currituck Schools, and that this document be in printed form not later than April 1st next,

The following step would be to look over your April 1st staff of teachers. Many of them may have good qualifications. Many of them may desire and have the ability to teach these advanced methods, It is but fair that they have the first chance. Make your selection of those you wish to retain, explain your plans to them. Let them read your curriculum book,and books like "New School for Old" and then let those selected go to one of the summer teachers' school where advanced teaching methods are taught. There are two or more such schools.

In this way you will probably start the next school year with many of your old teachers filled with a new enthusiasm for the advanced methods and will have a definite gauge to size up new applicants.

Finally our plans will never fully succeed until you have as the head of Moyock, Poplar, Branch, Currituck, and Knott's Island schools, a person of the type as Mrs. Johnson, Prof, Meriam or Dr. Patri -people who believe in "learning by doing" who have the ability and tact to lead in community life, who love their job and believe that it extends from January through December and ever many more hours a day than merely the school hours. With four such leaders we can and will succeed. Therefore, we simply must find them. So I earnestly hope the school board will delegate these duties to you; the preparation of the curriculum book, the finding of four people for the key positions.

Very sincerely,

Joseph. P. Knapp

I have to say for a college dropout, J. P. Knapp had a Masters, perhaps even a Ph. D., in Common Sense and knew full well what type of effort it would take for just about any worthwhile endeavor to succeed. Gordon Jones goes on to say, that the minutes of the school board reveal that Knapp's letter # 3 was adapted immediately and 1 & 2 several weeks later on Nov 6th. And there was great excitement for all the members of the school board and they overwhelmingly expressed their willingness to support such drastic changes proposed by Knapp. These were ordinarily slow moving farmers, whose actions so pleased Knapp that on November 15th he composed another letter that just knocked them flat. To the astonishment of the entire board, J. P. Knapp withdrew his original offer as it was proposed and now declared it to be a GIFT rather than a loan! Then added in that although he would not contract to return bonds bought by him in the amount of annual interest paid, that he was not withdrawing his intent to do so, as stated in his earlier letter.

To further aid the Board in gaining the support of the people, and to insure that the basic contents of the Department Of Interior Bulletin were widely known, J. P. paid to have it printed in the Independent as an advertisement. There the people could actually read how a "Federal Agency" summarized the existing terrible conditions of their schools. The details supporting the findings are fascinating to read. Imagine sending your child to a school today with no bathrooms, or where their buildings also were used as barns. W. O. Saunders, the Independent's editor who wrote his first story on Knapp and his 40 Bulls, went on to tell his readers that Knapp had no interest in any publicity for himself, and he kept them informed of "Knapp's School Project" as it progressed with editorials like this one from January 26, 1923.

"Mr. Knapp's interest in education, is just an out-cropping of his deep and fundamental interest in universal education. If you read Collier's Weekly, you must have noted that it is giving a lot of space to education. Collier's believes that every boy and girl in America should have the same educational opportunity and very best a nation can provide. That's a Joe Knapp idea passed on to a great weekly periodical. This newspaper has called Mr. Knapp a practical visionary, or something like that. He is a modern combination of idealist and business genius."

As 1922 drew to a close things started to really move at the school board in Currituck. On December 16th it accepted Knapp's first gift of $2,500 to pay off the old mortgage at Moyock school. Knapp soon made a second gift of $500 to pay for modern homes, which he helped to design. Then a $2,000 gift was given to establish a Home Economics department at the Poplar Branch school. He promised another $25,000 gift to the schools, "if a fair amount of community spirit were shown and sufficient taxation was levied to run the schools for nine months."

Spirit must of been shown, because in April of 1923, J.P. arranged for Miss Maud C. Newbury, who had made and written the school survey, to come from Washington in order to do more planning. She met with the Board and brought several other experts with her. Also at that time Cox and Knapp drew up further detailed plans for a progressive consolidation of the county schools and a modernization of their programs. J. P. with the full backing of the board, persuaded Miss Newbury to take a leave of absence from Washington and accept the position as Supervisor for 5 years, with the option of resigning after one year if the experiment did not prove to her satisfaction. Her salary was $4,000 a year plus a new Ford coupe and travel expenses. To keep the public informed, Knapp started a local monthly illustrated small newspaper The Picayune, which included his paying for a writer- editor and paying The Independent to print it. The first issue did a story on Miss Newbury's summer recruiting drive to find teachers from far and wide that "had the requisite education and interest to make the coming school year a success" The partial list held names of 24 college grads with 10 coming from out of state. Prior to that, the entire area only had 5 college graduate teachers. The little 12 page paper caught the attention of news papers and journals throughout the state among them Raleigh's News and Observer that commented:

Currituck, long noted principally for ducks and sweet potatoes, has climbed into the limelight from an entirely unexpected quarter. The Tar Heel county has undertaken to set the pace for rural school efficiency in northeastern North Carolina and starts right off the bat with a record that is going to be hard to beat or even equal. All the school work above the sixth grade in Currituck, will be done in two superior junior-senior high schools which will be accessible to almost all the children in the county by motor truck (bus). These schools will run for nine months in the year, and will make it possible for all the children in the county to have the advantage of a high school education, which is something few counties in the state can boast of. The High School Journal published by University of NC mentioned in an article reviewing Currituck's effectiveness : the larger and wealthier counties would do well to follow Currituck's example.

That first school year got off to a good start, but it was not total smooth sailing with problems caused by past methods. Newbury's early testing showed that reading, spelling and math levels were several grades behind and she commented in the fall of 1923 " The inequality in education available to Currituck's boys and girls, which Mr. Knapp had sensed, was now being discovered by modern educational tests and could hopefully be remedied by the new instructional methods he was making possible". And there were bumpy roads ahead too when unforeseen future events created a serious political problem of having out of state teachers employed when the depression hit hard. But Knapp's immediate main concern in the first year or so after he knew he had some major people and things in place was, how can the whole system be maintained?"

In his effort to solve this problem, he offered the board a special fund of $100,000 and a plan for its use. The money would be controlled by a Board of Trustees consisting of 5 members, one of which would be a member of the board of education. The purpose of this fund would be to cover expenses not covered by the tax rate. If used carefully Knapp said "It should last eight to ten years, which I hope would suffice to prove that these new improvements that included better instructors, and methods of practical teaching with longer school terms will have of demonstrated their usefulness in making the county more prosperous through the better education of it's young people."

According to Jones' review of the minutes of the school board's meetings, things happened very quickly in 1923. New building projects and diversity of financial transactions such as building contracts, maintenance, teachers vouchers for supplies etc were all handled by Mr. Cox. Knapp had previously strongly recommend (Letter #3) that Cox be relieved of clerical duties from the beginning, but was ignored on that point. By January of 1924 it was evident that accounts were not being kept in a business like manner and Superintendent Cox could not produce an accurate figure of existing indebtedness. At one particularly heated meeting that Knapp and Miss Newbury were present at "by invitation", the indignant Mr. Cox offered up his resignation in a considerable huff. Knapp was then asked to leave the meeting but later recalled. When he returned he found that the Board had accepted Cox's resignation, paid him for his salary to date, but he had left with all his records and the minute book. With no fiscal records at all, they decided to stop all work throughout the county on school buildings until some method of accounting could be set up.

A few days later Cox requested that his resignation be withdrawn and threatened a lawsuit if it was not. The Board refused and demanded he return the minute book. Mr. Knapp then came up with three questions that he wanted an immediate answer to. When the Board learned that they as individuals could be held liable, they wasted no time searching for answers to:

1: How much money does the Currituck County Board of Education owe and how can it be paid?
2: How much money will it cost to run Currituck County's schools as they are now run?
3: What is school income from all sources for the present year?

"The Check's In The Mail"

A special meeting was held within a week later and Maud Newbury was unanimously requested to accept the position of Superintendent while retaining her position as supervisor. She accepted with some reluctance and was awarded the additional new title and responsibility complete with a salary of $1 per year! At Knapp's request, Dudley Bagley, an officer of the Bank of Currituck, was put in charge of setting up an accounting system. Bagley would become a life long friend of Knapp and wrote an unpublished manuscript titled "The Joseph P. Knapp I Knew". This manuscript sits buried in the archives of the UNC at Chapel Hill. Although it has long been my desire to read it in it's entirety, unfortunately the University's quoted copying costs of over $400, from several years back, have kept it out of my reach, just as the distance and expense of traveling from Nashville to Chapel Hill to read it there and going on to Currituck to revisit so much of J. P. Knapp's history has become a fading hope as I endeavor to finish this manuscript. However as I already stated, I am grateful that inquisitive people like Mr. Jones have made good use of tidbits of Bagley's manuscript and that I have at least been able to include them here.

Bagley with the help of Mr. Frank Edmundson of the State Board of Education was able to set up a standard school accounting system and their report showed a deficit of just under $50,000 by the end of the school year, with $15,500 being overdue. Upon giving these figures to JP, Bagley quotes him as saying to the Board "I helped get you into this jam and I will get you out of it. A check for the $15,500 will be in the mail to you from New York next Monday. along with a plan for paying the balance of it." At the next meeting, Knapp presented a nine point plan for canceling the obligations of the Board and for running the schools until June 30th. The Board, the Trustees and Knapp all signed off on it. Among its provisions was a 30 cent tax to levied uniformly throughout the county in return for which Mr. Knapp offered to provide a special gift of $16,000 to build and fully equip a school building at Shawboro, where the voters had been especially antagonistic about any special levy for schools, even though they resided in the richest farm land in the county. A school tax referendum held in July was voted in by a vast majority in every district in the county. There is also a note in the minute book of an acknowledgment of Mr. Knapp, of his making a special gift that allowed for the employment of a school dentist. There was not even a practicing dentist in the entire county at that time. The new doctor was charged with examining every child and performing necessary cleaning and preventive therapies in an office established for him within the schools.

The original 1921 survey had made no mention of colored schools which of course were separate then and for decades after, but they too received attention from Mr. Knapp. In Feb of 1925, a letter from him was read into the minutes, where he requested complete details and drawings for a first class school, auditorium, teacher-age and playgrounds for the Jarvisburg Colored School district. When these were completed Knapp said, "My idea is start out to see whether I cannot find the money." He would discover, though, finding the money, would not be the main object in his way, in what was still the Jim Crow south.

From the very gitgo, Knapp had promised the people of the area he would always be there to help as long as the people were willing to share the expenses in proportion to their means of doing so. He would find out they always supported this concept, but he would also find out from a house to house survey conducted by Miss Newbury, that the poverty level in the area was much worse than he ever imagined. This resulted in his ever diminishing request or mention even of matching funds in his letters to the county as time went on. It also probably led in large part to his creation of The Knapp Foundation of North Carolina to aid in the smoother transaction of funds to where they were most needed. During the rest of 1925, by either matching funds or outright gifts, teachers of commercial subjects were added to the faculty, as were several vocational teachers whose salaries were 10% above the rest of the state to insure getting the best qualified people available. He also raised the salaries of two High School principals, established a clinic and employed a county home demonstration agent and kitchen equipment for four schools "so that overage elementary school girls and those taking Domestic Science in the high schools, might learn better methods of serving meals." In December of 1925, the Board received a letter from Mrs. Knapp[1] offering to defray the cost of constructing a free public school at Knott's Island with the postscript "I will advance whatever monies are required to pay bills connected with the above building." Joseph P. Knapp

Potholes & Detours Dead Ahead

Things really seemed to be going smoothly for the schools over in Currituck. The excellent academic results being achieved also resulted in the towns people working harder at the management of funds. In October of 1926 The Independent carried a four column story, comparing them to what they were just four years earlier. Conscious of Mr. Knapp's policy of desiring to keep a low profile, editor Saunders did not mention Knapp's philanthropies in the article. The article closed with "This marked advancement in education in Currituck County is due to CO-OPERATION on the part of it's citizens. They have worked individually and collectively for the school system they now have. There are in the United States today 186,000 one room schools, but not one of them are in Currituck."

By 1927 a report noted that Currituck teachers ranked first in the state's rural areas and above 15 cities in the nation. There was a even a surplus that a paid for books for all students at both the white and colored schools. Currituck also had a new school that was entirely paid for by Knapp except for $1000 for grading and paving the road. The condition of the roads got Joe Knapp's attention as well and he felt that the placement of future schools (that he also would contribute a whole lot of money to) be built on main roads for ease of transportation. For the most part the board usually went along or always seriously considered his advice and suggestions. The first sign of some political discord shows up in the board minutes of March 1929, regarding the hiring of teachers. It seems some members lobbied for the same consideration of relatives and friends of the board as those of other teachers. The referring paragraph was removed at the April meeting. It seems the leader of the discord was a former state representative named E. R. Johnson. Some rumors of protest reached Knapp about Miss Newbury not hiring local teachers and Knapp doing too much to help the Negroes. Things would escalate throughout the next year and Knapp let the

---

1 This of course would be Margaret Rutledge, as are all Currituck references to a Mrs. Knapp after 1923.

board know that he found these rumors "disquieting"

In a letter from Knapp, that was read at a Board meeting in April of 1930 , he said if they approved at their next meeting the erection of an elementary school at Grandy and the remodeling of the Poplar Branch High School, then he was prepared to ask his foundation to grant $175,000. He also mentioned the rumors: "We in the county, before making any changes, should consider carefully the merits of our present system which has been highly complimented throughout the State and the States. A few years ago we were ranked very low in school rating." He pointed out the improvements that were made each year by the Superintendent had made the schools vastly superior to anything this county ever had before. "Now we are right at the top. In my opinion politics and properly run schools do not mix, and I had an experience in Currituck some years ago that would seem to confirm this. Consequently I must now advise the Trustees of the Knapp Foundation only to supply funds for the Poplar Branch and Grandy work when this question is definitely settled."

The Board immediately but reluctantly authorized that Mr. Knapp be advised that "If the Knapp Foundation Trustees will not consider expending funds for a new building anywhere except on the main highway, then the Board favors erection and renovation according to his suggested plan." However it did not end there. Edwin R. Johnson was a politician first and for many years exercised strong control over the affairs in Currituck. Like many politicians he liked to take credit for things he really didn't do. He took the initial credit for bringing Knapp to Currituck, though he didn't. It was Thomas Dixon and his tales of ducks so thick the sky was black.

J. P. did not want to get involved in local politics, unless they infringed on his main concern–the children and their schools. So he wrote to the Board again this time proposing four variations on his initial plan. He also told them they might want to consult with outside experts to help them choose what might be the best course to follow and if they did, he would also advance another $2,000 to cover that expense. The Board declined the offer of experts and instead assembled a special committee of which E. R. Johnson was a member. They also remained deadlocked on the choice of sites. Johnson who seemed to clash frequently with Superintendent Newbury was looking for ways to get her to resign. Also in April Miss Newbury explained to Knapp and the rest of the Board that she needed a prolonged vacation after working steadily under many pressures since 1922.

At a meeting in which Knapp was invited, he stopped them all in their tracks when he read his own letter in person to them that he now thought because they could not come to a definite conclusion, he was advising the entire matter be dropped and all his previous offers concerning it withdrawn. He was also surprised to note the county had reduced the tax from 22 to 17 cents but said his Knapp Foundation was prepared to make up the difference. so that the program already in place would not be curtailed. Up till this point not many of these decisions of the board had received much public attention. But what happened soon afterwards took on slugfest proportions and the deceit of dirty politics at its worst. Johnson made his move to oust Newbury and introduced a bill in the House Of Representatives to expand the board to get two additional members who would vote with him. The local newspaper headline on April

23, 1931 was KNAPP INTERVENES FOR RETENTION OF NEWBURY AS HEAD OF SCHOOLS. The story reported the details of Johnson's bill and said that Knapp, who they called the Godfather of Currituck's schools, had declared that "no change in the present system of school government should be forced on the county by one man or a set of men without the consent of the county as a whole." A delegation of 100 angry Currituck citizens descended upon Raleigh with a petition supporting Knapp's view and carrying the names of 1,253 names of the 1,600 voters in the county. More headlines in all the papers read Currituck Folks Up In Arms Against Tampering With Their Superb School System. The April 29 the Norfolk Virginian Pilot read: CURRITUCK SCHOOL BILL DISAPPROVED AFTER FIREWORKS.

Johnson did not take it gracefully and in a vindictive speech accused Knapp of meddling in Currituck politics and as having carried his township Republican in the last election. Another delegation of angry citizens descended on Raleigh indignant that Knapp had been attacked and armed with facts and figures to prove Johnson wrong. Knapp sent this telegram to state senator Charles Whedbee and it was reprinted in the Daily Advance on May 5, 1931.

THE PEOPLE OF CURRITUCK HAVE EMPHATICALLY EXPRESSED THEIR wishes. Attempting through legislation to win out in a trivial, personal quarrel with our present superintendent in order to gain a small fight, being willing to interfere with and possibly tear down a school system that is admittedly most successful, not only amazes us but it is resented by all the thinking people in our county —E. R. Johnson is not representing but misrepresenting at least four fifths of the voters in this matter. We all appreciate his helpfulness in the past, but he has certainly slipped a cog this time and his position is truly incomprehensible.

Maud Newbury was re-elected as Superintendent and brought Currituck schools to their high point of excellence over the next two years in spite of the depression and shortages in tax collecting. When the County Commissioners were no longer willing or able to provide funds to keep the schools open for nine , Knapp, provided the funds. The school budget for 1932 showed county taxes produced $19,000 and Knapp contributions were $27,965. His help was made public by James A. Taylor, the County Registrar of Deeds in a letter to the Independent on May 23 that year, in which the Registrar explained why the county had the lowest tax rate of any county in state. He said that ever since 1923, Mr. Knapp had donated large sums of money for construction of school buildings and contributed thousands annually to help with expenses. " He has given us more this year than what we paid in taxes and this is the best way I know to explain a 69 cent tax rate for a rural county like Currituck that leads the state in schools."

Lest you think its only politicians of the last few decades who just make things up, in 1932 E. R. Johnson, while running for state senate was quoted as saying "Through my efforts the taxes in my county are now perhaps the lowest of any of the 100 counties and I shall not rest if I am sent to Raleigh as Senator from the First District, until every county in the section has a like reduction" This was not left unnoticed by W. O. Saunders. who wrote in his editorial in the Independent that "The only way Johnson could bring a low tax in other counties of the district would be to find a Joe Knapp for each one. The voters should resent Mr. Johnson's crass and will full misrepresentations " And they did, in a major walloping at polls and Johnson the one time political boss of Currituck was also relieved of his Chairmanship of the Democratic Executive Committee that he had held for 39 years.

One of the very first items I ever discovered about Joe Knapp, some 8 years ago were these two remembrances that were posted online regarding his involvement with education.

A Secret Garden
While surfing the Internet I ran across this page under the Alta Vista Search Engine about a future Knotts Island Home Page. Please keep up the effort for those of us not fortunate enough to live in that Garden of Eden. I am now almost 73 and live in Los Altos Hills, CA. I still visit Knotts Island every year or so to see relatives and to just enjoy the area.

I was raised on Knotts Island having moved there when I was six weeks old from Creeds, Va. I left to work with the Corps of Engineers in Norfolk in 1940 and on into the Navy in 1942. In 1946 I enrolled at NC State and I believe I was the first State graduate from Knotts Island. I still credit much of my success in life to the great beginning at the school on Knotts Island built and almost run in my day by Joseph P. Knapp. We had about eight teachers for 85 to 90 students and a curriculum that much of the country is still dreaming about- sex education, music, home economics, drama, etc. We also enjoyed a balanced diet thanks to the lunch program and milk and veggies from Mackay Island.

I could go on and on about life in the 20's and thirties on Knotts Island, but I'll stop for now.

Tunis Corbell

A Loan From Mr. Knapp
Prior to 1932, the Knotts Island menfolk often guided for wealthy sportsmen to support their families. My grandfather, Edgar Wright Brumley, was one such individual. He had five children - Nita, Adell, Ruth, Edgar and Paul. During that particular time, it was decided by the "powers that be" that to legally operate your Battery (a type of boat, outfitted to be used like the duck hunting blinds of today) a special license would be necessary. However, only so many licenses were to be made available to the Currituck County guides and Papa Ed did not receive one. He, however, took his Battery out and was promptly issued a citation, which resulted in a trip over to the Courthouse. Mr. Joseph Knapp was also there that day, as apparently were a lot of Knotts Islanders upset over the latest methods to keep the poor folk from earning a living off the water. Apparently my Grandfather had to pay a fine because Mr. Knapp came up to Papa Ed and spoke these words, "Mr. Brumley, it is not fair that someone like you, who is trying to feed your family is denied a license and someone like me without a large family to feed, is given a license. If you ever need any help for your family, come and see me." My grandfather did not forget that friendly offer which came from Knotts

Island's most wealthy part-time resident/sportsman.

In 1932 his two daughters, Nita and Adell, expressed a wish to go away to college and become teachers. The money was not available, but my grandfather remembered Mr. Knapp's offer. He hitched the old mule up, set off with his lantern swinging from the wagon and went to Mackay Island where the beautiful estate of Mr. and Mrs. Knapp was located. He went up to the Clubhouse entrance, was received politely and invited inside. He came away with a promise of a loan for whatever was needed for both girls to receive two years of college instruction. In those years, young unmarried women were allowed to teach with a 2-year certificate. The very next day their father took them to Norfolk where a cardboard suitcase apiece was purchased, and one trunk to be shared between them for their clothing. There would be no trips home for these two until the Christmas break. This was a loan and both girls were to repay it after they became teachers. Both did complete the two years required at East Carolina Teacher's College and both became elementary teachers. My mother, Adell Brumley Fentress, ended her teaching career in the late '60s teaching "little folks" at the same school in which she herself attended as a young child - Knotts Island School. I grew up hearing her repeatedly mention this wonderfully kind benefactor who made her dream of teaching become a reality. That she was able to share her love of teaching at the school which first nurtured her was, I think, a fitting closure to her 30 years of teaching. Mr. Knapp would have smiled at having been the instrument that made it all possible so many years ago. —*Sue Fentriss Austin*

I have already touched briefly in chapters 28 and 29 on some effects The Great Depression had on Knapp's business interests. Not surprisingly, it also effected his philanthropy. A later chapter deals with his methods of coping to protect his businesses, his workers, and friends—even his proposals to the Government to help them. Here, however, is how he focused on the events in Currituck that threatened to dismantle all the progress he made with the school system.

Throughout the state of North Carolina which was primarily agricultural, prices for cotton, tobacco and other crops fell far below sustainable. Farmers faced bank foreclosures en mass and both the state and local governments could not meet their own financial obligations. By the start of 1933 forty counties were in default on bond payments. If the schools across all of North Carolina were to be kept open, even more financial burden was placed on the state. The state wound up having to take over support of the system and taking drastic measures like reducing teacher salaries, slashing programs and enacting a state sales tax to try and raise sixteen million dollars they needed to operate a uniform one size fits all educational system.

A new law was passed that effected schools statewide, which were operating on six to eight month schedules and even though Currituck Schools were enjoying a nine month program and having their financial needs met by Knapp making up the deficits, this new statewide law that went into effect on May 15, 1933, effected them as well. Ironically and somewhat mysteriously, there was a clause in the new law that stated, "It was unlawful to operate schools in Currituck County for more than eight months and no supplements shall be allowed."

This clause was inserted by then Representative James A. Taylor, the very same gentleman who when he was Currituck's Registrar of Deeds, explained just why Currituck had the low tax rate it enjoyed! —One J. P. Knapp— This clause which greatly dismayed J.P., who had just turned 69 years of age the day before it was enacted. It certainly made things more difficult for him, but as you know by now, this man was not without his resources of all types. His own words that he spoke before the school board in 1924, "I helped get you into this jam and I will get you out of it," may have came back to him as he found ways to get around this restrictive law of equalization. To add to Knapp's difficulties, the depression may of been the last straw for Maud Newbury and in Feb. of 1934, his main architect of reform announced she would not stay on past June 30th. The newspapers pointed out that her loss was deeply regretted by all and that during the 11 years she was the main force to carry out Knapp's ideas and hopes for the schools, she had transformed the most backward and hopelessly rundown school system in the state into the second highest ranked one.

Even though the schools still experienced political interference, Knapp pressed on and found ways to get votes of exception from the state to allow his foundation to keep assisting the schools in his county. Money for summer schools, supplemental salaries for teachers and principals, entire salaries for music teachers, orchestra instructors, testing programs, and libraries. One of the most fondly remembered gifts however, was a personal one from Margaret Knapp, that became a tradition during the time she wintered there (1923 to circa 1946) and probably beyond. I have heard about this from many sources including Joe Lewark, a retired hunting guide I interviewed via phone in 2007. Mrs. Knapp would personally shop for and beautifully wrap a Christmas gift for every child in the school system. Usually they were items of warm clothing, sweaters, flannel shirts etc and were much appreciated by all.

In 1940, when the schools at Poplar Branch and Powells Point were consolidated and the one at Moyock which tragically burned down was rebuilt, it was large funds from the Knapp Foundation that got them up and running. Also the new school at Poplar Branch was named in honor of Dr. W. T, Griggs with Knapp's blessing even though Griggs had often sided against Knapp with E. R. Johnson. And perhaps a final crowning triumph J. P. would live to hear about, was the construction of a new Negro school in 1949 in which he matched the funds raised to equip it.

Even after his death, the Knapp Foundation guided by his widow Margaret, continued on with aid to Currituck's schools. In 1959, the state found it was short on funds to build a consolidated high school in Currituck and that the gymnasium would have to be left off the plan. Margaret presented them with a check for $100,000 and The Joseph P. Knapp High School complete with a gym opened it's doors on March 8, 1960. March 8 it should be noted was also the birthday of Phoebe Palmer Knapp. Holy Jumping Jacks Mr. McFarland! Bill McFarland, was one of my gym teachers at Wm. Floyd and although gym was far from my favorite class, he was genuinely nice man.

The Mastics in the 1930s:
Days of Discovery and End of an Era

Four months into 1930, the federal census was taken for the first time in the new four year old town of Mastic Beach. Of the less than 30 people the census taker found living there on April 17, about half were families that were employed at the private estates of Lawson, Floyd and Knapp. Next door, eight year old Mastic Park had close to triple that, but many of their residents too were employed at the estates of Dana and the other Floyds August and Emma. By 1940 most everything had changed.

Mastic Beach developer, the Home Guardian Company, was already feeling the pinch of the depression by 1930. In a press release of June 1930 they state that 1,200 lots of the available 3000 in their newly opened sections 4 & 5 were sold. Sections 4 & 5 were comprised of the colonial Richard Floyd -Robert estate that once totaled over 3000 acres and was reduced to just over 200 acres when it was sold outside the family in the 1920s. By August of 1930, the final remaining 12 acres that included the manor home built in 1741, was now in the hands of playwright, Hollywood screenwriter and part time resident John Howard Lawson. The writing was on the wall for the future of the Mastic area great estates, but the stock market crash of 1929 had slowed things down a bit. Especially in the transfer from the wealthy and privileged few into the hands of Bob Bluecollar from Bensonhurst, Brooklyn. As a contrast in 1926, their first year of sales, Home

Guardian had sold 10,000 lots of their Lawrence & Woodhull estates (sections 1, 2, & 3) that bordered on the east and west sides of the Knapp Estate to daily readers of the Brooklyn Citizen newspaper. Average home sites were 3-5 lots, but my 1930 aerial photos show many were still just that, home-sites minus the houses. In an interview he did in 1949, Paul Schulte, a pioneer businessman in Mastic Beach, only recalled a handful of bungalows (4-5) existing there in 1928.

In the Mastic Beach Directory, there are year by year notes of the progress of the town. In 1931 it states "Nothing going on— Perhaps the Depression." By 1932 electricity had started to come in, as an incentive to help sell land (the estates had long used their own generators), but by 1932 Home Guardian had ceased buying additional land to develop with the small addition of a few acres called Section Six, just west of Elder drive, to help flesh out the 5 corners area that was being developed and promoted by Paul Schulte as "New Town". By 1934 Home Guardian was giving away 3 Room Bungalows with the purchase of 4 Lots to help sell their land. (Total price for bungalow and land was $384.00 with no interest —I'll take several thank you— those original bungalows albeit improved with indoor plumbing and other amenities, sell today for well over $200,000).

Though the depression probably slowed down what eventually would occur to Mastic Beach, none the less the decade of the '30s also marked the biggest major change of all for it. Much of that change hinged on the actions of one Dodi Knapp. The changes in his personal life effected those of others to come for several decades. Or as I simply used to say to people (especially old friends from the area) who asked me many times over in the beginning of my research, "What was the big deal for me, as far as the Knapps were concerned? ...All there was in Mastic Beach, when we were young, was a mansion that they no longer lived in and no one seems to really know or care about who they were." My somewhat flip answer, based on just what I knew then was, "If Dodi Knapp hadn't done what he did in 1938, most likely all of us would've had to grow up someplace else, and therefore our lives would probably be somewhat different, not to mention you and I would of never known each other."

Back in 2001, I thought I had already came to the end of Knapp Road, as far as learning anything more than I already had about the Knapps and especially their time in Mastic Beach. I noticed though that posting what I had learned on the internet, it would from time to time lead me to another tid bit or contact with info that in turn would encourage me to continue searching. Besides that, it reconnected me with some old friends and acquaintances that I hadn't seen or heard from in over 40 years and also made new friends for me. That alone more than countered the negative feedback I had received from the Knapp heirs, whose main rationale for being against what I was doing seemed to hinge on the fact that I was putting it on the internet. And so pilgrim that I am, I pressed on somewhat innocuously. One of the last questions I ever asked Sibby, when she was still talking to me in 2001 was, "Did anyone know whatever happened to Marion Knapp?" The answer was "No— she just sort of disappeared after 'Uncle Dodi' died." At that time I wasn't even aware of his first wife Gertrude.

There also was a second epiphany for me in originally concentrating on my home town area. I was learning much more about the area than ever had been written about it in anyone place before. I soon realized there was enough there of interest to write a second book. And with that I started researching more and more just about the Mastic area itself. Much of that info with photos, I put onto my ever growing website, not knowing it would have overlapping fringe benefits. These findings will be published in book form under the title of "The Mastics_ from Blueblood to Blue collar" covering the little known history of the area from before the American Revolution till up to post WWII.

One of the old acquaintances I made over the internet, was a fellow named Marty Van Lith, who I went to junior high and high school with. Marty who still lived near the area, was also a hobby historian if you will, and over the course of the last several years, we got to know each other far better than we ever did in our school days. Since then we have always shared info on the things we would find.

One of the things the locals who kept in touch with me, always seemed to mention as astonishing, were my findings about the Tangier Development Company and their chief spark plug; CEO Frederick J. Quinby. Briefly, Tangier was a multi million dollar boondoggle of a development in 1910 of 10,000 acres of the nearby Tangier Smith estate, that included an ocean side Atlantic City style resort on Fire Island, just across the narrow bay at Smith Point. Quinby's target market was the wealthy country club set, but he miscalculated and the whole thing went belly up with just one manor home built and a temporary wooden bridge, leading to a barren ocean beach. That was all that remained along with a big set of surveyed plans that post WWII developer Walter T. Shirley would turn into a 1950's boom town named for himself.

Marty mentioned to me he had a neighbor friend name Fred J. Gillespie, who not only was born in Tangier in 1916, but was named for Fred Quinby by his Dad, who it turned out actually worked for Quinby, as a construction foreman and built among other things the original Smith Point wooden bridge. I certainly wanted to talk to this guy and so I did, in February of 2004. Just like Marty said, Fred was very sharp at 87 years of age, and he was an absolute delight to talk to. I learned a lot more about all that Tangier & Quinby stuff (Like in the 1940s Walter T. Shirley paid the Gillespie family, liens that Fred's father had placed on Tangier Development Co. as far back as 1912 and also that the Tangier Smith sisters Eugenia and Martha of the Manor of St. George, offered to send Fred to college, if he wanted to go. Fred instead went into the Army, where he was on a B-17 flight crew.

I then asked him what he did for recreation as a young man out there in the sticks. Without missing a beat he said, "We would drive down to Mastic Beach and chase girls!" Well knowing that there were only a handful of places then where a young man could per-sue that hobby I then said, "Well I guess you were in Paul Schulte's Tavern a time or two." "Oh sure," Fred said, "Now that guy sure had a lot of dough." Knowing Paul Schulte (1876-1956) and his family from back when I was a kid, I also knew that he was a successful and very resourceful businessman, whose activities involved bootlegging in the twenties. He actually opened his saloon, that, right after Prohibition was repealed in 1933. I was pretty certain that Paul had dealings with Dodi Knapp, (he wound up owning several Knapp estate outbuildings) if only through fellow German immigrant Willie Schluder (Knapp's estate foreman) So I just threw out the next question to Fred in total knee jerk fashion. "Did you ever hear of a guy named Knapp?" never expecting what I was about to hear in the phone. "You mean Isle of Palms Knapp—the millionaire?" ... As soon as I picked myself off the floor I said "YEAH; ISLE OF PALMS KNAPP," a term I had never heard before to describe Dodi Knapp, yet knew instantly Fred was talking about my guy. (All the deeds to the Knapp Estate in Mastic Beach I have, that Dodi signed in the 1930s and '40s, list his address as 410 Isle Of Palms, Ft. Lauderdale, Fl.).

"Well if you have some more time, I can tell you a story about him too." — *"Take your time sir, I'm all ears."* — *"Well he married a girl named..."* "Gertrude?" *I asked (by now I had known about Gertrude O'Brien being married to Knapp in the 1930's).* "No it wasn't Gertrude," *he said,* "it was, um...Murdock. But her first name escapes me." *Before I could say it, he said,* "Marion, it was Marion Murdock...but she was married at the time to a local fellow named Milton Murdock" *(Chapter 22, The Edey Murder).* "Marion Murdock took off to Florida with Knapp along with her daughter Shirley, who was a beautiful girl, classmate and good friend of my younger sister Ina. Shirley sent Ina a post card from Isle Of Palms. Now Milton, who was a bayman, an auto mechanic and a very nice fellow, was reportably paid 25 to 35 thousand dollars by Knapp to not contest Marion's divorce."* Note: Marion Murdock's Florida divorce record of 1937 states it was contested. I have heard both figures from others, but the divorce contest could explain the two different figures. Milton's pal, bayman Toddy Englehardt, recalled going to New York City with Milton for a lost weekend divorce party. That said, however, Milton didn't live too long to enjoy whatever settlement he got from Dodi Knapp. Milton Irving Murdock died in 1941.

H OLY SMOKES I THOUGHT AFTER WE HUNG UP ALL THAT INFO AND years of questions, answered just by my asking about what he did for laughs as a young man, not to mention Knapp wasn't even the reason I talked with him in the first place. It would lead me to an entire new area of looking into Dodi Knapp's affairs (pardon the pun) and would also give me the most plausible reason for why he sold most of his Mastic Beach estate off, when he did in the spring of 1938.

In doing so, it allowed the then two separate towns of Mastic Beach that his estate had been dividing for over ten years to finally unite. East west thoroughfare Neighborhood Road was opened again. At first he retained the mansion and 12 acres of property around it, but it too was on the market by April of 1939, for a very low price of $11,500. Finally twenty months later on New Years Eve of 1940, Home Guardian bought it from him at the absolutely ridiculous price of about $4,800 turning it over a week later to hotel manager George Sutter of the Bronx for $6,000.

Dodi Knapp's Florida divorce from Gertrude was not finalized until April 5, 1938 (he married Marion on April 17), and according to his will, he had been paying $10,000 a year alimony to Gertrude since November of 1936. Seeing he was "retired" and living on his trust and stocks income for 10 years, he too may have been feeling a bit of a squeeze. Gertrude was living in New Orleans by 1938 and lived on in places unknown to me until she passed away in 1959.

In the first Mastic Beach Directory, published in 1937, it listed 46 winter residents and about 700 summer residents. By 1940 the winter residents listed numbered 86, although one of the first is listed for the very first time, Joseph F. Knapp, who had actually been there since October of 1916 (more than a decade before there was anything called Mastic Beach) probably only made a token appearance in 1940, perhaps to take some antiques or furnishings back to the Isle of Palms, if he even showed up in Mastic Beach at all?

CHAPTER
33

Claire Was Here, There, & Everywhere

I don't think your Aunt Claire will ever be happy living in just one place"
Arthur Penney recalled his mother telling him that as a young boy in
the 1930s It was probably easy for his mother to think that, never having left
Moriches her entire life. Edith Penney may well of uttered that thought as
Claire made her latest move in 1933 to Red Cedar Point out in Hampton Bays,
In the seven years since Edith's brother in law Willis had married Claire, she
had moved from Mastic, to Yaphank, to Stony Brook, Long Island, to John's
Island, South Carolina and now back to Long Island.

Arthur Penney's Dad, the multi skilled Clarence (carpenter, landscaper,
house mover, road builder, dock builder and man of all work) had probably helped make at least two of Claire's residences Mastic (for certain) and
Yaphank and perhaps even Stony Brook, into the showplaces they were. Arthur saw that in person as a high school grad, when he would visit with his
Dad, his aunt Claire's former mansion in Mastic, as it sat lifeless and looking for a new owner in 1939. Clarence may of also been employed to do work
at the new one she was building on the old Barrett estate at Red Cedar Point
on the shores of Peconic Bay out east in Hampton Bays,. I say that because
Arthur recalls the newest "Clairedale" as having a lot of green paint everywhere because that was Aunt Claire's aunt Netty's favorite color. It was J. P.'s

sister Antoinette K. Brown, who helped Claire financially, to build the place that history would prove Edith Penney wrong. Claire Knapp Penney Dixon remained there for the rest of her life. Green may of well been the right color too, because it represents spring and renewal and by the time middle aged Claire (44) moved to Red Cedar Point with Willis (35) and their two young daughters Margaret (6) and Ann (4), Claire was certainly in need of renewal.

Prior to Red Cedar Point, it was both heaven and heart break at John's Island, South Carolina. Claire's firstborn daughter Margaret recalled it in a 2003 interview with author Kerrin Winston-Churchill. Churchill was doing a two part history of both Margaret and her Mother's historic thoroughbred kennels Pennyworth & Clairedale for Dogs In Review magazine. "Living there with those Chows, in that gorgeous country, what more could a child ask for? I was in heaven," recalled "Peggy" Newcombe.

Johns Island, South Carolina started as a winter home when the Penneys lived in Yaphank and Stony brook, but it seems it became Claire's main residence for a short time until tragedy struck. For the last several years the Chows that were being raised at Clairedale Kennels were considered to be some of the very best available in the world. Dogdom world honors and awards had followed Claire for close to a decade from Mastic, to Yaphank, to Stony Brook and now it would all come to a halt in South Carolina. For along with all that southern charm among the Spanish moss and lowlands of South Carolina, came the mosquitoes and with the mosquitoes came the microscopic heart worms for which there was no cure available then and when their symptoms were discovered in a dog it was already too late. "Oh my poor mother. She lost her entire kennel (about 30 dogs) of Chows except for "Son Too" and his son "Little Pal".

That's not to say mosquitoes were strangers to Long Island. Knapp Mastic neighbor, Ed Tolfree, a well known breeder of St. Bernards and Westminster Kennel official, who lived in Fred Quinby's manor house at Tangier from the 1920s -1945, lost his kennel there to the same disease. My own Irish Setters were stricken with heart worm when I last lived in Mastic in the 1970s, but by then at least, there was a treatment for it. It was harsh, but Red and Rusty pulled through. Years later when living at Red Cedar Point, Claire herself would write in an article about her experience at John's Island for Popular Dogs " After concentration on one breed for a period of sixteen years, this experience would be calculated to take the joy out of any optimist's life and we found ourselves in a muddy bog, after having worked for years to establish a certain type of dog—successfully I believe"

A Penney For Your Pooch

There were probably many decisions Claire would have to make regarding the construction of her new southern colonial styled home and grounds at Red Cedar Point, but probably none was more difficult than deciding what to do with her kennel program. She had lost all her brood matrons and young hopefuls in South Carolina. She looked at what was available in the Chow line to rebuild and found it not of the type she strived for and felt strong about. She truly was disappointed and felt that fads were taking over as she declared herself a breeder of the old vintage when she wrote "Type in Chows has vanished to some extent, probably I am a hard -headed[1] breeder and fancier, but I do prefer very little variation in type in all breeds, and feel that many different ones harm all of us."

Although she vowed to always know and love the Chow, she now turned her attention to a breed she called "little varmits and rogues". With her entire family being dog lovers, it was not unusual for the Penneys to spend their entire days at dog shows in which they competed. Over the years they had compiled a list of ringside must watch, whenever they attended a show. One breed that Claire followed extra closely for a number of years was the Sealyham Terrier. One of Claire's early dog mentors was Cora Charters, who she had met in England before WWI. Charters was described equally by other dog fanciers as "immensely knowledgeable, arrogant, fun loving, and a lady of great character, it is a no brainer that Claire would turn to Cora, who had by the 1930s raised a dozen Champion Sealys when she sought out stock to start her own program. These two great dog ladies on both sides of the ocean began exchanging letters filled with passionate ideas, dreams, advice, and observations etc. Claire who was regaled in America by other kennel owners as a dog woman of the highest calibre, always gave credit to Cora Charters and her St. Margaret kennel as the reason she would achieve the success she did with the Sealyham breed. But I don't think any real sharp dog breeder thought it would happen so quickly.

In 1933, Cora Charters bred her male St. Margaret Snowman with a bitch named Burdon Bliss from the kennel of Mrs. A. Wilkerson. In lieu of a stud fee Cora had pick of the litter. The puppy she picked was in her words so perfect she named him "Magnificent". In no time at all Magnificent had finished his English Championship and Cora thought he would make a great contribution to the Clairedale. So in September of 1935, St. Margaret Magnificent set sail for New York Harbor. On American soil the name Clairedale was tacked on to end of his name and Claire drove him to meet veteran dog handler Len Brumby in Hicksville, Long Island. Brumby like what he saw and agreed to handle both "Benji's" (his call name) show career and outside breeding commissions.

Margaret Newcombe remembered Benji fondly. "Like all Sealy's, Benji was a clown and my mother was smitten with him." Claire spoke of Benji in her words, " He has a sense of humor that is rare and will bring down the house even if you have a bad case of the blues." Claire was so impressed with Benji that she sent word to Miss Charters to send more breeding stock. And she did, among those she sent were St. Margaret Sweetness, Superman and another English champion Wolvey Noel.

As for the actual physical kennels that Claire built at Red Cedar Point, Peggy recalls them well, "They were not fancy, but they were very good and everything and everyone that was built, bought or hired, was done so with the dogs in mind. At it's height, she had up to sixty Sealys and enough people to properly care for them."

Benji was first shown in September 21, 1935 and would go on to win best of breed 13 times under 13 different judges by the time The Big Show at The

---

1 a Knapp family trait I recognize harking back to her grandfather and I mean that affectionately

Garden rolled around 4 months later in Feb. of 1936. Breeders and dog show reporters certainly took notice and many would write that "With the new boy in town, things look dim for a American bred Sealy to take the breed class. Others were not that kind and said green eyed things like " How very satisfactory for Mrs. Penney to be starting from the place it has taken some of us several years to reach."

When "The Big Show" arrived Benji found himself at the head of the class in the Terrier group, but also in fierce competition with Scottie Ch. Flornella Soundfella. It was Scotsman vs Welshman with both of them strutting their stuff in the ring with their little tails held high, before judge W. Edgar Baker[2] placed the 1st place ribbon on Benji.

On the next night Benji found himself up against a ring full of heavyweights, There was the crowd favorite Irish setter Milson O'Boy, a pure white Greyhound named White Rose, Mrs. Hartley Dodge's German Shepherd, Ch. Dewet von der Starrenberg, and more including the standard poodle of Mrs. Sherman Hoyt, Ch . Nunsoe Duc de la Terrace of Blakeen (how's that for a name?) who came out of retirement to defend his crown of Best In Show at Westminster from 1935.

But before the big prize was awarded, the crowd would have to wait for the judges to award Best Brace in Show. A brace is a group of dogs that allowed each kennel to show off their breeding stock. When that ribbon was bestowed, it fell upon St Margaret Sweetness and Magnificent of Clairedale. Now it was time for what everyone had came for, and every seat was full on the night of February 12, 1936. Time to pick the best dog out of the 2,940 that were entered that year.

When the house lights dimmed each winner of their group entered the ring to be judged by C. Frederick Nielson. The setter Milson O'Boy had received the most press during the show and was still by far the crowd favorite. It should be noted that Nielson a long time Irish Setter breeder himself, was at one time a financial backer of O'Boy's career. The fact that he had stepped aside from that duty, did not diminish his love for that dog and many were betting he would follow his heart. Every time Nielson would look at the setter the crowd roared. But as a modern terrier man, Bill McFadden would caution, "Anything can happen at the Garden" When all six finalists, a Pomerainian, Setter, Poodle, Greyhound, Shepherd and Sealy were assembled, Nielson took his time and went about his business of sorting them through. Reports said the Pomerainian was fiery, White Rose, the Greyhound wasn't feeling well that night and did not perform well. The German Shepherd was perfect, but the crowd was still going wild over the setter. Meanwhile Neilson later said he was torn between the Poodle and the Sealy. He asked the last two dogs to move again and studied them carefully. Finally he walked to the book, signed it, picked up the big rosette and silver bowl, walked passed the Setter and the Poodle and placed it next to the little Sealy. His decision was both confident and bold and he would later tell the press he knew there would be those who would disagree with him,

---

2 The professional dog world I have found is a very small one and I don't suggest anything here other than to note that W. Edgar Baker, a noted architect, Airedale expert and AKC Judge, was also Ella Dana's first husband and a Knapp neighbor in Mastic from 1916 - 1928.

but in his opinion on this night the Sealy was the best dog there. I don't think anyone was prepared though for what happened next.

As the clapping began, loud jeers and boos erupted. In the entire history of Westminster, this had never happened before. Even though the press tried to downplay it, the fact that it was mentioned in almost every report about the show speaks volumes. And as for Claire, it's impossible for me or anyone else to feel what mixed emotions she must have had that night. Her daughter Margaret who would follow in her Mom's footsteps and make history herself in 1964 with a Best In Show win (the only Mother & Daughter to ever do that) recalls it this way. "We were not there that night, instead my sister and I were at a boarding school in Garden City, we were not allowed to receive phone calls after Seven O'Clock, so it would be the next morning when my Mother and Father called almost in tears to tell us We Won, We Won!. I didn't find out about the booing 'til later, but boy did I find out! It wasn't just O'Boys fans in the bleachers. My mother never talked about it too much with me. She was too proud, but you can imagine how she would feel. How would you feel if you worked your entire life to get somewhere that grand and instead of being cheered for your accomplishments, you were booed? That just broke my mothers heart. She never got over it. She didn't talk much about it, but you could tell that it bothered her. It was always there".

Now for those who recall reading in Chapter 7 "Happy Thanksgiving To You Too" you know that Margaret Newcombe, only ever spoke thirteen words directly to me. That would be in November of 2001, when I called her the day after Thanksgiving, as a follow up to letter I had sent her asking if I could interview her. The call went like this "Hello Mrs. Newcombe, this is Ken Spooner did you get my letter?. Her reply was "Yes I Did, and I Don't Want To Talk To You About ANYTHING !— Although I always respected her wishes, even though I never understood them fully, I would find out about a year or so after she passed away in 2007 from Ms. Winchell, that she felt Margaret had come around a bit as far as her feelings about my research. When Kerrin asked her for a few more details about her Mother's history for a documentary film she was making, Margaret told her that "Ken Spooner, who has that web site thing, probably knows as much about my family's history as anyone."

As much as I regret never having had the opportunity to interview both Margaret or her sister Ann, who has never spoken to me, except through her lawyer, I did get some comfort in hearing her say that, if only second hand. I also have wondered if it was any one thing that I had posted on the internet that swayed her opinion of me or if it was everything combined. If I had to say it was one thing that might of turned the tide a little, I would hope it was the history of Clairedale Kennel, that I have on the web site and perhaps it was on how I felt about Claire's big night in 1936, 11 years before I was even born. I also included this editorial from Popular Dogs published a few weeks later in March of 1936

Booing, hissing and premature applause it seems have always been with us, and human nature being what it is we can do little about it except to periodically pronounce it rude and unseemly. But even out of booing good can come and so the fancy may well congratulate itself that there are still judges courageous enough to make awards without benefit of applause.

In that final Westminster line-up stood six dogs as splendid as any that have ever trod American show boards. There have been other years perhaps when one or two have gotten into the finals that should of not been there. But this year no one could complain. They were six of which any breeder or owner the world over might be exceedingly proud.

Now no matter how knowing a ringside may be. dogs cannot be judged from outside the ropes. Neither can they be judged on the basis of popularity or public sentiment. They are judged on breed character, anatomy, show shape, and soundness. Judge Baker who put up the Sealyham in the group, knows his terriers. he has judged them for years and cannot go far wrong. Judge Neilson's experience too is wide and his opinion valuable, while as for George S. Thomas who made the dog best of breed, there is no better judge on either side of the pond. Surely if there had been anything radically wrong with the winner these men would of found it.

One might of thought that the onlookers from high up in the galleries had found something wrong and that to show how smart they were, they booed the selection. But anyone who takes a mob decision seriously does not know human nature. At the drop of a hat a mob applauds or vociferously condemns merely to let off steam and to relieve the tension of the moment. In other words, mob acts are not the result of intellect but of emotion and consequently mean little.

It is unfortunate however that the rightful march of a good dog to the top should be attended by such uncontrolled expression of ill feeling which if considered seriously can constitute an insult to the club, the judge, and the winning exhibitor.

To her credit, Like she did when Zulal threw her in 1911, Claire got back on the horse and back in the show ring. Benji the Magnificent, went on to win six more Best in Shows in 1936. His lifetime career included Twenty Six best of Breeds, Twenty Terrier Group, Eleven Best in Shows and he sired 19 champions. He passed away in 1942 of kidney failure. Wolvey Noel, who was next in line, coming out of the gate racked up nine best in shows in 1936 and eight in 1937. Clairedale was more than on the map in the late thirties, it was at the top of its game.

I visited Red Cedar Point twice in 2002 and 2005, I never got to see the actual house Claire and her family lived in out there except from a satellite view of it taken just months before it was torn down in the fall of 2005 (which was why I never found it in 2005—I was about two weeks too late). I was given the heads up on it's location and fate from web site reader Jeff Schulz who grew up there in the 1960s, after Claire's daughters sold the Clairedale estate to a developer. Jeff's parents bought a small piece of it that included the house that Claire's longtime nurse lived in.

About twenty miles west of Hampton Bays, Dodi spent one summer with Marion and her daughter Miss Shirley Murdock in Shirley's and somewhat co incidentaly, his own childhood hometown area of Brookhaven - Bellport in 1940. Moored at the Bellport yacht club, was the new 50 foot Matthews custom cruiser "Storm King Too". While the Mastic Beach mansion was on the market from April of '39, until it finally sold in December 1940, I'm not sure if Dodi ever stayed in it again. Perhaps he tried and couldn't adjust to the townspeople building their little bungalows all around him, on his former land right in sight of his bedroom terrace? The following summer of 1941, Joseph F. & Marion H. Knapp of Isle Of Palms, Ft Lauderdale, FL, would move out to Hampton Bays, Long Island and spend the rest of their summers together there.

When Marion & Dodi started summering in Hampton Bays, they stayed on the south shore about six miles from Claire's Peconic Bay estate, renting for the first few years there right on Tiana bay, before buying a home in 1949 on Smith Creek. There just off their east verandah, they docked a new slightly smaller, 38 foot "Storm King III", also built by Matthews. Like his scaled down cabin cruiser, the last home he had in Hampton Bays was nothing like the 22 room behemoth he sold in Mastic Beach. But Dodi Knapp was still very much living the good life, and enjoying himself in Florida and New York.

CHAPTER

34

Mr. Knapp Goes to Washington
(and Vice Versa)

JP was not the first Knapp to go to Washington, though he might have been the last, at least on official business. His father was registered at hotels there in the 1860s-70s, probably in connection with the western geological survey lithographs that Sarony Major & Knapp did for the federal government. I am not sure if Dodi Knapp ever went to Washington on any official business for American Litho or not. I do know his original "Storm King" was moored there in July of 1975, but that was over three decades and five owners since Dodi sold her in 1940. Laughlin Morgan Currie's "Storm King" made the newspapers when she caught fire at the Washington Marina and sustained $8000 worth of damage to her cabin. She took out another cruiser moored next to her, but Storm King was saved to sail on and be sold again. She may still be floating around somewhere.(her last registration with the Coast Guard I found was in 1980) Also in the 1980s, Claire's daughter, Antoinette would go to the White House as a dinner guest of the Reagans , but that's another story.

When the great depression officially kicked off with the Wall Street Crash of October 29, 1929, J. P. Knapp was 65 years old, a multi millionaire and in very good financial shape, just having sold American Lithographic at a premium pre crash price to boot. He could of easily kicked back and withdrew somewhat from his business affairs and curtailed his newly formed philanthropic activities that he had been involved with for the last decade. Instead, he threw himself into trying to help solve the economic disaster that was about to envelope the United States and much of the world, with the zeal of a multi tasking twenty year old on his way up the ladder.

Besides dealing with the complexity and political aggravation of trying to improve North Carolina's education problems, it was his coming awareness of the depletion of the fish and wildlife (their abundance was main reason he built his principal estate there) that would involve J. P, in perhaps what would become the center piece of his great crusade of the 1930s. In doing so, he helped to relieve some economic hardships and even hunger, that some American's would be facing for the next ten years.

Knapp Is For The Birds

By the time he noticed there weren't as many wild ducks as their used to be, J. P. Knapp had probably blasted enough birds out of the sky, to put one on every table of every member of the conservation group known as Ducks Unlimited. Well perhaps not todays membership level, of over 775,000 members, but possibly close to the 225,000 folks that carried D U membership cards just a decade after Knapp founded the organization in 1937. Add in the total of pigeons and quail J. P. had taken out, since he was declared one the top wing shots in America in the 1890s and you might of had enough tasty birds to feed the current DU membership? That said, by the late 1920s, J. P. knew something wasn't quite right with the numbers of ducks he saw in the sky (They were no longer blacking out the sun in Currituck) Add in just his friends, who often went gunning with him, and those of his neighbors in Currituck and it took a person with the vision and drive like Knapp to steer the ship of ducks, that already had hit the iceberg and was taking on water fast. When he started to take action with his original group "More Game Birds In America" in 1930, one could truly say to JP's face that, he was for the birds and he would say thank you.

Although I have relied on many sources for the variety of Knapp duck info I have found over the years, the main source that I'll be referring to here came from the Ducks Unlimited organization itself. More specifically a DU 40th anniversary book titled "A Singleness of Purpose" by Jon Tennyson, who was the editor for Ducks Unlimited magazine. I also will say, I may have returned the favor somewhat to DU's main headquarters in Memphis,Tennessee. In late 2007, they asked me if I could supply them with a high resolution photo of their founder "suitable for printing" and I was only too happy to comply.

Although I am not a duck hunter, I do own an autographed copy of Jon's lavish book. I'm sure old J. P. would be enjoy it too, just for the printing quality alone. In preparing his book, Jon called on Arthur Bartley, at his Long Island bungalow in the mid 1970s. Bartley born in 1891, was the last living member of the original Board of Directors of Ducks Unlimited that was incorporated in Washington, DC on January 29, 1937. In the first chapter of his book "A Radical Idea", Tennyson writes of their initial meeting: " In response to my obvious first question on how Ducks Unlimited and it's conservation program all began, Bartley walked over to a low bookcase and picked up a framed picture of the most severe look-ing gentleman I have ever seen[1]. "This man, Arthur said as he tapped the glass in the frame, "is the one who started it all."

"The Sage of Currituck" and Ducks and Bucks

The sage of Currituck is the term J. N. "Ding" Darling sarcastically called J. P. Knapp (and perhaps quite unwisely) in 1935 when he wrote a magazine article about conservation that singled out Knapp for heavy criticism. Darling, a news-paper editorial cartoonist from Iowa and life long conservationist, headed a Fed-eral agency and designed the first US Federal "Duck Stamp" in 1934 and seemed to be in Knapp's good graces for a time. He actually wrote a article for American magazine, not about conservation, but about his being a farm boy and trying to live in NYC in 1919. I also recently discovered a newspaper editorial cartoon of Darlings published in 1924 that depicts Knapp walking along Wall Street, dis-cussing his dental care program with Thomas Lamont. Darling may have come up with the sage term in regard to Knapp's solutions for North Carolina's educa-tional problems. As for his conservation piece, Darling went on to say in 1935 that Knapp had spent more of his personal fortune on ducks than any man in the United States. It seems by then a storm was raging in Washington over solutions to the problems about diminishing ducks and wildlife in general, between the US Biological Survey that Darling headed and Knapp's More Game Birds in America organization, (which has been described by Tennyson as really just an extension of Joseph P. Knapp) but I'm getting ahead of the story here.

It appears that J. P. was a voracious reader, especially of material with prob-lem solving ideas. He also liked spreading good ideas around via his ability to publish them with the hope that they would catch on and yield great results for all of us on the planet. His own personal funding of his Mentor Magazine, that was far from a commercial success, certainly supports that observation.

Major duck hunter that he was, it could very well be that when he read an arti-cle, first published in 1912 by St. Louis attorney Dwight Huntington, that Knapp hatched his idea for More Game Birds In America. Huntington proposed some very radical ideas for their time of not only conservation of wildlife, but also of propagation (the breeding) of same as was being practiced in Europe by game keepers of the country gentry. It is highly likely that Dwight Huntington's writ-ings, which were still very radical, except to visionaries like Knapp, were passed on to J. P. by Dwight's son John C. Huntington, who after WWI headed his fa-ther's Game Conservation Society and later his Game Conservation Institute. The principal aim of the Institute, that took two decades to get off the ground, was a two year school for game keepers that had no counterpart in the entire world, teaching wild bird management and breeding. It was initially and logi-cally funded by the Sporting Arms and Manufacturers Institute in 1928. The SA

---

1 The picture Tennyson saw is the official portrait photo of J. P. Knapp from the 1930s. A notorious camera shy guy, I would not call that photo severe at all. J.P. looks quite warm and friendly there, at least compared to the steely eyed stare he gave to renowned photographer Arnold Genthe in a series of four official portraits Genthe took in 1928. Now those could be intimidating!

& MI pledged about $60,000 with the principal sponsor being the E. I. du Pont de Numours Company. They are the folks who made all that gunpowder for all those shotgun shells. The actual school was eventually established at Rutgers University in New Jersey, with the state chipping in $10,000. But as the skies darkened over Wall Street, fat cat financial support started to drying up quickly. The school went from one financial crisis to another. When the manufacturers dropped their financial support citing the depression a "prominent sportsman of means, who wished to remain anonymous" came forward to pick up the slack. In 1930 Knapp would wind up tapping John Huntington along with Arthur Bartley to be his day to day chief executives of his newly founded More Game Birds organization and they found themselves running both the school and More Game Birds In America. However the charter for the Game Institute prevented More Game Birds itself from assuming financial responsibility for the Institute, so the money had to come from other sources.

The Depression hit everyone and that "anonymous sportsman" who was funding the school, was also saddled with a boat manufacturing company with two factories in Connecticut, that had its workers using select marine grade mahogany for firewood, because you couldn't sell Sea Sleds, even at below cost. He also had a magazine and printing empire with hundreds of employees and printing plants across America to keep afloat, so J. P. Knapp had to finally drop his financial support for the Game Conservation Institute in 1934, but not his belief in it's worth. He actually had been applying many of Huntington's ideas at his Currituck estate and was breeding wild ducks there. Under the supervision of his "Duckologist" Issac Doxey, who also was his estate superintendent, 3556 mallards were raised in one season at the Knapp estate in the early '30's. This reinforced in Knapp's mind the idea of wild game propagation as a means of solving many problems the nation was facing.

Falling Through The Quacks

Like his father, who really had no taste for political office either, J. P. Knapp never ran for office, but he certainly recognized the value and advantages of having friends in offices of all levels of government, to help him get the things he wanted done. A lifelong Republican, he had direct access to Herbert Hoover and Thomas Beck his right hand man and more at Crowell-Collier, was a personal friend of future president Franklin D. Roosevelt. The first person Knapp tapped to head up his More Game Birds In America was, US Senator from Missouri Harry B. Hawes. In the spring of '29 Knapp had read Hawes' book "My Friend, The Black Bass" and started corresponding with the senator. An offer was made in August of 1930, and a big announcement of Hawes accepting the More Game Birds position appeared in the major newspapers in September 1930. The article stated that the Hawes would eventually succeed Knapp as president when his senate term expired in 1933. He was to be paid a salary of $50,000 per year. It also stated the projected endowment for the organization would amount to $10,000,000 to carry out a wide variety of proposed wildlife conservation projects. It is highly likely these figures came directly from Knapp, but when the

NY Times tried to confirm it by calling on J. P. at his Park Ave apartment, he declined comment, as did Hawes, who was in NY City at that time. Come September everything seemed to be in place and on October 6, 1930, after a meeting at Knapp's Currituck home with Clarence Stouch, Sea Sled CEO and Knapp's treasurer at Publication Corp., More Game Birds In America became an official corporation. The Hawes honeymoon was brief however, for within two months the senator released this letter to the newspapers that the NY Times printed on November 12 under the headline : Hawes Quits Post In Game Bird Body.

"Nov 11, 1930 — Dear Mr. Knapp: It is with sincere regret that I find it necessary to withdraw my acceptance of the presidency of More Game Birds in America a foundation. My acceptance of Aug. 15 was based upon your positive assurance that the headquarters and executive offices would be located in Washington and that the foundation would be national in character all of which is contained in the printed foreword which has been widely circulated.

Your subsequent determination to maintain the headquarters and executive offices in New York instead of Washington, contrary to our agreement and over my vigorous objection, and your selection of all officers from New York City in my opinion robs the foundation of its proposed national character and limits its activity to a restricted objective which will not meet with a popular support.

In a letter to me written by you on Aug. 20, you personally assumed a financial obligation of $35,000 a year for a period of six years- a total of $210,000—which under our contract was to have been paid to me beginning with the expiration of my term in the Senate. My withdrawal releases you from this obligation.

My interest in conservation and replacement of out door life cannot be influenced by personal consideration. It is a broad,national problem, and its future is greater than any one man or any one organization. My determination to devote my future years to it has not changed, but I believe my efforts will be more effective in a broader field.

Your one objective, the raising of game birds by the English poultry incubator method, may be of some assistance in the broader national undertaking. To this extent your endeavor to assist the good cause will be approved by some sportsmen. As my letter of acceptance and the announcement of my retirement from the Senate to accept the presidency of your foundation was given wide publicity, I am releasing this letter to the press.—Sincerely Yours, Harry B. Hawes"

I know a lot less about Harry Hawes than I do about J. P. Knapp, but there was most likely more that went on behind the scenes than is revealed in Hawes' letter. He was a conservative Democrat, although he was opposed to prohibition, a lifelong conservationist, sportsman - hunter, Born in Kentucky in 1869, he spent most of his life in Missouri and was a Democratic party leader there from the time he went into the state house in 1913. At age 47, he enlisted in WWI. He was both a US Rep and Senator from 1920-1933. He wanted the office to be in Washington DC, which is understandable as he had larger connections there, but must of enjoyed life in Washington well past his Senate years, as DC was where he died in 1947. I suspect the major disagreement that Hawes had with Knapp or foresaw coming, was that Knapp was going to control the organization no matter who held the title as president of it. But on the other hand it was being funded almost entirely out Knapp's pocket and you can't blame J. P. for wanting to keep a close eye on how things were done. Knapp located the executive offices initially at 500 5th Ave in NYC, just across 42nd St from the NY Public Library and then moved them up the block into his 580 5th Ave Publication Corp headquarters by 1931. Knapp may of not forgot his own nightmares dealing with the Washington DC crowd in 1907, trying to get a contract to print envelopes (chp 25) Another factor is as both a lawyer and a politician, Hawes had to understand power people and Knapp's handpicked board of directors were extremely powerful and all mainly his friends and associates. But again this was not a taxpayer funded deal, but rather coming from the deep pockets Knapp and his friends.

In any event Knapp got one of his board of directors, Colonel Arthur F. Foran of New Jersey to be Hawes' replacement. Foran was the head of New Jersey Republican party, a former state senator and had an interesting background. He was controller of customs for port of NY, under Presidents Harding and Coolidge, where he came under intense fire from the anti-saloon league for looking the other way over prohibition laws. History of course proved prohibition to be one of the more dangerous, dumb and unenforceable laws ever enacted. J. P. had no use for dumb, unenforceable laws. The Colonel also was the father of Dick Foran, the famous B movie actor.

The 25 member board of directors of More Game Birds of which Knapp and Clarence Stouch were also on, consisted of Knapp associates and friends. Most were duck hunters and they also were some of the most powerful people in America at that time. Many of them appeared on the cover of Time Magazine. Topping the list would be world banker, J. Pierpont Morgan, and his now full partner Thomas Lamont, who was also a semi silent Knapp business partner for years. Then there was Frederick H. Ecker (chp 13) who had known J. P. since they were boys By 1930 Ecker was a long, long way from the office boy he was at Met Life in 1883, where he watched J. P.'s father intently and learned the insurance business from the ground up. He was now the President of Met Life, which was rapidly becoming one of the largest financial concerns in America, if not the world. Jeremiah Milbank , a close friend of Herbert Hoover, was a bank director at Chase. He too was a philanthropist and had started the Boys & Girls Clubs of America. The afore mentioned Ogden M. Reid, was publisher of the NY Herald Tribune, Knapp Currituck neighbor, big time duck hunter and possibly the guy who introduced J. P. to Margaret. George T. Slade, a railroad tycoon, Myron C. Taylor, longtime friend and business partner of J. P.'s was head of US Steel, William E. Corey, ex US Steel president and Currituck Knapp neighbor. O. Max Gardner was the current one. Cameron Morrison, was the former governor of North Carolina, C. Edward Murray powerful New Jersey political leader, Walter C. Teagle, Oil Man, bankers Charles S. Sabin, of Guaranty Trust and Daniel E. Pomeroy, of Bankers Trust, Dr. John A. Hartwell of Cornell University was a teaching surgeon with an amazing life story, and a leader in anti vivisection legislation, Then there was super salesman, Thomas H. Beck, who although was not a hunter, was almost a de facto son for JP in the 1930s and 40s. Beck became JP's main go to guy and trouble shooter at Crowell-Collier during this period. There were others whose generic incomplete names has made research on just who they were too time consuming. I know they were VIPs who could be helpful or Knapp wouldn't of had them on his board and last but not least J.N. Ding Darling, who although was at one time head of the US Biological Survey in Washington, would often be at philosophical odds with Knapp and Beck and the entire More Game Birds organization. With movers and shakers like this, you would think Knapp would not have any trouble getting the things he wanted done for More Game Birds, but there were rough roads ahead. Undeterred he pursued this project with the fervor his namesake grandparents the Palmers did their Holiness Movement and was totally committed especially to the aims of his organization that appeared on the More Game Birds letterhead : More Farm Revenue, More Employment, More Food, More Land Value, More Outdoors, More Shooting—Knapp did not stop with just a board of power brokers either. He wanted results and he wanted them yesterday.

As early as 1904, Washington attempted to get involved with migratory bird protection and hunting regulations. A Migratory Bird Law was not passed until 1913 with the Dept Of Agriculture being the agency to make the regulations. It became obvious that these regulations were useless without an international accord with Canada and in 1916, a fairly detailed 15 year international treaty was drawn up to protect migratory game. Although it was somewhat helpful, when More Game Birds got organized, they quickly pointed out that it only helped to save threatened stock. There were no provisions for refuges and other constructive waterfowl measures. Another factor the legislators did not take into account or foresee, was the severe drought that started in 1929 and continued until 1934 (the same one that created the dust bowl in the western United States had severely damaged waterfowl breeding grounds in Canada) In 1931 More Game Birds found themselves at odds with the findings and recommendations of the US Biological survey which was under the control of the Dept. of Agriculture. J. P. felt that the Bio Survey in advocating for a severely curtailed hunting season, was unsound both biologically and economically and would put a undue hardship on the people who depended on the season for much of their livelihood. He advocated for a two to three month season with rest periods, With the Bio Survey curtailing it to just 30 days, he also felt the natives might vent their frustration by illegally increasing the kill of wildfowl for both market and food purposes. Needless to say the Bio Survey regulations were passed as law, and J P got busy making up charts to take to Washington that compared the merits of the "Proclamation Plan" 30 day season with those of his alternative "The Rest Plan 33". The Bio Survey's "Proclamation Plan" Knapp pointed out was a "shocking mistake to make at this time" for it shortened employment from three months to one *and* there was DEEP RESENTMENT to it from all classes of people, especially from those whose livelihood will be affected. He further pointed out that "little or NO cooperation could be expected from game officials of various states for the Proclamation Plan" This was mid September 18th and the season was about to start when Mr. Knapp took his charts to Washington to show a friend of his. Upon his arrival he made it clear that "I am here representing Joseph P. Knapp, not More Game Birds, as I have no authority to represent them." That friend was Herbert Hoover at 1600 Pennsylvania Avenue. He told the President that he did not believe the Bio Survey had the support of the States it claimed and cited a state game official as telling him " Now that the Proclamation has passed I will try to support it but it is a rotten regulation." Knapp told Hoover "that quote was recorded as an approval. No wonder they could get 48 states to back it if that was an approval!" Hoover upon hearing Knapp out and looking at his charts (which no doubt were beautifully illustrated and printed!) said. "The Waterfowl Advisory Board must be called and I shall tell the Secretary of Agriculture" On October 7th the regulation questions were reopened.

As Arthur Bartley smiled as he told told this story to Jon Tennyson he said, "Joe Knapp never pulled any punches, he said exactly what he thought. He did that with the President of the United States or anyone else, he was tough and he wanted results."

Mr. Knapp Writes

"I hate waste. Economic profligacy to me is not only deplorable but detestable. It is a crime against life. We Americans are incredibly, fantastically, wasteful of Nature's bounty." — J. P. Knapp

Those words that still resonate today, were the opening ones of J. P. Knapp for an magazine article he did titled," Let Game Birds End Farm Depression". It was first published in February of 1931 in Nation's Business and then in condensed form in Readers Digest that spring. For someone who was raised with the immense wealth, privilege and excess of the gilded age, it just shows what a fine job his parents did in instilling lasting real values in their son. The very private man that he was, most of his writings were in the form of personal letters that usually contained some of his thoughts. However this one gave the general public and the Washington crowd, that had to know by 1931, something was very wrong with the country as a whole, and something to think about.

... Others have said all this to careless and indifferent public. Talk gets nowhere. Somebody has to do something. So we started the Foundation "More Game Birds In America" Its one an only purpose can be found in its title. It will create a new crop for the American farmer; provide him with another source of income,sure, lucrative and demanding from him little increase in labor. This new crop is game birds_our fine old native American game birds, wild duck and geese, bobwhite, quail, partridges and wild turkey. These are all but wiped out now.

The only way to make game birds abundant,as is well said by the State Ornithologist of the state of Massachusetts, Edward Howe Forbush, is to commercialize them. Make them mean something to most people or to a lot of people, in the way of money. Then they get interested.

Early in the 19th century the United States had a greater variety and number of wild food birds than any other country. In the past 50 years this great natural resource, once considered inexhaustible, has decreased tremendously. In fact the abso-

lute extermination of game birds in America has been predicted. Yet we have passed more game laws than any country ever had and amended them more often.

But the more laws we have passed, the less game we have had. All this legislation was almost wholly restrictive and no attention whatsoever paid to propagation or to the great economic, commercial possibilities of wild game birds as a national crop, as a source of new income for the farmer.

To bring about a complete change in the present method of game bird control, conservation and replacement will take years and a lot of money. You can't work for a year or two getting people interested, and then shut up shop because no money is left to pay the rent. We organized More Game Birds in America so this movement can get going and stay going. The foundation has a million dollars to start with and can get more as necessary.

The British in six years replaced their wild game birds, almost totally destroyed during the War. What has been done on the grouse moors of Scotland and the partridge and pheasant preserves of England can be duplicated on a far grander scale in America. We have a more favorable terrain, one tenth of the British population per square mile and fairly well distributed wealth- everything needed for success.

The Game Act of Great Britain passed in 1831, has been the basic law of that people for a century. In all that time only minor details have been amended. Since the act was passed, partridges have increased more than 200%, pheasants more than 100%. Game birds are killed in tremendous numbers every year during the long open seasons. They have a wonderful game reproduction and thorough replacement system.

That system had a severe test during the World War and it is this test which convinces me we can make it work in America with splendid commercial results. When the War started, most of the 12,000 British game keepers went into the service and after the second year game production virtually came to a standstill.

Naturally vermin increased rapidly. Foxes, weasels, stoat — and all manner of greedy little creatures multiplied and took a heavy toll of wild nesting birds. At the Armistice the number of game keepers had been greatly reduced and less than 10% of the annual carry over of game birds for breeding purposes was available. It looked as if game in Great Britain was done for.

Not a bit of it. Using their old, well tested methods, the British put their supply back to normal in those six years from 1919-1925 an increase of 900%, and the game bird industry once more began to play an important part in the economic scheme of things _ a part we here in America scarcely comprehend. It once more gave employment to thousands, pleasure to men of moderate means as well as to the rich, and sent to the market at poultry prices a fine food supply.

Game farms and game keepers wasted no time in bemoaning the situation and changing the law. They bred and released game birds. They killed of the vermin. They don't set bag limits, but landowners are too intelligent to permit encroachment upon basic breeding necessities. If you lease a moor in Scotland and go there to shoot grouse, you pay according to the number of birds you will be permitted to kill in the season. If the land can stand it you may be allowed 5000. Or it may only be 500. The gamekeepers know down to a bird just what can be done. When you *have shot your quota you are through.*

But there is no idea of preserving anything but the basic breeding stock. They believe over there that game birds were meant for man. When a shooting party kills a 1000 or so they can't eat them all of course, so they send them to market, at poultry prices. In Scotland alone, 10 million dollars is paid to the landowners every year for shooting privileges. In addition to that sum, hunters who go to Scotland for grouse must spend ten times that amount there annually. Think what such funds would mean to our farmers. Some people have estimated that it would produce some 300 million dollars a year in shooting privileges alone. Personally I think a shooting industry can be built up totaling a half a billion a year.

So we organized the Foundation. Many keen businessmen and sportsmen have put $50,000 each into it, not for sentimental reasons, but because they see the economic value of the plan.

Recently Governor Garner of North Carolina, one of the founders, called a conference of game raisers, sportsmen, farmers, educators and legislators to take steps to make his state a model in game bird laws and in research, education and experiment. The More Game Birds Association of North Carolina was brought into existence.

The first act of the Association will to be establish a model breeding farm. The farm will act as a laboratory for classes in breeding and raising now being set up at State Agricultural College. A legislative committee has been formed to consider existing game laws, and draft a new bill that will supersede all present laws in conflict.

Probably not more than 100 men in the United States today are fully qualified to raise game birds. Great Britain has 12,000 game keepers. America, at the same ratio of population, should soon have three times that number, which at salaries of $2000 a year or more, would mean a vast amount in wages for a vocation hitherto practically unknown in this country.

Don't let the old Tarheel State get too far ahead of yours, for they are out to make that state the "Scotland of America." And remember that propagation is the keynote-propagation and not restriction.

Because the depression had already started in full force and government money was scarce, one of the aims J. P. had was to get a shell tax of a penny on every shotgun shell sold to help finance the programs he felt were sorely needed at both state and federal levels or the ducks would just disappear entirely. I have some letters from the early '30's that JP both wrote and received to support this idea that again gave me a small glimpse into the personality of the man. They also touch upon the politics of the day and his ideals. The earliest letter is to J. P. from Harry F . Byrd (1887-1966) written on New Years Eve of 1931. Byrd was the son of a Virginia newspaper publisher and the governor of that state from 1926-30. He became a US Senator 1933 - 1965. His brother was north pole explorer Admiral Richard Byrd. He wrote to J. P. regarding his running Knapp's idea of a shell tax past Jacob Raskob, one of the very top executives at Dupont, Although Raskob's office was just down the street from Knapp's, in the brand new Empire State building, it just shows the wisdom J. P. had in reaching out widely and utilizing contacts to get things done.

Mr. Joseph P. Knapp

580 Fifth Ave,
New York City
December 31st 1931

Dear Mr. Knapp

I was in New York yesterday and had a talk with Mr. Raskob in regard to the proposed shell tax. He said that while he had not had an opportunity to give it consideration, it appeared to him to be an excellent idea. He said he would be delighted to arrange an interview for you with Pierre Dupont. His office and du Pont's are adjacent in the Empire State Building. I thought it important to get Mr. Raskob's approval as he is a very influential and large stockholder in the Dupont companies. He said he would be glad to communicate with you for the purpose of arranging an interview at your convenience. I am delighted to be of service in this matter and if there is anything further I can do let me know.

Wishing you every possible happiness and prosperity in the New Year, I am
Cordially yours,
Harry F. Byrd

To which JP replied a few days later on January 5th:

My Dear Governor

Many thanks indeed for your kind letter of December 31st and your endeavor to arrange the duPont interview. I will promptly write to Mr. Raskob.

When you are next in New York, do let me know. Perhaps I can persuade you to take dinner and spend the evening with me.

Ever sincerely,
Joseph P. Knapp

And things started to really pop in the New Year for Knapp regarding this idea. On the same day he wrote to thank Harry Byrd he received a letter from L. du Pont the president of the company at their headquarters in Wilmington, Delaware.

Dear Mr. Knapp

Mr. F. S. du Pont has referred to me your inquiry as to a conference in regard to the one cent tax on shells, proceeds of which should be used one-half by the Federal Government for duck and other game protection and one - half by the state for similar purposes.

In our organization, matters of this kind are handled by our Smokeless Powder Department. which is in charge of the vice-president Mr. A. Felix du Pont. If it is agreeable to you, will you not get in touch with him regarding an appointment?

Yours very truly,
L. du Pont President

J. P. also wrote to Jacob Raskob informing him of what had transpired and re-questing the pleasure of meeting him. Raskob replied on the 7th of January:

Dear Mr. Knapp:

I thank you very much for your letter of the sixth in reply to which would advise that Mr. Felix du Pont is the proper man to see and I hope you will be very success-ful in your talks with him.

I should like to give myself the privilege of talking with you sometime about political affairs. I think we have reached the time where there has to be a realign-ment of people under our political parties and those of us actively in the Demo-cratic party are trying to bring that Party back to the sound principles on which it was founded in the hope that we can win the support and confidence of the people and have the people enjoy a sense of security in the Party that will be for the best interests of all of us as citizens.

Upon my return to New York next week I will call you in the hope that you may find a little time to give me.

Sincerely,

Jacob Raskob

A Penny For Your Shells

Interesting to note: John J. Raskob (1879-1950) and Joseph P. Knapp apparently first met over a proposed penny-a-shotgun shell tax. And yet among Ras-kob's many credits, he was the driving force behind the Empire State Building. Knapp, as finance director at Met Life, was the one of the prin-cipal financial backers of the same. Raskob rose from Pierre du Pont's per-sonal secretary in 1902 to be treasurer of both du Pont and General Motors. A bullish stock market person in the 1920s, he once wrote an article entitled "Everyone Ought To Be Rich" suggesting every American could become very wealthy by investing just $15 per week in common stocks. (Ironically, it only goes to show just how out of touch the very wealthy can be, average salaries being only $17-20 a week in the '20s.) A devout Catholic and father of thirteen children, Raskob had a large falling out over politics with GM's President Alfred P. Sloan and resigned in 1928. Raskob strongly supported Al Smith, who prob-ably lost the election because he was Catholic. Sloan supported Hoover. Ras-kob then sold his GM stock to start the financing the Empire State Building. He also became head of the DNC and turned much of his attention to supporting Al Smith again for the nomination for President in 1932.

In the following group of letters between Raskob & Knapp, their political ideology takes center stage over ducks. This first one on January 14, 1932 is written to Knapp just after they have met face-to-face for the first time where the staunch Democrat and staunch Republican both undoubtedly agreed only that things in America had to change.

Dear Mr. Knapp:

First again let me express the pleasure and enjoyment I had in meeting and having luncheon with you this noon.

I am enclosing herewith the following papers which I promised to send.

Copy of recent questionnaire, Copy of my letter to the committee, Copy of my address in Washington last March in which are outlined briefly some views on the Five Day week and the tariff along the lines we discussed. There are other suggestion in this address that may interest you too. I do not want to burden you unnecessarily, but I am sending these in line with the promise I made you in the hope you may find them of interest.

I appreciate more than I can tell you your suggestion that through cooperation you and I might be able to do a good deal of splendid work in getting better principles instilled in the conduct of our government and I want you to know that I am ready at all times to do my part and that you may feel free to call upon me or command me in any way that you feel will be helpful.

Sincerely yours,

Jacob Raskob

I WOULD'VE LOVED TO HAVE SAT AT THEIR TABLE THAT DAY AND HEARD what JP said to him. I would infer that ideas and frustrations came out of both men. I get the feeling by now that Knapp saw the handwriting on the wall for the future of Hoover administration that he had always supported. Knapp acknowledged Raskob on the 16th with a short reply:

Dear Mr Raskob:

Many thanks for your letter of January 14th with enclosures which I will read with great interest. I sincerely trust that I may have the pleasure of spending more hours with you. Very sincerely yours, Joseph P. Knapp

Then three days later J P wrote:

Dear Mr. Raskob:

Perhaps in this letter I may convey the thoughts that are running through my mind.

Last night I read your address to the National Committee, March 5, 1931. It impressed me <u>exactly</u> as did your talk at luncheon. You think carefully and profoundly, and then express your convictions, soundly economic, in few words.

Your advice, if followed, would make this the great and contented country of which Jefferson dreamed. The other day I said that if Young[2] should be nominated he would be overwhelmingly elected and my vote would be for him. Now I have found a second man for whom I would vote. His name is Raskob. His religion might make his election as president impossible, but in that position he would prove the third party to be unnecessary because he would give new life, new aims and new dignity to the Democratic party. This is not flattery- I mean it.

---

2 Owen D. Young was counselor to several US presidents and the founder of RCA in 1919. He was also on the WWI Reparations Committee with Tom Lamont in the 1920s and came up with a fairer second plan for Germany's repayments, only to have it fall apart with the stock market crash. In 1929 TIME named him Man of the Year. A Democrat, he ran for the party's presidential nomination in 1932.

Enclosed is a cartoon look at it carefully. From it you and the Democrats can gain valuable ideas as to how your platform should be worded. The cub reporters effusion is typical of all former platforms of both parties. At the bottom the editor however tells the truth in the fewest possible words.

Why not build your platform along these simple lines. Thus it will be totally new in style, read and understood by all. That certainly would be a <u>great novelty</u>!

After reading your address, I suggest to the Democrats that in the preparation of the forthcoming platform they make Raskob the author and editor. As such, you, in your simple, convincing style, should tell the people, after quoting from our glorious Constitution and Jefferson, the plain truth and the "right read" in the fewest possible words - and those all of "one syllable". In numbered paragraphs - to help gradually in "digesting" and for ready reference - set forth your plans.

If any Democratic orator insists on interjecting his poetic effusions, shoot him on the spot. With such a platform and with a strong man as a candidate-- why, of course: you win".

In this campaign as never before, the platform will be of supreme importance. Set forth plainly what your speakers are to say and make them stick to it. Describe minutely just what you have to "sell" Otherwise and without such guidance, they surely will run amuck.

Ever sincerely yours,
Joseph P Knapp

JP received a short reply from Raskob's secretary informing him that he was on a brief vacation. It appears that if Raskob did respond, he did by telephone. On March 1st, Knapp wrote again when it seemed apparent that Owen Young was no longer in contention for the nomination. Knapp never mentions Roosevelt in these letters, but Raskob and financier Bernard Baruch opposed FDR. After the election Knapp would later confer with Roosevelt administration officials at his Park Ave apartment as well as call on them in Washington to offer his advice.

Dear Mr. Raskob:

Can you let me have your opinion on what you think of Byrd's chances of securing the nomination? Some friends of mine in Virginia suggested that I ask you. I do not know the governor very well[3] but like him tremendously and think him a most attractive man. However, I have been saying that it did not seem to me that he had any chance because of lack of national prominence.

Perhaps you would prefer to talk on the above rather than write? If so, it would be fine if you would give me an opportunity of having another lunch with you at the Links Club.

Ever sincerely yours,
Joseph P. Knapp

---

3 The old sage of Currituck may be playing naive here or he may not? But I think if he knew of Byrd's weak support for education, he would not even be talking about him.

He apparently met with Raskob again and the last letter I have from Knapp to Raskob was written on April 2, 1932

Dear Mr Raskob:

Many thanks for sending me the Sam Crowther pamphlet on "Your Money". I shall read it and undoubtedly be interested. Sam always writes entertainingly and generally wisely.

Whenever you feel inclined to have another luncheon party, be sure to let me know. I shall hope that our next one is not interrupted by anyone who talks a lot, says nothing, and has a bad cough.

Ever sincerely yours,

Joseph P. Knapp

I'm not sure if the Sam Crowther referred to here is the early Boy Scouts of America leader or not. In any event, when Roosevelt got the nomination Raskob withdrew from active politics. I do not know if he maintained contact with J. P. Knapp past this time.

After Roosevelt was elected in a true landslide, his administration called on the nations business leaders and bankers to help find ways to resuscitate the country. Knapp had more than a few ideas about economic recovery that went beyond ducks. He had a plan—"The Knapp Plan"—that was presented in Washington along with the "Harriman Plan" which was the one that the administration eventually morphed into part of National Recovery Act. In several Roosevelt administration memoirs this next passage written in the 1940's appears about the time life long Republican Joe Knapp became part of Roosevelt's "New Deal" His new dealings seemed to be concentrated around the election of '32 as much of the country was loosing their shirts, homes and most everything else. The big city tycoon Joe Knapp, who we know loved the country, aligned himself with two Iowa farm boys: Wallace & Wilson. Secretary of Agriculture Henry Wallace who would also become Roosevelt's Vice President during the third term, and Wallace's right hand man Assistant Secretary of Agriculture economist Milburn L. Wilson:

...It is extraordinary, the emotional appeal that the second strain in Wilson's agricultural thinking exerted upon widely diverse and often powerful persons around the time of the 1933 bank holiday. "We seek the security of the earth," Clare Leighton has written, "when all around us trembles."

JOSEPH KNAPP, LARGEST OWNER OF THE CROWELL PUBLICATIONS, WAS not trembling. Other people attend to that for "Uncle Joe." But he was certainly amenable to Wilson's vision of a part time modern peasantry, semi-removed from the tumult and strain of commerce. And there can be no harm now, at this late date, in telling how on two occasions, Uncle Joe Knapp, warmest-hearted of tycoons and among the most irascible, almost joined the New Deal.

The Old Man, as they call him at the Crowell shop, has a big place in coastal Carolina. His love of the land is expressed in large-handed local benefactions and in a passion for ducks. "Ducks Unlimited" is his slogan. Arthur Hyde, Mr. Hoover's Secretary of Agriculture, was also somewhat duck-minded. Hyde published a piece in a Crowell magazine on the tragic irony of the barns and busted banks and the Old Man read the piece. He called in lawyers and went into a burst of national planning for open price covenants in industry. The attraction here was in some part that which had attracted Henry I. Harriman to Wilson's farm allotment plan; it foretold for industry a large out from under the antitrust laws, such as was later attempted under NRA. But Knapp's ideas were different from those of the Chamber of Commerce, under Harriman; Knapp wanted to induce industrial cooperation largely by baiting the offer with cheap governmental credit. (He would have been surprised to know how many dread liberals such as Rex Tugwell and Jerome Frank nourished similar plans).

Right in the middle of all this, Knapp's The Country Home magazine came out with a piece about Wilson. Now the phones at Crowell really began to chime. The Old Man wanted to see this fellow, Lord, who had written the article. His friend, Arthur Hyde, told him the Wilson idea was no good. He wanted to see this Wilson, too. Wilson was in New York for a day. The interview was arranged. A couple of harassed Crowell executives took us in a cab to the Old Man's big Park Avenue apartment. "Try, for heaven's sake," one of them urged us, "to get him back on ducks!"

We were shown into the Old Man's presence. His profile is like the face on an Indian penny, his skin a rugged red, his bearing erect and peppery. A grand old Tory, if ever there was one, and he liked Wilson right away. We started talking about farm allotments, indicating-in deference to the Old Man's gamey notions- that there might well be feed in the "surplus" strips and fields for migrating wild-life. A long distance call came from Washington and Wilson left the room. One of the minions leaned forward and remarked in a placatory tone, "You're going to like Professor Wilson, Mr. Knapp." The Old Man switched a steely, imperious eye and answered: "Of course like him. I know a man when I see one."

We sat there waiting. Wilson returned and settled into a chair comfortably. With slow words and gestures he showed that the Hoover-Hyde plan of retiring only unproductive or marginal acres would not sufficiently reduce production and maintain prices. Then he developed the business or industrial implications of an openly planned production. The Old Man listened, asking sharp questions. Then Wilson unfolded his legs and rose. He walked over to where the Old Man sat by a wide, curtained window in a high-backed chair.

"Now, Mr. Knapp," he said, "you and I have agreed just about perfectly so far. But now I'm going to say something I don't believe you'll agree with. I'm going to tell you what I really want." He took hold of a thick brocaded window-drape and drew, it back. There was Park Avenue, St. Bartholemew's Church, the apartment palaces, the elevated and the Westside slums beyond. "I want to destroy all this," said Wilson.

He went on talking quietly, standing there by the window. "This is no way for people to live. I want to get them out on the ground with clean sunshine and air around them, and a garden for them to dig in, if they like. I want to get all these children off of streets, out on the land again. Spread out the cities, space the factories out, give people a chance to live so they'll know what life is all about-that's what I want."

"Mr. Wilson," the Old Man told him as we were leaving, "I've never voted for a Democrat in my life. But if that's your New Deal, I'll vote for it; and I'm with you 100 percent."

A few weeks later, still in that happy time when the Deal was really New and all the cards were being played face up with spirit and abandon, the Old Man and three aides came to Washington to talk with Wilson and Secretary Wallace about Industrial (as compared with Agricultural) Adjustment. The Knapp plan was being circulated in typescript. Many New Dealers in agriculture liked it better than the plan furthered by Harriman and the Chamber of Commerce (later NRA). Under a loose cooperative arrangement then rather common, I was working on loan from my company-Crowell-as an assistant to the Secretary, and I took the delegation in to introduce them to Wallace. With his customary air of amiable diffidence Wallace came from behind his desk to shake hands. He said a few words of praise for certain features of the Knapp plan. Then we all sat down.

"Young man," said the Old Man, abruptly. "You're tired. But you're young. I envy you. You have the greatest power and the greatest opportunity in your hands at this moment of any American who ever"- He broke off abruptly, and, "My God!" he cried. "What's that?"

A white rabbit had come out from under a radiator, gently ambling and nibbling at the carpet. "It's a rabbit," said the Secretary. The Old Man passed a hand across his eyes. The rabbit misbehaved. An alert colored man, Edward, then the Secretary's messenger, came scurrying to scoop up the rabbit with one hand and the droppings with the other. They went away. The Secretary explained that the rabbit was his boy's, Henrys'; and it was sick; so he had brought it down to have a friend in the Department, a vet, look it over.

Everybody laughed and there was some attempt to get the talk back on the subject of the Knapp plan; but no go. The Old Man rose abruptly. "Can't you see this man's tired?" Then to Wallace: "God bless you!" They passed into the anteroom. "Now," said the Old Man, "where do I find Wilson?" We took him up to Wilson's office as chief of Triple-A's new wheat section, and they talked for the better part of an hour. From this and subsequent conversations, grew the report of the Thomas A. Beck-J. N. Darling -Aldo Leopold committee on Wild Life Restoration, and from this came "Ding" Darling's breezy spell of service as chief of the Biological Survey. But that visit was, so far as I know, Uncle Joe Knapp's last appearance in Washington or anywhere else as a hundred percent New Dealer.

CHAPTER
35

If it Walks Like a Duck, Get Its Address...and Don't Forget to Sing to the Salmon

At the risk of repeating myself, it seems that during the 1930's, when much of the world and America especially was in great difficulty, J P.Knapp was humming along like a man of 25 on his way up. He would be 76 by the end of the decade and the energy he poured into all his varied projects, business, personal, and philanthropic during the 1930s was astounding. Not that everything was smooth sailing and trouble free. because—"Trouble still knows where you live"—K.S.

No Limits !
Although More Game Birds was headed up by and funded by men of great wealth and power, I doubt none of them knew just how much effect the Depression and the drought was going to have on their ability to really turn things around those first few years. Ducks were far from a high priority of the budgets of both governments of the US and Canada. It is probably largely because of Knapp and his drive of getting long term pledges from his original founders, that they were able to do what they did. Even at that, economics played hardball and when three of the original founders felt they had legitimate reasons to renege on $150,000 worth of pledges. they were pursued past the point of hard feelings and into litigation.

But J. P. Knapp saw ducks as a crusade and part of the solution to many of the economic problems facing the country. He didn't let set backs and disappointments stop him. Setbacks like not being able to get the regulations on the hunting season, that seemed to be set in stone by the Biological Survey, changed during Hoover's last year in Washington, even after his personal visit to the oval office. Nor the disappointment of having his economic recovery Knapp Plan, that he presented to FDR's New Deal, passed over in favor of the NRA. His own modest successes at propagation of wildlife at his estate in North Carolina and at the Game Institute in New Jersey, were proof to him that the theory worked and the US and Canada could only benefit, if they could just be applied on a wider scale. The total amount of money he personally poured into this effort will never be known because he did so much of it anonymously, but it was well into the hundreds of thousands of dollars, during days of songs like "Brother Can You Spare A Dime". Bear in mind that he also had other philanthropic commitments as well as a huge publishing and printing business to keep afloat. Economic realities set in, as the depression years wore on. The high salaries of his executives at More Game Birds, like Arthur Foran's $25,000 in 1931 were reduced by up to 40% by 1933. I don't know if he was much of a dancer, but J. P. sure had a lot of tap dancing and juggling to do in the 1930s.

Of course he had good help too. In 1934 he sent Tom Beck to Washington on his behalf, as Beck was a personal friend of FDR. Beck presented Roosevelt with a "Memorandum for Consideration" that began with, *Mr President , attached hereto is a plan that is urgently needed, national in scope, in accord with the National Industrial Recovery Act, of great public interest, in complete accord with the policies of your administration, of great economic importance, and ready for immediate action which will produce quick results.* It went on to spell out point by point in numbers, that no President could ignore for the economic benefits that could be achieved by adopting it. Roosevelt responded by naming Beck as chairman of his first Wildlife Restoration Committee, a three man group along with Professor Aldo Leopold (an ecologist, forester and environmentalist) and political cartoonist Ding Darling. Roosevelt's critics jumped on the inclusion of Darling in this committee as *"a buying the silence of his most feared critic"* They obviously didn't know dick about Ding. Darling created a storm the very day he hit Washington, only to find Beck (who was really representing JP) was not going to be pushed around. In the middle of it all, was the soft spoken Prof. Leopold.

In 1954 after both his fellow committee men had gone on to that big nature preserve somewhere, Darling wrote an article for the National Parks magazine that reflected those stormy days: *"When the names of the committee were announced, it must of seemed to the sportsmen, as well as to the trained scientists and natural history technicians, that probably never had there been a more incongruous group."* According to Darling, Chairman Beck, who was neither duck hunter nor scientist, but representing Mr. Knapp, was both violent and outspoken and whose only mission it seemed to be was to throw the findings of the Biological Survey out the window body and britches. A howl of derisive and ribald criticism greeted us on the morning of our first meeting. It seemed we were condemned from the start. Secretary Wallace loaned us a spare room and some chairs and a table and at FDR's request, turned over an accumulation of White House mail containing advice and recommendations that for most part were quite unpractical, but by a wide margin the most popular method to save the ducks was to *"Stop man from shooting them."*

Overall though, Darling said there were no practical programs that they could use or adapt, that seemed any more enforceable than the late lamented prohibition experiment was. He then mentions "A privately supported organization known as More Game Birds in America, with an expensive technical staff, largely financed by the aforementioned Joseph P. Knapp owner of Crowell Publishing company, a fabulous sportsman, made a determined effort at considerable costs to replenish the depleted ranks of wild ducks by artificial methods. Knapp was not one to spare the horses, and every possible device was used in his hatcheries. The best thing Knapp's early organization ever hatched was Duck's Unlimited" which is doing in Canada what the U S Fish and Wildlife Service is doing on this side of the border—our committee fell apart with all the violence of an exploding powder magazine. Tom Beck, who had a resonant voice of a sideshow barker, could out shout both Leopold and me. He held the floor against all attempts to get a word in edgeways, and insisted on stating in the report to the President that the Biological Survey was incompetent and unscientific and should get the ax and he wanted to be present to see heads roll."

In spite of their differences, the report they submitted was very thorough and comprehensive. A few of the conclusions and recommendations were: Incontrovertible evidence of a critical and continuing decline in wildlife resources, especially migratory waterfowl, caused by the destruction and neglect of natural breeding areas. They called for projects comprising of programs for wildlife restoration on 5 million acres divided into 5 parts of, 1: Migratory waterfowl and shore birds, 2: Upland game including wild turkey, quail, rabbit, 3: Song and ornamental, which were of great economic value in insect control and of major importance to both spiritual and recreational purposes. 4: Mammals, including big game and fur bearers who had not been considered at all before this and 5: The creation of a new agency to coordinate all these restoration and conservation efforts in a business like manner.

The 5th part raised the sticky question of administrative changes within the Biological Survey which was still the controlling group. By February of 1934, Henry Wallace, the Secretary of Agriculture had the Beck report on his desk along with the resignation of Paul Redington chief of the U.S. Bureau of Biological Survey. By March Wallace appointed Ding Darling to take his place, making him in effect the first director of the US Wildlife Service. When Ding designed the first Duck Hunting Stamp he quipped, "Just because a hunter has this new stamp, they are under no obligation to shoot a duck, nor is there any rule to prevent them from purchasing several, because every dollar will be devoted to the cause of conservation. Duck propagation was bounced back in Knapps court and his next move, which caused a major rift between Darling and himself was also was instrumental in the formation of Ducks Unlimited.

Getting his ducks in a row

In July of 1935, More Game Birds decided to carry out the first international wild duck census. Think about what an effort organizing a human census must be. Then add in the complications of trying to count wild birds! The census covered the duck breeding grounds on Canadian provinces of Alberta, Manitoba and Saskatchewan and the States of North and South Dakota and Minnesota. A total of about 995, 631 square miles. It is hard to believe, owing to the difficulty of organizing this task and the resources available, that no prior preparation was done prior to July of 1935, as was More Game Birds claim. Could it of been a J. P. Knapp back burner, low profile project since the start of his merry group?

One of the true innovations to come from the duck census, was the development of the techniques used to survey populations from the air with 1000's of low altitude photographs taken in specially equipped aircraft. Trained observers focused on groups consisting of 25, 50, and 100 ducks approximately. These aerial surveys were used in conjunction with ground surveys. Although those conducting the survey believed there were probably 65,000,000 ducks on the continent in August 1935, they reported a grand total of 42,700,000. Another conclusion they came to, was due to the plentiful water supply after a long drought, that the 1935 duck crop was expected to be the largest in six years. So it came as no surprise when Ding Darling announced further restrictions for the 1935 hunting season, that those who worked long and hard were not happy. Darling took it personal and felt that the optimistic results of the census focused intense criticism on the regulations coming from his bureau. Or as Jon Tennyson surmised, most likely from talking with Arthur Bartley, Darling was still most likely still smarting from his run ins with Beck, who he believed just was doing Knapp's bidding. In any event Darling lashed out at the Wild Duck Census and Knapp specifically in an opinion piece called "The Wild Duck Racket" he wrote for Today magazine that was published on November 2, 1935 This paragraph was in the middle of Darling's piece

"Old Joe Knapp, the sage of Currituck, who was one of the best wing shots and has spent more of his personal fortune on ducks than any man in the United States, finds his shooting restricted to 30 days, no baiting and no live decoys. To the treetops men! There's a wounded lion loose in the tundra! He sends his number one ramrod, Colonel Arthur Foran, President of More Game Birds in America to Canada to count the ducks and prove that all those who contend that there is a shortage of ducks are fools; to Illinois to contest in the courts the rights of government to restrict shooting, and to organize a revolution against all those who stand in the way of the inalienable right of every American to shoot when and how he pleases. Joe loves to shoot. Certainly if by his efforts he succeeds in breaking down the only control that exists over taking of migratory waterfowl, the days of the ducks and the duck shooter will be numbered."

Four Days later Tom Beck sent this letter to the trustees of the American Wildlife Institute which was one of Darlings pet projects.

Gentlemen :

Jay N. Darling's inexcusable, wholly false and vicious attack (in the magazine Today issue of Nov 2) on my longtime intimate friend and business associate, makes it impossible for me to continue with an organization that is under the necessity of doing business with him. I, therefore, ask that you accept, as of today, my resignation as trustee, member of the executive committee and president of the American Wildlife Institute.

Cordially

Thomas H. Beck

J. P. also responded to Darling's charges, not in public via a magazine piece which he could of easily done, nor in several magazines with twenty times the circulation of Today magazine. Instead he wrote a personal letter to Darling which said in part:

I was out of the country when the advisability of a waterfowl census was decided upon by the Foundation. You, however, had full knowledge of it weeks before the 1935 regulations were issued. As you know, the census was made for the sole purpose of finding the true facts regarding the status of ducks.

After you personally examined at the New York office, the work of the Foundation in the 1935 duck census, you stated to Mr. Beck that the job had been efficiently done and that the figures were both accurate and conservative.

I did not send Colonel Foran to Canada to count the ducks and prove that all who contend there is a shortage of ducks are fools, nor did he go to Canada for this or any other purpose during the year. I did not send Colonel Foran to Illinois to contest in the courts the rights of government to restrict shooting, nor to organize a revolution against all those who stand in the way of the inalienable right of every American to shoot when and how he pleases.

The statement, "Certainly if by his efforts he succeeds in breaking down the only control that exists over the taking of migratory waterfowl, the days of the ducks and the the duck shooter will be numbered," is, as you know, a deliberate and malicious misstatement of fact, because the efforts you mentioned in your article were not made.

YOU made these regulations. In seeking to justify them, you have said they were necessitated by a shortage of ducks. Concerning the actual duck crop, you knew little or nothing and the Foundation census has proved there was no shortage, but that the ducks were actually on the increase.

In your "Today" article are you not knocking those who made you?

Your appointment as Chief of of the Survey was the direct result of your membership on the Presidents Committee on Wildlife Restoration. It seems necessary to remind you.

First, that the idea of a federal wildlife restoration project originated with More Game Birds in America and that the appointment of this committee resulted from a memorandum prepared by the Foundation and submitted to President Roosevelt by Mr. Thomas H. Beck who later served as the Chairman of the President's Committee.

Second, that in preparation of the committee report, which you, which you as a member signed, a major portion of the work was done by members of the Foundation staff, whom you profoundly thanked for their untiring efforts.

Third, that in accepting the position of Chief of the Bureau of Biological Survey, you did so with the condition that certain members of the Foundation staff were made available to assist you.

Fourth, that the report of the Presidents Committee on Wildlife Restoration embodied a sound , national program, which President Roosevelt approved. As a member of that committee and as Chief of the Bureau of Biological Survey, it was your clear duty to see that the program was carried out to the full extent of it's tremendous possibilities.

In the report of the President's Committee, which again I remind you bears your signature, I find the following: "The work of putting into effect this or any national wildlife restoration program and carrying on the essential conservation cannot be done with the requisite speed or resourcefulness by the pre existing personnel or through pre existing procedures ... much of the talent required for the above position is available in the Biological Survey, a misnamed, quasi-scientific bureau quite unequal to the present task."

The truth of the statement that the Bureau is quite unequal to the present task has been amply proven by it's record under your leadership. I quote again from the report of the President's Committee. "We find the plan in its general aspects and intent, practical, vitally necessary, national in scope, and of great economic and social importance."

This was a statement of fact. To make it successful calls for executive and administrative ability of a high degree which you do not possess.

Very truly yours,

Joseph P. Knapp

On November 15, 1935, thirteen days after Darling's Knapp attack hit the newsstands, he resigned as director of the Biological Survey, citing he went to Washington thinking he could make a difference, but felt as helpless as a cork in the ocean. In February of 1936, he was elected president of the General Wildlife Federation the forerunner of the National Wildlife Federation. This group would find itself at times aligned with the goals of Ducks Unlimited, but mainly worked against it.

Of the many findings that came out of the duck census, the most alarming and significant one to Knapp's thinking was the fact that if prompt action was not taken in regard to preserving the breeding grounds in Canada, then nothing else that More Game Birds or the US Government for that matter did would matter. To deal with it, he started a Canadian foundation called Ducks Unlimited and presented a tentative draft of the foundations goals and purpose to the Premiers of Alberta, Saskatchewan, Mantioba as well as Canadian game officials and sportsmen of each province. All Ducks Unlimited financing was to be covered by More Game Birds and every dollar subscribed for Ducks Unlimited would be spent to produce more ducks in Canada, where for one dollar, at least 5 times as many ducks could be produced than back in the US.

When author Jon Tennyson asked Arthur Bartley how they came up with the name Ducks Unlimited, Arthur said " *At the very first meeting, which I was held at Knapp's Fishing Lodge on the Beaverkill River in 1936 , Knapp simply wanted to call the new foundation "DUCKS," when I reminded him that Canadian corporations were identified as "Limited" and therefore the name would be Ducks Limited, Knapp just EXPLODED! and jumped to his feet "DUCKS LIMITED!", he cried, "WE DON'T WANT LIMITED DUCKS!" All right said Arthur, "Ducks Unlimited" "THAT'S IT", said Knapp.*

When J. P. and his hunting party, were given a summons for having 5 ducks over the bag limit in the fall of 1936, some Knapp enemies (Friends of Ding) had a field day with the news. The trial did not get underway until March of 1937. Nature magazine reported on it in June that year and presented only the parts and half truths that supported their obvious agenda of taking Ding's side and making Knapp look like a conservation hypocrite, who thought the rules applied to others. However at the trial itself (in which all 4 defendants did not appear, but were represented by council) Mr. Dozier, J.P.'s lawyer made the following summation speech before the judge. *"The respondent Knapp has taken up the torch from failing hands and passed it on, and the wave of interest for the preservation of wildlife now evident in America and the Dominion is largely due to him. If the officials of this generation, can not properly appraise him and appreciate him, those of the future will, for when the ducks, geese, and other wildfowl again swarm over Currituck Sound and nearly black out the sun, the credit will be his, and his prosecution will then appear in it's true and ridiculous light."* The Judge's decision said *"...it seems to me that this matter is rather frivolous and I'm going to dispose of it by imposing a fine of one dollar each."*

Initially Ducks Unlimited was to be a 5 year plan for restoration of the Canadian breeding grounds, staffed and funded by More Game Birds in America. In spite of many obstacles both economic and political, it grew rapidly with many members in the states and in 1938 the first annual meeting of the US trustees was held in Chicago and a United States headquartered organization was formed. By 1940, J. P. Knapp folded the More Game Birds tent and turned over all of its very considerable assets to Ducks Unlimited. Nay sayers, who in the 1930s were proclaiming wild ducks as history, had to whistle another tune. Over seven decades of DU conservation history is now on the books since J. P. Knapp convened his band of merry men at his fishing lodge and said "Let's just call it DUCKS!" Today with nearly 800,000 subscribing members, DU is the leading organization in North America for wetlands conservation and all things waterfowling.

Gone Fishing

As wild as J. P. was about ducks, he was also fanatical about fly fishing. The husband and wife team of Elsie & Harry Darbee, who were considered to be the foremost professional fly tiers in the world, recalled Knapp in the Ed Van Put's 2007 book "Trout Fishing In The Catskills" "One of our biggest customers in the 1930's was Joseph P. Knapp. He owned 4 and a half miles of the Beaverkill river, leased a stretch of the Nastashquan in Labrador and fished all over the world. I remember one day he was picking up an order of flies and he remarked, " It takes a lot of flies to make a living, If the time comes that you and Elsie don't have any orders, my friends and I will take all you can tie." We thought that was the kindest thing anyone had ever said to us, especially in the depths of the Depression, but we were able to make ends meet without having to take advantage of his offer.

In a June 29, 1964 Sports Illustrated article titled *"He Deftly Ties The World's Fanciest Flies,"* Darbee also mentioned Knapp's kindness: *"Ever since 1928*

Harry Darbee has been tying flies professionally. He and Elsie, whom he married in 1933 after she came to work as an assistant, weathered the Depression easily since the Big Rich tightened their budgets by fishing instead of larking off to Europe for vacations. Still, there were some customers who wondered how the Darbees could manage. One of them, the late J. P. Knapp, chairman of the board of Publication Corp., felt such pity that he gave Darbee a standing order to tie flies whenever he hit a slack period. At one time Knapp had some 250,000 flies in the house. "Knapp," explains Darbee, "used to say, 'When I get a good fly, I like to keep it around.' "

It was "Sibby" Penny, J. P.'s great grand daughter who first told me about J. P.s passion for fresh water fishing and his "fishing camp" in upstate NY. At that time I wasn't even aware that I had a 1917 deed with the Knapp's upstate Hardenburgh address on it stashed in with my big stack of deeds. I had already copied on that first fact finding trip in early September of 2001. Not that I would of known what kind of place they had there. I have heard several descriptions of Knapp's upstate place ranging from one that looked like Jefferson's Monticello in the hills of Hardenburgh, to the roughest of fish camp lodges. It seems the Knapps actually had two places there. I read someplace in the history of Roscoe and Livingston Manor the two nearby towns. that the Monticello style Knapp house caught fire in the 1940s and was destroyed, But he kept the fish camp at Lew Beach near Roscoe along the Beaverkill River. Sibby described his fishing lodge as very rustic and it was now the Lee & Joan Wulff "Royal Wulff" Fly Fishing School. Something didn't quite make sense because she also said during the Depression J. P. kept his caretakers busy, by constantly redoing landscaping projects, feigning that he changed his mind, because he didn't want to them to feel they were taking charity. I can't seeing him that doing that to a rustic fish camp. His wife Elizabeth's name is on that 1917 deed too and with what I know about Elizabeth, she did not appear as the type of person who enjoyed roughing it, nor did any of her social activities that were reported in the papers ever mention fishing and hunting.

Margaret however was definitely a fly fisher woman and most likely one of the eight charter members of the Woman Fly Fishers Club of the Catskills that was incorporated in 1932. Again in the book Trout Fishing in The Catskills, there is this remembrance of both of J. P. & Margaret. "Although the Catskills was the Woman Fly fishers club home waters, club members traveled all over the world in their pursuit of game fish. Some members were married to men who were avid fly fishers and along with their husbands, they owned unique stretches of private water along Catskill trout streams. Although they may have roughed it at times, members had some remarkable and memorable outings, especially along the Beaverkill and on the waters of Margaret & Joseph Knapp."

The Knapp water was located between Lew Beach and Turnwood and was a favorite of early members, not only because of the fine fishing, but because of their midday luncheons, which were "Fabulous" The Knapps entertained their guests by dining at stream side,at an opening in the woods, on a long lace-covered table with "nine silver champagne coolers" A whole salmon was flown in from Canada and dinner would include "2 roasts of beef."

He Sings To The Fishes

Not with the fishes, that's MAFIA stuff. When the book "Atlantic Salmon Fishing" was first published in 1937, J. P. Knapp was 73 years old and considered to be one of the world's leading fly fishing anglers. On salmon alone, which present some of the greatest challenges, he has caught 7,054 over 22 years on 7 different rivers. He most likely continued fishing for at least another decade. I tell you this to support the fact that this next story taken from the above mentioned book is no fish story.

An instance of the resourcefulness in salmon fishing is the way Mr. Joseph Knapp of NY takes fish in a certain pool on the Natashquan. He sings to them. He has discovered that the fish in a certain pool rise best when a fly is cast beyond them and dragged over them; and as he drags the fly over them, he sings to them. He once had two guests at his lodge who made a wager as to which of them would catch more fish the next day. Giving them two of his best pools the next morning, Mr. Knapp went on up river. When he came back down that evening, he found that the gentleman fishing the upper of the two pools had taken only two fish all day. Going on down to the other pool where the salmon must be sung to, he found his other guest, who also only caught two fish. Mr. Knapp asked him why he hadn't caught more. *"There are lots of fish here,"* he replied, *"but I can't raise them."*

"Did you sing to them?" asked Mr. Knapp. *"Sing hell. Don't be silly"* *"All right give me a rod."* said Mr. Knapp. And taking it, he cast out beyond where the fish lay. As he dragged the fly in over them, he sang at the top of his lungs, and just as he was singing his loudest, a big salmon rose and took the fly. Mr. Knapp caught him and passed the rod back to his guest. *"Now,"* he said, *"you sing to them. I want you to catch one and win your bet."* The gentleman took the rod, burst into song and caught a 23 pound salmon and won the bet.

How many wooden nickels am I bid for this wooden fish?

In November of 2004, Lang's Sporting Collectibles, listed the following item in their fall auction catalog:

Wood Fish Weathervane Taken From Lee Wulff 's Barn. Originally installed by Joseph P. Knapp around 1917 when he purchased the property. Knapp was the owner / publisher of Collier's Magazine and The Saturday Evening Post (sic) and one of the original founders of Ducks Unlimited, which was founded on his property in 1936. A plaque was installed in his honor, marking D. U's birthplace in 1996. Knapp, an avid fisherman owned 2400 acres and several miles of the Beaverkill River adjacent to the property. He called it, "The Beaverkill Stream Club".

Joan's son Douglas spoke with Mary Simpson (Van Steenburg) who with her husband George were the caretakers from the early 1930's through the 1950's. She stated *"it was up there when we got here."* Mary died in 1999. Lee and Joan bought the property in 1978. The weather vane was mounted on a wooden ball with the spike you see going through a hole in the middle of it. There were 4 directionals screwed into the ball, which are included here. The ball, rotted and held together with paint, fell apart when taken down in 1997. This vane has been on a wall in the barn since then. With a length of 39", this weathered fish has remnants of the original green and white paint, has cracks and a worn finish and not only is it a fine example of folk art, it has historic significance with it's passing through the Knapp's and the Wulff's ownership. Estimated sale price $3,250-$4,250.

I contacted the auctioneers to see if it sold— It did! I also told them that there was a glaring error in their catalog description. If J. P. Knapp saw himself being listed as the owner of the Saturday Evening Post, that weather vane would of spun faster than Linda Blair's head did in the Exorcist !

The Knapps Lived Here,
On the Water

Wallabout was the very first place on Long Island that the Europeans settled in 1624. The first Knapp Mansion in Williamsburg, was just over two blocks away from Wallabout Bay on the East River. In the 1890s, the second generation Joseph Knapp family, Joseph P., Sylvia T., Miss Claire A. and Master Joseph F., lived just off of Riverside Dr., almost directly on the Hudson River in NY City. When they went out to the country for "the season," Bellport on the Great South Bay was their choice. Their habit of living near or on the water never really changed, and almost half a century later, though all four had gone their own ways and had lived and traveled all over the world, at least three of them would still be living year round on a river, lake, or bay regardless of which home or what season they were in. As for Sylvia, who was in Paris, she too could not of been very far from the river Seine. That said, the last move J. P. would make from his Park Avenue apartment in the center of Manhattan isle would come as no surprise to me.

River House
This 1930s era residential tower at 435-447 East 52nd St., was surely one of the most luxurious and well situated ever built in New York City. Until the FDR Drive was completed in the 1940s, a private dock allowed tenants to moor their

yachts right at their front door. Thirty stories high with just 64 apartments that originally sold for up to $275,000 in 1931, River House has been synonymous with wealth and power from the day it was built. Residents have included Angier Biddle Duke, Henry Kissinger, John Kenneth Galbraith, Cornelius Vanderbilt and many more. In the 1980s, Gloria Vanderbilt was denied permission to buy a Riverhouse apartment. She sued on the grounds that the co-op board had rejected her because of her friendship with cabaret singer Bobby Short. The board defended their actions by saying she could not afford an apartment at the then going price of over 1.1 million — a typical River House apartment has twelve rooms, six baths, two fireplaces and a spectacular view of the East River— *from the book "Living It Up" by Thomas Norton & Jerry Patterson. pub 1984 Antheum*

During the same week of 1936, that Claire Knapp Penney & St. Margaret Magnificent of Clairedale moved into the Westminster Dog Show record book at Madison Square Garden, this item ran in the New York Times: Large Suites Taken In East Side Houses Feb 12, 1936: Several leases of large apartments and penthouses were included in rentals announced yesterday. Douglas Gibbons and Co. leased from Vincent Astor his 903 Park Ave Suite of 18 rooms and seven baths for a client. Other rentals through Gibbons & Co, were Joseph P. Knapp at River House, 12 rooms and four baths.

Claire and Willis and her newly crowned champion dog, Margaret Magnificent and brood, may of dropped in that week to see her Dad and step mom's Margaret's *"magnificent River House apartment with windows that seem to hang out over the east river"—* Fortune Magazine, August 1937 or perhaps even stayed with them there?

What Would J.P. Do?

Gloria Vanderbilt, the great great grand daughter of one New York's original 400 Bluebook families, was not the only notable reject who applied to purchase an apartment at River House. Others included actress Diane Keaton and Richard M. Nixon. But probably none brought as much unwanted publicity to River House as Gloria Vanderbilt's lawsuit did. It led me to wonder if J. P. was on the co op board, what would his vote be on Gloria, Diane or Tricky Dick? Or if Collier's was still in business, would it of run this story?

Gloria Vanderbilt Charges Bigotry But Co-Op Says She Was Snubbed On Her Merits

Maybe the late Bob Paley was wrong. You can be too slim, too newly rich, or that anyway was at least the ugly explanation of why the board of Manhattan's exclusive River House co-op rejected Gloria Vanderbilt's $1.1 million bid to buy a two story co-op.

In affidavits filed with both the New York State Supreme Court and New York City's Commission on Human Rights in, Vanderbilt, a sleek 56, charged that the River House directors had acted on the supposition that black entertainer Bobby Short, her frequent escort, was the man she would be bringing home to dinner and domicile. Added Vanderbilt's lawyer, Thomas Andrews: "The seller's attorney asked whether Gloria intended to marry Mr. Short. It is none of their damned business." Then the directors, stung by the publicity and the taunts of some of their East Side neighbors, denied that race had played any part in the Vanderbilt decision. Their real objection to Gloria, suggested board president Carl Mueller, was that she is a Seventh Avenue designer now better known for her jeans than for her genes (she is the great-great-granddaughter of Commodore Cornelius Vanderbilt). Though River House has several celebrity owners in residence, including Henry Kissinger and Josh Logan, Vanderbilt's renown was apparently regarded as tacky. "Fame which attends public service and professional achievement," Mueller declared loftily, "is to be distinguished from publicity which is the result of constant cultivation to promote commercial self-interest —I believe that the ceaseless flow of gossip column items about [Vanderbilt's] comings and goings would attract unwelcome publicity to the River House."

The directors also questioned whether, given the "up-and-down nature of the fashion business", if Gloria's listed net worth of more than $7 million would be sufficient to back up her offer. "We are convinced that the longer she can drag this out, the more jeans she can sell," declared River House attorney Marion Epley, though he confided privately: "My daughters are furious with me for being against the 'Blue Jean Lady.' —People June 9,1980

Dead End

Built on a dead end street on the site of a former cigar factory, River House first received unwanted attention of what it represented as contrast between the haves and have nots, the year the Knapps moved in, when playwright Sidney King used it to set the scene for his dramatic play "Dead End" The Broadway play was adopted in 1937 into a successful movie of the same name starring Humphrey Bogart. The highest critical praise for this typical gangster film of the '30s though was saved for its set, in which River House loomed ever present. The film also marked the first appearance of group of dangerous street tough youths, whose Hollywood persona would be radically altered in subsequent films, as they were morphed into a wise-cracking, comedic group of harmless B movie buffoons. They were led by icons Leo Gorcey & Huntz Hall and would be forever known as the Dead End Kids.

What follows is the stage directions from the original 1936 play: STRANGE SIGHT, set plumb down in the midst of slums, antique warehouses, discarded breweries, slaughter houses, electrical works, gas tanks, loading cranes, coal chutes etc the very wealthy have begun to establish their city residence in a huge palatial new apartment. Theatre critics were quick to point out the poignant metaphor at the heart of Dead End; The apartment house, once a place for the poor and déclassé, had become an ivory tower.

How's this for some low profile living: In 2006 this anonymous apartment listing appeared, the River House board insisted neither the name or address be listed. The ad took the "enquiring mind" of a NY Post reporter to uncover its location or perhaps he just asked his publisher Rupert Murdoch. "Baronial Granduer" in Midtown east "arguably the city's finest, if not the worlds finest apartment building" 8 bedroom duplex—$39 million.

I HAVE SEEN SEVERAL PHOTOS OF VARIOUS INTERIORS OF RIVER HOUSE through the years, but nothing would grab my interest as much as a 2007 photo I would discover of The Knapp Room that is located in the new Knapp-Saunders building on the campus of University of North Carolina. It seems that when widow Margaret Knapp moved out of River House in 1954 and back over to Park Ave, one of the many donations she made of Knapp furniture and art to UNC, was the actual pine that was used to panel their living room in River House. It looked instantly familiar to me, mainly because of its unique color that was not like most other pine of that era that usually was much lighter in color and boldly showed it's knots. This photo was just like looking at the Mastic Beach Knapp Mansion's empty ballroom, I first walked into that summer of 1955. When I first recalled the ballroom in my "The Mansion" short story, I thought because of its grain and dark color, that it was a hardwood like walnut, but was later enlightened by discovering the NY Times classified ads when Knapp put his Mastic Beach mansion on the market in 1939-40. Those ads mentioned as one its many features, "$7,000 of imported pine on the walls of the large 25 x 50 foot living room." It is highly likely the only way Dodi Knapp knew what his living room paneling cost was, if he had it installed years after he bought the place in 1916. And that probably was when his father did likewise at River House. Why else would Margaret have it removed when she left? I know if I ever do get to visit UNC at Chapel Hill (and I certainly hope to someday along with Mackey Island in Currituck) that walking into the Knapp Room will evoke a strong case of De-ja-Vu , if not a 100% confirmation that it is indeed the same beautiful wood that caused a whole bunch of little kids to stare with open mouths back in 1955, as we slowly spun around, looking at that huge empty room, exclaiming like a gaggle of little Gomer Pyle's "GOL-LEE!"

410 Isle Of Palms

I knew of Dodi Knapp's home on The Isle of Palms in Fort Lauderdale, very early on because it was the address on all of his Mastic Beach deeds, going back to June of 1938, when he sold off chunks of his estate piece meal to Home Guardian. I even have the one that lists the lot #s my boyhood home would be built on in 1941.

When I spoke with Sibby, his grand niece back in 2001, I asked her if she ever visited his Florida house. She told me she may of been there once or twice but could not recall many details other than it was big and it was on the water. She did have pretty vivid memories of being at River House as a young girl though and playing under her great grandfathers huge desk.

The first person who gave me line on the exact location of 410 Isle of Palms hacienda of one Joseph F. Knapp, was Merrilyn Rathbun of the Fort Lauderdale Historical Society. Merrilyn sent me a detailed property map along with two copies of pages from the Ft Lauderdale City Directories, one from the 1938-39 and one from the 1952-1953. The listing in 1938 said: Knapp, Jos F. 436 Isle Of Palms and the one from the 1952 listed it: Knapp, Jos F (Marion H) 410 Isle Of Palms, & Hampton Bays, L.I. The house number difference Merrilyn attributed to the Post Office renumbering the Las Olas Isle area.

Now besides giving me another initial associated with Marion's name (I had both E & H) there were other Knapp names in that directory that were real eye openers for me. Not their last name of Knapp, but rather their first ones. For there like ducks in a row, were almost all of the relatives of one Mike J. Knapp that he spoke to me about. Elaine , Minerva, Arlette, Oscar, and Henry. You may recall "I'm Forever Blowing Bubbles-Mike" (chapter 5) who led me on that initial Knapp merry go round back in 2000-2001. Mike did so by relaying tales his grandfather Henry who told him, when he was a kid in Ft. Lauderdale, wild stories of a the family country estate complete with a mansion "somewhere in the countryside of NY" and of vast fortunes lost and stolen.

So in retrospect Mike Knapp, whose very eccentric behavior, when I discovered his family were not the Knapps I was looking for, and whose extreme hostile reaction to my findings nearly caused me to abandon the whole project, could of also been a victim of stories. Stories that could of well been passed on in the 1930s - 1950s to Mike's family from one Dodi Knapp, who I have on eyewitness authority, was no stranger to all the better watering holes in Ft. Lauderdale. As a next canal neighbors to "Isle Of Palms" Knapp himself. for that is just where some of Mike's relatives lived in the 1930's.I am reasonably sure they knew him.

The Venice Of America
The entire area around Knapp's Isle Of Palms home is known as Stillwell Isles and is a series of man made finger peninsulas that run north and south off the main east west road known as Las Olas Blvd. Las Olas runs from the Atlantic Ocean into the downtown city of Ft. Lauderdale. Homes built there have waterfront on both front and rear of the house. In the Knapp's back yard was the man made Sunset Lake, which in reality is just a wide connecting body of water that leads to even more canals and isles. You can moor a bigger yacht there. The entire eastern Lauderdale area was developed around the New River and along with the canals, man made lakes, small bays, it gave the city of Ft. Lauderdale the nickname, The Venice Of America. Some of Mike Knapp's family lived on Royal Plaza Isle in the 1930s and 40s. The canal between Royal Plaza and Isle Of Palms is about 200 feet wide and the walking distance door to door from both Knapp houses via land, is less than a half mile. So what are the odds that these two Knapp families may of met during the decade or so they were next canal neighbors? Pretty Strong!

The first person who sent me photos of the actual house as it is today, was a fellow named Ben Conley back around 2002. Ben read my stuff on the website, he lived in the area and so he helped out. Ben's photos were taken from the street and although much of the house was shaded and covered by palm and other trees, I could make out it was a large home of the Mediterranean style with the typical red tile roof. They were followed up by Skip Clement another web site reader from Lauderdale about a year later and were pretty much the same shots. Skip said he was going to boat around to Sunset Lake and get some from the rear of the home too, but they never showed up. Much of the front of the house is well hidden by the trees.

Also around 2002 using the internet search engines, I found in the archives of a library at University of North Carolina at Ashville, a dime store scrapbook with the name Joseph F. Knapp of Ft. Lauderdale written on it's cover. I contacted the school and they made me copies of its contents, which were fairly cryptic as far as the writings in it, but also contained some photos and many missing photos, but none the less were of great interest. The dates that appear in it are all circa 1938-40s. Among the photos, are one of a definite Florida home, though it was quite a bit smaller than the picture of the one at 410 Isle of Palms. Could this of been 436 Isle of Palms that Knapp was also listed at? A second photo showed a casually but well dressed gentleman sitting in a lawn chair in a yard with palm trees that was on a body water. The shape of shoreline on the opposite side of the water was identical to what Sunset Lake looked like directly across from 410 Isle Of Palms.(It has a distinctive angular cut) Could this be the mysterious Dodi Knapp I thought? I posted it on my web site with the caption *"Dodi Is That You?"* For three years I got no answers. Today however it sits on my site with an ID. But I'm getting ahead of myself. There was also a photo of a middle aged dapper looking man in an Army uniform holding a Scotty dog. He too remained unidentified for quite some time, but I had some strong suspicions on just who he might be, based on some photos I had of a family I thought he was connected to. That hunch would eventually prove to be right when I received a 1940s photo of Lenoard, Clarence and Willis, the three sons of Merritt Cash Penney. This scrapbook had a photo of Willis Oliver Penney, first husband of Claire Antoinette Knapp! I believe the dogs name was Peaches. But what was he doing in an Army uniform? I would much later find out that when he and Claire got divorced, Willis enlisted during WWII. There were also several photos of some African Americans in the scrapbook along with news clippings about life in Asheville area. I inquired to the library as to where they got the scrapbook. They furnished me with the donors name, who lived in Texas. A phone call revealed that he found it in a house he bought and because he went to College in Ashville, when he saw the local clippings, thought his alma mater could use it. He had no idea at all what the Ft. Lauderdale stuff meant or who Joseph F. Knapp was. Once again the power of the internet as a fantastic research tool resonated with me. But as good as that was, it was paled by the internet connection I would make with Marty Van Lith, an old classmate that eventually led to that innocuous phone interview in 2004 with Fred Gillespie, regarding his father building the wooden Smith Point Bridge, in 1910 that would eventually lead me to the KNAPP JACKPOT !

Where There's A Will—There's A Way

When I told Marty Van Lith about Marion and Shirley Murdock and the "Isle Of Palms Knapp" story, that I accidentally learned from interviewing Fred, he took me to the next level. Marty has been involved with historic preservation of old Brookhaven area cemeteries and as it turns out another Murdock relative, "Jebby" was also involved with taking care of one of the cemeteries with him. This one happened to be where Marion's father in law, Gardner Murdock (the 1912 Edey murder in Bellport) and her ex husband Milton is buried. Jebby confirmed some of the Murdock family history he too heard about Marion and Milton and Knapp "the millionaire". He also told Marty that some years ago (in the 1980's) another Murdock relative named Allen Davis, had contacted Marion's daughter Shirley about chipping in for some headstones for her grandfather and father. The only problem was, Jebby wasn't sure of what Shirley's married name was and Allen Davis had passed on. I knew Marion had died in the mid 1980s, only because I found Stanley Conley, her third husband's 1987 obit that mentions he was predeceased by Marion H. (there was that darn H bomb again). I only knew of Stanley Conley, because that was Marion H. Knapp's new name on the deed as of 1954 when she sold the Hampton Bays home that Dodi died at in 1952 . Keeping with our chapters theme here, once again we have another Knapp home on the water. Still with me?...Deeds can be handy as they usually reference the past in great detail. Through the Social Security system I found a Marion Elizabeth Conley on her application for Social Security. Her maiden name was Hurd and her Manhattan address was the same as the one in Stanley Conley's obit. I was definitely on a roll. Marion was born in December of 1906 in New Haven, Ct. It turns out there were a bunch of Murdock relatives in that same town. But I still did not know what her daughter Shirley's married name was or if Shirley was still alive.

Using a paid people search system that searched via maiden names, I turned up a few possibilities in the Ft. Lauderdale area, but all turned out to be dead ends except for one. Only thing is the one that turned out to be Shirley's address, was her long ago former address and several months later the letter was returned to me with the notation "moved unable to forward." Bear in mind all of this took place over a period of about 18 months. I then thought about the possibility of obtaining Dodi's will? Knowing that he died in New York, I assumed his will was filed there just like his father's was. Then I was given a price for researching and copying it by the Suffolk County Clerks office and it was way past my budget. Well over $100 plus another $90 search fee which was too much for me to risk on a hunch to find one name. But then I thought the fact that his permanent address was Ft. Lauderdale, perhaps there is a document in the Florida Vital Statistics? There was indeed! There was the last will and testament of Joseph F. Knapp of Fort Lauderdale filed October 31, 1952 and a copy could be mine for $1 per page and a modest search fee (I think it was about 5 bucks) The will itself was 22 pages long and worth every dollar, for not only did Dodi's step daughters married name appear on page 3, it revealed a whole lot more info, including a fact that there was a separate New York will, but that didn't matter, because I now had the name of Shirley Murdock Cheaney.

My elation was fairly short lived however when I checked the SSDI online. For there I found that Shirley M. Cheaney had passed away in August of 2001, the very same month that I started my Knapp research in earnest. I paused to reflect what a strange trip this travel down Knapp road has been all these years.

Looking through old Ft. Lauderdale news papers via Lexus Nexus, I found Shirley Cheaney's obituary. It turns out she was living in North Carolina when she died. Because she was a longtime resident of Ft. Lauderdale, she was remembered very fondly there. It also listed the names of her husband and children. I found some Cheaney addresses in that area of North Carolina and wound up writing some letters of introduction and what I was looking for. I'm sure in retrospect the letters had to strike the recipients as somewhat odd. Anyhow I mailed them off mid week and prepared to wait for what I thought was probably going to lead to another dead end or worse, no response at all. Three days later my phone rang!

The Cheaneys Lived Here

I remember it like it was yesterday. It was a Saturday evening July 2, 2005. Anne and I were watching The Grass Harp, one of my favorite movies. I rarely watch any movie more than once, but when I do, it's because it's a favorite. The Grass Harp has a great cast of characters. Sissy Spacek, Walter Matthau, Jack Lemon, Piper Laurie, Charles Durning and more, plus a fantastic soundtrack. It is a Truman Capote story about a lot of things, but central to it all is that when the wind blows the tall grass in a field, if you really listen and are open to it, then stories of those who came before us will be passed along to you.

The person on the other end of the line was Susan Cheaney, Shirley's daughter. Her Dad had received my letter and because he recently had a mild stroke, he asked her to call me to say YES. He knew Joe Knapp since the late 1930's, when he started dating his step daughter. Philip was pilot in WW2 and he married Shirley after the war. They had family photos of Marion and Joe and Joe's sister Claire and more and that he would be happy to pass along copies of them to me. Susan and I talked very cordially for about a half hour, I told her a little about about the web site and my research of how I found her family. We exchanged e mails etc. and Susan said she would get some copies of the family photos made the following week. When we hung up, all sorts of thoughts were running through my head, not the least was, I'm finally going to see the lowest profile Mr. Knapp of all. Dodi, or was it Doty? or was it Dod - Die? That question remained unanswered for oddly enough, no one in the Cheaney family had ever heard him called that and yet on Long Island that's the name that was stuck to him, like the hull of his capsized sail boat, he clung to for 5 hours in Bellport Bay in 1911. The Cheaneys only knew him as Joe Knapp.

Several days later a nice letter arrived from Mr. Philip Cheaney explaining that yes, I had the right family, he had family photos and a few stories to tell about Joe Knapp and life in Ft. Lauderdale in the 1930s and 40s, but that because of his medical condition, he would have his daughter Susan get in touch with me. And true blue Sue, also e-mailed me and sent off a nice package of photos too. They were far and beyond all my expectations. I can still recall the first time I saw an 8 x 10 sepia toned photo, of a casually and well dressed middle aged couple sitting on a very nice leather and rattan chaise lounge, with palm trees and flora behind them. There was no more guessing about what Dodi Knapp looked like. He was first and foremost a Knapp. Like his sister Claire (who I got a portrait of back in 2002) he had many of his father's features. His face seemed a bit rounder though and when I finally got a photo of his mother Sylvia in 2008 (Her passport photo from 1920) I could see some of her features too. But the first thing I thought after finally getting a good look at his face (the picture from a great distance in his Sea Sled in 1925 did not reveal much) or should I say heard was, a song from the soundtrack of the Grass Harp. It was a Benny Goodman live recording from the 1940s of a tune called "Close Your Eyes", a smooth dance number that just started playing in my head and does just about every time I look at that photo or if I hear the song I see that photo. Don't ask me why—but that's just what happens. If I don't hear that one, I hear the haunting Grass Harp theme. Other photos showed Marion sitting on the cabin roof of The Storm King Too,The Isle of Palms house from the rear in 1937, the dock on Sunset Lake, and many pics of Dodi and Marion out on the town in various night spots and restaurants in both NY and Lauderdale with family and friends, including all the Cheaneys, his sister Claire, his long time personal secretary and friend Ed Kiely, his niece Margaret and her husband Jack Raynor, Also several taken at the 1939 Worlds Fair,

Now there were several unknown photos of big mansions in the snow (perhaps J. P.'s Catskills home?) and one that looks like it may be the back part of the Currituck Mansion. And there were several of folks that had no IDs on them that no one in the Cheaney family knew who they were. But I am very happy to say I was able to ID one of them for the Cheaney's. It was of a gentleman in his 30's or early 40's, smiling nicely and standing by the water. I had a hunch who it might be and when I showed it to Fred Gillespie—BINGO ! with no hesitation at all he said " That's Milton Murdock" So for the first time, Susan got to see her Grandfather. It seems. that her mother never spoke much at all of her early life on Long Island to the family. As I mentioned, Shirley was around 12 years old when she moved to Ft. Lauderdale with her Mom and step father. Several of Fred Gillespie's younger friends, like Benny Savage, who is in his '80s and went to school with Shirley, told me all the boys at school were heartbroken when she moved away. Her childhood photos are indeed of a very pretty girl, but as an adult WOW! RADIANT is but one adjective, STUNNING is another. Those boys back in Brookhaven would all be crying in their beer to know such a pretty woman slipped out of town before they ever had a chance to ask for a dance.

Susan and I got to know each other over the next year and she was extremely helpful in asking her Dad questions or trying to find answers from wherever she could. But not only that, she really surprised the heck out of me when she journeyed to Long Island in November of 2006 for a reading, I gave at the Mastic-Shirley Library on this book and its Mastic area connections. It was a most perfect day and the turnout at the library was standing room only, about 200 folks that included several of my former school teachers, going back as far as the 5th grade, kids I went to school with, kids I played in the Knapp Mansion with, and all sorts of Mastic area residents both pioneers and newcomers. I in turn totally enjoyed giving Susan a tour of the area, her mother started out her life in, including the 1828 Old Southaven Church her Mom was baptised at in 1930, her childhood home, the little school house she walked to and of course the "Knapp Estate Tour" of Mastic Beach.

Growing up in Fort Lauderdale, where her Dad would commute to work by boat, I could tell we had a kindred spirit of the sea vibe going. We visited the dock where Knapp's Storm Kings first were berthed and she told me tales of her Mom catching fish on the same boats in Lauderdale. She took to the south shore of Long

Island, like a duck takes to a Knapp! We also drove over the Smith Point Bridge to Fire Island to visit the new the TWA Flight 800 Memorial on the ocean. Susan, who resembles actress Shirley McClaine, was a flight attendant for TWA for many years. She lost several co workers and friends on that ill fated 1996 flight and I lost a musician friend, who was on his way home to Paris. On a much brighter, but still highly emotional note, I introduced her to then 90 year old Fred Gillespie, who just by talking to me about his life in 2004, made all of this possible. I took a picture of the two of them sitting together, looking through her mother's Ft. Lauderdale scrapbook, that puts a lump in my throat.

Clairedale At Red Cedar Point

I mentioned, that I never found Claire Knapp's home on Peconic Bay at Red Cedar Point on the north shore of Hampton Bays. The first time I went out there was January of 2002 and it was snowing pretty good. I did not want to get stuck on some desolate roads in the woods, especially the one that ran along the edge of the Peconic Bay, and I still needed to get over to the South Shore of Hampton Bays and try to find Dodi's three 1940s-1952 Hampton Bays homes. The snow was coming down off and on but at least I had the name of the roads Dodi's homes were on. The second time I tried to find the Clairedale house out there was in October of 2005, not knowing it had been torn down that September. I thought I did find it as I discovered on Red Cedar Pond, a large 1930s era rambling Georgian Colonial that fit the description. It would turn out, I was just a stones throw (if you were Hercules) from where Claire's fine house once stood. The house I thought was hers, was built in the 1930s by a US Senator.

By being a native Long Islander and knowing the lay of the land, that just by driving around out there on Clairedale Drive and other rambling roads at Red Cedar Point, I always felt I had a pretty good visual of the way it was when Claire lived there from 1933-1959. It is still highly wooded and much of it is now a state woodland preserve. I must confess though, I was also very fortunate, because of the power of the internet, to get a very nice remembrance of what life was like especially on the water in the 1950s at Claire K. Dixon's. That story came from Stan, her only grandson that I never knew existed, until an e mail came in from out of the blue in 2003. But Stan's story is a wee bit more complicated and will have to be dealt with in another chapter. That said, I'll now dive like a submarine, leaving you with this observation. The name Knapp means top of the hill, but by the sea was where these Knapps always seemed to be at home.

CHAPTER
37

Business as Unusual Part III

Back in high school, I wrote a term paper on Andrew Carnegie and one of his most famous quotes that resonated with me then was, *"Put All Your Eggs In One Basket..."* which is often misquoted as *"Don't Put All Your Eggs In One Basket."* The rest of what Carnegie said, that is often left out was, *"And Watch That Basket Carefully."* Now Carnegie who became the richest man in the world, was of J. P.'s father's generation, and his childhood was far different than J.P.'s. Andrew made most of his fortune during a period of almost no regulation aka The Gilded Age. I wonder how he would of dealt with the Great Depression of the 1930s? J. P. who was already very secure financially at the start of the depression, seemed to use some of Carnegie's wisdom during it. (it is well known he always kept his eye on all his baskets) During the 1930's he adjusted his business empire placing a strong focus on his major source of income, magazine publishing. In 1937 as the Depression was starting to light-en somewhat, he allowed Fortune Magazine to publish the most in depth look anyone would ever get at his magazine empire at Crowell-Collier Inc. Fortune's August issue, would print 14 , 11" x 14" pages with 27 photos including one of the rarely photographed J P. In this chapter, which is based on the Fortune article and memoirs from books of some of his inner circle, you will learn a little more about not only J.P.'s business acumen, but also of how he interacted with some of his real good eggs, a dedicated and trusted group of basket watchers, who kept a close eye on things when J. P, was somewhere out in his duck blind.

"*SIRED BY LENIN OUT OF MARIE ANTOINETTE!*" Is how political. economic, and social journalist, John T .Flynn (1882-1964) once summed up J. P. Knapp. I have to be honest and say I never quite fully grasped exactly what Flynn meant by that, other than perhaps Knapp was a man of such great contrasts, that Flynn thought those two extremes were the best description he could think of. Flynn, was an associate editor, who wrote articles for Colliers and Woman's Home Companion during the 1930s, He would prove to swing a wide path in his ideals from the 1920s to 1950s as he moved from arch liberal to arch enemy of FDR and the New Deal and then arch supporter of Joe McCarthy and finally to obscurity. In recent years, his later books, essays and ideas have been embraced by the Libertarian party. However Flynn's impression of Joseph Palmer Knapp has remained like Knapp has to the general public—very obscure and perhaps only fully understood by his Crowell-Collier and Publication Corporation basket watchers.

I don't think Flynn was one of Knapp's basket watchers. But Lee Maxwell sure was. Lee Wilder Maxwell 1881-1948 was a career "Ad Man" and longtime Knapp inner circle executive at both Crowell and Collier. He joined Crowell around 1913 and rose to be both President and then Chairman of the Board of Crowell-Collier when Knapp merged the two. An excellent lifelong golfer, he lived in Greenwhich, Conn., on an estate he purchased for $300,000 in September of 1929, just a month before Black Friday. He kept apartments too, in NY City during the years associated with Knapp. Maxwell was always on the top paid executive lists published in the NY Times during the Depression. He was also on the boards of several banking trusts with other Knapp friends and associates.

Ed Anthony (1895-1971) was at Knapp's magazines from 1924-1954, rising through the ranks all the way to publisher of both *Woman's Home Companion* and *Colliers's* in the '40's. In 1960 he wrote of Maxwell, Knapp and the Depression in his book *This Is Where I Came In*: "*Lee Maxwell announced in the early '30's that he was reasonably confident that Crowell-Collier could weather the storm without the dismissal of a single employee, if everyone understood the need for salary cuts, which would begin with a big slash in his own pay—with the support of chief stockholder Joseph Palmer Knapp, Maxwell had successfully carried this program through; and in accordance with his promise, the cuts in compensation were restored a few years later when things improved.*" It seems you could take to the bank, the word of people who worked for J. P. Knapp.

Anthony also wrote of the subscription selling crews in the rural areas where folks expressed a desire to buy the magazines in 1930-34, but just didn't have the cash. Many subscriptions were bartered for with chickens and eggs and many crews carried crates in their cars to house the chickens they accepted for magazines.

And of J. P. Knapp himself, Anthony recalled all the different appraisals of him, that both he and his associates would experience over the years Like his "explosive nature", that terrified all around him, (mouth corners drawn down, voice raised to a quivering roar, blue eyes swimming in tears) of his "*impractical editorial ideas*" some quite grandiose, like solving the countries labor problems by locking up a group of industrial chieftains and labor leaders in a hotel at Collier's expense, with Collier's having exclusive rights to publish what occurred in the room. In looking back, Anthony thought that full measure of the man, always far outweighed these minor criticisms.

He was the longtime Chairman of the Crowell board when Lee Maxwell had a falling out with J. P. Knapp in 1937 over J. P. taking sides in a dispute Maxwell had with then number two man at Crowell president Thomas Beck. As a result Maxwell resigned. It was this act that led Knapp finally to emerge from what was his very comfortable behind the scenes shadow and become in print, the head of what he already had been for over three decades. This was done in typical Knapp style (as low key as possible) and in the fall of 1937 the name Joseph P. Knapp, Chairman of the Board, first appeared in the masthead of his 4 magazines, American, Woman's Home Companion, Collier's and Country Home. Their combined circulation in 1937 was 9,496,841 which brought in $37,000,000 revenue to the Crowell-Collier coffers.

After resigning, Maxwell however did stay on the Crowell executive board. The four man "executive committee" consisted of himself, Tom Beck, "Cap" Winger, and "The Old Man" (J.P.) . In the 1940's Maxwell struck out on his own and became publisher of PARADE, a Sunday News Magazine imitator of Knapp's THIS WEEK that J. P. started in 1935.

"Hello Country Bumpkin"

That would be Wheeler McMillen (1893 -1992) An academically educated farmer-journalist from Ohio. I would not call Wheeler a bona fide Knapp basket watcher, but because he writes so honestly about his personal experiences at Crowell in his memoir "Nine Decades In The Human Race" I want to include it. I feel he helps fill out the portrait of life at the Knapp magazines and perhaps the admiration Joseph P. Knapp always seem to hold dear for country folks and country life.

Wheeler's first dollar he ever earned from writing, occurred in 1910, the year he graduated high school and the magazine that paid him was Farm & Fireside. In the early 1920s Wheeler, had written a few free lance articles for them, for what was considered to be very high pay for an unknown writer ($75 per article). At the magazine they considered him a regular contributor and asked for a photo and bio. One day in 1922, he was sent a telegram asking him if he would come New York at Collier's expense to discuss a job offer. There editor George Martin took him to lunch at the Ritz-Carlton and put him up in a first class hotel for a week to let him get a feel for New York. before offering him $5,000 a year to become an associate editor (a reporter basically) That was more than Wheeler needed to accept the job. As a comparison, an average white collar salary in 1922 was about $1,100. A careful and conservative man, Wheeler returned to Ohio and talked it over with all of his family before leaving the family farm in the hands of a hired man. His Dad was semi retired by then, making Wheeler's big move to NY a little easier. Within a year his wife joined him.

Wheeler's impression of Tom Beck was, that Beck cared little about what the magazines printed as long as the circulation and advertising rates kept pace with main competitor Curtis ,who published the Saturday Evening Post and Ladies Home Journal. In 1929 Tom Beck decided that "Firesides are out of date_ everyone has radiators now" and that Farm & Fireside needed a major make-over into a much slicker publication to compete with their major competitor Curtis Publications, *"Country Gentleman"*

George Martin whose personal depression was all ready preceding the stock market crash, phoned Beck from a speak easy where he was keeping company with W. C. Fields at four in the morning. Martin wanted to let Beck know where he could stick Country Home. Resignation accepted. Wheeler then found himself answering to a new editor named Thomas Cathcart, who came from an advertising background and could care less about agriculture. He proved to be far more difficult to work for and tried to jettison McMillen via difficult assignments (like interviews with Henry Ford and then Governor Franklin Roosevelt) only to have McMillen shine at the tasks and come back each time looking better and better in the eyes of Tom Beck.

The first early encounter Wheeler had with J. P. is mentioned that it came in a letter. It was in the regular reader mail in regard to an economic article Wheeler authored on the effect of a Hoover administration program, the Reconstruction Finance Corporation was having on farmers. Knapp mentioned that Mr. McMillen had left off three zeros in his figures. The amount should be billions not millions of dollars. Obviously a number that was not often in Wheeler's thoughts.

By 1934, with the magazine's new direction making little progress for Knapp's bottom line, Beck decided to move Country Home's direction back to a solid farm emphasis. Wheeler was given the editors spot and Cathcart was moved "up" to editorial director. When the two walked back to their offices, McMillen asked Cathcart how he interpreted Beck's directive. Cathcart said " Well if I am the editorial director, then I expect to direct" To which McMillen answered "Well OK... if I am the editor, I expect to edit and if I need any direction I'll call you." A few months later Cathcart moved over to Knapp's, This Week Sunday news magazine

Wheeler mentions that Knapp who had recently acquired the rights to a high speed roto gravure process, decided to utilize Country Home as his first magazine to use the new process rather than letter press. McMillen said Knapp did not listen to his press people, who said it wasn't quite ready and "My red Duroc Hogs came out purple and the dignified Angus cattle that every cattleman knows is black, came out looking red or yellowish." They had to suspend the series while the process was tweaked.

Although he would make some considerable contributions to Country Home's modest rise in ad revenues over the years, Wheeler found himself being promoted to Editorial director in 1937 and started to feel useless. He looked around for new opportunities, taking a position with the Farm Journal in March of 1939 staying with that publication until 1963. Just a few months after Wheeler left Crowell-Collier, Knapp pulled the plug on Country Home.

"Best Man In The Business"
That would be how J. P. characterized his most senior magazine executive, Gertrude Battles Lane (1874-1941) She had started at Woman's Home Companion

in 1903, which was three years before Knapp bought it. In 1912 she became its editor in chief and rose to be a vice president and director at Crowell-Collier. She was also an advisor to American and Country Home. During the World War, she was a member of Hoover's Food Administration and when he became President, she was an advisor on several White House Conferences including Child Health and Protection, Home Ownership and Building. In the 1930s her budget for the Companion was over $800,000 and her salary was $52,000, which was only exceeded by a hand full of women in the entire United States. Fortune who said Knapp was rarely, if ever seen at the offices of Crowell, nonetheless was "The Unquestioned Boss Of His Domain" Ed Anthony supports that observation when he writes of an encounter J. P. had with Gertrude in late 1936.

"...Quick tempered, frequently cantankerous, an absolutist who took a dim view of those who disagreed with him, he managed nevertheless to emerge as a strong character, when you least expected it. Gertrude Lane, the brilliantly successful editor of The Companion, once told me how Knapp stormed into her office to repeat the low opinion he had expressed in a letter he'd sent her, savagely attacking a new type of art work in the Companion that had been introduced by the talented new art director Henry Quinan and was being hailed in the trade as a welcome departure from the stereotyped magazine illustration.

When Knapp reached the shouting stage, she ordered him out of her office, pointing out as she did that her middle initial B stood for the name Battles and she hoped he grabbed the significance of that! I recall how the rumor gained currency that Knapp was so resentful of having been shown the door, that he planned to fire Miss Lane. And I remembered how many surprised people there were around the office when Fortune showed up about six months later and published a comprehensive article about the Crowell operation and in it Knapp described Miss Lane as "The Best Man In This Business" Knapp - Lane hatchets were permanently buried when Miss Lane read Mr. Knapps handsome compliment!

I don't know if they had smaller battles prior to 1936-37, but I would not be surprised if they did. If so, they may of also carried over to the home front, for Gertrude lived in the same apartment building at 330 Park Ave as the Knapps did, prior to their move into Riverhouse. Although having a no nonsense look in the photos I have seen of her, similar to those stern matrons who were leaders of the anti saloon league, it was headlined in Gertrude's NY Times rather large obituary, that she was a staunch opponent to prohibition.

Colliers and Chenery

Collier's was undoubtedly the best known magazine that Knapp owned and the only one that carried the name of its founder. When he took it over in 1919, the one time revered publication was not in very good shape, thanks to the carelessness and high style living of the last Collier. Had Bob Collier's friends like Conde Nast, not wrestled it from his control shortly before he died of a heart attack in 1918, there's a good chance the magazine would of been nothing but a footnote in publishing history. That said, just because Knapp took it over at the initial purchase price of 1.75 million and invested millions more, it did not have a very fast turnaround. The immediate problems he faced were a paper shortage from the war, a printers strike and business depression. His long term problem of finding the right guy to fill the editors chair, proved much more difficult to solve. Turnover at that position was such in the early '20s that there was an inside joke in the trade that you did not want to wait more than twenty minutes for an appointment to see the editor, because there was a good chance he would not still be there after that!

In reality there were only three editors in the first six years before William Ludlow Chenery (1884-1974) took the position in 1925. Chenery stayed as editor for 18 years and then publisher for another 7. Collier's was on life support from Knapp's other Crowell magazines when Will first came there after many years working as a newspaperman. His 1952 book "So It Seemed", offered up many insights and stories into his life and times at Collier's magazine and more importantly some more glimpses of J. P. Knapp's personality,

Chenery commented at several different times over the years that, Knapp never wrote a single line that appeared in Colliers's during the time he was its editor. But Knapp was not at all shy in sharing his opinions of just what should be in his magazine. He would however always defer, sometimes very painfully to all involved, to the decisions of his editors. This heated incident occurred just weeks after Chenery's arrival, when he received a memo from Knapp proposing an article. "I answered Mr Knapp in the journalese of a newspaper shop. "Is this a must or am I to use my judgement?"...a few days later Mr. Knapp came to my office (UH OH!) in a mood of perfectly restrained fury. He opened up directly "Chenery! How many times do I have to tell you that there are no MUSTS in this office?" I said, "Mr. Knapp, you are the principal stockholder in the company that owns this magazine. I respect the rights that goes with ownership. If you want to have that editorial line taken, that is your privilege. If however, you want me to use my judgement, then I am going to use it and do what I think is best for the magazine. Mr. Knapp said grimly: "You have got to use your judgement." I said, "All right, I will" Then he followed "Are you going to publish that article?" I said, "I am not" For a long and angry hour we discussed the question of the article. He insisted on my making the decision, but he fought to bend my judgement to his will. I did not yield.

Chenery went on to say that he felt J. P. Knapp's insistence on the editor making the final call is part of what brought success to Collier's over the years. I believe these two developed the utmost respect for each other and they must of become pretty close confidants too, because Chenery is the only person I have read (after J. P's passing) that in regard to the big falling out with his own father in the 1890s, J.P. told him that his father never forgave him and he only wished his father could of lived to see his success.

One early decision that Chenery made, that cost Collier's a few subscribers, had the full backing of J. P. Knapp and probably everyone else at the Crowell shop. Collier's decided to do an extensive investigation into how the prohibition law was working. Chenery sent three reporters around country to look into it at all levels. The resulting articles concluded there was a complete breakdown in law enforcement, which was a real hot button issue in those days. Collier's became the first big league publication to call for repeal of an unworkable law. In doing so it lost 3,000 outraged subscribers and picked up 400,000 new ones.

In spite of these strides, in 1927 the major stockholders were getting very nervous at the red ink that was still flowing at Collier's. Ten million had already been spent to turn things around. So J. P. called them together for a dinner in which he showed them a chart. The chart showed that it would only take three million more to make Collier's totally self supporting. There were a lot of doubting Thomas' at the dinner, so he then offered them Plan B. He would fund the magazine himself in exchange for their stock. They went with plan A and by 1929 the magazine was in the black. In most of the years that followed, Collier's was second only in circulation to the Saturday Evening Post, which remained a thorn in J. P.'s side for the rest of his life.

Chenery built up his staff and the contributing writers he hired, were some of the country's best. P. G. Woodehouse, Kathleen Norris, Ring Lardner, H. G. Wells, Sinclair Lewis, and Zane Gray. It may of came as a Big Fat surprise to Ernest Hemingway, just a few years after the Big Fat Slob incident to find himself on Collier's payroll too, as a war correspondent.

Thomas Hambly Beck

As I would find out in 2007, from Joan O'Connell, daughter of Dodi's right hand man, Ed Kiely, Dodi Knapp had a major fight with his father in 1929, leaving the family business for good and retiring at age 37. As I previously stated, if there is one person I think that filled in the roll of a son, in a father and son business relationship, my vote would go to Tom Beck. In researching him I found some other parallels to Dodi Knapp in regards to Beck's interests, particularly in aviation. He first flew in 1912 and was a lifelong proponent of civil aviation, flying all around the world, as well as having his own plane to commute to the Springfield, Ohio printing plant. Therefore my profile of him here will go far beyond those of his coworkers at Crowell-Collier.

Beck was born in Oakland, California on July 24, 1881 and you may recall, he was criticized by Ding Darling, for being nothing more than a stand in for JP to do his bidding on the Presidential Wildlife Restoration Committee. The fact is as a boy, Beck fished the streams and roamed the hills out in California, providing memories that would stay with him for life with his involvements on behalf of conservation both with J. P.'s organizations and independently.

Young Tom was a super salesman. He started out selling soap door to door for Borax and quickly made a reputation as the most amazing soap salesman in the business. He once said "If you know how to sell soap or Fuller brushes, you can sell anything." He was sales manager for Proctor & Gamble before joining P. F. Collier publishing, around the start of WWI, only to be tossed out the door there along with Cap Winger and several other young turks over editorial differences. They encouraged J. P. K. to buy Collier in 1919, moved back in with him and stayed for life. He was President of Crowell-Collier from 1934-1946, then succeeded Knapp as Chairman of the Board when Knapp finally retired in 1946.

Fortune reported on the goings on at President Beck's office in 1937 thusly: *The two doors to Tom Beck's office are never closed. Through them all day long moves a procession of Crowell executives and editors. Albert E "Cap" Winger, the able vice president and treasurer, who along with a mass of other duties, directs Crowell's huge purchasing program: bald pated John Brehm, whose circulation department is perhaps the best in the publishing business: James A. Welch called "Judge" because he looks owlish, who is director of advertising; Malcom Smith who is considered by many outsiders as the shrewdest promotion man in the field; William P. Larkin, a jolly Irishman who runs the Collier book business, Gertrude Lane, especially smart editor of Woman's Home Companion, and a thoroughgoing executive; William L. Chenery, quiet scholarly editor of Colliers, Through those contacts, Beck exercises the active management of the company. But nowhere in that group, even in Tom Beck, do you find the Big Boss. You do not even find him at 250 Park Ave, but in a tower 4 blocks away, whither Tom Beck can leg it in nine minutes when the boss man wants to talk business.*

A glimpse of Beck's positive outlook was revealed in this short anecdote. When asked one time if he played the violin, Beck's answer was *"I don't know, I never tried."* He would ask rhetorical questions until his listener found themselves saying yes every few seconds. There was a framed sermon from Beck in many a Crowell office titled *"The Viewpoint Of A Salesman"* There is a chapter in Ed Anthony's book titled "The Well Nigh Incredible Beck" in which Anthony starts out by stating *"The most colorful human being I have ever known, was Thomas Hambly Beck — or should I say most astonishing. He conformed to no pattern and was almost completely unpredictable. If I could devote the time and money to the project, it would take two or three years and a small fortune in travel expense, I would like nothing better than to address myself to a full scale biography of Beck."* After reading all the great Beck stories involving Einstein, FDR including one that offered Beck "incontrovertible proof " directly from FDR, that he would not seek a third term, Harry Truman and more that Anthony crammed into just one chapter, I would have to say, if Ed Anthony had pursued a book about Knapp, I would of no doubt been doing something else these last eight years.

Here are some glimpses in Ed's chapter on Tom. Anthony himself described Tom as "having that elusive quality known as personality" and of being a combination of "George F. Babbit, Don Quixote, Benjamin Franklin, Baron Munchhausen, Jesse James, Richard The Lion Hearted, Raebalis and other warring elements." Bob Ripley, the cartoonist of Ripley's Believe It Or Not, who also had a Times Square museum of oddities, said to Anthony after meeting Tom for the first time "I'll Never Be The Same, Why Don't We Make A Fortune By Putting Him On Permanent Exhibit." One associate who wanted to remain anonymous said: "Life is too short to try to figure out the gyrations of Beck's mind. He often would cancel out on Tuesday, what he declared to be company gospel n Monday."

Web Blanchard was his personal secretary for 5 years and offered up these observations: He recalled him as a GIANT with a tremendous mind. He could discuss technical items with the engineers and scientists, who were employed by our advertisers on their own levels On my first visit to his home, I noticed the "5 Foot Shelf Of Books " of the World's Great Essential Literature, that Collier's Books sold to subscribers. I asked. "If he thought anyone ever plowed through them all." He said, "He knew of at least one person who did— himself." One of those volumes in the 5 foot shelf was Adam Smith's "Wealth Of Nations" published in the 19th century that was a favorite of Beck's. Once at a party at his home, Beck remarked that for non conformity "the world whips you with its displeasure" to which a friend replied " I suppose that is from the epigrams of one Thomas Beck?" and Beck replied. "No—you'll find it in the essays of Emerson, a feature of the Harvard Classics. Available on easy terms. No home should be without a set. Published by us, of course". And with that, he produced some sales literature from his desk and handed it to his startled guest.

His recollection of what he read was often reliable, but he certainly had his off moments too. He once told a luncheon companion that prefab housing had actually been a thriving industry in 18th century England. He said he had read about it in Boswell and Johnson. The companion challenged him and Ed Anthony wound up with the assignment of finding the passage that would prove Beck right in the 1000 page book, finally finding this obscure reference. *Pray do sir. We will go pass the winter amid the blasts of St. Kilda, We shall have fine fish and take some books with us. We shall have a fine vessel built by some Orkney men to navigate her. We must build a tolerable house, but may carry with us a wooden one ready made, requiring nothing but to be put up.* Beck's friend wasn't buying that as proof of a thriving pre fab industry, so Tom sent Ed to dig deeper. Nothing more was ever found

The merging of Crowell and Collier by J. P., helped set up some of the friction that eventually caused the spat between Beck and Maxwell causing Maxwell to eventually resign. Anthony described those days this way. "Beck was at his best as a salesman, even his detractors around the office of which there were many agreed with that assessment—at one time you found yourself labeled either as a Crowell man or a Collier's man. Beck lacked some of the orthodox approach that some of the older Crowell crowd expected out of an upper-echelon publisher, but eventually he won over those who viewed him for some time with suspicion and a touch of alarm. He was always controversial, but his detractors shrunk as his methods, frequently startling, improved even the good financial showing under Maxwell. Eventually he became Crowell-Collier's most successful CEO, getting his opportunity to show what he could do when Lee Maxwell broke with Joseph Palmer Knapp over Beck's methods. I don't know if this one was the big one for Maxwell or just one of a series of Beck's antics that steamed his clams, but Anthony described it detail.

The Last Straw on the 13th Floor?

Beck was always talking about showmanship. Our reception rooms were lacking in this quality, he felt, especially the one on the thirteenth floor. That floor, at 250 Park Ave ran north and south from 46th to 47th Street and east to west from Park to Vanderbilt avenues_ a square block, in other words housed the chief editorial and executive offices.

Writers, author's agents, big advertisers, whom Beck and many others knew— many of them important, well-known people, wound up in the thirteenth floor reception room and Beck decided to give them a little showmanship. He arranged to have a UP news ticker placed in the reception room. Beck seldom stopped to figure out where his authority ended and that of President Maxwell began. It never occurred to him to get Maxwell to approve the installation of the ticker.

Maxwell, normally calm and collected, seldom exploded. But this time he did —with a loud bang. First he sent Beck a blistering inter office memo. This he followed up with a verbal blast. By what authority did Beck think he could change the character of Crowell's main reception room? And how could he even think of making such a move without consulting his associates?

Beck said the reception room was dead. He wanted to impart some showmanship. *"Fine showmanship!"* Maxwell retorted, " *We leave our magazines lying around on tables so our callers can look at them while waiting and you decide to take their minds off our own product with this new toy of yours."*

Maxwell's memo had called for the immediate removal of the ticker. So Beck had it moved, but not off the premises. He set it up in Collier's editorial department. This department was badly crowded and there was no place to put it where it would not interfere with the work of busy people. Nevertheless it was installed and immediately became unpopular with editors when employees from other departments strolled over to look at the news. The chatter of the visitors became a distraction and one day the ticker was removed.

One editor remarked *"Tom was always playing games and this one allowed him to play make believe newsman. I overheard him tell a big advertiser he needed it to keep up with events as they happened or else he felt lost. The advertiser was very impressed"*

The Big Shuffle

In 1942 Beck asked Anthony if he would like the job of publisher at the Companion which was vacant for a year with the passing of Gertrude Lane. Ed said he would and Tom said he was going to recommend him for the post. A week later Ed found himself at a luncheon with Beck, Cap Winger and J. P. Knapp. J. P. made it official that day, telling Ed that it had been decided he would become the publisher of the Companion effective Jan 1, 1943. Ed did very well as publisher there and when Beck took Knapp's place as Chairman of the Board in 1946, Cap Winger moved into Beck's old President chair. In 1947, Winger noting how successful Anthony was with Companion, sounded him out about taking over as publisher of Colliers. Anthony said he was flattered in the confidence, but for personal reasons wanted to stay out of the Collier's picture. Winger approached him again a few months later with the same results and then again the following year, spending an hour or so in closed door meeting, telling Anthony it was his duty to take the position. Winger made it clearly known he was not pleased with Anthony's rejecting the offer. Ed Anthony's major reservation was that he felt his mentor and longtime friend Beck, did not want him to take that job. Because at that time Beck himself was wearing both hats as Chairman and Publisher and trying to succeed at putting an ailing Collier's back on it's feet. What Anthony didn't know and perhaps Beck didn't either too, was that Beck himself was getting sick and his personality was changing, especially towards Anthony. When Ed felt he had to talk to Tom about the pressure Winger was placing on him and what his advice was. Tom told him that taking the job was "Entirely Up to You."

Unknown to Anthony at that time, upon Beck taking Knapp's place as Chairman, it was agreed with Winger taking over as President, that Winger alone had the free hand to make all of the personnel decisions and changes. (I would not be surprised if perhaps this was not J. P. Knapp's final executive decision) It would prove to be a reluctant assent by Anthony, as he wound up running both magazines and his relationship with Beck changed radically the last few years of Beck's life. Tom became increasingly hostile towards Ed, but he probably was not aware at first that he was a getting very sick. Beck resigned as Chairman of the Board in the spring of 1951 and would be dead by the the fall. None the less in his memoir Anthony recalls all the good times with Tom Beck as far out weighing the tension that existed between them at the end.

By The Numbers
Because much of Fortune's readership was and probably still is comprised of big picture and big number executives, I am including a few of the numbers that Knapp's basket watchers kept an eye on for him in 1937. 70 plus years later they are still pretty impressive. The presses in the eight story one city block Springfield, Ohio plant turned out 84,666,000 magazine pages a day. One days supply of paper to print his 4 magazines weighed 610,661 pounds. The Weiss Speed Dry patent, that Knapp wisely bought up, but took some initial tweaking to apply to his needs, allowed him to speed up the RPMs on his 122 presses from 3,500 to 15,000 per hour. The ink was dry within 5 feet of the paper leaving the point where it was first applied. 468,000 pounds of special highly volatile ink was used in a years time, at a cost of $745,700. Second class postage to mail magazines to subscribers then cost $2,635,000.

Stranger Than Fiction
In writing this chapter, I had a touch of deja vu of an experience I had in the late 1990's. I initially was approached by and then flown first class to NYC to have a meeting with a major book publisher, for a project they wanted to explore the feasibility of getting into. It seems one of their editors had read my stock car racing books and pitched me to the big deciders as "Our Guy To Write Our NASCAR Project"

I recall getting some new clothes for the big meeting. The fight to NY was early, but uneventful other than being the first time I ever flew up front in those wider seats. I spent about an hour or so past our appointed time in one their outer offices being plied with caffeine and danish. I skimmed through some of their publications, but mostly passed the time looking out the windows at east and south views of mid town Manhattan. They sent an assistant in several times to apologize for keeping me waiting, then took me to a very nice lunch, at what I would later learn was considered to be the finest Chinese restaurant in Manhattan. There were dishes on the menu, that I never saw on the one at the Patchogue Royal, where I first sampled Chinese food as a kid in the early 1950s. A sentry stood attentively at our table the whole time, solely to refill our water glasses when ever anyone took a sip. I'm sure his salary was reflected in the bill, which I caught a discrete glimpse of as it was passed over to the big boss. Lunch for the four of us was higher than a months rent at my then three bedroom Nashville apartment.

The meeting that followed was a strange one, as I watched my companions crash into each other over a series of what seemed silly arguments, that led me to look out the window and wonder what time I would make it home. By the time we wrapped it up around 4 PM, I saw the whole deal "going out of the park" to use a stock car term of when a car goes over the wall.

For the trip home, it was a big tip to the cabbie for driving like Dale Earnhardt to make my flight. Only to be delayed well over 2 hours at La Guardia airport because of weather in Chicago. I wound up getting fed a full course dinner on America Airline's nickel. My hunch on going over the wall with their "NASCAR project" came to reality after several frustrating months dealing with them via the phone, only to be the last to know the big boss had pulled the plug on the whole shebang at least two months prior. Did I mention the publishers name? Collier Books! which in the 1990s was an internationally owned corporation and 4 decades past Knapp's ownership.

CHAPTER

38

The War Years

Funny thing about the title of this chapter, if you said it or read it during the era I was playing with my friends in the abandoned Knapp mansion, it usually meant only one thing: World War II. Even though there was something called the Korean War that was still going when we dragged the WWI airplane and radio parts (we saw the dates on them) out of Knapp's barn.

This chapter is going to cover a range of people, places and events in the decade that might have been called the fabulous '40s had it not been for The War Years. In thinking about the term in the context of most of the Knapps who were living at the end of the decade, War Years included the Civil War, the Spanish-American War, World War I ("The War To End All Wars"), World War II and the start of the Korean War. In terms of history, it boggles my mind that Joe and his sister "Netty" Knapp were young children when Grant accepted Lee's surrender at Appomattox. Incidentally, President Grant was also a guest at their childhood home on more than one occasion, as was Lincoln during his first campaign. Years after their parents' presidential guests had gone home, Joe and his sister would still be witnessing history in the 1940s. The fact that both of them saw the end of so many bloody conflicts give way to the terrifying atomic age really puts a perspective to the war years.

For Sale By Owner

Ahhh the lexicon of real estate advertising. It sure hasn't changed much over the years. Consider this classified ad that appeared for the first time in the NY Times on July 23, 1939.

MASTIC BEACH (Monroe Dr and Dogwood Rd) Charming old colonial residence of 14 large rooms, 4 baths, 2 lavatories; overlooking Great South Bay and Fire Island; pine paneled living room (cost $7,000); 6 fireplaces, random wood floors, sun deck, solarium, General Electric oil furnace and humidifier, brass pipe, largest Fridgidaire: perfect condition ; with 3 landscaped acres $11,500. 9 additional acres of lawn with tennis court and outbuildings available; caretaker will show; exceptional opportunity for hotel, club or sanatorium. Owner, Room 3202 580 5th Ave. City

True this home was sitting on property that went back to pre Revolutionary war colonial days. It's probable builder, Frank M. Lawrence, certainly had the colonial pedigree of America's founding fathers. Captain James Lawrence, uttered his immortal words "Don't Give Up The Ship" during the War Of 1812. His lesser known words were "Fight her till she sinks" as his men carried him below decks aboard the USS Chesapeake on June 4, 1813. Well in July of 1939, it certainly appeared that Dodi Knapp was giving up his country "ship" and the last piece of the grand estate. It was his country seat if you will, since shortly before the US entered into WW1, when he and his buddies took the skies from his waters edge to hunt German U Boats.

Over the years of studying deeds, maps and property atlases, I believe that the actual mansion I knew as a kid, was built by Frank Mauran Lawrence, circa 1899-1900, I recently have found some Lawrence estate journals, that describe Frank's sister Emma as living in a very opulent residence, compared to the 18th century mansions in Mastic nearby at that location in 1904. Actually the initial classified ad is very accurate. I know that after both Claire and Dodi bought it in 1916, they kept many of the local towns people busy constantly making improvements to the house and grounds. Cut Redin's grandfather installed the oil burner, that replaced the coal furnace. Center Moriches masons, Barber and Smith installed the livestock ponds for Claire and the artificial streams for Dodi's golf course that Clarence Penney built. As for the total amount of rooms, I guess we kids must of counted two walk in closets as rooms, they certainly were big enough. I recall on the first day the gang of us set foot in there, we counted 22 rooms including all the bathrooms and lavatories on all three floors, at least three times.

In 1939 as the curtain was finally being torn down on the terrible economic cloud that had devastated much of America, it was lifting in Europe on a far worse drama. On September 1st, Hitler invaded Poland. The combination of the two, may of been the one reason that no one had bought the Knapp place during the summer of '39, in spite of the very attractive price of $11,500. I would love to have known, if any one actually drove out to look at it based on that ad. A few days after WWII officially started, this slightly revised one with an even lower price appeared on September 23.

MASTIC BEACH - SACRIFICE - *$9,750 Cost over $40,000 Jefferson Dr. and Dogwood Rd. Charming Colonial residence with 3 landscaped acres overlooking Great South Bay; 14 large rooms, 5 baths, paneled living room, 6 fireplaces, sun deck, solarium, oil furnace, brass pipe, Fridgidaire. Perfect condition. Caretaker will show IDEAL FOR HOTEL, CLUB or SANITARIUM, Additional land, tennis court, outbuildings available. Owner, Room 3202 580 5th Ave, N.Y.C.*

Note: the original price the Knapps paid for the estate in 1916 was $35,000. Of course that was with the 188 acres of land around it , but they probably conservatively put $50,000 or more into just home improvements alone over the quarter of century they lived there. The initial asking price of $11,500 was a real bargain, $9,750 was a real steal. and the final selling price just boggles my mind.

About the same time that I started writing the short stories that would grow into this book, Darby Penney was recording an oral family history from her father Arthur. I know that neither of us could of imagined (we had yet to even meet via the internet) that some of the stories Arthur told his daughter, would play important parts in this book. Because of his father's work, Arthur would grow up being in and out of all the estates in Mastic area. His Aunt Claire had already left her Mastic estate in 1925, when Arthur was quite young, but he recalled a visit there with his father, just before Arthur went off to college. This again would of been either in 1939 or '40 and at the time he said the mansion was up for sale and unoccupied. "There were antiques of all types. musical instruments, a piano, organ and beautiful furniture and fine artwork on the walls. I mentioned previously, that Louise Mauran, was a summer boarder at Arthur's grandmother's home around 1900 and it's where Frank Lawrence courted her. Arthur, who was the first member of the Penney family to go to college, went to Brown University in Providence RI. While there he wound up working part time as a butler for the Mauran family. He said in the interview that the widow Louise (Frank died in 1920) who was pretty well up there in age then, was reminiscing about her days in Mastic and said *"If we only knew what kind of people those Knapps were, we would of never sold them our estate."* Now keep in mind, this is before Darby Penney knew of me or had ever even heard anything at all about the Knapps. So she asked her Dad quite innocuously. *"What did Louise mean by that?"* Her Dad just said , *"I guess the Knapps lived a little too fast, for the very prim and proper Louise C. M. Lawrence"* I had also heard Arthur once describe his Uncle Willis as "a fast liver" and by looking at Willis' photo, I could tell just what he meant. In the 1930s ,Willis bought his Father a new Ford V8 Roadster. Now Merritt, who had never driven anything faster than a Model T, remarked after he lost control of his new Ford and nearly put it into a tree *"The Devil's In That Car—Did You See It Aim Right For The Tree?"* Ahhh, Fast Living With A Hot Rod Ford V-8!

I have often thought too about what Louise meant or how she knew "What kind of people the Knapps were" for I believe after 1916, Frank and Louise Lawrence did not return to Mastic? Yet news of the lifestyles of Dodi and Claire Knapp, must of reached them somehow. Perhaps via the Penney or Ross family grapevine? Whatever, it appears Mrs. Louise Carlo Mauran Lawrence just did not approve of the Knapp lifestyle.

An interesting side note about the Mauran family in America, who both Frank & Louise were part of (Yes Virginia, cousins do marry, just ask the royal family) The founder was Italian, Joseph Carlo Mauran, a shanghai victim at age 12, who after two years imprisonment at sea, ran from his English captors upon touching American soil during the mid 1700s. Settling in Rhode Island, and concentrating on ships and shipbuilding, he became one of the founders of the US Naval fleet during the Revolution. He saw service as both a privateer and a captain of a the war ship Washington. The Maurans and the Lawrences of New York intermarried. The Mauran family of Providence, are still in shipping, banking. Frank Mauran Lawrence's mother was originally Sarah Mauran, a founder of Sarah Lawrence College.

T HROUGH THE FALL OF 1940, DODI KEPT DROPPING THE PRICE FROM $9,000 to $7,000 and the final advertised price, I found in October was an unbelievable $4,950 which was more than $2000 below what he had invested in just the pine paneling alone for his 50 foot living room. When he finally found a buyer, America was just about year away from going full force into WWII and on New Years Eve of 1940, Dodi and Marion signed over the deed to the mansion and the 3.5 acres immediately around it, to the Smadbeck's Home Guardian Company. They in turn would resell it a week later for about $6,000 to George Sutter, a Greek immigrant, who managed the Grand Concourse Hotel in the Bronx. Sutter's wife Lillian, had purchased several other properties from the Smadbeck brothers before, so there is probably little doubt Warren and Arthur had themselves a buyer before they literally stole the mansion from Dodi Knapp. At that price, I'm surprised that one of the brothers didn't keep the home for themselves. Although their customers who were now building little bungalows, just a few hundred feet from the ballroom door, may have been too close for comfort. The Sutter's reportably had relatives summering in Mastic Beach in the 1930s, so they were probably well aware of the bargain showplace they had just bought. Their plans were to turn it into a summer boarding house and combination vacation home for themselves. The Smadbecks would also purchase the remaining property and scattered out buildings that consisted of homes and barns of the Knapp Estate. In 1938 the two towns of Mastic Beach were joined together and now sections 9 & 10 of Mastic Beach, were no longer separated by the remaining Knapp property. The earliest homes that went up on those grounds listed their address as The Knapp Estate. On some maps today, you still see this large square blank space in the dead center of Mastic Beach that represented Knapp's mansion 13 acre property hold back from 1938-1940. I doubt few who see it now, have any idea of what that blank space means.

In January 23, 1941, the local paper The Moriches Tribune reported: The remainder of the Knapp Estate including the original houses included in the original estate have been recently sold. Mr. and Mrs William Schluder have moved from the estate to their new home on Neighborhood Road. Willy and Honey Schluder, who were the last caretakers at the Knapp Estate, lived for most of their remaining years in Mastic Beach in the little gate house on the southeast corner of Monroe Dr. and Neighborhood Road. The gate house which had a tunnel that connected it to the Mansion a quarter mile to the south of it, has caught fire at least two times, most recently in 2005, but remains standing. I mentioned near the end of chapter 3 that Willy Schluder could well of been working at his part time custodian job at the Mastic Beach Fire House in 1959, when the alarm came in for the Knapp mansion.

The old 19th century barn on the east side of 1 acre Schluder property, finally fell completely down in 2003. The southern part of Knapp Road originally had passed on its way to the mansion between the barn and house. It was reconfigured into Monroe Drive in 1938, when Knapp sold the northern acreage, that became Section 9 of Mastic Beach. After Knapp left Mastic Beach for good, Willie took a job as a chef at Camp Upton in WWII. Both he and his wife Honey, remained active in social affairs of the town, especially with the fire department. They used to tell people, my Mother included, that Knapp gave them the gate house and property as a reward for their years of faithful service from the 1920s-1940. That said, the original 1938 file map of Section 9, does show their home and property remaining the property of Jos F. Knapp, but the deed to their home was between Home Guardian and themselves? I believe the Schluders stayed in Mastic Beach until about 1970. No one seems to know where they wound up, and Social Security does not have a record listed of their last known address. They never had any children.

In March 30, 1941, the Moriches Tribune ran this short item in the news of Mastic Beach. George Sutter of the Bronx drove down on Wednesday to look over his property. Mr. Sutter is the new owner of the old Knapp house and part of the Knapp estate. Mr. and Mrs. Sutter and family expect to spend their summers at the beach at their new home. As early as 1942, the Sutters started advertising in the NY Times offering "Beautiful Rooms and Country Boarding in Mastic Beach" Believe it or not, one of their early boarders was Dodi Knapp's right hand man Ed Kiely and his daughters. His daughter Joan told me that was the only time she was ever in the mansion. When Knapp owned it, the Kiely family stayed in the secretary house, just a stones throw from it. Her mother did not care for that situation at all said Joan, "We had no electricity and just a hand pump in the kitchen. My mother who was raised in NYC, did take well to living out in the sticks. She only came out there with us a handful of times in the 1930s."

In May of 1943, this ad appeared in the Times:

MASTIC BEACH - *for rent mansion, season, year, furnished, large garden, near beach, boating, fishing. reasonable, Sutter JErome 7- 7400*

The phone number was for the Grand Concourse Hotel. Frank Campbell, a pioneer Mastic Beach resident and high school friend of my sister, told me he used to see fairly large crowds at the mansion in the summers during the war years and he recalls feeding Sutter's cow apples. I do not know if George Sutter ever found a full time renter during the war years, but in 1949 he found himself not only a full time boarder, but also a future owner. That would be Father John P. Skelly, the newly appointed priest at St. Jude's R. C . Church in Mastic Beach.

Fr. Skelly certainly enjoyed himself living in the mansion and set about plans to convince his Brooklyn Diocese to eventually purchase it from George Sutter.

Meanwhile Out East

In 1941 Dodi and Marion Knapp started summering in Hampton Bays. Dodi's sister Claire had lived out there with her husband Willis, and daughters Peggy and Ann full time since the mid 1930s. Peggy whom her mother used to tease by saying "You were weaned by a Chow, I had nothing to do with it" was out of high school then and managing her mother's Clairedale kennel. Clairedale had expanded to a few other terrier breeds besides Sealyhams and in 1940 Peggy also started her own kennel there. Pennyworth would soon make a name for itself with the Whippet breed. In 1942 Willis and Claire divorced and Willis moved to Florida. Terry Hooper, his grandson by his first marriage to Dorothy Terry, visited with him in the 1960s and Willis told him the reason for the divorce was he wanted a son and Claire did not want any more children. She was almost 36 when she married Willis in 1925. By the time they were divorced she was 53! In October of 1942, two months before his 45th birthday, Willis enlisted in the Army and served stateside as a private during WWII.

Of Weddings and Weirdness

In 1943 Willis would remarry a woman named Lucille Rice in Florida. They had a son in 1944 and named him Willis Oliver Penney. I believe he may still live in Florida or Georgia, but I was never able to contact him. Claire also remarried around 1943-44, to a longtime Knapp family friend, Thomas Dixon aka Thomas Dixon Jr, which was the name his famous, one time celebrity father also used sometimes. We first met young Tom, as he was clinging to the overturned sailboat in Bellport Bay with Claire's brother in 1911 and later when he was a charter member in Aerial Coast Patrol at the Knapp Estate in 1917 and doing loop the loops with Lawrence Sperry over Pattersquash Island.

The Knapp-Dixon marriage went for a loop too and they separated after a short time. Claire's grand daughter Sibby told me that "That marriage was very brief, because Thomas Dixon was a very strange man.". This statement would become only slightly clearer, as I discovered more odd, albeit somewhat circumstantial facts and events about him. It appears that his life and fortunes revolved entirely around his fathers fortune and misfortune. As a boy he enjoyed a fantastic and privileged lifestyle on a beautiful waterfront estate in Virginia and fine town home on Riverside Dr. in NYC. In the early 1920s, he lived in Los Angeles, representing his father's motion picture interests, that seemed to fizzle after the success of Birth of A Nation. Sylvia (Claire & Dodi's mother) also lived in Los Angeles at that same time, for reasons unknown before moving to Europe. Tom wrote a letter of character reference that appears in Sylvia's US passport application in 1923. Sylvia would later write in her affidavit re: her lawsuit against the US Customs in 1925, that the reason for her move to Europe, was over disagreements with her children.

I have thought long and hard about including this next story or leaving it out because it may or may not be entirely connected. But there are certainly some facts that connect it to some highly unusual circumstances, that if it were any other family, but the Knapps, would probably of never made it into this book. I also thought of a another brief statement Sibby told me in 2001 upon learning of my intent to write a Knapp history, "My family has some very wild characters in its past that you may discover " Finally I thought that there was no way the Mike Knapp merry go round, I stepped onto very early in 2000, could be connected either, only to discover his family was Ft. Lauderdale neighbors with one Dodi Knapp! That only taught me you cannot assume anything when it came to trying to piece together the Knapp story. A tale which I have long ago concluded, can never be entirely told. With that caveat dear reader, you may proceed.

When his father went bankrupt in the '30s, Tom Dixon drifted, living in various places in New York, North Carolina and Washington, DC. A big question remains, namely if he may have been the same Tom Dixon who became involved with the American Fuhrer, Fritz Kuhn and his German American Bund activities of the late 1930s. This would seem ironic, as just a decade before, young Tom took to the skies from the shore of the Knapp estate to hunt German U-Boats in WWI. But in the light of reason, it is not that much of a stretch, due to fortune's fate of his racist father, who seemed to suffer huge losses from bad Wall Street advice given to him by "Jewish bankers." Then of course, their was his strong admiration and championship for the original Ku Klux Klan, which he had chronicled into fortune and fame in the early 1900s via his books, plays and film. The reconstituted Klan of the '20s, whose tactics the enigmatic senior Dixon disavowed, would loosely join forces with Kuhn's Bund in the '30s to fight communism, Jews and to propagate all sorts of hate and fear as they lobbied sympathetic Americans to keep "The Jew Deal" (as they called Roosevelt's administration) out of getting involved in the affairs of Europe.

The Bund's surreal rallies drew masses of goose-stepping, Nazi-uniform-clad sympathizers at their recreation camps like Camp Seigfried in Yaphank, Long Island. And in New Jersey and Wisconsin, the Bund grew with thousands of German-American citizens saluting Heil Hitler. In the little town of Mastic Beach, Bund leaders from Yaphank tried to recruit Paul Schulte at his tavern to join their ranks, only to be physically thrown headfirst out the tavern's door. Both Paul Sr. and Jr. were always proud of their German heritage, but they were apparently prouder of being Americans. I often wondered if the Schulte's German pal Willie Schluder was also there to help them escort the Nazis off the premises that day.

Kuhn visited Hitler a few times (once during the 1936 Olympics) but Hitler and his inner circle just wanted Kuhn and storm troopers to take a hike. When District Attorney Thomas Dewey of NY indicted Kuhn and his henchmen for embezzlement, they fled New York after a rally at Madison Square Garden, only to be arrested in Krumsville, Pennsylvania. A man only named as "Thomas Dixon of New York" was in the car with Kuhn and his comrades, but Dixon was released the following day. Kuhn went to prison and was deported after WWII. The Thomas Dixon who traveled with Kuhn also went under the alias of American Cherokee Indian "Chief New Moon" and Thomas N. M. Dixon. He gave hate speeches at the Bund's rallies. Life Magazine published a photo of him in 1938 on a stage, behind a podium emblazoned with a Swastika. Poorly focused, perhaps shot secretly, it's inconclusive evidence, but there are definite similarities to the photos I have of Tom Dixon from 1917. The major difference is the weight gain, but the senior Tom too, in middle age looked nothing like the slim dashing author and preacher he was in his younger days. Arthur Penney's remarks about the failure of the Knapp-Dixon marriage are simply attributed to Tom's heavy drinking, which could have been all there is to it. But the Dixon family background, always framed in controversy, keeps pulling at me.

Author John Roy Carlson wrote of his experiences as an undercover agent for the FBI who infiltrated the Bund in 1943. The book titled "Undercover, My Four Years In The Nazi Underworld Of America" mentions Carlson's brief encounter in New York with a Tom Dixon after the arrest. Carlson said Dixon was now very disillusioned with the Bund as Kuhn had made lots of promises, but Dixon had never been paid for all his work writing and distributing anti war leaflets and with Kuhn in jail, he did not know what he was going to do next.

Along with his WWI draft registration card, I also have a copy of the then 50 year old, Tom Dixon's WWII Draft Registration card from 1942. The most interesting revelations on it are that he lists, 580 5th Ave. NYC for his address (J. P. Knapp's offices) He states in three separate places, that the contact person at that address is Mr. Joseph F. Knapp, who will always know the whereabouts of the registrant. He also states he has no occupation or employer. It is signed Thomas Dixon Jr.

After he and Claire separated, Dixon moved back to Los Angeles to work as a writer at Universal Pictures, perhaps arranged through Antoinette's husband, Paul G. Brown, who sat on Universal's Board of Directors. Dixon's once famous father (his last public hurrahs seemed to occur in the 1930s as he backed Al Smith to run against Roosevelt) was still turning out novels, but they were mere rehashes of his work from 3 decades earlier and were largely ignored. There was also screenplay about a thinly disguised Bund and German takeover of the world, but it got shelved by the studios. The man who sold his Currituck island hunting retreat in 1918 to J. P. Knapp, would pass away in April of 1946. Claire never did actually divorce his son and she kept the name Claire K. Dixon.

A much longer lasting union started out in Ft. Lauderdale on February 19, 1945 when Mr. Joseph Fairchild Knapp walked his step daughter, Shirley Marion Murdock down the aisle to marry Army-Air Corp Major, Philip Norbourne Cheaney. After the war ended, Shirley and Philip spent most of their lives and raised their family in Ft. Lauderdale, Florida, before moving to North Carolina in the 1990s, Shirley passed away in August 21, 2001, which I find somewhat ironic as that was just a week from when I started out for New York on my initial research. As I stated earlier, I will always be deeply indebted to the Philip Cheaney and his daughter Susan for providing me with the only photos of Dodi and Marion Knapp that appear in this book, along with some stories on the lives and times of the Knapps at the Isle Of Palms and in NY.

In the late '40s, Philip and Shirley would become the guests of Dodi and Marion and take a sleeper train trip to New York. There they visited with J. P. and Margaret at River House and went to one of the ALCO printing plants where they watched Dodi change the roll of paper on a proofing press. They also ventured out to Hampton Bays and visited Claire's estate and kennel, picking out a pooch for their children back home. "Sir Suchcrust of Clairedale," a miniature Schnauzer, was later flown to Florida in the airline pilot's pocket!

Susan Cheaney and I have discussed and speculated on more than one occasion what her Mother's reaction might have been to my inquiries and findings, had I started this book say in the 1990s and found her. Susan told me her Mom never talked much about her early life before her own mother married Joe Knapp. I'm certain I would have enjoyed meeting Shirley. That said, I have always been extremely grateful to have discovered all the bits and pieces that came my way from such scattered sources over the years. It's amusing that back at the start I never thought I would ever have more than a short biographical sketch to write about the Knapps.

The Winter Of His Life

The '40s was a decade when Joseph Palmer Knapp lost several of his close friends and business associates. Samuel Untermyer, a former Columbia classmate and world famous attorney, who advised J. P. that he could successfully buy out his father's control of Major & Knapp in 1890, passed away in March of 1940. Untermyer was also partners with Knapp and Thomas Lamont in the initial purchase of Crowell in 1906. Lamont who was a full partner and CEO at J. P. Morgan, passed away in Florida on February 3, 1948. J. P. was named as an honorary pall bearer, but did not attend Lamont's New York City funeral, held just a few blocks from Knapp's River House apartment. I believe it may be because, J. P. was severely impaired visually at that time and did not want to be seen in that condition. I don't think it was because he was in North Carolina, as his health problems had led him to stop wintering at Mackey Island about 1946. The vision problems seemed a very cruel fate to have happened to a person who once had magnificent hand eye coordination. The kind that helped make him a champion at billiards, golf and marksmanship. Stating that 82 was a good age to retire, J.P. stepped down from his Chairmanship at Crowell-Collier in the spring of 1946. I don't know what the relationship between J. P. and Lee Maxwell was at the time, Lee passed away in autumn of 1948, but they were together for far too long for me to believe it remained as strained as it was in the 1930s, when Maxwell resigned as Knapp's Chairman of The Board.

Mother Daughter Suites

On September 17, 1948, while a guest at the Hot Springs Resort in Virginia, Mrs. Antoinette Knapp Brown would pass away at the age of 86. No details were revealed, but I couldn't help noticing that she died in a place very much like her mother did forty years earlier. The large rambling Victorian Hotel at Hot Springs, was very reminiscent of the mansion house Phoebe was at in Poland Springs, Maine. Somehow it seemed proper, that both ladies would pass away in splendorous surroundings, not unlike their original Knapp Mansion in Williamsburg. Antoinette was buried in a private ceremony in the Knapp family circle at Greenwood in Brooklyn, next to her teenage son Edward along with her Mother and Father, the baby brother Francis that she never knew, her grandmother Antoinette, Uncle William and two members of the Ballard family, who I believe were very close friends of the Knapps? Josephine Ballard, who is not buried there, was a close friend and traveling companion to Netty for many years. Within two years Antoinette's last husband, Paul G. Brown would also be laid to rest at her side.

Some Unfinished Business in North Carolina

This story actually started out in the 1920s as Joseph P. Knapp educated himself in the workings and failures of local government, seeking to help out the overwhelmed and underfunded school system at Currituck. It was then that he befriended Dudley Bagley, a local banker, who helped him sort out the financial mess his philanthropic and well-intentioned efforts had put the school board into. The jam was due to the board's inability to manage accounts effectively. Bagley, you may recall, authored an unpublished manuscript titled "The Joseph P. Knapp I Knew" that sits buried in the archives of UNC at Chapel Hill, NC. I still hope to be able to read it someday. In the '40s, Bagley, then a state senator, told J. P. Knapp about the efforts of a UNC law professor named Albert Coates. He was trying to teach public officials to be better at their jobs with an Institute Of Government course. Intrigued Knapp wrote this letter to Mr. Coates.

My dear Professor

Senator Dudley Bagley was discussing with me the question of training for public service and he said that in the book on "The Institute Of Government" I would find much interest.

I would be glad to have the opportunity of reading it, and if not too much trouble, will you kindly ask the proper people to forward it to me, with bill.

Sincerely,

Joseph P. Knapp

Coates sent him the book and other materials describing the work of the Institute of Government and received this letter in reply

My dear Professor:

It would be difficult to express sufficiently my appreciation of your letter of January 1st and of the merits of the publications and "Popular Government" which you so kindly sent to me at Mackey Island. They will be preserved carefully read and re-read. After I have had the opportunity to study them, I will write you again.

But Albert Coates did not hear again from J. P. Knapp. He did get a call though from Dudley Bagley, saying that he was going to "see the man who has expressed an interest" in helping the Institute of Government and he would let him know how things came out." Coates wouldn't hear any more about it—until 1951.

CHAPTER
39

Home Again

Well here we are back in the good old 1950s again. Wait a minute isn't this where we started out some umpteen hundred pages ago? Must be that frisky "Flux Capacitor" acting up in the old Delorean again, that has brought us around to this point. Wow! what a trip down Knapp Road it's been though. From the 1950's forward to 2001, then back to 1832 and slowly back up the ladder. Who would've thunk it?—a little kid, his big brother and their friends, a couple of old barns with some airplane and radio parts, and a big old empty mansion, would of led to all this?

I'm calling this chapter *Home Again*, because it was the title of the last chapter in the first really big book that I ever read all by myself. As I recall, I spent a week or so up in my loft bedroom of my Mastic Beach house (the one that sat on the former Knapp estate) reading that big book and I remember it like it was yesterday, The Wizard Of Oz, was written by L. Frank Baum in 1900, and was in my family long before I came along. I think my parents got it for my big sister when she was little or it may well have been my Mother's when she was a girl, sadly like too many things from my past, it has been lost to the ages, other than in my memory. It had green hard covers and wonderful drawings in it by W.W. Denslow, to illustrate Mr. Baum's story that held my attention from cover to cover, and if you have made it this far dear reader, then I have done my job.

A task and a trip that started when I tried to draw a picture of what the Knapp mansion looked like, for my own five year old son in the 1980s. I got frustrated and started to look for a photo of it instead—Now let's follow the Yellow Brick Knapp Road, the rest of the way and see how this thing turns out shall we?

Sutter Signs Her Over

On Thursday, May 4, 1950 (my brother's 6th birthday), George Sutter, who was then living at 39 West 46th St. in New York City, signed over the deed to the Knapp mansion in Mastic Beach (It was never known by another name from 1916-1959) to the Roman Catholic Diocese of Brooklyn. The IRS Tax stamp on the deed was for $19.25, which put the actual sale price at about $16,000. I don't know how much money if any George Sutter put into the place, during the 9 years he owned it, or how many boarders he actually had, but his property taxes were not that high, as Mastic Beach had no school of it's own yet. So I think getting 10 grand over what he paid for it, he didn't get hurt on the deal. My discovery of that deed, put to rest the long ago folk lore that existed around town when I was a kid, that the mansion was gift to the church from the Knapps. Ironically it was converting it into a school, a parochial one of course, that Father Skelly, had in mind for it. As the head of St. Jude's Church and the spark plug who convinced Bishop Molloy at the Diocese to ok the purchase of the place, Father Skelly had big plans for the mansion and more. He would hit a few minor bumps in the road at first, but it looked liked smooth sailing for him by the time my family arrived out there in the fall of 1950.

The Devils In The Details

A lot of this stuff, as it relates to the period of St. Jude's ownership of the Knapp mansion and its demise, was touched upon in the early chapters, but here you will get the details, many that I discovered right off the bat, but belong here as the curtain falls.

In March of 1950, two months before George Sutter put his John Hancock on the deed's line, Fr. Skelly announced his plans for the Knapp place and weekly paper reported on a subsequent town meeting held regarding those plans.

WILL PROCEED WITH ST. JUDE'S BUILDING PLANS

Moriches Tribune, April 14, 1950: Despite opposition expressed at a recent meeting of the Mastic Beach Property Owners Association, St. Judes's R. C. Church of Mastic Beach will go ahead with a $200,000 building plan for expansion of Parish facilities it was revealed this week. Though opposition was limited to an announcement from an unidentified member of the group, that a bloc was being formed to combat the church program, it was learned that a proposal to establish a parochial school was drawing the heaviest fire. Present plans are for a school to open in September 1951.

Residents opposing the school, claim it's establishment would lower residential values in the neighborhood and that pupils would damage property on their way to and from their studies. Others backing the church plan said that parochial school students are carefully supervised both in and out of school.

If plans go through, the school will be located on a three acre tract on the corner of Dogwood Road and Monroe Drive on what was formerly the Knapp estate. The Knapp mansion would be converted into a school structure. Included in the plan is a proposed auditorium-gymnasium community center that would be available for both youth and adult activities.

The building program was announced late last month by Rev. John P. Skelly, pastor of the church, who said that the plan would be raised during a campaign which will be launched in early June. A home exhibit will be a campaign feature and a fully equipped summer bungalow will awarded at the end of the summer. Proceeds of the church bazaar slated for July will also go to the building fund.

The lone anonymous voice from that meeting, may of spoke too soon regarding a bloc, or the bloc amounted to just two or three folks? The MBPOA went on record as being in favor of the plan. The following week the paper reported St. Jude's was now the new owner of the Mastic Beach landmark known as the Knapp mansion. Fr. Skelly held an open house that Sunday afternoon. Always a community minded guy, he invited everyone from around the town to come look at their new community house, which was his immediate plan for the ballroom in the mansion. Church member Charlie Stevens, who lived just across the road on Locust Dr., was a professional photographer and took photos for Fr Skelly that day including the main 3/4 view I have of the front. I'm reasonably sure he took many photos,including interior shots and had always hoped to see his negatives, which were given to a neighbor that still resides there, but I received no cooperation from him. Probably if I had, this book would not exist. Anthony Torre, a kid I went to school with, recalled going to that open house and walking right into the opening of huge ballroom fireplace to look up the chimney and getting yelled at.

In June of that year, they held a big ceremony and ground breaking for the new auditorium in the back yard of the mansion. Thirty other clergy from the Diocese attended, but Bishop Molloy did not (which I found strange) However the Bishop Of Reno, Nevada came in his place. I don't think they played Bingo that day, but by all the newspaper accounts, a splendid time was had by all including the fifty some Mastic Beach church members who attended, in-spite of the highly unusual chilly weather for June. Many women who were there are shown wearing fur coats in the backyard photos taken at the ground breaking. The architect for the new auditorium, Mr. Berlenbach also spoke to the crowd and his drawing of the building with the mansion behind it was unveiled.

A true man for all seasons and denominations, the activities Fr. Skelly held for everyone in the mansion were well received and well covered by the press. He had concerts, recitals, card parties, breakfasts and dinners in the ballroom. Groups like the Girl Scouts met there. Nicola Pesce, who was St. Jude's choir director, arranged for his former opera and piano students from NYC to come out and perform. For most of the folks in Mastic Beach, it was their first look inside the place that once divided their town in two. Dorothy Jendral, whose family moved to Mastic Beach in the 1930s. told me of listening to a classical piano recital in the ballroom on a beautiful soft breezy summer evening, gazing out the ballroom doors across the lawn and thinking about what it must of been like to have been a Knapp and lived within all that splendor for all those years. Loretta Clune, a founding church member, was no stranger though, as she returned to the home she once cooked in for the Knapps. Shirley Kohan wrote "*Of trying to visualize Loretta ever working there, where everything was so big and Loretta so small*" That first and second year, they had barn dances and a summer camp for kids, with most of those activities held outside on the grounds. Two months after the groundbreaking, the church had raised $58,000 of the $75,000 they needed to put up the auditorium behind "*the mansion*" which by then was all you had to say in town, for those to know what you meant.

Change of plans

What happened in two years that followed, was never really publicly explained by St. Judes's or ever mentioned by the press. I found the local presses omissions very odd, for they would print the most mundane events to fill spaces on their pages. If your Aunt Tilly came to visit or your neighbor was down with the flu, you could read about it in the weekly papers. What actually happened was theorized by many whom I interviewed and it ran from reasonable to wild rumors, that only supermarket tabloids, which were still a decade away from appearing, would print.

In 1952, the Moriches Tribune re ran the same architects drawing from 1950 showing the auditorium and the mansion behind it. The caption under it reads GRAND OPENING of a grand new showplace, the $160,000 St. Jude's Youth Center in Mastic Beach is scheduled for Sunday. Brainchild of the Rev. John P. Skelly, pastor of St. Jude's, the new center is one of the largest gathering places in Eastern Suffolk. This architect's drawing of the building shows how the building and grounds will look when landscaping is completed. At present workers are rushing the structure to completion for opening ceremonies.

Besides the new building running more than double of what it was announced to have cost two years prior, there was something very strange with them showing that two year old drawing. They could of easily printed a photo of the new building, that had to have been under construction for at least 6 months or more. The exact new building in the drawing was about to really open its doors all-right, but it was no where near the Knapp mansion. It was a half a mile away across the street from the church itself! Carefully checking all newspapers for the two year span, there is no mention of the change of location, the actual start of the construction, or its progress as it neared completion.

It certainly peaked my curiosity and sustained me in my early quest for any info at all on the good ol' Knapp Mansion and so I started to investigate what had happened. In 2001, I first enquired at the St. Jude church office and they knew nothing about it or that they had any affiliation with any mansion for that matter. Deeper inquiries involved dealing with two NY Diocese'. Brooklyn and Rockville Center (Rockefeller Center had taken over Brooklyn's Long Island jurisdiction in 1957) and the overall Diocese archives, housed in a separate location in Huntington. Brooklyn was a dead end, Huntington mailed me some highly redacted papers, but only after the Rockville Center lawyers viewed them. I also received a xerox copy postage stamp sized picture (the Charles Stevens photo) All of the local folks still around, who were adults when the auditorium was built, never even recalled that it was originally supposed to go up on the mansion grounds. Old friend, Adolph Almasy, lived just behind the mansion. He was only 3 when he was at the ground breaking with his parents, who were active church members, and he offered this plausible explanation. The extra clergy that used to come out in the summer to help at the overflow services, used to stay at the mansion and complained about walking a half mile to the church and carrying all their stuff. That really didn't seem to make too much sense, because they didn't sleep in the auditorium either. And if the auditorium which is where they held services with the extra clergy was built in on the mansion property, there goes that theory out the window. However not long after the auditorium was built, two old houses were moved behind the church to serve as a parish house. I thought along with some others, that perhaps the church could not get the proper fire safety permits to turn the wooden Knapp mansion into a school and so the big plan was abandoned.

But what they did next has no rationale at all. They just completely walked away from it. Leaving it fully furnished and the doors unlocked. This was around 1954. For a very brief time, the place was left untouched, as I have spoke to several kids who were a few years older than me, who used to go in there just to look around, only to get chased out by Mr. Almasy, who tried to keep a close eye on the place. One of those "kids" took the big brass key out of the front door as a souvenir, but has regrettably since lost track of it. The most improbable stories came from a local tomboy, who lived just up the block from it. Her house was directly across the road from the gate house that Willie & Honey Schluder wound up living in. Her father, who was a police chief and Father Skelly were great friends and she was in the place many times when St. Jude's actively used it and after it was empty. She had heard that *"a priest committed suicide there by leaping out the top floor window!"* And if that wasn't enough,*"that there was a satanic alter discovered on the grounds, that made it impossible for the church to continue to use it"*

It didn't take long before the locals started carrying everything that wasn't nailed down (and even things that were) out of the place. Paintings, furniture, antique firearms, instruments, sporting goods, and gambling equipment. I was told by Roland Penney, grand nephew of Willis, that Dodi Knapp was said to have ran a casino there in the '20s and '30s. The roulette wheel that my friend Larry Schulz saw in there as a kid, could of well belonged to St. Jude's as the Catholic church also ran games of chance for fundraising, until they were outlawed.

Father Skelly got transfered out of St Jude's back into the city around 1954. He was replaced by Fr. Reilly. I'm pretty sure it was a kid aged 12-25, that through the first rock through a window there. After that it didn't take long for the mansion to become the haunted mansion. When we first gathered up the nerve to go in there in 1955, most every window was broken and the paint was peeling from the ceilings. It had a real musty smell and there were quite a few holes in the plaster walls.

As I said in the original mansion story, by 1958 the place was really torn up and dangerous for anyone to be wandering around in. The circular staircase was ripped away from the wall and the banister completely gone. That fall one of neighborhood kids ,Willy Conklin, fell from the top roof, down two stories and onto the roof on the front verandah, breaking his leg. That story got around fast and I'm sure Father Reilly heard it and wanted to do something about solving the churches liability problem of having a dilapidated and vandalized building on the their hands. Exactly what he did or didn't do, is still unknown to me. He may of looked into the cost of having it torn down. He may of just expressed his frustrations quietly or may of said something from the pulpit. Or he may of said or done nothing. But two young local yokels did. At least one, possibly both, were members of the Mastic Beach Fire Department in the winter of 1959. One of them for certain, was still living in Mastic Beach as 2006 and is still active in civic affairs. I have known both their names for over 6 years, but have decided it serves no purpose to print them. Besides the place was heading for the wrecking ball in due time anyway. To me the real crime was not that these two jerks decided to light the place up that Sunday afternoon of Feb 15, 1959 for grins or for fire fighting practice. My brother and his friend Doug, initially went over to play in it earlier, before I got home that day. They saw a vehicle on the mansion grounds and decided to turn around. By the time the three of us went over there, perhaps an hour later, the arson was well in progress. The fire department still could of put it out when they got there, but a phone call was made to Father Reilly and he told Chief Mike Gilewski, to just let it burn. Mike only lived across the street from it and was probably unaware of what one or two of his firemen were up to just an hour or so before. The real crime to my way of thinking, was that St. Jude's let the place get into that condition by their total irresponsibility over the years. When Fr. Skelly first moved out of it, it was probably as perfect as the day Dodi Knapp had left it over a decade before. It still contained personal items the Knapps left behind, like the antique firearms hidden in the wall safes behind the paintings. Some of those guns could be worth about $50,000 today. The church did keep the building insured for $18,000 and probably collected all or most of that after the fire. In chapter 4, I mentioned that in 1962, I was driving an old car that was dumped there, around in circles on the property. That lasted for a few days before the town towed it away. I have thought about those days several times, as I went around in circles gathering the info for this book. In the 1970s, the church used the property for a youth baseball team. In the 1980s they finally sold the 3.5 acres for about $83,000.

Today there are three large houses on the north, south and west sides, that share a sort of communal backyard, which ironically is the actual foot print of where the mansion once stood. There is still a trace of the sidewalk, that ran on the east side between the east front entrance and the kitchen entrance. I visited with two of the homeowners in 2003 and was given a brick that was laying in the bushes. It had came from one of the chimneys and didn't get buried with the rubble. It was made by the Sage Brick Company in Greenport, Long Island. who were still operating in 1910. The bricks of which there some on the nearby Dana estate too, were probably brought to Mastic via boat. One of the homeowners showed me something else man made that was lodged in the fork of a tree. As soon as I saw it, I recognized it to be a piece of a post from the master bedroom terrace rail that was over the ballroom. It had most likely landed in that tree when the flames brought down the roof and walls.

Back At Riverhouse

On Tuesday evening January 30th 1951, Joseph Palmer Knapp went to bed and did not wake up Wednesday morning. He was four months shy of turning 86 years old. The New York Times ran a two column obituary with his portrait photo on Wednesday, which strongly suggests they had it well prepared. Besides a featured obit, The NY Herald Tribune, co publishers with Knapp of the then 10 million weekly copies of "This Week", ran an additional editorial on the life and times of Joseph Palmer Knapp. Their last sentence of the tribute *"Here was surely a masterful American"* is engraved on his tombstone. On Feb 3rd (Dodi's 59th birthday btw) The Times reported that 400 people turned up at St. Thomas' Cathedral on 5th Ave for J. P.'s funeral. His honorary pallbearers were all executives and friends with Crowell-Collier and Publication Corp including Thomas Beck, Ed Anthony, Clarence Stouch, and Sumner Blossom. Dudley Bagley carried J.P.s ashes back to Currituck and buried them at Moyock Cemetery.

Widow Margaret took over as his voice and vote at the Knapp Foundation. In 1952 she sold the Mackey Island estate to lumber dealer and home builder James J. Standing of Virginia Beach. She did not however sever her ties or those of her late husband with North Carolina. In 1954 she moved out of Riverhouse and back over to an apartment on Park Avenue. She donated some furnishings and antiques from both Riverhouse (along with the imported pine wood from the living room) and the from the Knapp Lodge on Mackey Island to the University of North Carolina at Chapel Hill. Some of the small furnishings, eg. Chinese porcelain and art collectibles and personal effects like his golf trophies were put on display at their Akland Art Museum on campus, the larger items would initially go into temporary storage and reemerge on a much larger scale there.

The Knapp Building

Of course the news of Knapp's death was big news in his adopted state of North Carolina too, where he had made a big difference in the lives of many. It certainly did not go unnoticed by Albert Coates, who now knew he would never be hearing again from Joe Knapp, as he once thought he would according to J, P.'s last letter to him . He would however hear from Dudley Bagley, who explained to him just why Knapp had grown silent regarding *"The Institute of Government"*. Coates found himself a visitor at Bagley's home where he learned that J. P. had indeed summoned Dudley to New York to discuss ways in which Knapp could get involved with helping the institute. He had even written memos to his editors at Colliers and American magazines suggesting one of them do a feature story on the institute to call attention to what J.P. thought was a very worthwhile and purposeful organization. The week that Bagley arrived in New York for their meeting, Saturday Evening Post ,which as I previously stated was always a major thorn in J. P.'s side, had ran a large spread on the Institute. Well J. P. was livid that his arch competitor had beaten him to the punch. Bagley said there was no way that week that J. P. wanted to hear another word about helping anything or anyone.

Then Bagley told Coates about the Knapp foundation of N. C. and that it was interested in continuing to carry on J. P.'s work in the state. Dudley's wife Ida added that while Margaret had been discussing continued work with wildlife and fisheries, she also mentioned that she would like to see her husbands name on a building that symbolized his life interests in helping out the citizens there. It was there in the Bagley's living room that Coates told him of his dream of a building for the institute.

The dream was soon put in motion and at a Knapp foundation meeting in 1952, where they had already approved a quarter of a million dollar gift to the project, Margaret Knapp spoke her mind. "Joe Knapp pulled his weight in everything he did as long as he lived, and he will keep on pulling it in everything done in his name. as long as his name is in my keeping." With that single sentence the gift was lifted from a quarter to a half million dollars. The second half million was matched by the state. As the Joseph Palmer Knapp building at UNC Chapel Hill neared completion in the spring of 1956, Margaret visited it. Coates said "We turned on every light from the cupola to the basement in her honor that evening and Margaret reveled admiring it from every angle possible." In later years she approved an additional $100,000 and had Francis Vandeever Kughler, her favorite artist, paint murals on its interior walls, depicting historic events in North Carolina history. One of them shows a very young Margaret and J. P. in full colonial southern dress, at a large outdoor plantation gathering. Other Knapp family members and workers at the Mackey Island estate are depicted as revelers.

We Three Kings and more

It's probably because of the big dock down the road from our Mastic Beach house, that Knapp's boats have always been of special interest to me. When I first discovered the name of the yacht Storm King in the big fat slob story, I used the research facilities at Mystic Seaport in Conn, to try and find out more about the boat. In 2002 they came up with three Storm Kings for me, all listed in the yacht registries to Joseph F. Knapp from 1931-1951. For a time his Storm King Too, a 50 foot Matthews, did double duty. as did the first Storm King at both Ft Lauderdale and in Hampton Bays, Long Island during the summers. I assumed that after he sold Storm King III which was home ported in Hampton Bays in 1951, that it was the last boat he owned. Silly me: never assume with a Knapp. Because he also lived in Ft. Lauderdale and owned several boats. I asked Philip Cheaney, if he recalled Dodi's last boat. Not only did he recall it, he sailed on its maiden voyage when Dodi took delivery of it in January 1952 at the Huckins boat yard in Jacksonville.

Phil recalled the trip was ill fated, as they ran aground in Stuart about two thirds of the way between Jacksonville and Ft. Lauderdale and had to put into Palm Beach for repairs. The boat was a Fairform Flyer, which was the design name of all Huckin's yachts. It was a 34 footer Pro Bono model, which was in keeping with Dodi replacing each previous Storm King he owned, with a smaller one. He went from 53, to 48, to 38 footers. The Fairform Flyer was a totally new name and surprise to me. I decided to follow it up by researching Huckins Yachts. As it turns out they are quite the exclusive boat company, going back to the 1920s, when the first Fair Form Flyers were built. In WWII they were one of the manufacturers of PT Boats and many of their post war boats carried on that styling. They published a beautiful coffee table book titled *Huckins: The Living Legacy*, that listed the original owners of all their boats and sure enough there was Joseph F. Knapp in 1952. The book mentioned they also kept extensive records, so I wrote to company and they provided me with copies of not only the build sheet, the cost $23,000 (over twice the price of an average house in 1952) and delivery date and further history for this boat and for another one that Dodi ordered in June of 1952, that proved to be very intriguing.

The House On Hampton Harbor Road

After renting in Hampton Bays for 8 years. Dodi and Marion bought a custom built cape cod home in 1949. "Cove Point" sat on 3 acres and had a private mooring on 560' of shorefront on Smith Creek, that led into Tiana Bay. They paid $1,000.00 less for the 4,000 sq foot 4 bedroom home than they would for a 34 foot boat two years later.

After owning Storm King V for 5 months (I don't know if there ever was a SK IV?) Dodi placed an order on June 19, 1952 with Huckins for a larger boat. He ordered a Corinthian Model, which was 47 feet long. The typed order sheet for hull # 280 says it is to be christened Storm King VI and its hailing port is Hampton Bays. Besides the NYC address and phone of Publication Corp., it lists the contact phone number HB2-0001. which was for Knapp house on Hampton Harbor Road. What is most intriguing about this document is, what is written in pencil very boldly across the entire order. "*Cancelled Oct 17th, Deposit Returned —Deceased.*" I find it intriguing. because of the date which shows no sign of erasure. It was not for another week later on October 23, 1952 when Marion Knapp awoke to find Dodi had died in his sleep. Cause of death was heart failure and according to Ed Kiely, the autopsy showed that his arteries were very severely shrunken. Now could he of had a stroke a week or so before and the cancellation of the boat was called in? Possible, but that does not explain the word Deceased and that date.

October 23, 1952, also happened to be Claire Knapp's 63rd birthday. Short obituaries ran in all the major NY Papers and in the Hampton Bays weekly paper. It just stated he was the retired Chairman of American Lithographic Co, survived by his wife Marion H. Knapp, and sister Claire K. Dixon and nieces Margaret P. Raynor and Anne P. Willumsen. Dodi was the first to be buried in a new Knapp family plot his sister most likely purchased in the Southampton

Cemetery. It is very private and surrounded by hedges. A large anchor stone that says Knapp, sits at the rear of plot His very small headstone reads IN LOVING MEMORY JOSEPH F. KNAPP Feb 3, 1892 - Oct 23, 1952. Not more than a few 100 feet away, are his step family: Elizabeth Laing Knapp whose large stone also says, Wife Of Joseph Palmer Knapp, her son, Archie McIlwaine who was the Navy flyer in WWI, his wife Caroline and their son Navy Flyer, Archie III, who went missing in the Pacific in WWII.

In June of 1954 Marion H. Knapp, who was now remarried to a commercial photographer from NYC named Stanley Conley, put "Cove Point" up for sale. It sold very quickly for $55,000. The house is still standing today and is probably valued near 2 million. She also sold the Isle Of Palms house around the same time, which is a multi million dollar home today.

There is also a typed in notation on the paperwork that says "Mr, Knapp died before actual construction of the boat had started and hull #280 was completed for Harold A. Reilly who christened it Grahar. The boat was fully restored in the early 1990s and is now known as the Poseidia hailing from Miami Beach. The 34 Foot Storm King V was re-christened "Mischief" and was last registered in Southern California.

Although she expanded somewhat on the variety of breeds she would handle, Claire herself naturally slowed down with her kennel activities during the 1950s. She had several illness some associated with advancing age that required a live on the premise nurse. Her daughter and others now did the actual day by day running of both Clairedale and Pennyworth. They also did joint ventures,with dogs like Ch. Alfonco von der Goldenen Kette, a standard poodle that won numerous awards in the mid '50s including Best in Non Sporting Group at Westminster 1956.

J. P. Drops The Big One On The Big Apple

Back in New York city things were rapidly changing at Crowell-Collier by the start of the '50s and within the months following J.P.'s death. Even though he was officially retired from his company for over 4 years before he died, his persona was firmly chiseled in stone there. Physically the biggest change started on March 2, 1949 with the very unique laying of a cornerstone for the Crowell-Collier 19 story office building on the site of what once was the William Vanderbilt mansion at 5th avenue and 51st Street. The atomic age was upon all of NY City that afternoon as J. P. Knapp symbolically dropped The Big One on what was once Mr. Vanderbilt's huge mansion, that once nestled or should I say elbowed itself between the St.Thomas & St. Patrick Cathedrals. Before it was torn down, the Vanderbilt mansion represented everything associated with wealth and power in America.

According to the news account, seven hundred people witnessed this event. The master of ceremonies was my grandpa's closest old pal, James Farley. Along with him, Nelson Rockefeller, Mayor Impelliterri, and Fred Ecker. the Chairman of the board of Metropolitan Life Insurance who started out at Met in 1880s with big J. F. Knapp was there. It does not state whether or not J. P. attended or any members of the Knapp family, but the fact remains that this day would of not happened, if not for one Joseph Palmer Knapp.

At the push of a button, a two ton piece of polished granite was put in place without any human hands, by a miniature nuclear reactor operated by Dr. Dunning, a professor of physics from Columbia University. I wonder if he had a city permit? The good doctor used a 1/2 gram of Radium Berryllium to bombard the 10, U-235 Atoms, that released 200,000,000 volts for each split. That in turn generated electrical impulses, igniting a magnesium flare imbedded in a ceremonial ribbon. As each atom split, a bell rang and a large fluorescent tube lit up. The ribbon then parted, with a flash of light and a loud explosion on the tenth and final split. This in turn activated a motor hoist that lowered the stone one foot precisely onto the spot. It does not mention if Mr. Reuben Lucious Golberg was consulted or if he was in the crowd that day? It does state that Oliver Back, construction foreman for the building's contractor Starrett Brothers, was favorably impressed and quoted *"We won't have to move the stone one bit —just have to put a little mortar around the bottom"*. Seriously though, Dr. Dunning was quoted as saying " the energy symbolized the great advances man has made and the hope of the world that rightly used, will mean an era of peace, and help bring the better life to an ever increasing fraction of the world's people OR— *"A Crowell magazine in every home around the world"*— *Tom Beck*. Tom who was developing a new international magazine for Crowell in the post war era, I'm sure played no small part in the organization of this memorable day. He in-fact had a small safe placed next to the stone in which he placed 300 "hope letters" written by social, business and civic leaders of the day. The safe was to be reopened on Jan 1, 1954 to see how many hopes and predictions had come to pass. The December 3, 1949 of Colliers Magazine cover was adorned with the modern new building and they ran a large feature story on the entire Crowell magazine organization. Christmas was coming and they certainly had earned the right to blow their own horn.

Then There Were Three

There of course were a few more, but the fact is J. P.'s closest inner circle at Crowell-Colliers was shrinking fast. Three of the men who were with him back when his magazine empire started to really build were Cap Winger, Tom Beck and Clarence Stouch. Two months after J. P. died an ailing Tom Beck left as Chairman of the Board to head the Knapp Foundation. Winger who started out working for JP at American Lithographic, moved up as Chairman of the board. By October of '51 Beck was dead. Clarence Stouch who wore many hats for JP over the years, came over from Publication Corp to be president of Crowell-Collier. Winger would retire in 1953 and Clarence moved in the Chairman slot. Stouch, born in 1891, would be the last of the original Knapp men to hold that position.

It seemed that things at Crowell-Collier publishing, in respect to their three remaining magazines, changed rapidly and radically around the time of J. P. Knapp's death and in the immediate years after. Some of it was brought on by retirements of long time Collier's editors, like Bill Chenery in 1950, and the ever diminishing Knapp executives and some by a changing world. The new medium of TV, that first took its toll on the movie business, was also changing things on Madison Avenue. Advertising, not circulation, is what keeps magazines in the black. In 1953. the annual board of Directors meetings reported Crowell was in the red due to it's magazines to the tune of over 4 million dollars. Colliers then went from being a weekly to a bi weekly magazine. In 1954 there was a major shake up and all of its last generation of editors and publishers that were from the Knapp era were let go, reassigned and or had quit. And in 1954, just as the late Tom Beck said they would back in March of 1949, the 300 letters of hope from the likes J. Paul Getty, Pearl S. Buck, Jack Benny. Walt Disney. George Gallop, J. Edgar Hoover, Ernest Hemingway etc. were taken from the cornerstone safe and quietly put in a file cabinet and quickly forgotten about. They were only rediscovered twenty years later. On May 1, 1974, the NY Times published a feature on them titled, *"It Was 1949, Here's How Notables Viewed The Future"*. Like the personalities who wrote them, they were all over the map, from the generic scribble you would find in any high school yearbook, to quite the specific and constructive. Hemingway, who was already dead for 14 years then, wrote somewhat true to character, "I Hope no wars, all my kids ok, that I continue to write well, and that William Chenery goes out and hangs himself!" The Times contacted Chenery, the 90 year old ex editor who had steered Collier's for 25 years into the place of prominence it held, all the while holding J P Knapp at bay. He was living in Big Sur, California now for twenty years and in spite of a recent fall, was enjoying himself quite nicely. He would pass away three months later. In 1955, Clarence Stouch resigned as CEO at Crowell and went back to heading Publication Corp that oversaw everything Knapp related including This Week magazine, which was still flourishing. Eight other top execs followed Stouch out the Crowell door in '55, including Sumner Blossom who once was the editor of American Magazine and Irving Miller, who was one of JP's personal attorneys and would become the executor of his estate by personal request of both Margaret and Dodi Knapp.

Like Rearranging Deck Chairs On The Titanic

That's the way it seemed at Crowell Collier shop by the mid 1950s, in regard to their magazine business. In 1955 they announced they were back in the black, but their troubles were not over. The new guard had also announced they were looking into purchasing radio and TV stations. Though they agreed to initially spend 15 million to buy radio and TV stations in the mid west and west and Hawaii, which was still 4 years away from statehood, but obviously a great destination to head for, they may of been a day late and a dollar short. I have often wondered what J. P. would of done in this situation? I'm not sure, but I don't think he would of let his ship sink.

In March of 1956, three attorneys whose names do not have any Knapp connections, let's just call them Moe, Curly and Larry, petitioned the United States Tax Court on behalf of Crowell-Collier Publishing seeking tax relief. I have the actual document, which is over 60 Pages and has about 175 numbered paragraphs. Their history of the company, especially regarding the Knapps, is filled with errors. For example they state that " *Joseph Palmer Knapp's FATHER Joseph F. Knapp, who was also the founder of Metropolitan Life was a member of*

Crowell's Board Of Directors up until 1942" Nice Legal work there counselors, glad your not representing me. Of course they were speaking of Dodi Knapp, who being his late grandfather's namesake, also caused some confusion for me at the start. In paragraph 15 they kill off *"JOSEPH PALMER KNAPP, THE PETITIONER'S MOST IMPORTANT STOCKHOLDER"* somewhere between 1946 and 47. Like Mark Twain, rumors of JP's death is greatly exaggerated here. But I don't think their sloppy history, mattered to the judges, who had to wade through this case that is loaded with charts and numbers going all the way back to the 1920s. They also characterize "Knapp" as he is referred to from there on as a "dominating, positive, and forceful person, who exerted a strong influence over petitioner's top executives and board of directors, of which he was a member. He kept close track of and exercised his influence on all phases of the petitioner's business. He had no marked ability as an editor, but sometimes attempted to fix basic editorial policy.

As Will Shakespeare said in Henry VI, *"First thing we do, let's kill all the lawyers."* (Mr. Alex Turpin. my high school English teacher and a major influence on my becoming a writer, always called him Will and it has stuck) The lawyers were seeking reimbursement for the hundreds of thousands of dollars that Knapp did not charge to Crowell for his services in the 1930s and for the extraordinary costs involved in the switch over from letter press to total roto-gravure printing! I do not know what the final decision was or when it came down, but I do not think they made their case or if they did, they did not get the total amount of tax relief they sought. I wonder what their fee was?

In August of 1956, Crowell stopped the presses on American Magazine. Started as Frank Leslie's magazine in the late 19th century, Knapp had owned it since since 1911. Then announcing losses of over 7 million in 1956, and just ten days before Christmas, Crowell-Collier announced that it's last two magazines, Collier's which had been in print since 1888 and Woman's Home Companion since 1897, would cease publication by January 1957. Look Magazine, would pick up the existing subscribers. 2,400 jobs were effected, including well over 300 at the new NY editorial and advertising office that had started with an Atomic blast just 7 years before.

1959

And speaking of seven years, by October of 1959, the tall grass was already growing waist high over the footprint where the remains of the Knapp Mansion laid buried in Mastic Beach. In Southampton, the Knapp family plot still had but one family member in it for seven years now since Sunday afternoon October 26, 1952, when Dodi was laid to rest there. It only seems fitting he would be first be joined on October 28th, by his big sister Claire. For on Sunday October 25, 1959, just two days after her 70th birthday, Claire Antoinette Knapp Penney Dixon would pass away. Like her brother, her funeral services were also held at the quaint St. Mary's Episcopal Church in Hampton Bays.

Claire's obits in both the NY Times and Hampton Bays paper were that of the ordinary citizen. The exception came in a large memorial page in the

December '59 issue of American Kennel Magazine. Upon my showing it to Barbara Kolk at the AKC in NYC, she remarked that this was truly extraordinary because *"our organization did not normally memorialize, nor single out its members to anywhere near that degree."*

I knew Claire was ill for sometime, but have wondered if the news of the fate of her Clairedale Farm, as the Knapp Mansion in Mastic was first known by in 1920, ever reached her in those last 8 months of her life? It's probably 50/50, and not important to anyone but me, but I would like to think, she cared about the Mastic Beach place on Narrow Bay, just as she did about the last Clairedale in Red Cedar Point on the Peconic Bay. Her grand daughter Sibby told me in 2001, she had never heard anything about her Grandmother owning a mansion in Mastic. It could well of been that when Claire left it behind to her brother in September of 1925, that she never looked back.

I don't know where or exactly when it happened, but according to Dodi Knapp's trust, his first wife Gertrude O. Knapp, also passed away in 1959. I last found her living in New Orleans in 1937 according to the divorce papers. I thought for a time, I had actually found her again, living in Huntington on Long Island's North Shore in the 1940s and 50s, as there was a woman listed in the phone book there as Gertrude O. Knapp, who was the same age as Gertrude O'Brien Knapp. After receiving her Social Security application. I found the O stood for her maiden name allright, but it was not O'Brien, I was a wee bit curious, because of all the other similarities I discovered, like Gertrude O. Knapp was born on Sept 3, 1893 just ten days before Gertrude O'Brien Knapp was, and she too was divorced from a millionaire! But then—she was a KNAPP!

The '6os

It seems that the fabulous fifties decade had not been all that fabulous to the Knapp family. but life goes on. It was the decade that I first became introduced to them, in my subconscious while having a grand old time as a little kid, exploring where they once lived in a style far removed from anything I could imagine. Then to have all of them re emerge in ways I could not fathom then or even now a half century later, was a mind blower. As was learning far more than I ever really wanted to, while simply searching for a few photos of one of their grand homes. The one that cast shadows and light in my own backyard,

It had also been almost a century since Joseph P. Knapp was born, when this obituary appeared in the New York Times on the first week of January 1960. MRS. JOSEPH P. KNAPP — Mrs. Margaret Rutledge Knapp of 605 Park Avenue, widow of Joseph Palmer Knapp, former board chairman of the Crowell-Collier Publishing Co. died yesterday (Jan 4th) in Summit, Miss. after a long illness. Her age was 73. She was visiting a sister, Dr. Elise Rutledge Lockwood. Mr. Knapp, a principal stockholder in the Publication Corporation and a director of the Metropolitan Life Insurance Co. died in 1951.

Mrs. Knapp a skilled flycaster and duck hunter, had shared these activities with her husband. She was a member of the Woman's Fly Fishers Club and a former volunteer worker for the American Red Cross. Besides her sister, a brother and two-step grandchildren survive.

Margaret's ashes are also buried in Currituck along side of J P.s

1961

1961 is probably the only upside down year that will appear in our lifetime. It seems fitting that sometime during that year, the US Government purchased the 2,500 acre Knapp Estate on Mackey Island from the Richardson Brothers Lumber Company, who had been cutting down trees there for a number of years. The Government's plan for it, was to turn it into a game preserve, which they did do and still maintain today. I am confident this would of met the approval of both J. P. and Margaret. However there seems to be a joker in the deck, who obviously did not have the benefit of the schooling, the Knapp foundation had made available at The Institute Of Government. For whomever placed the rubber stamp of approval upon this last deal, is probably still in J.P's & Margaret's gun-sights. It seems that a house wrecker named Kermit Land, purchased the three story, thirty seven room replica of George Washington's Mount Vernon home , that Knapp built in 1920 from a government official for the grand total of $57.52 ! No that is not a typo, allow me to spell it out: Fifty Seven Dollars and Fifty Two Cents! (pray tell, what the hell was the 52 cents for?) Then Kermit dismantled it and floated it away on barges. He later resold it one piece at a time. I understand many pieces of it, like bathtubs, windows, paneling. doors etc, still exist in all the better homes in Currituck County.

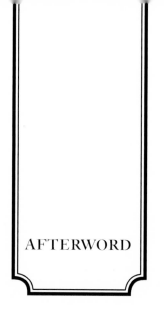

This is My Story, This is My Song;

Blessed Assurance written by

Fanny Crosby and Phoebe Knapp

On FRIDAY AFTERNOON, AUGUST 22, 2008 I REALIZED AS I WAS writing Chapter 39 of the manuscript, that not only was it going to end this day, but that it was ending on the same month that it really started in earnest in 2001. As that thought started to hit me, I doubled checked with my perpetual calendar,and the realization got even stronger—the facts were bordering on the supernatural. This was in no way planned, yet here I was finishing the book on same afternoon seven years ago, that I touched down at Islip airport on Long Island to begin my research of the Knapp story (chapter 6) With that driving me on, I started playing the soundtrack to the Grass Harp (chapter 37—Cheaneys Lived Here) which and finished the last few pages. I then emailed a handful of family, friends and Knappsters, some who have been with me since the gitgo, to tell them, IT'S FINALLY FINISHED! Then sat in shock for a few minutes surrounded by piles of files, books, photos, old magazines and stacks of CDs with more files on them, that seemed to get totally out of hand these last few weeks, as I worked towards a self imposed deadline of Labor Day 2008. I had myself a Yuengling Black & Tan beer (America's oldest brewer since 1828 and related by marriage to the Knapps) while sitting in the chair, surrounded by framed photos of my central cast of characters and listened to Randy Travis warble Blessed Assurance. Old friend Larry Schulz suggested via e mail, that I have two Yuenglings! I might of, had I not a house to put in order as Anne was due home from work in about 90 minutes! Plus Claire was coming to visit that evening (no not that Claire; Claire Orologas, Anne's sister). Today as I write this, it is very early Sunday morning, of that very same weekend seven years ago, when I was first poking around in Mastic Beach talking to folks like Mrs. Schulz, who told me stories of being a little girl in the 1930s, sitting on the deck of Knapp's boat, and of her father being invited to go out on the town drinking with Dodi Knapp, which she added her Dad was extremely proud of. It was also the first time I ever heard the name Dodi Knapp and wondered which Knapp was that? As my wife Anne would say many times over these last 8 years— *"It's just too much."* When I first pressed her for an explanation, she just said *"You and the Knapps and what you find out... it totally overwhelms me ... it's just too much."*

Believe it or not, there is still much more to this Knapp Story, some of which I know and have chosen there is no purposeful need to tell and some of which I know, I will never know— at least not in my lifetime. Simple things like where and when Claire & Dodi's mother, Sylvia T. Knapp passed away. I believe it was France or possibly Germany. Or, what was the exact spelling of Joseph Fairchild Knapp's nickname: Dodi, Doty, Dodie? I would love to have been able to sit and have a drink or just a talk with any one of three Joe Knapps, but am still extremely grateful I was able to talk with folks who did "hoist a few" with two of them, J. P. and Dodi.

Because this is also my story and my song if you will, I feel there is a need for a few more afterthoughts, rather than a few more beers. I still approach all of my books, like I would as if I was writing a song, I would have to say though that if The Knapps Lived Here was characterized as a song, it would exceed the subject, length and meanings of Bob Dylan's: Rosemary, Lily and The Jack of Hearts, Sad Eyed Lady of the Lowlands, Masters Of War, Like A Rolling Stone, Gordon Lightfoot's; Wreck Of The Edmund Fitzgerald, Lennon & McCartney's Hey Jude. Jimmy Webb's Sandy Cove, and Don McLean's American Pie combined. I also realize that it is my song too, the one of being a little kid and experiencing the traces of Knapp life, when and where I did, that is the real reason behind all the words that preceded this.

I also want to say a final word about the Knapp family privacy and what honestly seemed to me in the beginning, as their acting paranoid about me? Just as I am sure that my fledging research was being viewed by them as threateningly inquisitive. As I stated in my 2001 response letter to their attorney, I have always honored my original pledge to Mrs. Sylvia "Sibby" Penny, (chpts 6 & 7) who told me after she spoke with her family that it was ok with them to write about the deceased Knapps, but that the living members of her family wished to be left out of my history, I believe I have truly honored Sibby's request, other than use comments and history she initially told me and point out, what I thought was a history making event, that was well covered at the time with both photos and story by Life Magazine, the NY Times and many more. That being of course, when Sibby's aunt, the now late, Mrs. Margaret "Peggy" Penney Raynor Ritchie Newcombe, became the first daughter of a former BIS winner at the Westminster Dog Show, to do likewise in 1964. I am absolutely sure, Claire would of just bust her buttons to have been there with her! I would like to think her Dad Willis, certainly did upon hearing the good news.

To be totally honest and totally human, I have to say through out the beginning years of my research, I took their rebuff personally and way too much to heart. I had already been warned prior to our confrontation, that the Knapp heirs were very sensitive about privacy matters and I was to use caution in dealing with them. That said, I have never dealt with them in anyway other than laying what few cards I had on the table from the gitgo and letting the chips fall where they may.

But in an effort to understand what all the hub bub from them was about, I naturally poked around a bit, but like most everything else that I discovered along the way, the real eyebrow raisers, always seemed to come to me quite innocently and with no intent on my part to disparage the Knapp name. Prior to our direct confrontation, I had already known the public details of the *"Nancy Reagan White House China incident"* that made all the papers in 1981 and early 1982 where Mrs. Ann Vojvoda (Claire Knapp's younger daughter) reluctantly came forward to announce it was the indeed the Knapp Foundation that donated the $210,000 for a new set of china for the White House. The SASMM (short attention span mainstream media) ran that story for a few days in the fall of 1981. Picking it up again on Feb 3rd 1982, of all days, at a State Dinner, where the new china was used for the first time. The SASMM never questioned, except one time, flippantly by a gossip reporter, why a foundation whose charter and purpose, that was set up by in 1929 by J. P. to aid wildlife conservation and for educational matters, e.g. the Knapp Library project that provided libraries to many public schools in America that could not afford them—why a foundation like this, would want to buy a set of dishes for the Reagans. Other than being true Republicans, I would add that I believe their real motive was political to insure a separate move of the Knapp Foundation of NY, that was laying quite dormant, but was being blocked from from being folded into the coffers of the main Knapp Foundation, they controlled in St. Michaels, Maryland. It seemed to me perfectly within the heirs rights to do so, but I am not a lawyer or legal scholar. The matter, Alco Gravure versus The Knapp Foundation, had come to the attention of Edward Meese, Reagan's attorney general and was slated to be argued before the Supreme Court.

And though I had honored my word to the Knapp heir attorneys, about ever contacting the family again, nothing was ever said about any Knapp family members contacting me, which you don't have to be a lawyer to know is perfectly within their rights to do so. Three of them did. One of them was the granddaughter of the woman whose attorney sent me the warning letter that appears in Chapter 7. She wrote explaining just who she was, in relation to the family and that "I would love to chat with you about my family history and inform you of anything I may be able to help with." I responded to her by saying I believe she might want to check with her grandmother first, as we had an understanding about my having any direct contact with her immediate family. I never heard from her after that.

I also received an e mail from a Mrs. Peggy Norton, one of the daughters of Claire Knapp's oldest daughter Peggy Newcombe and that was an entirely different story. Again I responded with my caveat, only to learn that Peggy Norton certainly did not need to answer to her aunt or any other member of the Knapp family. Truth be told, upon hearing her story, I feel they needed to do some 'splainin' to her! But it is a highly personal situation and would serve no purpose for me to get into here. That initial contact, led to a sincere friendship over the last 5 years and even a personal visit at my home no less by Peggy and her husband Charles, who ironically is an attorney and advised me that everything I had published on the internet or proposed to write in this book, was indeed public information and beyond actionable by anyone. Peggy in turn introduced me to her brother Stan Newcombe, who I have also had the pleasure of sitting down face to face with for several hours in 2003 in Clearwater, Florida, just around the corner from my former home. Wait a minute —The Knapp Mansion was just around the corner from my house in Mastic Beach! Stan told me stories about his childhood at Grandma Claire's Hampton Bays estate, while I was being absolutely stunned by his physical resemblance to the patriarch and to my way of thinking supreme authority on the Knapp Family—Mr. Joseph Fairchild Knapp (1832-1891) or as I like to refer to him, BIG JFK!

I will always be great full to have met Peggy and Stan, along with the others I have along the way like members of the Cheaney, Clune, Penney, McIlwaine and Kiely families, all whose full names are in the acknowledgments and are related to or have had direct contact with the major Knapp players in this story. I was also thrilled to have been able to enlighten them at times with some of my research and photo discoveries. That said, some of the stories, I have heard from all of them would serve no purpose in telling or propelling this Knapp story any further.

In closing this really big chapter of my life, I am still looking forward to posting new discoveries if they find me, about both the Mastic area and the Knapps on my website. I also still hope visit Currituck and Chapel Hill, North Carolina someday, to pay my respects to Joseph Palmer and Margaret Rutledge Knapp, and to return once again to Greenwood Cemetery in Brooklyn, New York to play at the graveside of Phoebe Palmer and Joseph Fairchild Knapp, my CD with 15 very different, but all very fine versions of Blessed Assurance. And finally, what might seem the simplest thing of all, to someday see a photo or two of the interior of the Knapp Mansion in Mastic Beach. the way it was when—The Knapps Lived Here.

—KEN SPOONER NASHVILLE, TENNESSEE, AUGUST 24, 2008

As we go to press, a gift to me of author Thomas Dixon's last novel The Flaming Sword, cleared up the question of how Dodi spelled his nickname and why Arthur Penney pronounced it Doad. It is inscribed, *"To Joseph F. Knapp 'With a thousand memories of a happy boyhood'"* — *Sincerely Thomas Dixon*

Under that is, *"**Dode**: May I be permitted to insert my oar into the above sentiment and add 'manhood'"* — *Love Thomas Dixon Jr. July 28 '39*

I had never seen Dodi spelled that way. Research shows a 1907 Cincinnati Red's outfielder, George "Dode" Paskert, known for his speed. As late as 1949, Joseph F. Knapp, still enjoyed demonstrating his running ability.

Aknowledgements

FOR THEIR AID AND SUPPORT ABOVE & BEYOND Anne Spooner, Erik Spooner, Kenny Vitellaro, Marty Van Lith, Fred Gillespie, Philip & Susan Cheaney, Darby and Arthur Penney, Mildred & Kathy Clune & Family, Estelle & Larry Schulz, Doug Percoco, Adolph Almasy, Ed & Marilyn Albano, Dan Acernio, Lynn Allen, Christina & Rebecca Anselmo, William & Gloria Baessler & Family, George Barnes, Jeb Barry, Nigel Brassington, Phillip Brown, Steve Calabro, Frank Campbell, Carolyn Capel, Dr. Walter & Bunny Hoest Carpenter, Jacque Chapman, Philip Cheaney , Susan Cheaney, Kerrin Winter-Churchill, Skip Clement, Kathy, Len & Monica Clune, Mildred Clune, Anita Cohen, Ben Conley, John R. Cox, Jimmy Cutro, Steve Czarnieki, Bob DeBona, Joe Dionisio, Kay Ann Donaldson, Kevin Doxey, Peggy Earhart, Rose Estes, Ray Farmer, James Fender, Van Field, Fred Gillespie , Paul Haberle, John & Janet Heyer, Marty Himes, Terry Hooper, Dorothy Jendral, Archie Johnson, "KNAPPSTERS!" (*y'all know who you are*), Linda Knel, Mallory Leoniak, John LiBaire, Pam Light, Bob Lee, Don Martin, Jane McIlwaine, Gary Messinetti, Bill Murphy, Emily Muse, Robert Muse, Dorice Nelson, Stan & Marian Newcombe, Peggy & Charles Norton, Alicia Patera Norwick, Joan Kiely O'Connell, David Overton, Dawn Pack, Edie Padilla, Arthur Penney, Darby Penney, Roland Penney, Sylvia W. Penny, Doug Percoco, Phyllis Potts, Bill "Cut' Redin, Mark Rothenberg, Merrilyn

Rothbaum, Jack & Dot Rutigliano, Ashley B. Saunders, Roy Sawyer, Estelle Schulz, Larry Schulz, Brad Shupe, Susan Silvestri, Bob Siriani, Warren Smadbeck, JoAnn & Phillip Strong, Mac Titmus, Anthony Torre, Greta Speiss Tucker, David Trevallion, Marty Van Lith, Ken Vitellaro, Phil Van Tassel, Jean Wassong, Josephine Wuthenow, Jim York.

PUBLIC LIBRARIES OF Mastic-Shirley, NY; Patchogue-Medford, NY; Center Moriches, NY; Hampton Bays, NY; Southampton, NY; New York Public Library; Queensboro, NY (Long Island Division); Nashville, TN; Clearwater, FL; Library of Congress; Smithsonian Air & Space Library, Washington, DC.

UNIVERSITY LIBRARIES OF State University of New York at Stony Brook, NY; Vanderbilt University, Nashville, TN; University of North Carolina at Chapel Hill and Asheville, NC.

HISTORICAL SOCIETIES Suffolk County, Riverhead, NY; Post Morrow Foundation, Brookhaven, NY; Brooklyn Historical Society, Brooklyn, NY; New York Historical Society, New York, NY; Ft. Lauderdale, FL.

MUSEUMS Cradle of Aviation, Roosevelt Field, NY; Museum of the City of New York; Suffolk Marine Museum, Sayville, NY; William Floyd Estate, Mastic Beach, NY; Manor of St. George, Shirley, NY; Smithsonian Institute, Washington, DC; Mystic Seaport Museum & Library, Mystic, CT.

And even though I played enough hookey for an entire student body,
I cannot leave out some very influential
WILLIAM FLOYD SCHOOL TEACHERS From My Elementary, Junior High and High School Days: Janet Tribble, 3rd Grade; Lorraine Rosado Paszkiewicz, 5th Grade; Bill Profreidt, 7th grade English; Gerry Holzman, 8th grade History; Jane Cass 10th grade English; Alex Turpin, 11th grade English; Don Collins, 11th grade History.

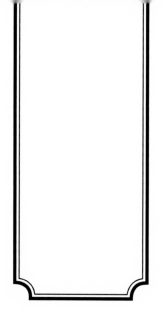

Bibliography

Anthony, Ed *This Is Where I Came In* Doubleday 1960

Arthur, Reginald W. *Contact The First Naval Aviators* Register 1917

Baker, Carlos *Ernest Hemingway selected letters 1917- 1961* Scribner 1981

Baker, Carlos *Ernest Hemingway a life story* Scribner 1969

Blumhofer, Edith *Her Heart Can See* Wm B. Erdmans 2005

Bok, Edward *The Americanization of Edward Bok* Scribner 1920

Brown, Kenneth *Walter Palmer the beloved physician* Hazelton Press 2001

Carlson, John Roy *Undercover* E P Dutton 1943

Chenery, William L *So It Seemed* Harcourt Brace 1952

Conrad, Clemens, Jonsson *Huckins The Living Legacy* Ortega River Books 1998

Cook, Raymond *A Fire From The Flint* J. F. Blair 1968

Coppedge Bud, Johnson Archie *Gun Clubs & Decoys* CurBac Press 1991

Dixon, Thomas *The Life Worth Living* Doubleday Page 1905

Finney, Ben *Feet First* Crown 1971

James, Marquis *The Metropolitan Life* Viking Press 1947

Paine, Ralph *The First Yale Unit* Riverside Press 1925

Phair, Charles *Atlantic Salmon Fishing* Derrydale Press 1993

Robie, Bill *For The Greatest Achievement* National Aeronautic Ass. Smithsonian 1993

Ruffin, Bernard *Fanny Crosby* United Church Press 1976

Saunders, Ashley B. *History Of Bimini,* New World Press 1989

Saunders, Keith *The Independent Man* , Saunders Press 1962

Slide, Anthony *American Racist Life &Times of Thomas Dixon* University of KY Press 2004

Tennyson, Jon *A Singleness of Purpose,* Ducks Unlimited 1977

Wheatley, Richard *The Life & Letters of Phoebe Palmer* Palmer & Hughes 1884

Periodicals
American Architect December 1914 Sept 1922

Aerial Age Weekly July 2, 1917

American Kennel Gazette August 1926 December 1959

Flight Journal June 2001

Fortune Magazine August 1937 Crowell

Knapp. Joseph P. *Let Game Birds End Farm Depression* Readers Digest March 1931

Brooklyn Citizen 1920 - 1930

Brooklyn Eagle 1855 - 1902

DogDom June 1920 March 1936

Dogs In Review The Great Ones June 2003

Dog World Showstoppers Feb 2007

Hampton Bays News Hampton Bays, NY Oct 1952 - Oct 1959

The Independent Elizabeth City , NC Sept 21, 1921

Moriches Tribune Center Moriches, NY 1938 - 1959

Nashville Banner Nashville TN May 11, 1928

New York Times 1851- 1982

New York Herald Tribune Jan - Feb 1951

Patchogue Advance Patchogue, NY 1894 - 1959

Popular Mechanics December 1926

Popular Science December 1926

Rudder Magazine March 1931

Southampton Press Weekly Southampton NY 1917 - 1922

Time Magazine 1920 - 1984

Washington Post 1910 - 1982

Wooden Boat June 1991

Working Mans Advocate July 14, 1832

Misc
Bagley, Dudley *The Joseph P. Knapp I Knew* (unpublished manuscript) UNC Chapel Hill, NC

Graham, Gertrude *A History of Mastic Beach* MBPOA 1976

Jones, Gordon *Introduction Of Modern Education in Currituck County NC* 1971

Knapp Building Dedication Booklet Institute Of Government UNC Chapel Hill Nov,1960

Knapp Joseph F (Mrs.) *Notes of Joy* Walter C. Palmer 1869

Knapp, Joseph F. *Bookshelf Scrapbook of John Dawson Collection*, University Of NC at Asheville NC

Lloyds Registery of Yachts 1932, 1939, 1941, 1955, 1979 editions

St. John's Methodist Episcopal Sunday School Manual 1869

Social Register of NY Social Register Association 1909, 1918, 1920, 1936, editions

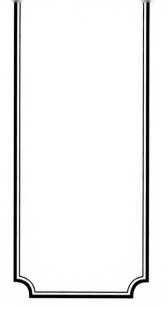

Image Appendix

Our House in 1950 on the corner of Elm & McKinley

Butch, Boots, and Me on Elm Road in a 1928 MB Fire Engine.

"The Mansion."

Mr. Clark's barn, 2001.

Best Laid Plans: St Jude's Auditorium.

Joseph Fairchild & Phoebe Palmer Knapp, circa 1855.

The Patriarch Knapps, circa 1880.

Knapp Mansion, corner of Bedford & Ross, circa 1880s, and the Music Room, below.

The Met Tower: A New York City Landmark.

Left, a young JP Knapp, President of American Lithographic Co. Above, JP at the Knapp Lodge in Currituck, 1930s.

Sylvia T. Knapp, mother of Claire & Dode,
Passport Photo 1920.

Margaret & Claire, 1940s. Only mother
& daughter to ever win Best in Show at
Westminster.

Elizabeth McIlwaine Knapp, 1910.
(Mrs. JP Knapp II).

Naval Aviatior Archibald G. McIlwaine, 1917.

Marion & Dode Knapp, 1930s.

Margaret Rutledge, Mrs JP Knapp III

Thomas Dixon, center, on the Knapp Estate, Mastic, 1917.   Willis Oliver Penney, circa 1947.

Dode & Marion Knapp with Philip & Shirley Cheaney, Ft. Lauderdale, 1947.

"Miss Demure," Dode Knapp's Sea Sled in Mastic, 1924.

Storm King in Ft. Lauderdale, 1940s.

322 72nd Street, NYC, JP Knapp's home ca. 1890s, as seen in 2002.

The Savoy Hotel, Phoebe Knapp's home, 1894-1908.

Tenacre, JP Knapp's Southampton, LI home, 1920s.

Clairedale Farm,
Greenlawn, 1914.

Knapp Lodge in Currituck, NC.

Isle Of Palms, Ft. Lauderdale, 1937.

JP Knapp's last residence, Riverhouse on the East River, NYC, 1930s.

Dode Knapp's last residence, "Cove Point," Hampton Bays, LI.

Knapp Estate, Mastic 1917.

Unit 3 Aerial Coast Patrol on the Knapp Estate.

LW Bonney and his Gull in Mastic, 1920s.

Knapp Helicopter 1930s.

Above, Knapp family cook Lorretta Clune and her children Mastic, 1921. Below, the Clunes at their Caretaker's Cottage with Clairedale Chow Dog, Mastic, 1920s.

MASTIC BEACH
SUFFOLK COUNTY
LONG ISLAND, N.Y.

1938

Mastic Beach Directory
Published by
St. Andrew's Community Church
Mastic Beach, N. Y.

KNAPP ESTATE

— LEGEND —

A—St. Andrew's Community Church
B—Mastic Beach Club House
C—U. S. Post Office
D—St. Jude's Roman Catholic Church
E—Five Corners
F—Woodhull Mansion
G—Mastic Beach Yacht Club and Lagoon
H—Democratic Club House
I—Old Cemetery; Gen. Woodhull Grave
J—East End Fire Department
K—West End Fire Department

Knapp Mansion, Mastic Beach, 1956.